Jesus and the Muslim

Jesus and the Muslim

An Exploration

Kenneth Cragg

London
GEORGE ALLEN & UNWIN
Boston Sydney

**George Allen & Unwin (Publishers) Ltd,
40 Museum Street, London, WC1A 1LU, UK**

George Allen & Unwin (Publishers) Ltd,
Park Lane, Hemel Hempstead, Herts HP2 4TE, UK

Allen & Unwin Inc.,
Fifty Cross Street, Winchester, Mass 01890, USA

George Allen & Unwin Australia Pty Ltd,
8 Napier Street, North Sydney, NSW 2060, Australia

First published in 1985

British Library Cataloguing in Publication Data

Cragg, Kenneth
Jesus and the Muslim : an exploration.
1. Christianity and other religions——Islam
2. Islam——Relations——Christianity
I. Title
200 BP172
ISBN 0-042-97046-6

Set in 10 on 11½ point Plantin by V & M Graphics Ltd,
Aylesbury, Bucks
and printed in Great Britain
by Billing and Sons Ltd, London and Worcester.

Acknowledgements

The publishers and the author acknowledge with thanks the use of copyright material from the following publishers and sources:

Dr Hasan Askari for a paragraph from his *Inter-Religion*. Aligarh, 1977 (chap. 10, fn 1).

The Associated University Presses, Cranbury, New Jersey, for seven lines from the poem of Can Yucel, trans. M. Nejmet-Nejat, in *Contemporary Turkish Literature*. London, 1982 (chap. 5, fn 22).

E. J. Brill for sixteen lines from Dr F. Rosenthal's *Sweeter than Hope: Complaint and Hope in Medieval Islam*. Leiden, 1983 (chap. 3, fn 38).

Jihad-e-Sazandegi for an extract from Masih Muhajeri's *Islamic Revolution: Future Path of the Nations*. Teheran, 1982 (chap. 11, fn 11).

Alfred Knopf & Co. for thirteen lines of verse from R. Hingley: *Basil Pasternak*. London, 1982 (chap. 3, fn 8).

Mizan Press for quotation from Hamid Algar's translation of Ali Shari'ati's *On the Sociology of Islam*. Berkeley, 1979 (chap. 3, fns 20 and 21).

Muslim Information Services for three extracts from Muhammad 'Ata al-Rahim: *Jesus, a Prophet of Islam*. London, 1977 (chap. 11, fns 14, 16, 17).

The Open Press Ltd for material from Kalim Siddiqui: *Issues in the Islamic Movement, 1980–81*. London, 1982 (chap. 11, fn 12).

Paulist Press, Ramsey, New Jersey, and SPCK, London, for lines from Paul Jackson's translation of Sharafuddin Maneri's *Hundred Letters*, 1980 (chap. 3, fn 46).

Secker & Warburg for an extract from Dan Jacobson: *The Story of Stories: The Chosen People and its God*. London, 1982; and for a paragraph from Thomas Mann: *Joseph and His Brothers*, in the translation by H. T. Lowe-Porter. London, 1978 (chap. 9, fns 18, 24).

Student Christian Movement Press for words from J. Jeremias: *The Prayers of Jesus*. London, 1967, trans. by J. Bowden and J. Reumann (chap. 5, fn 27).

Contents

study: redaction: why four Gospels?: the Epistles as revelation: pastoral nurture and the imitation of Christ: liberation from idolatry: the point of precedents: the churches and the state: Paul's letters: James: Peter: *Hebrews*: John the theologian: Christian apocalyptic and martyrology: *Acts of the Apostles*: Luke as historian: Stephen's death: Peter's discovery: the saga of Paul: elders of Ephesus: the riot over Diana: the open end of *Acts*: the New Testament Canon and its formation: the text and textual scholarship: Codices and Papyri and consensus.

5 Jesus as the Christ 125

'The kingdom of God' and the Messiah: the kingdom both present and to come: Jesus' role within it: his teaching: truth through personality: the Beatitudes, their nature and significance: Jesus in indictment of society and religion: implications about Jewry: Jesus and liberation: moral authority: the parables: Jesus healing: need not credulity: compassion its own sufficient reason: cure and forgiveness: 'signs' and significance: communing with the disciples and with the Father: the crisis at Caesarea Philippi: the rising tide of hostility: the watershed of the story: the Lord's Prayer and its clauses: Jesus reading the Messianic clues: the options and the temptations: the map in the mind: Messianic logic and its inner springs in Scripture and in Sonship: the Palm Sunday entry: the meaning of the final supper: the nativity hymns according to Luke.

6 Gethsemane and Beyond 166

A clear intention to crucify: its implications about evil and for vocation: the Cross affirmed in the Qur'ān as human deed: the Cross strongly inferred in the Qur'ān as Jesus' fidelity: the excluded dimension of 'God in Christ': the meanings of *shubbiha lahum*: 'he' or 'it'? as within 'illusion': mistaken identity or non-fatal crucifixion: a prophet's credibility: the esoteric ideas of the Docetics: another sense of the 'seeming': other passages and their bearing on Surah 4:157 f.: other Islamic rulings: it did not happen historically: it should not happen morally: it need not happen redemptively: the theology at issue: only one Cross?: Resurrection, fact and symbol.

7 The Decisive Faith: 'God in Christ' 189

'Behold, I am here': crucial history, perceiving community and divine credentials: Surah 3:31 with John 16:27: reckoning God rightly by *ḥaqqa qadrihi*: a decisive monotheism via the insignia of Messiah: the movement into faith: the movement into community: the movement into creed: 'Jesus – Lord': 'sonship' language: does this faith 'compromise' God?: or unduly 'humanise' divine will, sovereignty and mystery?: or set God under 'necessity'?: is Christology *shirk*?: the Christian confession of the unity of God.

Preface

Medical people say that taking the history of a patient is no less important than the physical examination. The latter may well be straightforward, a matter of clinical diagnosis, while the former may be vague and confused. If the doctor has to have the history from the patient only through an interpreter, because they do not speak the same language, the difficulty is compounded.

A comparable situation to this in the service of health occurs also in the study of faiths. There is not only what academic search may examine and establish in analysis. There is also what people have lived and undergone, as they themselves tell it of themselves in the case-history of their convictions.

The purpose of this book is to study, as scholarship may, the Muslim situation in respect of Jesus, or ʻĪsā as he is known within Islam. What are the facts of Jesus in the case of Islam and what do Muslims have to say of their sense of him? Who *is* the Islamic Jesus – a question at once involving objective investigation and subjective experience, needing to be answered both from fact and from life.

It can hardly be asked or answered, however, in dissociation from the Christian awareness of Jesus and the history of that awareness within Christian experience. It must surely entail something like an introduction, for Muslims, to the New Testament where Christians told their case about Jesus in definitive form via a documentation in and from which they found their identity as the community of his recognition. This must mean an introduction which always keeps in mind the Islamic situation as belonging to another community with another *raison d'être* and an identity of its own. Our duty here is to consider the ʻĪsā of Islamic faith from within the perspectives of the New Testament and to interpret these perspectives to the people of the Qur'ān. Hence the sub-title, in both directions: 'an Exploration'.

This book is meant, therefore, for both Muslims and Christians, relating either to the other within the theme of Jesus of Nazareth, Messiah. Thus it is parallel to an earlier study concerning *Muhammad and the Christian* (Darton, Longman & Todd, London; Orbis Books, New York, 1984); it is also in sequence with two books earlier still, namely, *The Event of the Qur'ān* and *The Mind of the Qur'ān* (Allen &

Unwin, 1971 and 1973). These were studies of the Qur'ān and its *Tanzīl*, or incidence in history, its major themes, its vocabulary and its significance for the Muslim and for the non-Muslim. These two books deliberately excluded the 'Christian' issues in the Qur'ān in order to concentrate on the main concern of Muḥammad's mission with pagan polytheism and its overthrow by an effective and undeviating monotheism.

That counter-pagan thrust of the Qur'ān – its anathema against all *shirk*, or plural worship, in the name of *lā ilāha illā Allāh* ('there is no god except God') – is undoubtedly the primary theme of the Qur'ān to which the question about the other monotheisms, Judaic and Christian, is subordinate. Yet the demands and the passion of the major theme affected the temper of the minor engagement. Islam has always been strongly under the constraint of its originating call in its postures and relationships. These have instinctively assumed a vigilance against idolatry wherever it could be imputed or suspected, even if mistakenly. Though Jews and Christians were tolerated as submitting minorities (or *dhimmis*) immune for *jihād* by virtue of islamicising politically, their faiths remained always doctrinally dubious in Muslim eyes. For they had not islamicized theologically and, therefore, were liable to theological anathema.

In the Christian case, Jesus and the interpretation of his significance lay at the heart of this tense relationship. So the major Quranic theme of the two earlier publications in 1971 and 1973 required some further study of what I then thought of as *The Christ of the Qur'ān*. However, long subsequent reflection has made me aware that the theme is better shaped as *Jesus and the Muslim*, for there is more than the Quranic 'Īsā. There is the long tradition and the image of Jesus in Muslim philosophy, poetry and devotion. The Quranic 'Īsā is certainly the core of these, but by no means the sum. Furthermore, one could in no way isolate the Christ of the Qur'ān from the criteria of the New Testament. Any adequate, not to say responsive, study of the 'Īsā there must entail the need to introduce Muslims to the New Testament Gospels and to the rest of the New Testament.

A sensitive Muslim introduction to the New Testament has long been a need, unmet in our relationships. There can be no more urgent desire, in this field, than to have the New Testament seriously read and studied in the Islamic world. Yet its format and character present obstacles to Muslim readers as formidable as those which face the Christian student of the Qur'ān. Why four Gospels? Why Epistles at all? What of the relationship between event and record? What sort of a Scripture is it which God has not dictated? What of the history of the quest of Jesus and what of the bearing of it on Quranic authority? What is our responsibility with, for, or from 'revelation'? The questions multiply. The best way to face them is to merge into one the study of the Islamic Jesus and the New Testament Christ, to have the Christian literature through Muslim eyes and the Quranic Jesus for Christian perception.

Some may wonder whether this is not to fall between two stools. Would it not be better to separate an introduction to the New Testament for Muslims from a study of 'Īsā for Christians? Prudence and market factors in publishing might perhaps commend this, but this book proceeds from the conviction that they can not only go together but assist each other. Chapter 1 summarises what is involved in the juncture of the two. Chapters 2 and 3 present the Qur'ān, Tradition and much else Islamic in the portrayal of Jesus. Chapters 4 and 5 discuss first the documentation of the Christian Jesus and then the event of him as the New Testament literature describes it. Chapter 6 takes the story, as both faiths have it, into Gethsemane in order to study the contrasted climax – redemption or rapture. Chapter 7 concerns the theological significance of the whole. Chapters 8, 9 and 10 venture relational questions around salient personalities and themes concerning Paul the apostle, John the evangelist, and the Paraclete, and their bearing on the Islamic mind. Finally, Chapter 11 intends to locate all that might otherwise be assigned to scholarship or 'dialogue' within the living tensions of the contemporary scene. There, I find no occasion to be sanguine. Despair may at times be more instinctive than hope. Yet, where Jesus is the theme, despair is never apposite. 'When I look at him,' as the poet had it, 'I must permit myself a wonderful hope.'

However, we must be ready for what Robert Frost called 'trial by existence'. Since existence is increasingly co-existence and the trial it has of us is also mutual, we need to bring our case-histories together and see how the figure of Jesus constrains our understanding of God and of ourselves, and how, therefore, he constrains our wills to faith and discipleship. 'Even now,' wrote John Keats on 27 October 1818, 'I am perhaps not speaking from myself but from some character in whose soul I now live'. The New Testament writers were in no doubt that it was so, with them, about Jesus. Edmund Spenser caught their mood and meaning, and our task, in his lines:

> And from that love, we weighing worthily,
> May likewise love thee for the same again
> And, for thy sake, that all like dear didst buy,
> With love may one another entertain.

Oxford, July 1984 — Kenneth Cragg

Chapter 1

Mecca's Long Vista Towards Jerusalem

i

It has often been remarked that Jerusalem on her twin hills tilts towards Moab and Arabia beyond. The recent massive urbanisation and the growth of a metropolis may conceal this feature from the casual visitor today. But the geographer and historian of the Holy City at the turn of this century, George Adam Smith, was in no doubt. Describing this 'eastern bent and disposition of the City',[1] as he called it, he went on:

> In certain states of the atmosphere, and especially when the evening sun shortens the perspective by intensifying the colour and size of the Moab mountains, the latter appear to heave up towards the city and to present to her the threshold of the Arabian desert immediately above the hills of her own wilderness... It is as if Providence had bound over the city to eastern interests and eastern sympathies. Hidden from the west and north, Jerusalem, through all her centuries, has sat facing the austere scenery of the Orient. If the spell of this strikes even the western traveller he can better understand... why the Muslim as he looks down her one long vista towards Mecca, feels himself securely planted on her site.

Islam's tenure in Jerusalem, to be sure, rests upon much more than a fact of topography taken as a symbol, and there are other far more tenacious factors of possessiveness nourished by other perspectives. Yet symbol that eastward 'prospect towards Arabia' certainly is – and for more than geography tinged with romance. If we are spiritually as well as visually imaginative, we will learn to be vividly aware of Arabia in a mingled sense of distance and proximity, whenever we take bearings from Jerusalem. Most of all will this be so if, for Jerusalem, we read that central drama of Jesus' Messiahship in suffering achieved there, which is for Christians its most ultimate significance.

How, then, does their faith orient itself towards Arabia out of which Islam came? Some sixty years after its arrival Islam crowned the city's 'eastern tilt' with its earliest, and many still take as its finest, architectural glory – the Dome of the Rock. It gave eloquent expression to 'eastern interests and eastern sympathies' in what seems to have been a deliberate intention to supersede the Church of the Resurrection, then at its most splendid. The Dome's exquisite calligraphy has mostly to do with Quranic passages relating to Jesus. They were doubtless chosen because the location was Jerusalem and this was the city which witnessed the climax of his teaching. The Caliph builder, 'Abd al-Malik, may also have been purposefully celebrating Jerusalem's dignity as the initial *Qiblah*, or direction of prayer, in original Islam.[2]

Clearly, there is point in 'Jerusalem's long vista towards Mecca' – and point, too, if we reverse directions and ponder Mecca's long vista towards Jerusalem. Either way, there is distance and there is proximity. It is both that these chapters aim to study, borrowing a parable to quicken our imagination from George Adam Smith's observant eye. Our question is: how should the New Testament significance of Jesus, 'beginning [as it does] from Jerusalem', look into – and seem from – those 'eastern sympathies' which Islam defines? How is Jesus himself viewed from Muslim perspective? How may his Christian disciples see into Arabia as the cradle of Muḥammad and his people?

Islam apart, 'eastern interests' were not in view in the New Testament itself. Its preoccupation is all the other way. Apart from Philip the Deacon's journey to Gaza, the Acts of the Apostles is all 'westward ho'. 'From Jerusalem round about unto Illyricum' was Paul's measure of his travels, with hope beyond of Rome and Spain (Rom. 15:19). The recorded dispersion of the faith followed the languages of the superscription over the Cross: Hebrew, Greek and Latin. Whatever the undoubted penetration of the world to the east, whether by Thomas or Matthew or others, the Greek canonical historian, Luke, is not concerned to tell. The fact that his account of the expanding Church is the only one, in the Scripture that is definitive, has meant a strong emphasis on western criteria and Graeco-Roman ethos.

There are indeed those who see in the whole shape of Christianity – in the New Testament and after it – what they call, perhaps awkwardly, a de-Semiticising of Jesus, by which he was taken over into

Greek categories and away from the authentic prophetic tradition of his truly Hebraic quality. Muslims are often strongly minded to share this view, seeing their own religion as the salutary corrective which, in the 'Īsā (Jesus) of the Qur'ān, repossesses the true dimensions of the prophet of Nazareth. As final revelation, the Qur'ān, viewing from Mecca and Medina, retrieves Jesus from 'Christian' distortion and brings back, as it were from Europe, the Semitic story rid of theological philosophy.

This is to anticipate. There are many tangled issues here to be taken up later, especially in Chapters 3, 4 and 8, and it may be well to note that, in Paul's hands at least, the western direction had its origins in a vision in Damascus and rumination in Arabia. The immediate point, meanwhile, is to ensure ourselves a lively sense of the Muslim view and perspective as to Jesus and, from that sense, to respond.

ii

Some will query at the outset whether the sort of cross-reference between two faiths which we have here in mind is really possible and, if possible, desirable. Religion, for the most part, consists in the interplay of what we may call faith-data and faith-experience. Both these have a possessive and a possessing character not easily amenable to translation across a frontier of soul and into a different structure of identity. Despite their deep affinities, this is very true of Islam and Christianity. As well as wide diversities within each as to their proper definition, there are deep disparities between them as to what are the data of faith, while the faith-experience of either cannot well find a way to be inclusive of the other. That being so, is there sane hope of feasible and mutual discovery either of the other?

Scepticism in reply was assessed, in part, in *Muhammad and the Christian*[3] when diagonal relationship was attempted in the other direction. Venture is perhaps the best rebuttal. Now, when *Jesus and the Muslim* is the concern, we need not argue again the positive case. If it can be successfully illustrated, so much the better. It certainly will not be proved by neglect of its challenge.

If feasible, however, is religious cross-reference desirable? Are there not, on every count, practical needs in a world like ours which will be little served and may be much aggravated by merely religious discussion? Will questions of world economy, national politics, secular technology and cultural – or other – revolution, be resolved by a concern for the image of Jesus among Muslims, its history and present pattern? To this query we will return in a concluding chapter when we have a retrospect from which we may incur its point more intelligently.

If we are to aspire to diagonal relationship should it not be left to Muslims to develop their own account of the place that Jesus has with them and of how they see themselves and him? *Jesus and the Muslim* is properly a book for Muslim pens. Indeed, Chapters 2 and 3 will be concerned, precisely, with Jesus in the Qur'ān and in Muslim Tradition. But need contemporary Islamic formulations about Jesus, such as those we explore and those we await, be insulated from all commerce with Christians in the same field? Many of the historical issues, after all, are common territory. Matters of New Testament interpretation belong to both alike. There is a sense, conceded by perceptive Muslims themselves, in which Christian scholarship has a longer stake and deeper experience than Muslim authorship, and perhaps, too, a sharper familiarity with the techniques.[4] Christian writing may properly register, and aim to fulfil, an obligation to interpret – as here attempted in Chapter 4 – the documentary nature of New Testament literature. It is a subject sadly capable of misconception. Epistles look oddly revelatory by Islamic canons of what revelation should be, while it is unhappily notorious how differently construed the term 'Gospel' (*Injīl*) can be. It would be odd, not to say disloyal, for Christians to refrain from all converse with Muslims on these vexing points or to fail to offer their understanding of their faith-data and faith-experience as their New Testament enshrines it. Such converse, however, will in no sense be calculated to offset or deter the fullest Muslim initiatives of study and concern. Rather the intention can only be to serve and stimulate such study in competence and adequacy.

The enterprise has, moreover, a reverse relevance. There is a Christian constituency to educate in the significance of the place Jesus occupies in the belief and devotion of Muslims. The status he enjoys there has often been neglected or discounted by Christians. The reasons are not far to seek; for, as they see it, a sad reductionism has occurred. By New Testament criteria the Quranic Jesus is a very attenuated figure. Many of his most cherished deeds and sayings are left to silence and what the Qur'ān does with the final climax of Jesus' ministry, as we shall see in Chapter 6, has desolating consequences for Christianity. These tensions between us should not be allowed to prevent a lively Christian sense of the significance of the Islamic acknowledgement of Jesus as prophet, sign and servant, and of the Virgin Mary, his Mother, and of his disciples as 'helpers unto God'. Christians will best communicate the Jesus of their New Testament discipleship if they relate patiently and intelligently to the light in which Muslims see him. Those long vistas between Jerusalem and Mecca must be seen in both directions.

iii

In taking up that obligation it is wise, in this introductory chapter, to anticipate in general terms the four crucial themes in which, through much exacting detail, we will be involved. Jerusalem and Mecca may be said, at least for symbolic purposes, to be the poles of the axis around which they turn. To summarise here may help to indicate the sequence which logic seems to require in the order of the chapters and the areas they cover.

We begin, and end, with Jesus himself. Doing so in Christian/Muslim context, we find ourselves engaged in questions of divine revelation, its nature and form, its credentials and its due embodiment in scriptural document. Implicit all the while in Jesus and revelation are the third and fourth issues, namely, man and the human situation – how comprehended? – and the reality and rule of God – how realised and fulfilled?

Some would no doubt propose these themes in another order. In the end it matters little, for they belong together. In matters of faith it is always true that 'in my end is my beginning'. 'Revelation' might be said to matter first, since without it how can we know in whom to recognise that we are receiving it? So then we begin where we say we possess it – in Jesus, or any other figure availing for the role. Apart from the prior reality of God, how shall we look either for it (revelation) or for them (the bearers)? Shall we identify it, or them, as such in neglect of the phenomenon of man which they must illuminate and answer? Yet, without the key of revelation, will not our human situation remain an enigmatic puzzle?

It would seem, then, that any point of departure requires another. We are entailed in them all if we are to begin at all. This fact of our situation is neither for despair nor for indulgence in philosophic pleasure. It is simply to alert ourselves to realise that wherever, concretely, we start in faith these are the themes that stay with us, if with faith we are to end. It is Jesus who is here both our guide and our clue, as Muḥammad was in the earlier study (*Muhammad and the Christian*). If we are to see him aright, whether from Meccan or Jerusalem perspective, we must be ready for all that he will involve us in, both for open study and for honest discipleship. Whether we are Muslims or Christians, the ultimacy and the supremacy are always God's. 'You are Christ's', Paul wrote to his Corinthian friends and he went on, 'Christ is God's' (1 Cor. 3:23). It could be said that the whole of Christianity is in that sequence and in those possessives. All that *Jesus and the Muslim* should do, as a study, is to hold them together and do so – as Paul could not – with a mind for Islam.[5]

Our first duty, then, is to see how Jesus is portrayed in the Qur'ān. This is done in its own words, the entire text brought together in sequence from its several points of incidence within the Book. Because points of translation, especially in relation to Jesus' suffering, raise vital matters, direct translation – rather than use of existing ones – is offered. To have the Quranic Jesus in this way *in extenso* enables us to appreciate both the range and the limitations of the portraiture when set alongside that of the New Testament. Following the narrative itself, there is obvious call in the same chapter for some discussion of the major points at stake, such as the use of the alternative name, 'Īsā, and the title *Al-Masīḥ* (the Messiah), postponing to Chapter 6 the large issue of the climax. Since the point there is not whether Jesus suffered rejection but how the rejection eventuated, it is wise to entitle it: 'Gethsemane and Beyond'.

The Qur'ān, though, is far from exhausting the image and esteem of Jesus in Islam. From the earliest sources in Tradition, down to contemporary novels, essays and studies, there is a rich mine of veneration in celebration of 'Īsā, last but one of God's faithful prophets. This long tribute of Muslim piety to Jesus is the subject of Chapter 3, together with some observations and reflections on its implications, as these have to be carried forward into later chapters.

iv

Any effort to relate Islamic awareness of Jesus to New Testament Christianity at once encounters the question just noted as to how revelation might be understood, how its incidence in the human scene and the human personality might be recognised, and what such incidence might require for its perpetuation into Scripture. Here the Islamic assumptions and the New Testament situation are so sharply disparate that attempt must be made to clarify the confusions and surmount the contradictions. What is the role of the servant and the word? Can there be 'more than prophecy'? How is the revelatory activity constituted? How is its import secured in a text or texts? What is its appropriate book form? Behind these more immediate questions, there are still larger ones about authority, inspiration and human instrumentality under God. Exacting as these matters are, there is no care for a Muslim reading of the New Testament that can well ignore them. Without the sort of *raison d'être* which the Christian Scriptures, and Christians with them, presuppose, there can only be pitfalls and prejudices for the Muslim reader.

This calls, then, for what might be described as a Muslim introduction to the New Testament – something which is long overdue. Chapter 4 attempts one. It could easily occupy a whole book. What, we have to ask, is the nature of a 'Gospel'? Why four? If not one only, why not forty-four? What place can 'Epistles' claim within a Scripture when, far from 'coming down' – as Islam understands – in Holy Writ which descends from heaven, they travel horizontally, from here to there as personal correspondence taken up with local interests and problems of daily life? On every count they must surely fail to qualify for inclusion in heavenly *Tanzīl* joining God's Book and the Prophet's voice in direct line? While on every count appropriate, as we must show, to the Christian scheme of things, they are eminently suspect to the Islamic. Muslim understanding of what prophets, and their scriptures, should be conflicts radically with what the New Testament is both by origin in Jesus and through form from the apostles and evangelists.

Chapter 4, then, has a big task in preface to the crucial portrait of Jesus for which it must prepare in Chapter 5. We must keep firmly in mind that it is only for the sake of this that the task is undertaken. The aim is not abstract competition about scriptures in contention. It is to liberate the parables from obscurity, to take the full impact of Jesus and so appreciate the Incarnation, to live within the growing Church as it emerges from precisely those toils of idolatry and ignorance which Islam was set to destroy, to dwell within that pastoral nurture by which the apostles reared the Church and to enter with Paul via Romans into the whole pride of man and its submission to God. The Gospels and the Epistles have a great world of relevance into which to be translated when they meet Islam, if only they can be freed from crippling assumptions and confusions.

This exhilarating task is, of course, attended by several technical duties belonging with scholarship and history. As noted earlier, Christian studies have naturally had a longer discipline in this field and perhaps also a more congenial temper. Christian scholarship in the Qur'ān, though now a notable tribute and contribution to religious openness of mind and care for detail, was slow to develop the necessary objectivity and discipline of will.[6] In measure a reciprocal Muslim scholarship in the New Testament is still awaited and the necessary skills are not easily attained, whether technical or temperamental. However, they have to be looked for, since Islam is squarely involved in the central issues of New Testament literature and theology. In part, in the Aḥmadiyyah Movements and elsewhere, these have been polemically broached, but their full demand and measure have only yet rarely been taken.[7] The hope in Chapter 4 is that what the New Testament 'takes' in these respects may be illuminated and set forward.

There is one further consideration here. It is that the idea of scholarly obligations attaching to scriptural convictions tends to be either uncongenial or suspect among Muslims in general. The sacrosanct on this view cannot well consort with the critical. There must be an absoluteness, both of meaning and text, about religious authority. Scriptures are not for scrutiny by critics but for recitation by believers. The Qur'ān is seen as literal revelation, explicitly communicated in the Arabic language by celestial mediation to the Prophet who is ensured protection from even slips of the tongue. The Scripture, therefore, is divine, immune from verbal error and – all the more – from necessities of scholarship in its reception. It is not a Scripture remotely involving editorial responsibility. Perish the thought. The Prophet receives *verbatim* the given content in the given words. Subsequent inscribing is the exact reiteration of what was divinely mediated to his lips. That mediation, it is generally believed, did not imply any conscious meditation or circumstantial participation from him, in content or in phrasing. There was no conscious authorship. To imagine that there was is to misconstrue the very nature of the Qur'ān and the fact of its *Tanzīl*. The very notion that 'slips of the tongue' could be relevant to its status or a danger to its contents is in itself eloquent of how the Qur'ān perceives itself.

It is, of course, not this way with the New Testament. The resulting dilemma for would-be Muslim readers is sharp indeed. It has to be said that from time to time the very prolixity and, indeed, the vagaries of some Christian, or other, academics has not helped those readers. It can sometimes seem as though the New Testament situation altogether dissolves into a welter of minutiae or a maze of ideas. That it is in no way truly so is the confidence of Chapter 4. However, as long as New Testament scholarship remains a discipline in need of discipline, its more radical practitioners will have to be radically countered if confusions, especially in the Muslim direction, are not to be wantonly increased.

That apart, it is evident that Muslims are minded to approach the Christian Scriptures with their Quranic point of departure as to what those Scriptures should be. They will need to be met sympathetically on that ground. For example, a recent Malaysian writer, Syed

Muḥammad al-Naquīb al-'Aṭṭās, in *Islam and Secularism*,[8] writes: 'From the point of view of Islam, although western Christianity is based on revelation, it is not a revealed religion in the sense that Islam is.' The reason, he further explains, is that it possesses no 'revealed Law' (*Sharī'ah*) expressed in the teachings, sayings and model actions (i.e. *Sunnah*) of Jesus. There *was*, he says, an original oracular revelation to Jesus. Since this has undergone cultural and misguided interpretation by its recipients and heirs Christianity in its familiar form is 'a new religion, not intended as such by its assumed founder, nor authorised as such by the God who sent him'. Syed al-'Aṭṭās finds clear evidence of this in the very shape of the Gospels and Epistles and notes that these factors of 'mispossession' are in constant flux, so that the once-for-all directives given through the prophet Jesus are subject to 'adjustment' to the cross-currents of time and opinion as, he claims, Christian theology demonstrates.

All of this is apposite on Islamic grounds. That very fact gives us the measure of how much interpretation of basic principles about scripture is needed in the context of Muslim instincts concerning it. Muslims ask of the New Testament: How can such a book, so handled, be divine revelation? The answer needs much patience and care.

V

When the Christian understanding of how the event of revelation 'happens' in Jesus, of what it means and holds for faith-acceptance, and of how the writings enshrine in description and evidence both the event and its acceptance, we find ourselves taken into our third crucial theme – that of man and his situation. Christian faith *from* and *about* Jesus (the progression here is important) can only be understood alongside the Biblical sense of man and evil. In the events around Jesus the Gospel has at its heart a grim measure of the wrongness of the world. Chapter 6 on 'Gethsemane and Beyond' in sequel to Chapter 5 on Jesus in history, teaching, ministry and hostility, will disclose this. At the very core of this history there is that which forbids us to be sanguine or superficial about our human nature, as reliance on law or exhortation is sometimes prone to be. Sensitive souls who reflect with dismay, or even with despair, on the ways of society and human structures find that the drama of the crucifixion of Jesus comprehends them well. In its quality and its meaning it registers, in one event, what John in his Gospel called on us all to 'behold' as 'the sin of the world'. There could hardly be a more devastating commentary on our human nature than what happened on Good Friday in answer to the Sermon on the Mount.[9]

Seeing this drama as it is has made it impossible for the Christian mind to take lightly the waywardness of humanity, to suppose it manageable merely by education or legislation, or to see it measured only in individual lapses from decorum. Evil, as expressed in the Cross of Jesus, has an inner dynamism that may reject guidance, defy prohibition and persist in its own purposes against the light it knows. It is not, then, in want of knowledge: it is perverse in will. Its condition is more than *Jāhiliyyah*.[10] Sin is evident in the Gospel story, not simply in the compromises of private people but in the interests and the passions of collectives and of establishments – social, political, even religious – by which personal conscience is overridden and where evil masquerades as expedience or realism.

It is such an awareness of things, taught by the central event of New Testament faith, which explains a dimension of Christianity often puzzling to the outsider.[11] But why puzzling? It does not conflict with the essential goodness of God's creation: it only takes it seriously. It does not impugn the majesty of law: it takes law, for law's own sake, beyond law's own resources if law is not to be tragically denied its goals of righteousness. It surely reflects what personal self-awareness knows only too well about the way we are in our inner capacity for deviousness and pride.

Chapter 8 will attempt to penetrate this further in the company of Paul. The important point now is to see how it informs the Christian significance of Jesus and how the dark climax of his ministry in the experience of rejection is of primary significance for the understanding of Jesus. It means that the Gospel of Jesus and the Christian faith with it are inherently conversionist. 'Except you be converted...' were his words even to those of high religious esteem. For Jesus' Gospel, true humanness begins and continues in penitence. If we are to reach what we should be we must first acknowledge what we are. This should not be seen as a mistaken preoccupation with sin, a kind of morbid view of the self. The Paul who learned from Jesus to say of himself: 'O wretched man that I am,' could also cry in adoration: 'O the depth of the riches of the wisdom and knowledge of God...' (Rom. 7:24 and 11:33).

vi

This has brought us to our fourth vital theme in the range of thought that belongs between Mecca and Jerusalem, namely, the reality and rule of God. Here all our studies having to do with the person of Jesus, the nature of revelation and the human situation converge. God is always the question of questions. To insist so is the supreme virtue of Islam among the religions. Its constant cry is: *Allāhu akbar* ('Greater is God'). 'That God may be all in all' (1 Cor. 15:28) is the goal of the New Testament. 'The power and the wisdom of God' – so close to echoing the Qur'ān's *Wa Huwa al-'azīz al-ḥakīm* ('and He is the mighty, the wise') – was the ringing confidence and celebration of the New Testament by both the evangelists and the apostles. Within that common theism of both Muslims and Christians and within the interpretation of those same attributes of power and wisdom there are certainly sharp disparities. They should be seen as belonging with shared convictions.

So we reach Chapter 7 with its presentation of 'The Decisive Faith: God in Christ', using 'decisive' in the sense meant by Paul in the passage where he writes: 'The love of Christ decides us...' (2 Cor. 5:16) and makes up our mind, leaves us no different option, resolves us. Along with the whole New Testament, he takes his clue to God from the whole significance of Jesus. So it is here that we must undertake the several responsibilities that Christians have among Muslims in being interpreters of what is meant by 'God in Christ'.

This is where what we call 'Christology' belongs, where it also arises. We have to ask what we can mean, what we do mean, by 'Sonship' to God. There are terms here meant to carry, and safeguard, the significance of Jesus which among Muslims have all too often impeded it. These are not to be either offered or rebutted in partisan purposes. Though we cannot elude controversy, we must insist that it obtains only within common ground. We only properly broach the questions that belong with Jesus from the perspectives that belong with God. Christology is always within theology. What is distinctive to Christians, in and from their New Testament, cannot be separated from what is instinctive to Muslims as taught by the Qur'ān. The theme of God is the place both of convergence and of contrast.

The meaning, for Christians, of 'God in Christ' – a meaning understood from the entire significance of Jesus – will be seen to rest upon a conviction characteristic of all three Semitic faiths, namely, that God can be known by man only in conjunction with the human situation. The formula, so to speak, has always to be: 'God and...' How could it be otherwise? The term 'God' in total isolation or dissociation from the human could have no significance. In Judaism the central 'association' by which God is believed and known is peoplehood and covenant – 'God and His people'. In Islam, that which 'associates' God with humanity is prophethood, and supremely the prophethood of Muḥammad.[12] The Christian faith has the same trust in God's 'relationality' to man and history but locates it finally and inclusively in Jesus – in Jesus not simply as the spokesman of a message, but also as the 'event of grace' in which divine love is known in action. The community of that 'association', the community that lives in its recognition, is not ethnically constituted or covenantally limited but is open to all mankind on the one, and feasible, condition of response.

To identify the 'and' by which God is real to us as God, and to do so in the person and the event of Jesus, is the key both to Christian experience and to Christian Scripture. Their witness is to a word of revelation which enlarges into a life, to a significance (Quranically speaking 'a sign') which inhabits a situation, to a fidelity fulfilled in suffering and to a suffering issuing into reconciliation and peace. They say that God is known for who He is by what He does and that what He does He does definitively (though not unrelatedly to other history) in Jesus as the Christ.

These are the convictions that belong in Chapter 7, where they will be more fully explored and linked with convictions taught by the Qur'ān. Let it be clear that theology anywhere is, so to speak, transitive – has to do, that is, with God in operative concern with man. It has to do with man as the 'object' of divine grace, however understood, so that theology in turn may be about God as 'subject', as the source and ground of the relationship that defines our human being. 'He is,' in the phrase of Hebrews (4:13), 'the God with whom we have to do',[13] whether that 'having to do' is held to reside in submission to law, experience of covenant, obligation via prophets, or initiative in compassion. The truth that through all our differences all our Semitic theologies are this way should enable us to bring to our relationships the patience, the hope and the reverence they deserve. What we each have is an interpretation of the divine by reference to those areas of experience which we – or more likely our inherited faiths – have identified as those in which His relatedness to the world meets us for our recognition. The rest is worship.

vii

To complete, however imperfectly, a presentation of 'God in Christ' will leave us with certain matters at a tangent which will deserve elucidation, as being particularly the concern of Muslims. It is intended to gather these into Chapters 8 and 9. For reasons which will become clear, these are linked the one with Paul and the other with John. 'Paul and the Qur'ān' and 'John and Jesus' will admit of bringing together some further points about the New Testament picture of Jesus in relation with the remaining misgivings or feelings of disquiet that Muslims have about him in that Christian light. Among these are the significance of the sacrament in bread and wine, the question of the Paraclete (the 'other Comforter') and the actual progress of the spirituality of the Church both in thought and contemplation and in encounter with ongoing history. These engage Chapter 10, 'the abiding Paraclete'.

Perhaps it will then be seen why historical Christianity takes Jesus so crucially into its sense of God and so fully into its worship of God. Jesus is, for Christian faith, the warrant for confidence that 'God is love', but only because the warrant originates from God's own initiative. This is what is meant by 'Sonship'. If we say, as faith does, that 'God is where the action is', and further that Jesus being the Christ is 'the action', it will be an idle or a wishful faith unless God, authentically, is in the acting. This is where the Divinity of Jesus belongs.

Will it be a fruitless ambition to aim to clarify these meanings so as to do justice to the instincts by which Islam and Muslims are minded to call them into question? If not, then we may be ready for a concluding chapter looking outside our faith-relations into the contemporary scene.

viii

At the outset we began this introductory chapter with a reminder of the physical propensity of Jerusalem towards the east and towards Arabia. Contrasting it with the New Testament's interests westward, we used it as a symbol. Islam did not emerge historically until the seventh Christian century to be the bearer and sponsor of those 'eastern sympathies' of the Holy City which had been its first direction of prayer when Islam was Meccan only. History admits of being handled without confinement to chronology alone. So, was Islam a re-Semiticisation of Jesus in contrast to that westward bent of the apostolic Church and maybe, too, in protest? Islam was certainly much more than that and it is wrong to restrict its significance to an implication which its dynamism far exceeded. Yet the fact remains that Islam 'possesses' Jesus in terms which radically revise the New Testament image and it is, likewise, a basic fact that Islam has eastward and Arabian origin and that New Testament Christianity took definition 'in letters of Hebrew and Greek and Latin' in the west. It is also true that the eastern Christianity, so steadfastly 'instant, in season and out of season', on the far side of Jerusalem from Peter, Paul and John, nevertheless revolved its theology – through all disparities and nuances – around the same themes by which their western counterparts had understood the Lord.

Though Islam, then, in no way monopolises the eastern prospect from Jerusalem, may it not now be seen as presenting to us in characteristically simple form the perennial question about Jesus? Both faiths agree that he belongs vitally to each, either as the focal point of man's deepest experience of God or as the last but one in 'the goodly fellowship' of prophets. There *is* now a 'long vista from Jerusalem'. Looking west, what it tells is that 'God was in Christ reconciling the world unto Himself'. Since the reconciling was the world's the vista eastward is the same. But, looking from Mecca and as affirmed by Islam, Jerusalem presents a different face and Jesus in her. When Islam first worshipped in that direction, it was towards a symbol of the unity of God and a heritage of prophethood, both being renewed in the finality of Islam. When that *Qiblah* after the *Hijrah* was turned around to Mecca it was in token of this finality and in repudiation of that other symbolism for which Jerusalem was the sign of a divine unity fulfilled in more than prophethood and realised in the love that comes and suffers and saves.

The original *Qiblah*, of course, has never been restored. There is no chance after these many centuries that it will be. That should not be seen as Jerusalem's repudiation. Quite the contrary: it is the sign of an alternative index to God, to man and to Jesus. The hope of the chapters that follow is to look duly at this alternative Jesus from the perspectives that first identified him for the early Church. It is important to recognise, in doing so, that the issue is more than a concern of two religions. But certainly the historical quest for Jesus must incorporate Islam.

Notes

1 George Adam Smith, *Jerusalem: The Topography, Economics and History from the Earliest Times to A.D. 70* (London, 1907), vol. 1, pp. 11–12. Smith, in the final sentence of the quotation, uses 'Mohammedan' which we have changed to the sounder usage 'Muslim'.

2 The building of the Ḥaram al-Sharīf, as the Dome of the Rock iṣ known in Arabic, was completed in the last decade of the seventh Christian century. Mecca itself was not then in the control of the Ummayyad Caliphs in Damascus but was occupied by a heretical group. Some have suggested that part of Caliph 'Abd al-Malik's aim was

to upgrade Jerusalem and perhaps even prepare for alternative pilgrimage. The suggestion, however, is widely discounted. The choice of Quranic calligraphy certainly bespeaks his intention to affirm that Jerusalem, and Jesus, belonged properly to Islam. It is interesting to reflect that he was at the same time giving rich occasion to architectural and artistic skills nourished in Byzantium.

3 Kenneth Cragg (London, 1984).

4 In his interesting study, *L'Islam et Dialogue* (Tunis, 1972), Dr Muḥammad Ṭalbī recognises this fact and asks for more time in which Muslims could equip themselves for a thorough knowledge of Christian meanings and their Biblical sources. This would, of course, include familiarity with the Greek New Testament and the theories of literary criticism.

Among Muslim writers who have made careful study of Christian origins, Dr Ismā'īl Rājī al-Fārūqī (now of Temple University) is prominent, but his writings have a sharply polemical ring and a magisterial tone which offset his erudition and disserve his scholarship. See. *Christian Ethics: A Historical and Systematic Analysis of Its Dominant Ideas* (Montreal, 1967). See also his *'Urubah and Religion* (Amsterdam, 1962), esp. Ch. 3, pp. 58–120.

5 Paul's relevance to Islam, despite six intervening centuries, makes a fascinating study, attempted in Chapter 8.

6 Earlier writings, like those of Gottfried Pfander and St Clair Tisdall, studied the Qur'ān polemically. Foremost among pioneer Christian scholars in the positive critical study of the Qur'ān were Richard Bell (*Introduction to the Qur'ān*, 1st edn, Edinburgh, 1953) and Arthur Jeffery (*Foreign Vocabulary of the Qur'ān*, Baroda, 1938). On the continent Ignaz Goldziher and Hirschfeld were their notable mentors, with scholars like Wensinck of Leiden in the field of Tradition. Despite the current denigration of western 'orientalism' in some Islamic circles, there is no doubt that Christian contributions to Islamic studies have been monumental.

7 Examples are: Muḥammad 'Alī's translation of *The Holy Qur'ān* into English, with extensive footnotes (Lahore, 1916 and subsequent editions); Haẓrat Mirzā Bashīr ud-Dīn Maḥmūd Aḥmad's translation of *The Holy Qur'ān* with introduction and footnotes (Rabwah and Washington, 1955); and Al-Ḥājj Khwāja Nazīr Aḥmad's *Jesus in Heaven on Earth* (Woking and Lahore, 1952). The matters mainly at issue in these works will be noted later in Chapters 5, 6 and 9.

8 Syed Muḥammad al-Naquīb al-'Aṭṭās: *Islam and Secularism* (Kuala Lumpur, 1978), pp. 127 f. It is noteworthy that the author sees Christianity exclusively as 'western', and discounts any revelatory status other than that of a teaching content verbally delivered to, and by, Jesus. This criterion of divine revelation rules out dimensions of it implicit in Christian faith, western and eastern, from the beginning.

It is refreshing to find a Muslim thinker relating critically to contemporary western theology as Syed Al-'Aṭṭās does. There is point, too, in his reproach for its temerity and its cultural 'captivity'. He needs, however, to reckon more positively with the original sources and with the whole range of a theologian's duty today. Of this he seems to have little inkling. The immutables of religion impose no standstill on time.

His book is an indication of how the 'virtues' of western theological 'liberties' work havoc in the inter-religious field – the more so as they are not always 'virtuous'.

9 See Chapter 6; and see further: Muḥammad Kāmil Ḥusain, *City of Wrong*, trans. from the Arabic (Amsterdam, 1957), for a Muslim's reconstruction of the drama of Good Friday, which focuses it on the theme of collective evil overriding private conscience and leading religious system itself radically astray. Dr Ḥusain's study is replete with Quranic terms applied to interpret religious (and by implication Islamic) wrong measured in the will to crucify Jesus.

10 *Jāhiliyyah* denotes the 'time of ignorance' prior to Islam. It has something of the sense of 'untamedness' and 'lawlessness', rather than simply stupidity or a state of being uninformed. The term is sometimes used by Muslims today as having also a post-Islamic sense – the 'heathen' within the (Muslim) fold.

11 The difficulty is compounded by the misconceptions attending the phrase 'original sin' which is much cited by Muslim apologists, discussing Christianity and puzzled at what they take to be a Christian morbidity or fatalism, or a calling in question of the essential goodness of creation. The 'originality' of sin means none of these things but means its presence in the springs of our being and not just in external circumstances, or the body merely, or occasional lapses or infractions of social law. See further in Chapter 8.

12 For the meaning of this deliberately disconcerting word 'association' see *Muhammad and the Christian*, p. 111, where *Shirk* is discussed. The very urgent, common concern to repudiate 'association' of beings with God, which is idolatry, in no way denies the equally urgent recognition of God's 'association' with the human scene which can alone explain prophethood itself, not to say creation too.

13 Literally the Greek of the verse reads: 'All things are open and upturned before the eyes of Him to Whom there is for us the word.' It makes God the great addressee of mankind, whom neither shyness, nor secrecy, nor subtlety can elude. Though the Greek idiom 'upturned' is very gentle (the hand that wants to lift the downcast face), it is, one might say, a very Quranic verse.

Chapter 2

The Quranic Jesus

i

Our first purpose in this chapter is to state in full what the Qur'ān has to say about Jesus, and to do so in the chronological sequence of his birth and ministry, postponing all questions or elucidations until the Qur'ān has presented its entire picture. Only in this way will the brevity and the concerns of its presentation be clear. However, it is perhaps wise to have one prefatory consideration in mind, namely the fact that the perspectives of the Book are always closely aligned with the immediate situation of Muḥammad's preaching among his own people. That context of apostleship and resistance to it from the Meccans, with the attendant exchanges about God and unity, – precedents prophetic and attitudes pagan, – dominates all that has to do with Jesus in all the passages. Needless to say, this abstracts his whole story from the kind of setting which obtained in the Galilean and Jerusalem theatre of Jesus' actual calling and in the circumstances of Christian nurture within the first-generation Church where the Gospels of the New Testament came to birth.

What this transposition does to the feel and essence of the picture will be evident at once. An attempt to relate to the problematics will follow. The point can be illustrated graphically in a passage from Surah 43:57–59, and 43:63.

> And when the son of Mary's role as an example is put to your [Muḥammad's] people they will have nothing to do with it. They say: 'Are our gods better, or he?' It is only in contentiousness that they bring him up anyway in arguing with you. They are a contentious lot!
>
> Jesus was none other than a servant on whom We bestowed grace and whom We made to be a symbol to the sons of Israel.
>
> When Jesus came with clear truths, he said: 'Truly, I have come to you with wisdom and to make clear to you something of the things

about which you were at odds. So hold God in awe and be obedient to me.'

In this controversy the pagan Meccans are evidently familiar with the name of Jesus,[1] sufficiently so to cite him as one whom they reject in assertion of their own preferred names of worshipping, and clearly supposing him to be the alternative deity of others. Muḥammad disabuses them of this confusion and in that context insists on the servant-status of Jesus with which every Christian concurs. However, given the *onus* of that situation, there is no occasion or possibility for the assessments of Jesus to move from that very servant-status (as the New Testament does) to a sense of its expressiveness of God Himself so that the obedience to it (for which Jesus here calls) might point towards an acknowledgement of divine nature disclosed, such acknowledgement properly moving into worship. All these – which are the Christian logic and the historic New Testament process of faith – are excluded by the exigencies of the Qur'ān's immediate locale. It is comparably so throughout. Before looking at the consequences the whole 'portrait' should be seen.[2]

ii

In succession to them [Noah and Abraham] by Our will Our messengers came, and Jesus, too, the son of Mary We caused to come after them and to him We brought the Gospel. In the hearts of those who became his disciples We set kindliness and mercy.

Surah 57:27

One who guarded her chastity, We breathed into her [Mary] of Our spirit and We made her and her son a sign to the worlds.

Surah 21:91

God chose Adam, Noah, the house of Abraham, and the house of 'Imrān before all creatures, in a continuous line of descent. God hears and knows.

When the wife of 'Imrān said: 'Lord, I vow to Your service my unborn child: accept my offering. For You see and know all things.'

When she gave birth to her daughter she said: 'Lord, a daughter is born to me.' God was well aware what the child was. A female birth is not the same as a male. 'I have named her Mary: I entrust her into Your protection and her seed after her from the malice of Satan.'

Her Lord received her with gracious favour and under His hand she grew into a goodly child. The Lord gave her into the care of Zachariah.

Every time Zachariah entered the sanctuary he found her supplied with food. 'Mary,' he said, 'how do you come to have this food?' 'It is God's providing,' she replied, 'for God gives without stint to whoever He wills.'

Then Zachariah prayed: 'O Lord, hearer of prayer, grant me at Your hand a blessed offspring.' As he was standing in the sanctuary in the act of prayer, angels called to him and said: 'God, confirming His word, brings you happy news. It is about John, a prince of men and chaste, a prophet numbered with the righteous.'

'Lord,' said Zachariah, 'how shall I have a son when I am now an old man and my wife is barren?' 'God brings about what He wills. That is how it will be.'

Then Zachariah said: 'Lord, let me have a sign.' 'Your sign,' He said, 'will be that for three days you will speak to no one except by gestures. Celebrate the praise of your Lord evening and morning, and remember Him often.'

And the angels said: 'Mary, God has chosen you and made you pure. Truly He has chosen you above all women everywhere. Mary, be obedient to your Lord prostrate yourself in worship and join yourself with those who pray.'

This is a narrative of things concealed which We have given you to know. For you were not present when they cast their lots over who should have the care of Mary and you were not on hand to observe how they vied for the custody of her.

To Mary the angels said: 'Mary, God gives you glad news of a word from Him. His name is the Messiah Jesus, son of Mary. Eminent will he be in this world and in the age to come, and he will have his place among those who are brought near to God's throne. He will speak to men in the cradle and in his mature years, and he will be among the righteous.'

Mary said: 'Lord, how shall I bear a son when no man has known me?' He replied: 'The will of God is so, for He creates as He wills. When His purpose is decreed He only says: "Be!" and it is. God will teach him the Scripture, the Wisdom, the Torah and the Gospel, making him a messenger to the people of Israel, to whom He will say: "I have come to you with a sign from your Lord. Out of a clay I will shape for you the form of a bird and as I breathe on it it will become one, by God's authority. Also I will heal the blind and the leper and bring the dead to life, by God's authority. I will bring you word of what to eat and what to hold in store in your houses. Truly

miracles

that will constitute a sign for you, if you are minded to believe. I come confirming the truth that you have already in your possession, namely the Torah, and to authorise as lawful for you things that hitherto were forbidden. I am here among you with a sign from your Lord. Then hold God in awe and be obedient to me. God is my Lord and your Lord, therefore serve Him. This is the straight path."'

When Jesus realised the unbelief in them he said: 'Who will be my helpers on behalf of God?' The disciples replied: 'We are the helpers of God. In God we have put our trust. Witness, O Jesus, our surrender. Lord, we believe in what You have revealed and we follow Your messenger. Write us down as loyal witnesses.'

Men schemed. But God, too, has His scheme of things and His prevails.

Then God said: 'O Jesus, I am causing you to die and will exalt you to Myself, vindicating you from the people of unbelief over whom your followers will have victory at My hand and then, at the resurrection, is the home coming of you all. I will be arbiter between you about all that is in contention among you.'

'As for the unbelievers, I will afflict them sharply in this present world and in the world to come, and no aid will avail them.'

For those who believed and did good deeds We will ensure their reward to the full. God has no love for doers of wrong.

These verses as signs We thus recite to you and the Reminder that brings wisdom. God would have you think of Jesus as you think of Adam, created by God from the dust, saying to him: 'Be' and into being he came. This is the truth from your Lord, so do not be among those who are dubious.

Surah 3:33–60

The mercy of your Lord to His servant Zachariah is here recalled. In the secret of his heart he entreated his Lord, saying: 'O my Lord, I am a feeble old man, with snow-white hair. Yet never, when I called upon You, Lord, have I been left forlorn. I have a fear as to my kinsfolk after my decease and my wife is childless. Grant me, I pray, an heir at Your hand who will enter on my inheritance and that of Jacob's family also. Let him be a man to please you, Lord.'

'Zachariah,' came the answer, 'We give you glad word of a son, John his name, a name which We have not before now bestowed on any one.'

He said: 'O my Lord, how shall a son be mine when my wife is barren and I as old and decrepit as I am?'

His Lord replied: 'It shall be so – your Lord's word for it. It is no hard thing. When you yourself long ago were non-existent I brought you into being.'

'My Lord,' said Zachariah, 'grant me a sign.' 'The sign for you,' his Lord replied, 'is that for three whole nights you will not be able to speak.'

So he emerged from the sanctuary to his people and indicated to them that they should engage, morning and evening, in praise to God.

To John when he was still a child We gave authority, saying: 'O John, lay hold upon the Book with all your strength.' Tenderness and purity, too, We granted him. He was devout and dutiful to his parents and never overbearing or contentious.

Blessed be he on the day of his birth and the day of his death and the day when he is raised again to life.

Recall, too, in the Book how it was with Mary when she withdrew from her family to a place eastward, where she was hidden from them behind a curtain. There We sent to her Our spirit, who came to her in comely human form.

'I take refuge from you in the all merciful,' she cried, 'if you are a man of honour...' But her words were lost in his as he said: 'I am the messenger of your Lord. "I will give you a son, a pure boy", is what he says to you.'

Mary answered: 'How shall a son be mine when no man has ever known me, nor have I ever been unchaste?'

'So it shall be,' he said, 'your Lord's word is: "It is easy for Me and We will make him a sign to humanity and a token of Our mercy." What is decreed is utterly sure.'

So she became pregnant and withdrew to a remote spot, where pangs of travail came upon her beside a palm tree, and she cried: 'Would I had died 'ere now and gone without a trace!'

There came a voice from below the tree: 'Be not sad. See, there is a stream beneath you – God's doing for you. Shake the trunk of the palm tree and fresh ripe dates will drop down around you. Eat and drink and take heart. If any one accosts you, all you have to say is: "I am under a vow to the all merciful to fast and, this day, I hold converse with nobody."'

Then when she brought the child in her arms to her family, they said to her: 'Mary! for shame! whatever have you done? Sister of Aaron, your father was no profligate, nor was your mother a loose woman!'

Whereupon she simply turned their glances in the child's direction, and they retorted: 'How shall we address words to a child in the cradle?' And the child said: 'I am the servant of God. He has given me the Book and appointed me a prophet, and He has made me blessed where-ever I am. He has commanded me to pray and to do alms all my life long and to be duteous to my mother. What belongs to the arrogant and the wretched has no place in His will for me. Blessed am I in my day of birth, my day of death and my day of resurrection to life.'

Such was Jesus, son of Mary – the true word about him which is a matter of doubt among them. It is not for God to adopt a son. All praise be His. When He decrees anything He only says: 'Be!' and it is.

God is my Lord and your Lord. So worship and serve Him. For such is the straight path.

Surah 19:1–36

We commissioned Jesus, son of Mary, in the train of the prophets, attesting the truth of what is already in the Torah. We gave him the Gospel in which are guidance and light and which confirms what is already there in the Torah, as guidance and admonition to all who would be God-fearing.

So let the people of the Gospel judge according to what God has revealed in it. Those who do not judge in accordance with such divine revelation are surely ne'er do wells.

Surah 5:46–47

The Messiah, son of Mary, was simply an apostle. Apostles before him have passed away. His mother was a woman of truth. Both of them took food.

Surah 5:75

On the day when God shall gather together the messengers He will say to them: 'What response did you have?' To which they will say: 'Of that we have no knowledge. Yours it is to know things that are hidden from us.'

And to Jesus He will say: 'Jesus, son of Mary, remember My grace towards you and towards your mother when I aided you with the holy spirit, so that in the cradle and in your mature years you spoke to men. Remember how I gave to you knowledge of the Book and the wisdom, the Torah, and the Gospel, and how by My leave you fashioned clay into the shape of the bird and when you breathed into it it became a bird by My leave, and how, by My leave too, you healed those born blind and the lepers and how, by My leave again, you brought the dead to life once more.'

'Remember too how, when you came to the people of Israel with clear signs, I held back their antagonism against you, the unbelievers among them alleging that plainly it was all sorcery.'

'When I moved the disciples to put their trust in Me and in My messenger, their reply was: "We do so trust. Bear witness that we yield ourselves up to You."'

When the disciples said: 'Jesus, son of Mary, can your Lord bring down to us a table from heaven?' he said: 'Be in awe of God, if you are true believers.' And they said: 'It is our desire to partake of that table, that our hearts may be at rest in the knowledge that you have indeed spoken truth to us and thus we too may be witnesses of it.'

So Jesus, son of Mary, prayed, saying: 'O God, our Lord, send down for us a table from heaven that it may be to us for a festival through all our generations and a sign from You. Provide for us, for there is no provision like Yours.' And God said: 'Send it down to you I will. In time to come whoever among you turns to unfaith will have retribution from Me such as none else incurred in all the world.'

God said to Jesus: 'Jesus, son of Mary, did you ever say to men: "Adopt me and my mother as two gods in disregard of God Himself?" To which he replied: 'Glory be to You. It is not in me to say what I have no warrant for. If I had ever said such a thing You would have known it. For You know my innermost being. Knowledge of what is within You I do not possess. It is You who know altogether things unknown to us. I said to them only what You commanded me to say, namely: "Worship and serve God, my Lord and your Lord." As long as I was among them I bore witness to them and when You took me to Yourself it was You who were watcher over them. For all things are within Your scrutiny. If You submit them to chastisement they are Your servants, and if You forgive them it is because power and wisdom are Yours.'

God said: 'The truth of those who deal truthfully this day avails them well. Theirs are gardens watered with flowing streams, where immortality is theirs, God being well pleased with them and they with Him, where all is highest bliss.' God's is the sovereignty of the heavens and of the earth and of all that is within them. His is the power that rules over all.

Surah 5:109–120

The Messiah said: 'O sons of Israel, worship God, my Lord and your Lord. God has prohibited Paradise to every one who alienates worship from God. Their dwelling will be the Fire. Doers of evil assuredly have none to come to their rescue.'

Surah 5:72

We brought Jesus, son of Mary, the clear truths and upheld him with the holy spirit. Every time there came to you an apostle for whose message you had no appetite within you, you reacted in proud disdain. Some of the messengers you said were liars and some you put to death.

Surah 2:87

We brought Jesus, son of Mary, the clear truths and upheld him with the holy spirit. Had God willed those who came after him would not have fallen into strife with one another, seeing that the clear signs had been brought to them. But they did differ one with the other. There were those who believed and those who denied. Had God so willed they would not have contended with each other. But God does as He wills.

Surah 2:254

Jesus, son of Mary, said: 'People of Israel, I am the messenger of God to you, confirming the truth of the Torah which you have already and giving you glad word of a messenger who will come after me, whose name is more highly praised.'

When, however, he brought clear signs to them they said: 'All this is obviously sorcery.' Is anything more heinous than for someone to attribute falsehood to God when there comes to him the very call of God Himself to acknowledge that He is God? God's guidance will never avail for such who flout the truth.

You who believe, be true allies of God, as Jesus, Mary's son, said to the disciples: 'Who will stand with me in the behalf of God?' and the disciples said: 'We will be the helpers of God.' One group of the people of Israel believed, while another body of them denied the faith. Those who believed We sustained against their adversaries and they became the victors.

Surah 61:6–7 and 14

Truly they have lied against the truth who say: 'God, He is the Messiah, son of Mary.' Say: 'Who can arrogate sovereignty from God in anything? If God but wills it His power could annihilate the

Messiah and his mother and every one else in the world. To God belongs the sovereignty of the heavens and of the earth and all that is within them and He is omnipotent over all.'

Surah 5:17

People of the Book, do not go to unwarranted lengths in your religion and get involved in false utterances relating to God. Truly Jesus, Mary's son, was the messenger of God and His word – the word which He imparted to Mary – and a spirit from Him. Believe, then, in God and His messengers and do not talk of three gods. You are well advised to abandon such ideas. Truly God is one God. Glory be to Him and no 'son' to Him whose are all things in the heavens and the earth, their one and only guardian!

That he should be servant to God will never be disdained by the Messiah as beneath his dignity, nor indeed by the angels who dwell in the divine presence. Servants of His who take on arrogant airs and think themselves above serving – well, God will have them all summoned to answer for it.

Surah 4:171–172

As for their claim that they killed the Messiah Jesus, Mary's son, the messenger of God, the truth is they did not kill him, nor did they crucify him. They were under the illusion that they had. There is a lot of doubt about this matter among those who are at odds over it. They have no real knowledge but follow only surmise. Assuredly they did not kill him. On the contrary, God raised him to Himself – God whose are all wisdom and power. And before they come to die, the people of the Book, to a man, will surely believe on him. On the day of resurrection he will be a witness against them.

Surah 4:157–159

iii

The immediate impression on the general reader from what the Qur'ān has to tell him about Jesus is that of its brevity. There is no direct quotation or citation from Arabic Gospels[3] and no narrative descriptions of the ministry. The bare reference to healing and restoration of sight has no setting in incidents from which the 'sign' quality can be appreciated. It is further surprising that within the limits of some ninety verses in all no less than sixty-four belong to the extended, and partly duplicate, nativity stories in Surahs 3 and 19. This leaves a bare twenty-six or so verses to present the rest and some reiteration here reduces the total still further. It has often been observed that the New Testament Gospels are really passion narratives with extended introduction. It could well be said that the Jesus cycle in the Qur'ān is nativity narrative with attenuated sequel. The gentle piety of those passages and their celebration of divine mercy in birth and vocation might have been expected to lead into the significance which nativity inaugurates. Both John and Jesus are heralded in prelude rather than presented in action. The 'sign' of their birth is not interpreted into the destiny of their lives. Birth, to be sure, is a prior condition of biography. It can hardly substitute for it.

So it is that the deep veneration with which the role of Mary and the nativity of Jesus are held in Islam often preclude a close attention to the content of Jesus' teaching, his announcement of 'the Kingdom of Heaven', the Beatitudes, and the meaning of the servanthood of 'the Son of Man'. It is ironical that it should be so, seeing that the meanings thus left to silence are believed by Muslims to have been gathered into the more ultimate Qur'ān.[4] One of the urgent needs in Muslim/Christian meeting today is that this supposition should be vigorously reviewed.

It is, of course, this sense of the finality of the Qur'ān which explains the fact, already noted, that everything to do with Jesus is set in a context assumed to be parallel to that of Muhammad himself. The fact of antagonism to Jesus is an important feature of the Quranic picture which it will be our task to measure in Chapter 6. The hostility tends to be understood as if it were analogous to that which Muḥammad sustained in the contrasted setting of Mecca and the Quraish – different at almost all points from Galilee and the Pharisees. At times it is difficult to be sure whether a Jesus controversy has not passed over into a Muḥammad controversy. Jesus' question: 'Who are my helpers (*anṣārī*) in God's cause?' (3:52 and 61:14) has a very Arabian ring, this being the term used to denote the Medinan citizens who gave shelter to the emigrants from Mecca at the time of the *Hijrah* (9:100 and 117). The disciples in the Gospels at the time of Gethsemane were far from emulating those described by the same term in the campaign by which Medina was brought into Muḥammad's cause. When they did respond to Jesus' call to be his 'helpers' it was as itinerant preachers summoning their hearers to repentance and to 'the kingdom of God'.

It is such disparities within common terms and contrasted situations which make it necessary for Muslims, minded to understand the person of Jesus within the Christian tradition, to detach themselves firmly from the transference of the scene from Galilee to the Hijāz which the Qur'ān has made and imaginatively to return to his original environment of place and time.

That Jesus had a specific – some would say a limited – mission to Jewry is stressed in the Qur'ān. Only Muḥammad as the 'seal of the prophets' belongs to all times and places. The 'universality' which Christianity is alleged to have 'read into' Jesus, violating this more explicitly Jewish vocation, is seen as part of that de-Semiticisation of Jesus' Gospel which, as we saw in Chapter 1, is attributed to the early Gentile Church. By this very token it is all the more urgent, therefore, to set the figure of Jesus squarely in the Palestinian milieu, where the central battle was not for the unity of God against pagan idols but against the pride of privilege and the moral and spiritual compromises of the purest theism. Only as this altogether different travail is realised will it be also realised what a radically different Jesus it means.[5]

Beyond all particular points of detail, it is this radical readiness for new frontiers of thought which is required of those who start from the Quranic Jesus. It means an invitation into the measures of the New Testament.

Take, for example, Jesus' reported phrase about John the Baptist: 'Yea, I say unto you, and more than a prophet' (Matt. 11:9; Luke 7:26). On Quranic grounds one cannot speak of anything 'more' than prophets in divine dealing with the human world. In the divine education of humanity prophets are all we have and their guidance all we need. This or that prophet, it is true, may be more than another in respect of his range of message or spread of hearers, Muḥammad being more than all in the long sequence from Adam to himself. On such an understanding, Jesus' words have a strange ring. For they hint at other dimensions entailed by prophethood itself whereby truth could pass from verbal utterance, faithfully delivered, to the whole significance of the personality fulfilling that fidelity. Or again, prophethood, in its serving loyalty, could take such personal significance into depths of travail and tragedy where behaviour might speak with a deeper eloquence than words. This is just the kind of different possibility we have to explore in Chapters 5 and 6. John's being 'more than a prophet' would then consist in his role as a prelude to such a climax.

iv

There are many other examples of how a change of the perspective brings new question into old attitudes. This one about prophets serves well to take us into another issue that the Quranic account of Jesus brings to the fore, by its repeated reference to 'confusion' and 'conflicting views' about Jesus among his 'followers'. That this is a strong feature of the Jesus passages in the Qur'ān strikes every careful reader. Such a reader may be able to sympathise in a lively way with the Qur'ān's impatience over 'Christian Christology' if he knows his Church history. Some of the circumstantial factors affecting the Quranic presentation at this point will concern us in Chapter 10. Controversies indeed there were and there are precedents, both before and after the Qur'ān, for being round with them as theologically unhappy or tedious, intellectually unreal and spiritually sterile.

Yet is the short shrift the Qur'ān gives them the whole story? Do those robust negations end all question? It is true that the gist of the controversies is never explored. To do so was not relevant to the contra-pagan thrust of Muḥammad's whole *Risālah*, or mission-message.[6] As we must see elsewhere 'adoptionism' and 'docetism' do betray their presence in what the Qur'ān has to say about 'errors' concerning Jesus the prophet-servant, for which 'Christians' were responsible. Disentangling confusion about confusions is a taxing, and at times a desolating, duty.

The point, for the present, however, is simply that 'complexity' can hardly *not* be incurred when we have the 'more than prophecy' situation we have just noted. If that progression beyond verbal mission into personal travail is substantiated – and all we need for the moment is not a proof of it but only a mind not closed against it – then the witness to that wholeness of mission *cum* person might well involve its bearers in intellectual and spiritual adventure in the telling. Clearly it would be a far more exacting trusteeship than that of reiterated book-content loyally transmitted. It might well emerge as both served and disserved by the minds that brought it. Their inadequacies, or vagaries, in the telling of it might well be aggravated by the misconceptions, if not the contentious ill-will, in their hearers' reception. Together these might well hinder its due recognition or its authentic expression or conspire against the necessary patience with its burden both of mystery and fact. All this might be the more the case where, as in Jewry, the very traditions of virile theism had to undertake a new kind of hospitality to divine unity. It might well be the case, too, where the instincts of Graeco-Roman culture could readily mistake the intention of a new faith, and lend terms for it that were liable to misinterpretation. Centuries on, it might further be the case, when lengthening and precarious transmission had brought it into a context where vigorous controversy was championing theism against pagan pluralism.

Impatience with Christology has its point, but there is point in patience also, if only for the sake of doing justice to the very theism which the impatience is set to assert and defend. Such patience will discover that many of the issues which Christology found so controversy-prone recur in theology too – not least in the theology that relies on the simplest of credal statements. As the classical Islamic theologians demonstrate, the simplicity can be deceptively profound. The conflicts into which Christians fell in understanding the person of Jesus in the early centuries have features it is right to reproach, but to think that reproach is all disserves theology itself. An alert sympathy is necessary if denunciation is not itself to fall into the confusion it deplores.[7]

If it be asked whether a ground or sphere of faith as liable to controversy or 'confusion' as, by many, the New Testament is seen to be, is well suited to religious certainty or proper to God's 'efficiency' in revelation, the answer must take us back into the considerations reviewed in Chapter 1. What we can expect or require revelation to be tends to depend entirely on what we have taken, in our differing faiths, to be revelation. Can there be any tests, exterior to faith, of what we should think faith sees as appropriate? For Muslims, in the main, trust is properly satisfied in guaranteed certainty emanating from God in explicit terms. On those grounds a Scripture, like the New Testament, which only comes out of loving retrospect upon events and through the mediating interpretation of belief itself responding to the impact of a personality, must doubtless seem suspect. The instinct of Christianity, by and large, has been to see in that pattern of inner experience, giving written form to the sense of truth, the authentic shape of divine ways with men and of human response to the divine.

It is not well, then, to let 'dispute' obtain between us, in terms of clarity versus 'confusion' or simplicity contrasted with controversy, but rather to make ourselves accessible to the positive witness which was at once within and also beyond the complexities of thought and language that impatience would dismiss or condemn. That there *is* a fair consensus of historic Christian faith as to 'God in Christ', these chapters hope to show. However, they can only do so for Muslim readers who are minded to hold in suspense for a time the polemical temper which has its negative judgement already given.

There is a sharp example of this need for looking closely into Quranic reference to Christian themes in Surah 4:172. The passage insists that 'Messiah will never scorn to be a servant to God'. The term used, *yastankifa*, is uncannily close to the usage Paul has in the Greek of Philippians chapter 2, which is classic celebration of Christian faith about Jesus in the form of one of the earliest hymns, or poems, of devotion and liturgy. Its origin is probably earlier than Paul himself. It speaks of the self-emptying by which Messiah fulfills his servanthood.

'Taking the form of a servant... he made himself of no reputation,' his Messianic standing being fulfilled in self-expenditure, not self-reservation. The term used here in Phil. 2:6 – *harpagmos* – relates to that which one covets to retain at all costs. The modern notion of 'status' may help to an understanding of it. 'Status' is normally and actively protective of itself, does not allow of being mistaken for what is lower, insists on being acknowledged for what it is and makes vigorous and vigilant assertion of itself. The shaikh would not willingly be mistaken for a novice, nor the field-marshal for a mere lieutenant. All walks of life, and all professions, are this way. It might be possible to think of God Himself in these terms, or of God's Messiah as having a status, a supremacy, that must be perpetually asserted. There *are* forms of 'status', however, which are not in this sort jealous of prerogative, which in fact are all the other way, consisting in giving themselves away. Such is true love: its dignity is in its cherishing the other at its own expense.

So Paul, in Phil. 2 is saying, in line with the Qur'ān, that Jesus as Messiah will never consider servanthood beneath his dignity (this is the sense of *yastankifa*) but gladly embraces it as the self-expending task of love. He makes no reservation of himself in obedience to the costly will of God. This, as Paul sees it, is the very nature of Christ's Sonship. In Surah 4:172, the same readiness in Jesus for humility is stated and saluted. But the passage sees this servanthood as the very disqualification of the notion that Jesus is 'Son'. Clearly the 'sonship' here in mind is that of pampered 'status' which will not soil a hand, lest the heir be mistaken for a menial slave. Such is not the Sonship of Jesus in the New Testament. The logic by which, for the Qur'ān, Jesus can never be 'Son' to God is precisely the logic by which, for Paul and the New Testament, he is. Both Scriptures affirm his being gladly 'servant to God'. That is their unity. The Qur'ān, however, denies his 'Sonship' on the very grounds in which the Christian sees it to consist, namely a loving obedience to God. For the latter there is a quality of service which only the 'Son' can bring.

V

Though there are many others, a clearer example of the need for patient care would be hard to seek in what relates to the Quranic Jesus. Nor does this one turn simply on a single term/concept in two passages. It pervades the whole story. Excluding 'Sonship' rightly (as long as it is understood in status-clutching terms), the Qur'ān takes a truly 'Christian' satisfaction in the servanthood of Jesus. But it does not reckon with how, in fact, that servanthood was fulfilled in terms of conscious 'Sonship'. 'To do the will of My Father', 'the cup which my Father has given me ...', 'I must be about my Father's things ...'[8] These were the motives, the impulse, in Jesus' obedience. It was in that harmony of will with the mind of God that Jesus saw his Messiahship and the Church later formulated his significance. It would be fair to say that the entire course and cost of 'not scorning to be servant' are the essence of the Gospels. We find there, filled out in narrative and in event, the reality to which the Qur'ān alludes in this single clause, set in a context of dispute over 'confusion'.

It is useful here to consider the sense of the term 'Messiah' as applied to Jesus in almost all the Quranic passages concerning him. There are some Muslim grammarians who have linked it with the verb *sāḥa* ('to wander', 'to roam', 'to travel afar') which could conceivably yield *masīḥ* as one who does so. This coincides with the oft-repeated tradition in Islam that Jesus was 'homeless', with nowhere to lay his head.[9] A far more likely meaning is that of the cognate Hebrew verb 'to anoint'. As such it belongs with Jesus' supernatural birth and designates him a prophet of the divine word. His being 'the son of Mary' is always linked with his being 'the Messiah'. The New Testament implications of the term are not to be understood in its more limited Quranic import. The tensions which surrounded the relevance of 'Messiahship' in the Gospels and the travail Jesus had in wrestling with them both inwardly and publicly are not reflected in the Quranic usage because of the silence which envelops the actual course of Jesus' story there. 'Messiah', then, in the Islamic Scripture must be read within the framework of Jesus' significance as there understood. The 'anointing' is to be understood as an equipping and commissioning for the task of prophethood and teaching. The fuller sense of a crucial role within a redemptive purpose of divine initiative in the human crisis belongs with it only by association with Christian usage.

It is, therefore, appropriate that the disciples of Jesus in the Qur'ān, his 'apostles' and 'followers', are never referred to as 'Christians', the Arabic term being *Masiḥiyyūn*. They are always called *Naṣārā* (s. *Naṣrānī*) derived from the place name of Nazareth, scene of Jesus' youth and first ministry (Surahs 2:63 and five other verses; 5:14 and three other verses; 9:30 and 22:17). Within the ministry itself, though no individual names are given in the Qur'ān, the disciples are called *ḥawāriyyūn*, a term of debated origin usually held to mean 'pure ones', 'cleansed from defilement', 'tested and found free of defect', or perhaps even 'launderers' by profession[10] (Surahs 3:52; 5:112; and 61:14). The 'sifting' of discipleship, the testing of its mettle (to vary the metaphor), according to Luke (21:31) was how Jesus saw the situation at least in the case of Peter. Again one has to go to the Gospels to discover the vivid detail of how it happened.

Much thought has been given to the interpretation of the Quranic implication of the word *kalimah* in relation to Jesus. He is not called anywhere in the Qur'ān *Kalimat Allāh*, 'the Word of God'. In Surah 3:39 and 3:45 in almost identical phrases first Zachariah and then Mary are given good tidings, in the one case 'confirming a word from God' and in the other 'as to a word from Him', or 'by a word from Him'. In Mary's case the annunciation is followed immediately by the words 'his name is the Messiah Jesus, son of Mary...'

If these are taken strictly in apposition to 'a word' then it could be understood that 'a word' is Jesus and Jesus is 'a word', from God. This would be in line with another passage in Surah 4:171, where it is said that 'Messiah Jesus, son of Mary [is] the messenger of God and His word'. Alternatively, the reference in 3:45 could simply be to the annunciation itself, the tidings brought to Mary (as comparably to Zachariah) *about* the promised conception and child. If 3:45 is read in that way then 4:171 could be seen in the same light, so that 'His [God's] word' means, not any metaphysical status other than the dignity of apostleship, but simply the fact of birth by verbal promise to Mary and, as the story indicates, without the intervention of human paternity.

However, the clear commitment of the Qur'ān to virginal conception (which is, of course, the very heart of 'annunciation') in the case of Jesus marks his birth as coming from within a divine initiative and as an expression of God's directly creative power. For that reason it is probably more appropriate to read both 3:45 and 4:171 as celebrating a unique status belonging to Jesus – albeit for the purposes of prophecy – which gives him a significance altogether his own as 'God's word'. Since the creation of Jesus was as the creation of Adam (3:59) there could be said to be at least an 'association' of the vocation of Jesus with the genesis of humanity at large. In respect of both it was God who said: *Kun fa yakūn* ('Be! and there is').

vi

Some have wanted to think that this approximates to the theme of the Prologue of John's Gospel where 'In the beginning was the Word' corresponds, in the evangelist's thought, to 'and the Word was made flesh and dwelt among us'. Creation and Incarnation are there seen as associated initiatives of the divine purpose. Paul, too, has the same conviction when he speaks of 'the light which shined out of darkness' at creation having 'shined in our hearts to give the light of the knowledge of the glory of God in the face of Jesus Christ' (2 Cor. 4:6). However, it would be against the insistent themes of the Qur'ān to read this New Testament dimension into the *Kalimah* of the Surahs about Jesus. Indeed, it is quite possible to interpret them as intending no more than the fact of the angel's message to Mary. There are many Quranic passages where 'the word of your Lord' (e.g. 6:110; 7:137; 10:33) or even 'the word of God' (9:40) refer simply to occasions of divine speech, whether in pledge or warning or assurance.

In line with this more immediate sense of 'annunciation' there are those who see the angelic message as actually bringing about the virginal conception. It has been possible for some to link the very breath of utterance (breath and what is 'breathed' being very closely tied in Semitic thought) with the fertilising factor. Jesus would then be understood as begotten literally by means of the 'annunciation' which might then be the quite literal sense in which he might be described as 'His ['God's] word', or 'a word from Him'. Will it not be wisest, in the end, not to penetrate so crudely into Mary's experience but rather to recognise in the personality of Jesus a vocation divinely intended and therefore divinely brought to pass? The Qur'ān and the New Testament will still differ deeply in their common reverence for what that initiative signifies.

'Signifies' is a rightly chosen word. For the sense that Jesus and his Mother are 'signs' (s. *āyah*) is a distinct emphasis in the Quranic picture. It includes the fact and the nature of his birth, his mission as a prophet, the content of his message and his fidelity with it, and the drama of his experience of rejection and vindication. All the prophets in their individual spheres 'signify' the divine directive for mankind, in guidance, warning and counsel. Jesus, we may say, 'intimates' what God wills, and does so by virtue of the divine intention which gave him being. This 'sign' language may indeed help to mediate between the Islamic accent on verbal messengership and the Christian reliance on the entire significance of personality within the fulfilment of it, if the *Āyah* of Jesus and Mary may be said to point towards the theme of 'sacramental' situations where 'the word' is not only 'speech' but 'event' and 'presence'. Any such conjecture must appreciate that the *Āyah* altogether excludes, indeed upbraids, what John understood by 'the Word made flesh'.

It will be noted that the particular 'signs' in Jesus' service, within the inclusive 'sign' of himself, were all – as the Qur'ān has it – 'by leave, or authority, of God' (cf. 3:49, twice; 5:110, three times).[11] The phrase occurs in a variety of other situations relating to other prophets and to ordinary mortals. Nothing, in fact, is conceivably exempt from this proviso as to divine permission, but in the case of Jesus it represents, like the *Āyah* attribute just considered, another potentially mediating feature between the Qur'ān and the New Testament. The Jesus of the Gospels, it is true, claimed and exercised an authority impressively personal and direct, in contrast to the traditionalism or casuistry of those who taught by citation and appeal to texts. Jesus' independence of spirit was an independence of such human props and institutionalised authorities. As such it arose from a deep commitment to 'the will of Him that sent' him (John 4:34; 5:30; 6:38) while his teaching and his healings were derived from a commanding sense of what God had authorised (cf. Matt. 18:14).

The divergent understanding, by Muslim and by Christian, of the person of Jesus, therefore – wide as it is in their respective Scriptures – need not and should not obscure for us the unifying fact that everything in Jesus was by divine authority and leave. As in so much else, the disparity concerns a unity. What is at issue is how to understand and confess the divine authorising and the human fulfilling which came together in the personality of Jesus. 'By what authority I do these things' (e.g. Matt. 21:24) was a question often to the fore in Jesus' ministry, and the early Church came to see the authority of his Cross and Resurrection as the act and design of God Himself. It could reasonably be said that the long, meditative retrospect of prayer attributed to Jesus in John chapter 17 is the surest insight into Jesus' sense of authorisation 'by leave of God'.[12]

One possible hint to the quality of Jesus' education of his disciples there reviewed and his nurture of them is given in the brief suggestion of Surah 3:50 that Jesus 'authorised as lawful things that were forbidden to them'. Is it fair to see here a certain 'liberalising', or rather a liberating stance, lifting off the yoke of rigorism and what Arabic writers call *taqlīd*, the state of being hidebound? If so, for all its brevity, it coincides with a notable emphasis of the Gospels. Not that Jesus decried discipline and the Law. Surah 3:50 says: '*Some* of the things prohibited.' We must see in Chapter 5 the refreshing emancipation Jesus brought his hearers from the tyranny of legalism, from the minutiae of the fastidious and from the narrow horizons of the ethnic purists and the self-righteous. With him, the compromised might find a new beginning, the sick be recovered on the Sabbath, and even Gentiles demonstrate a faith not matched in Israel. It was, of course, precisely in thus defying the hard or static conventions of his day that Jesus incurred the hostility to which Surahs 2:87 and 4:157

relate – a theme reserved for Chapter 6. His challenge to the assumptions and prejudices of the time was an appeal for what the Qur'ān, in its own context, calls *Sharḥ al-Ṣadr* ('the opening out of the heart').[13] *Sharḥ* has an intriguing double sense in that it may refer to the 'exposition' which frees the import of a text from obscurity or distortion as well as to the loosening of the mind from narrowness and rigidity. Jesus' teaching brought the two together, bringing both meaning and minds into a larger room. It was as if he was saying to his hearers in the later words of his servant, Paul: 'You are straitened in your own selves; be enlarged' (2 Cor. 6:12).

Is this a possible context in which to understand the otherwise enigmatic phrase in Surah 3:49 about Jesus 'telling what [people] store in their houses'? This knowledge of them on his part, which will impress them 'as a sign', would seem to have to do with their 'privacies' of thought, linked as it is with 'what to eat'. Surah 24:28 and 24:61 make it plain that domestic territory is not to be 'invaded' by those outside the family unless leave is given. They are God-appointed 'places of rest' (Surah 16:80). The sanctity of Semitic hospitality is well known. It may well be, therefore, that the reference in 3:49 reflects the incisive quality of Jesus' preaching as that of one who read men's hearts and laid the accent on purity within. Some commentators take the verse to refer to literal hoarding and as an injunction to 'lay up treasure in heaven', perhaps balancing this, in the two halves of the phrase, by what good things may be enjoyed in this life. Either way, the analogy the hearth supplies for the heart seems the intended sense, though according to Al-Baiḍāwī it is the *mughayyibāt* – 'the hidden things', perhaps the 'transcendental things' of which they are not in doubt – which Jesus makes explicit for them. The verse could, no doubt, be read as denoting the kind of 'clairvoyance' a seer-style of 'prophet' might possess for the better convincing of his hearers.

vii

Postponing to Chapter 6 the sharp issues in the Qur'ān's reference to the death of Jesus as 'only apparent', there remains one other feature of its narrative, namely, the 'Table' passage which gives its title, *Al-Mā'idah*, to Surah 5. The disciples inquire whether Jesus' Lord can bring down a table from heaven, for they desire to be assured of his truth by partaking of it. In response Jesus prays to God for the sending down of a table from heaven 'that it may be a festival through all our generations'. God hears his prayer and promises to do so (5:114–115).

It has been thought that three different strands may be present in these verses. There is an echo of the query of the Israelites about the feasibility of 'bread from heaven' in the wilderness, prior to the granting of the 'heavenly' manna. There may be an allusion, if remotely, to the feeding of the multitude in Jesus' ministry. Thirdly, the passage may be associated with the 'table' in the Upper Room, particularly in view of the perpetuation of that experience as a 'festival through all generations'. In the Qur'ān the point of departure, however, is a request from the disciples, whereas the Last Supper, according to the Gospels, was entirely at the initiative of Jesus, the disciples having simply inquired about the location for the traditional Passover.

Any one of these three 'associations' of the passage would fulfil its 'sign' quality, but only the third has the sacramental dimension explicitly and the character of perpetuation. There is also the suggestion in the final words of 5:115 that 'the table' would be the touchstone of fidelity. If a link with the Christian Eucharist (however tenuous) is agreed, then there is particular pathos in the Qur'ān's attribution to the disciples in seeking it the words of a most cherished of Islamic prayers – that for *iṭmi'nān al-qulūb*, 'the experience of hearts at rest' (cf. 3:126; 8:10; 13:28; and 89:27). It may be legitimate, further, to align that interpretation with the famous passage in Surah 24:36 which almost certainly refers to the sanctuary light, or altar lamp, in the Christian monasteries that verse describes.[14]

Since the Qur'ān very properly inspires and determines Muslim attitudes of mind and heart, many of the aspects of the whole Quranic picture of Jesus will recur in the concerns of Chapter 3 for the larger canvas of Muslim awareness of him. There remain here two final matters in retrospect over the passages reviewed. The one is the deep veneration for Mary, the other the puzzle of the name 'Īsā.

Most Christians find their Biblical clue to the personality of the Mother of Jesus from the *Magnificat* which Luke's narrative presents in prelude to the Nativity. Its absence from the Qur'ān means the absence of the clues to her birth-experience which it suggests. Its lyricism and, more, its radical reversal of values are indeed clues to the subsequent significance of Jesus in active ministry. But even without them the exemplary piety and surrender of Mary to vocation have endeared her name and quality to the generations of Islam. Theirs has been a veneration strictly within the understanding of the *Kalimah* status of Jesus earlier discussed. This has saved them from the subtleties, though unhappily, not from misunderstanding, of the Christian theologies and cults of the Virgin.[15] These issues it is wisest to keep firmly within the theme of Jesus and *his* centrality to all else.

The Qur'ān's invariable insistence on his being 'Son to Mary' should enable us to do this. Motherhood ultimately, and certainly here, finds its benediction, given and received, in the Sonship its travail confers upon the world.

In his geographical history, *Al-Khiṭaṭ*, the ninth (Muslim) century historian, Al-Maqrīzī, gives a delightful picture of Mary's esteem among his people and, indeed, of the bond it might constitute between the two faiths.[16] Of the monastery of Al-Quṣayr in Cairo, his native city, he writes:

> In its sanctuary was a beautiful picture of Mary, peace be upon her, painted on a tablet, and people used to flock to this place in order to look at this picture. At the top [of the monastery] there was a chamber which Abū-l-Jaysh Khumārawayh (883–895 A.H.) son of Aḥmad Ibn-Ṭulūn, built with four windows, overlooking the four directions. He used to visit this monastery frequently because he was very fond of the picture located in it. He used to admire it greatly and repair there to look at it from time to time.

The traditional veto on representational art clearly had to yield, in the monastery penthouse, to the appeal and celebration of Mary.

What, finally, of Ibn Maryam, always named 'Īsā in the Qur'ān? In the passages above, 'Jesus' has been used for the simple, sufficient reason that 'Jesus' is the English to which translation was there committed. There is no doubt of the one identity. Yet equally certainly there is a strange disparity within it of which the alternative name is sadly symbolic. The name 'Jesus' is supremely cherished in Christian faith and discipleship, even if Christian usage does not invoke 'peace upon him', after every mention, as devout Muslims do when 'Īsā is spoken of. It is, therefore, painful to have his name made different in this disconcerting way. 'Jesus', it might be claimed, is itself some compromise of the original Hebrew Yashū', but via Greek and Latin, which were the other languages of the *titulus* over the Cross, it intends to be equivalent as 'Īsā with its reversal of vowels and consonants does not.

Explanations are far to seek and difficult to credit, such as the suggestion that the name was made to 'rhyme' in its last two letters with Mūsā (Moses) in line with certain other rhymed 'pairs' in the Qur'ān. But only in five of the twenty-five occurrences of the name in the Qur'ān is Moses involved. Changing the Hebrew and Syriac 'sh' to 's' (as is general, cf. *shalom* and *salām*), Arabic obtains Yasū' as the equivalent. Adapting the letters that serve as vowel lengtheners, one can say that 'Īsā alters the 1,2,3 order of Yasū' to 3,1,2. There are instances among Arabic verbs where variation in the order of consonantal 'radicals' yields identical (or near identical) sense (e.g. ḥ-m-d and m-d-ḥ, 'to praise'). However, there is no reason why this sort of device should be applied as explanation in the case of a proper name.

It is perhaps best to leave possible technical explanations of the 'Īsā/Yasū' question to silence and simply allow the puzzle to symbolise the deep distinction obtaining between the Christian Jesus of the New Testament and the Islamic Jesus of the Qur'ān. Two names, if remotely cognate, for one *persona*: one *persona* divergently revered and received.

Notes

1 The evident familiarity of the pagan Meccans with the name of Jesus and their apparent misconception of him as 'a (tribal) god' would fall for consideration in the context of a general review of what was current about Christianity in seventh century Ḥijāz.

2 The translation of the Qur'ān into intelligible, readable English is a difficult enterprise. A.J. Arberry's *The Koran Interpreted* (London, 1955) is deservedly prized, but he tended to aim at something like the English of the Authorized Version of the Bible, allowed himself little liberty with Arabic forms and so incorporated many odd Arabisms in his English usage. There are many points where the sense and the 'feel' of Quranic terms almost defy expression outside their Arabic original. It is in part this awareness which prompts the venture here of an independent rendering. Some of the basic points at issue, turning on crucial terms, will emerge later. On the general problem of Qur'ān translation see: Muhammad Asad, *The Message of the Qur'an*, (Dar al-Andalus, Gibraltar, 1980), pp. iii–vi.

3 The familiar clause in the Lord's Prayer is echoed in Surah 3:16, where God's servants are described as those who say: 'Our Lord, we believe: forgive us our trespasses and protect us from the punishment of the fire.' The Arabic words *ighfir lanā dhunūbanā* are identical. In 48:29 is a reference which approximates to Jesus' words about the seed springing forth impressively. E.G. Parrinder, *Jesus in the Qur'ān* (London, 1965) lists various Quranic allusions or turns of phrase which might suggest traces from the Gospels (pp. 100–104).

4 One textual focus of the claim that Jesus both anticipated and validated the more final prophethood of Muḥammad is the passage in Surah 61:6 relating to 'a messenger coming after me whose name is *aḥmadu*'. This will be studied in Chapter 10 because of its alleged connection with a crucial passage in St John about the coming of the Holy Spirit, 'the Comforter'.

5 One trenchant advocate of the Semitic nature of Jesus' mission and significance and the need, against western Christianity, for his 're-Semiticisation' is Ismā'īl Rāgī al-Fārūqī. See his *Christian Ethics: A Historical and Systematic Analysis of its Dominant Ideas* (Montreal, 1967), pp. 50–110. What was at issue between Jesus and the Judaism of his day prepares the way for the ultimacy of Islam and, in Fārūqī's view, quite disqualifies New Testament 'Saviourism' and Hellenised Christology.

6 *Risālah*, from the same root as *Rasūl*, means both the content of the message and the commission that brings it.

7 One familiar example of the need for mutual sympathy here in Muslim/Christian discussion lies in the fact that technically, where the Qur'ān remonstrates against Christian faith in Jesus' Incarnation, what it in fact accuses is not Incarnation but

adoptionism, itself a heresy. However, it serves little purpose for Christians to 'exploit' this and argue from it that the Qur'ān mistakes what it is rejecting and, therefore, might be claimed not to reject what Christians believe. This would be both barren and contentious, a disservice both to fact and to right intention. The operative term is *ittikhādh*, (cf. 17:111, 19:35, 19:92, 25:2, 39:4). 'God's not taking to himself a son' is a conviction Christians share. The phrase does not describe, and so does not in itself deny, what the Gospel means by 'the Word made flesh' and the Creed by 'the only begotten Son'.

8 John 5:30; 18:12; Luke 2:49. What we might well call 'sonship to the Father' within the praying of Jesus – and such 'praying' within the stresses and sequences of his active ministry in obedience – was the direct historical origin of the final faith of the Church about Jesus' identity as 'Son of the Father'. Like all else in the New Testament the Gospel *in* Jesus is the source, the warrant and the context of the Gospel *about* Jesus. The Church confessed the one in the possession of the other. There is no need to 'oppose' servanthood and Sonship: either belongs with the dimensions of the other. They are mutually definitive of Christ because they are mutually defined in Jesus.

9 See Chapter 3 for fuller data on this intriguing interpretation so naturally aligned with the Gospel's own words: 'The Son of Man has nowhere to lay his head' (Matt. 8:20; Luke 9:58).

10 That verbal association of 'laundering' with 'discipleship' is echoed in the suggestive but still puzzling passage in 2:138 – '...*ṣibghat Allāh wa man aḥsanu min Allāhi ṣibghatan*...' – where the verbal noun *ṣibghah* has to do with dipping and cleansing but is necessarily taken here in the metaphorical sense of 'baptism'. Some translators incline to the 'dyeing' metaphor in which we 'take our hue' from God. Grammatically the noun is in the accusative but lacks any governing verb. Clothes may be a parable of, if not an index to, character and thus the means of renovating the one be a symbol of the renewing of the other. See also Chapter 9.

11 In 5:110 the words 'by My leave...' as in direct divine speech.

12 The clue to the perspective of the Fourth Gospel will be studied in Chapter 9. Chapter 17 in the Gospel is the clearest index to its nature, where an apprehension only possible in retrospect is woven into creative literary narration of the history which generated it.

13 Surah 20:25 and 94:1. That the 'tightening' or 'narrowing' of the heart was one of the dangers in the experience of pagan opposition is clear from 15:97, in respect of Muḥammad's struggle against the restrictive mentality of hidebound tradition and human obduracy.

14 It *is* possible to take the point of recurrence of 'the sending down' (which, in 5:115, God Himself echoes in the form *innī munazziluhu*, lit. 'I [actively] sending it down') to refer to the habitual benison of the natural order perhaps responsively to the petition of 'the Lord's Prayer': 'Give us day by day...' The fact that 'iron' (Surah 57), basic element in the mineral world, is included in this formula of divine bestowal of what man utilises might be held to support that more general sense. The specifics of the narrative certainly favour the explicit context of the first 'Eucharist'. The two may be brought together in the quite central emphasis of the Qur'ān on 'eucharist' (in the literal sense) in the world relationship of man in nature as that of a creature of gratitude within a creation through and through sacramental. Cf. this author's *The Mind of the Qur'ān* (London, 1973, Chapter 9).

15 See V. Courtois: *Mary in Islam* (Calcutta, 1954). The steady care for transcendence in Islam makes for difficulty in the distinction between 'worship' and 'veneration' familiar to Christian tradition. Confusions of mind – not to mention spiritual *animus* – relating to the faith in Incarnation inevitably involved Muslims in controversy about the person of Mary, despite their faith in her virgin motherhood.

16 See trans. W.B. Bishai, *Humanities in the Arabic Islamic World* (Dubuque, Iowa, 1973, p. 100). The passage occurs in Al-Maqrīzī, *Al-Khiṭaṭ* (Part 2, Cairo, n.d., p. 502).

Chapter 3

Jesus in Muslim Awareness

i

For reasons which the picture itself suggests, this chapter will end, rather than begin, with the birth of Jesus. Even so, we may take a point of departure from a Muslim Christmas carol, written by Aḥmad Shawqī, a leading Egyptian man of letters early this century. He included it in his *Great Events in the Nile Valley*, among a collection of verses.

> Kindness, chivalry, guidance and humility were born
> The day Jesus was born.
> His coming brightened the world,
> His light illuminated it.
> Like the light of dawn flowing through the universe,
> So did the sign of Jesus flow.
> He filled the world with light,
> Making the earth shine with its brightness.
> No threat, no tyranny, no revenge, no sword, no raids,
> No bloodshed did he use in his call to the new faith.
> A king he lived on earth,
> But, wearying of his state,
> He substituted heaven for it.
> To his faith wise men were attracted,
> Humble, submissive and weak before him.
> Their submission was followed by the submission
> Of kings, common folk and sages.
> His faith found roots on every land
> And anchors on every shore

Egypt proved ready soil for those roots, as Shawqī hails 'the wise men of Thebes', greeting Jesus' emissaries, whose 'holy altar' – not least in Egypt – 'became a monastery, all splendid and radiant'.[1]

The reader should not imagine that Shawqī is giving voice to an indulgent Egyptian patriotism or making a generous gesture to the

Coptic tradition of St Antony and his desert monks, to which so much is owed by Christianity at large. The Muslim poet's salutation breathes the long tradition of Islamic veneration of Jesus which it is the concern of this chapter to explore. Milton's *Ode on the Morning of Christ's Nativity* is plainly in his mind,[2] but the 'peace' of which both writers sing belongs with the Qur'ān's own celebration: 'Peace is upon me...' in the mouth of the infant Jesus (Surah 19:33).[3] What the 'peace' or 'benediction' of Jesus, enjoyed in his quality as a divine messenger and bestowed in his significance for the world, means within Islam is now our theme.

It must be set within the framework of the Quranic outlines just examined in Chapter 2. These were widely expanded and elaborated in the long interaction of Muslim and Christian during the centuries that followed the rapid inundation of Christendom by Islamic power in the seventh and eighth centuries and the steady Arabisation of the surviving Christian elements through and beyond the same period. The role that the Qur'ān had assigned to Jesus in the economy of divine revelation, as understood by Islam, was deep and positive enough to ensure a vital relevance to those contacts with Christian faith and devotion. It was, however, a relevance entangled in controversy and puzzlement because of the strong negative features which, from the Christian point of view, it presented. Muslim awareness of Jesus drew heavily from Christian sources but conformed them to its own prescripts and premises as taught by the definitive Qur'ān. The silences of that Scripture might be eagerly filled but only in strict conformity to its rubrics. The result was a fascinating characterisation of Jesus which emerges at the same time as a fascinating characterisation of Islam. Just as many a work of art bespeaks the artist in the subject, and a history is in its findings a clue to the historian, so it is here. One may study the mind of Islam inclusively in its mind about Jesus, decisive clues being everywhere implicit in how it reads and 'places' him within history, theology and faith.

The literature is large and belongs richly both to the first five hundred years of Islam and to the last centuries where – for the most part – we will savour it. Exegetes, moralists, poets, historians, mystics and theologians, as well as imaginative writers, all contribute to its wealth and diversity. They deserve a book to themselves. Yet to compress them into a single chapter, however vexing to their claims, is a salutary discipline within the overall purpose we have set ourselves. Issues which are here only hints or allusions or ideas will come to fuller discussion in later chapters, especially Chapters 5, 6, 9 and 10. To know how these have seemed in popular, or in learned, Muslim awareness will be a useful prelude to the obligations such awareness lays on Christian scholarship and interpretation.

ii

It will be convenient here to follow a sequence appropriate to the entire Islamic framework of faith, starting with the actual teaching and message of Jesus as these are, for the Qur'ān, the essentials. Jesus being only and worthily a messenger, it is right to begin with a study of how Muslim tradition builds on the very tenuous Quranic notice of what his message and teaching in fact were. This will lead, naturally, into its version of Jesus' achievement, if we may so speak, its stress on what Aḥmad Shawqī called his 'weariness with earth' – that characteristic docility and meekness on which Islam so instinctively seizes and in which it finds sharp contrast with the robust activism of Muḥammad's visible success. For many Muslims, it is 'the manifest success', as the Qur'ān has it,[1] of the Prophet of Islam which constitutes the 'finality' of his prophethood whereas Jesus, in the circumstances of his day and the providence of God, was not granted that evident external vindication. Hence, of course as we must see, that other vindication of heavenly rapture.

It was a vindication thoroughly deserved, for in a hostile setting desirous of his death Jesus fulfilled his messenger-vocation with gentle fidelity. The hostility was divinely frustrated, not personally evaded by compromise or cowardice. The 'achievement' of Jesus, though lacking a Muḥammadan-style climax, was faithful – for Muslim eyes – in the perseverance of the spoken word. This throws the emphasis firmly back on the teaching dimension and so, in turn, upon the teacher's character. Both, however, are coloured, as it were, by the climax to which they tended of other-worldly quality and destiny. Steadily recurring through all Muslim reference to Jesus is this aura of a goodness only uneasily at home in the roughness of this world, having nowhere to rest, no place to lay the head.

Yet within it was a staunch tenacity which many Muslim writers see as educating, and oftentimes confronting, the privacies of Judaic self-understanding. His mission was to Jewish peoplehood and, as these Muslim assessors see it, needs to be duly 'Semiticised', against the Hellenising of Christian interpretations on the one hand, and the inauthentically 'Semitic' on the other. This inauthenticity of Jewry is variously alleged and in some cases involves the Qur'ān's own *animus* with the emotions of current politics.[5] These need to be patiently disentangled. The issues of New Testament study and scholarship in which the Muslim reckoning with Jesus is deeply involved will be dealt with in Chapter 4. Of prior importance is a due measure of what his word and quality have inscribed within the soul of Islam.

That portraiture, by its own constraints, calls for some discussion of eschatology and the role of Jesus in Muslim tradition of 'the end things'. His heavenly rapture left room for a future significance which actual demise on earth would have prevented. Christians awaiting a Jesus-to-come conveyed millenial hopes to Muslims which gave wide currency to his name and to anticipations of his destiny as the Muslim adversary of *Al-Dajjāl*, the antichrist. It was, in part, because of these expectations that the story of his earthly *sīrah*, or sojourn, remained important for a faith-community which possessed the otherwise all-engrossing, all-sufficing, *magisterium* of Muḥammad.

Exposition has a different task when it passes to the possession of Jesus by the Sufi mystics. Their literature and devotional piety give him fervent welcome, constantly invoking his name and his repute to exemplify a meaning or adorn a moral. Jesus the wanderer, the ascetic, the devotee, the master of disciples, the *quṭb* of the soul, or simply the beloved of Christians, comes often to mind in the writings of these *wālīs* of God, the practitioners of the divine presence. Muḥammad, to be sure, is the supreme *quṭb* exalted, in the *Taṣliyah* of love, to the ultimate *hypostasis* of God's satisfaction.[6] Jesus, in his meekness, his mystical sobriety,[7] his absorption in divine ends beyond the claims of flesh and hunger, fulfils his role as 'sign of God', and 'sign' for the wayfarer towards *ma'rifah*, or illuminative knowledge.

The mystical possession of the person of Jesus in Islam leads us into some study of Islam and Christology by way of the Muslim conviction about the birth of Jesus which, as we saw, has so large a share of the Quranic portraiture. How that aspect is possessed by the tradition and read by modern Muslims and how it might relate to a reckoning of either faith with the other are vital themes for our concern. With these in mind, we will take the peace salutation upon Jesus at his birth into a Christology of the heart as a spiritual experience which perhaps some in Islam may come to share – a Christology of the heart for which the Christology of Christian definition and formulation was always meant.

It is fascinating to observe how many in the contemporary world, outside a practising commitment to Christianity, are nevertheless wistfully participant in the mystery of Jesus as the clue to their art and their existence. Boris Pasternak, Russian poet and creator of *Dr Zhivago*, wrote of life as 'the dissolving of ourselves in the selves of others, as if bestowing a gift'. Through all his theological reticences,[8] there is no mistaking the Christ-source of his sense of things and in a final poem he has Jesus say:

> I shall descend into my grave,
> And the third day rise again.
> And even as rafts float down a river,
> So shall the centuries drift, trailing like a caravan,
> Coming for judgement, out of the dark, to me

There is no reason within Islam why Muslims should be exempt from the appeal which reaches from Jesus even if it comes – if need be – in spite of, rather than in line with, the Christian Christology. Nor need the familiar Islamic dissuasives be more resistant to such attraction than the sundry motives of reluctance that derive from secular scepticism or indifference. Perhaps it is the lesson of the long centuries of *doctrinal* encounter between faiths, and in particular between Islam and Christianity, that we should let the poetry of faith take over its commendation, as that for which the vigilance of dogma was always watchful when it was properly dogmatic. Credal phrases are liable to make us – and others – 'hearers only', whereas James, in his down-to-earth Epistle calls on us to be 'poets of the word'.[9] The Sufi awareness of Jesus, if we can do it justice, will best help us to find a tributary into a Christology of the heart from the springs within Islam. The hope will be the more realist if it reckons with how deep are the reservations in Islam about a Christology of the mind, and of doctrine. Whereas, in Christian thought, theology and Christology are mutually necessary and mutually definitive, in Islam theology is largely defined by the exclusion of Christology. The person of Jesus is where the contrast proceeds. It is only from him and through him that it may be overcome.

As long, however, as our common concern is God (and so theology), the issue we locate in Jesus will remain an issue about God, for what is due from man to God belongs with what is due from God to man. A famous Persian mystic of the seventh Islamic century, Najm al-Dīn Rāzī, in his *The Path of God's Servants from Origin to Return*,[10] has the point vividly. He wrote of Moses taunted at Sinai by angels who ridiculed his desire for divine law to guide his people. Was not that desire, Moses thought (though to himself), only the other side of a conviction that God sought things from man?

> When the angels on Mount Sinai impudently taunted Moses by saying: 'O son of a menstruating woman, what do you seek of the supreme Lord?' Moses drew in his tongue and fell silent.

> He did not answer them by retorting: 'You ask me: "What do you seek of the supreme Lord?" Why do you not ask Him: "What does the supreme Lord seek of dust?"'

A fair reversal. For a Moses, summoned by God to receive Torah for human obedience, cannot but mean a divine seeking of the human answer, though from dust it must be. Najm al-Dīn Rāzī drew back from such a bold logic and continued:

> We threw the ragged cloak of inauspicious remoteness from Him over the shoulder of safety and in the corner of tranquillity drew the skirt of submission over the foot of intent.

Both the florid language and the reluctance to be fully theist characterise the classical Muslim theologians. Najm al-Dīn Rāzī is no exception. It is the same instinct against a consistently confident theism which underlies the Muslim reckoning with Jesus. The reservations of, and about, deity are translated into the limitation of the relevance of Jesus to teaching, guidance, exhortation and direction, to messengership not incarnate Christhood and to a servanthood that cannot be sonship. To this Muslim awareness of the Jesus of heavenly words, we now turn.

iii

Muslim *Ḥadīth* sayings about Jesus and by him have been collected by numerous scholars and a tabulation need not be attempted here.[11] It is important to realise that the Muslim assumptions about the nature both of prophetic utterance and of 'scripture' require a concern with the actual words of Jesus, with what western scholarship would call his *ipsissima verba*. On Muslim reckoning there are no *verba* other than the 'actual', though the great Al-Ghazālī (1058–1111) justified his use of John's Gospel by his belief that God had granted to Jesus a special *khuṣūṣiyyah*, or personhood, whereby he was allowed to use theopathic language which had only metaphorical value.[12] However, even Al-Ghazālī laid prior stress on univocal speech. The issues here about the very nature of 'scripture' will be taken up in Chapter 4. The point now is that Muslims relate to sayings of Jesus reaching them through Tradition as to *dicta* by a Qur'ān-style speaking mandate possessed by Jesus, a mandate which gave the world the *Injīl*, or Gospel, first uttered, then recorded, only to be later distorted by Christians, largely lost, and retrieved fragmentarily within the Qur'ān.

Jesus' sayings linger and circulate in many fascinating places. The ruined city of Fatehpur-Sikri, south of Delhi, was built by the great Mughal Emperor, Akbar, to celebrate his victories. On the eastern side of the south gate of its great mosque are the words: 'Jesus (peace be upon him) said: "This world is a bridge. Pass over it, but build not your dwelling there."' Of all the *dicta* of Jesus this is the most famous. The world is a place of transition and properly meant only for pilgrimage.[13] This world and the next, Jesus said, may be likened to two wives. You will be pleased with one and angry with the other.[14] Travellers in remote regions of the Muslim world have been surprised to find that even illiterate peasants knew of Jesus as the one who said that 'the son of man has nowhere to lay his head'. This note of caution about the beguilements of the world is frequent. The Qur'ān exegete Al-Zamakhsharī (1075–1144) notes that 'in the sermons of 'Īsā, son of Mary, it is written: "Beware how you sit with sinners."' His successor Al-Baiḍāwī (d. 1286) has from Jesus: 'Be in the midst, yet walk on one side', as a directive about how to be *in*, yet not *of*, the world.[15] In his *'Ilm al-Akhlāq*, Fakhr al-Dīn al-Rāzī (1149–1209) attributes to Jesus the dictum that withdrawal and abstention suit the important things in this world more than effort to improve them.[16]

D. S. Margoliouth of Oxford, listed the sayings attributed to Jesus by Al-Ghazālī in his celebrated work: *Iḥyā' 'Ulūm al-Dīn* (*Religion: Its Meanings and Practice Revitalised*). To review his citations here will be a sound index to the theme, given Al-Ghazālī's outstanding authority and the wide currency of his work. Numbers in parentheses indicate the Book and Section of the *Iḥyā'*.[17] Throughout, the echoes – close or distant – of the Gospels are unmistakable.

> He who knows and does and teaches shall be called great in the kingdom of heaven. (1:8)
>
> Do not entrust wisdom to those who are not meet for it and do not withhold it from those who are fit for it, lest you do them harm. Be like a gentle physician who lays the remedy on the diseased spot. (1:30)
>
> Evil scribes are like ... the conduit of a latrine which is plastered outside but foul within, or like sepulchres the outside of which is adorned while inside are the bones of dead men. (1:49)
>
> If a man send away a beggar empty from his house, the angels will not visit that house for seven nights. (1:177)
>
> God revealed to Jesus: 'Though thou should'st worship with the devotion of the inhabitants of the heaven and the earth, but hadst not love in God and hate in God, it would avail thee nothing.' (2:119)

Jesus said: 'Make yourself beloved of God by hating evil-doers; bring yourselves near to God by removing far from them and seek God's favour by way of their displeasure.' They said: 'O spirit of God, then with whom shall we converse?' Then he said: 'Converse with those whose presence will remind you of God, whose words will increase your works and whose works will make you desire the next world.' (2:119)

They say there was no word of address Jesus loved more to hear than: 'Poor man'. 'There is no poor man poorer than I.' (2:154 and 2:168)

Jesus lay down one day with his head upon a stone. Satan, passing by, said: 'O Jesus, you are fond of this world.' So Jesus took the stone and cast it from under his head, saying: 'This be yours, together with this world.' (3:28)

Blessed is he who abandons a present pleasure for the sake of a promise about what is absent and unseen. (3:52)

O company of apostles, make hungry your livers and make bare your limbs: perhaps then your hearts may see God. (3:65)

Beware of glances, for they plant passion in the heart and that is a sufficient temptation. (3:81)

Devotion is of ten parts. Nine consist in silence, and one in solitude. (3:87)

Jesus one day walked with his disciples and they passed by the carcase of a dog. The apostles said: 'How foul is the smell of this dog.' But Jesus said: 'What pearls are its teeth!' (3:108)

Take not the world for your Lord lest it take you for its slaves. Lay up your treasure with Him who will not waste it. (3:151)

It is a mark of the evil of this world that God is disobeyed therein... Know that the root of every sin is love of the world. (3:151)

Woe to him whose care is this world. Who is he who builds on the waves of the sea? Such is the world: do not take it for your resting place. (3:153)

The world was revealed to Jesus in the form of an old woman with broken teeth and all sorts of adornments upon her. He said to her: 'How many husbands have you had?' She said: 'I cannot count them.' He said: 'Have you survived them all? Or did they all divorce you?' She said: 'No. I have slain them all.' Then Jesus said: 'Woe to your remaining husbands: why do they not take warning from your former husbands? You have destroyed them all one after the other and yet they are not on their guard against you?' (3:161)

The heart, so long as it is not torn by passion, nor befouled by desire, nor hardened by comfort, shall become a vessel for wisdom. (3:161)

Store up for yourselves that which the fire will not devour. They said: 'What is that?' He answered: 'Mercy.' (3:184)

Blessed is he whom God teaches His book and who does not die proud. (3:256)

If a man lifts his head up to the roof it wounds him, but if he bows down his head it shelters him. (3:261)

Beautiful raiment means pride of heart. (3:269)

Do not look to the wealth of the people of this world. For the glitter of their wealth takes away the light of faith. (4:157)

Jesus was asked about the best of works. He said: 'Resignation to God and love of Him.' (4:281)

He was asked: 'Are there any on the earth like you?' He answered: 'Yes. Whoever has prayer for his speech, meditation for his silence and tears for his vision, he is like me.' (4:354)

The recurrent note of austerity and withdrawal from the world belongs also in a long passage in the *Iḥyā'* (3:198) which is reminiscent of Matthew chapter 23 with its 'Woe to...' directed against hypocrisy of outward piety and inward wrong. 'What does it profit,' Jesus asks in a strange revision of the Gospel analogy, 'for a dark house that a lamp is set on its roof, when all is dark within?' Jesus, another passage records, took nothing with him except a pitcher and a comb. One day, seeing a man comb his beard with his fingers, Jesus threw away the comb. On another day, seeing a man drink from the river with his cupped hands, Jesus threw away the pitcher (4:182).

iv

It is interesting to speculate on the provenance of Al-Ghazālī's references to Jesus and the sources through which they reached him. In the dimensions of his great work on moral theology and the care of the soul, it is fair to say that he draws on an awareness of Jesus only in incidental ways and for merely illustrative purposes. He is there 'to point a moral and adorn a tale'. There is no deep grappling with the ethics of man in New Testament terms – which is the more unfortunate, given that Al-Ghazālī was so thorough and incisive a moralist in Islamic terms. Perhaps it is that very competence which marginalises Jesus within his analysis of ethical religion.

The teaching of Jesus finds more central place, and more explicit citation, in the writings of Abū 'Abdallāh Ḥārith al-Muḥāsibī, a ninth century Muslim moralist whose *Kitāb al-Waṣāyā* (*The Book of Commandments*) is one of the most searching scrutinies of the soul, a work that comes as close as any in Islam to the temper of the Sermon on the Mount. Perhaps because the first translations of the New Testament into Arabic from Syriac coincide with Al-Muḥāsibī's generation, his references are precise and incisive. He was, as his name indicates, a sort of 'accountant' of the soul, and he taught a rigorous self-interrogation and self-discipline with a lively sense of the deviousness of the heart and the urgency of inward sincerity. He used the parable of the sower in teaching 'a caring for the rights of God'. He deprecated anxiety for the morrow, reproached fasting and 'righteousness' which were only for outward seeming, and gave warning of the separation of 'wheat from tares'. He rejected oath-taking in the name of God as implying some right to be deceptive when not under oath. He drew from Jesus the repudiation of retaliation under wrong. Retribution lay in the hands of God. One should bless, not curse, the evildoer at whose hands one suffered. He echoed Paul, in turn echoing Jesus, in saying: 'Do not be wise in your own conceits ' (Rom. 12:16). He had a concern for what he called 'the springs of compassion' and cherished the habit of a constant gratitude toward God as sensing 'the Giver beyond the gift'. He wanted people to be free of envy and care, detecting the dependable mercy of God in the beauty of the flowers and the joy of the birds.[18]

Al-Muḥāsibī's Islamic awareness of Jesus is nowhere surpassed in the Muslim story. Approximations to the sort of currency of the teaching of Jesus, studied in these two writers, occur throughout Muslim tradition, ethical thought and theological discourse. Interest in the story of Jesus tends to centre around the areas of emphasis in the Quranic version, so that, in Al-Ya'qūbī, for example, (late ninth century) an almost verbatim summary of the Sermon on the Mount occurs only in the context of a primary interest in the birth narratives. Even so, Al-Ya'qūbī quotes two beatitudes, links them with 'the salt of the earth and the light of the world', rehearses the prohibition of murder, retaliation, adultery and oath-taking, and commends the duty of 'the second mile', of non-resistance, and the generous loan. The summary continues down to the parable of the house built on the rock. When he turns to Luke, it is naturally the Nativity narratives which most engage Al-Ya'qūbī, but he is careful to note and report the words of Jesus in the synagogue about the 'servant' in Isaiah chapter 61. He is clearly minded to record what the Gospels offer without the inhibition that limited many in Islam to those accents of the teaching Jesus – few as they were – which the Qur'ān actually enshrined, or left them to total silence on the ground that no attention outside the Qur'ān was required.

This is not the context in which to explore how this varied acquaintance with the corpus of Jesus' teaching transpired within Islam, whether in its diffuse and popular form or in the more erudite shape of scholarship, both historical and theological. Three exemplars here do scant justice to the wealth of reference, but it may be claimed that they represent its variety and character. What of the Muslim estimate of the achievement of Jesus through and beyond his actual teaching? For answer we will opt to listen rather to the moderns as our mentors.

V

As noted in discussion of the Quranic Jesus, the criteria are assumed to be rightly those of the Quranic situation of Muḥammad. Whether those criteria are proper or whether it is right or necessary to question them seldom arises. In consequence the 'manifest victory' held to have eventuated within original Islam becomes the yardstick by which the career of Jesus must be measured. In consequence, again, a certain incompleteness must attach to Jesus' messengership inasmuch as it did not emerge into 'manifest success'. This in no way detracts either from his status or his fidelity and divine mercy compensates in other ways for what Jesus was not permitted, alike by circumstance and providence, to attain. It also explains why it was an important duty of Jesus, as Muslims allege, to announce the coming of Muḥammad. They 'cannot think that such a major manifestation as Islam would have been passed in silence by Christ.'[19]

The 'incompleteness' of Jesus' achievement is seen as being only in part due to the circumstances of Roman power and the tenacity of Jewish religion, against which his mission was pitted. It was also attributable to his one-sided spirituality. Observing that 'whoever has no worldly life has no spiritual life', 'Alī Shari'atī,[20] the philosopher-revolutionary of contemporary Iran (1933–77), writes:

> Then came Jesus who directed society to concentrate on the hereafter so that Rome changed its orientation from pleasure and worldliness to asceticism and contemplation of the hereafter, the ultimate result of this being the Middle Ages.

He is not, of course, referring to the 'Rome' of Jesus' time but to a later 'Christendom' which he derives, with much telescoping of history, from the docility of Jesus. However, the point is clear. 'Ideal man,' Shari'atī goes on, 'holds the sword of Caesar in his hand and he has the heart of Jesus in his breast.'[21] These being compatible, Jesus lacked the first and therein lies the partiality of his mission and the superiority of Muḥammad. A detail survives in Al-Ghazālī's *Iḥyā'* about how Jesus took as a disciple a penitent brigand who had infested the highway for forty years. Could it be that Jesus should have recruited his violence rather than induced his repentance and so 'redeemed' him for effective revolution?[22]

It is not compatibility but rather complementarity which Khālid Muḥammad Khālid sees in Jesus and Muḥammad in one of his several popular books: *Ma'an 'ala-l-Ṭarīq: Muḥammad wa-l-Masīḥ* (*On the Road Together: Muḥammad and the Christ*). He sees them 'together', 'in the way of the Lord, and for the sake of man and of life'. Sharing the belief we explore below in a future role for Jesus, Khālid Muḥammad Khālid recognises and approves his gentleness and openness to suffering, quoting freely from the Passion narratives and acknowledging the significance of Gethsemane, while maintaining the contrasted necessity of Muḥammad's patterns in their time and place. Like many other Muslim contemporaries he sets Jewry at the core of reproach for Jesus' tribulations as the source of his mission's frustration. This he focuses in a final chapter headed: 'And Now – Barabbas or Jesus?' in which he avers that all society today is faced fundamentally with the same choice. Muḥammad, he believes, 'chose the Christ'. He goes on:

> The Christ was himself his message. He was the supreme example he left and gave. He was the love which knows no hatred, the peace which knows no restlessness, the salvation which knows no perishing. And when we realise all these things on this earth, we shall then comprehend the return of the Christ.... He is peace and love and truth and good and beauty. With Muḥammad the faithful we declare: 'Christ, not Barabbas, the true not the false, love not hatred, peace not war, life not extinction.'

The spirit of Barabbas, he says, glorifies force, violence and tyranny. Were there not one hundred and fifty million victims of the last two world wars? In looking to the future by the criteria of Jesus, which Khālid Muḥammad Khālid takes to be the meaning of Muḥammad's tradition of Jesus' return, the Prophet identifies himself with the ultimacy of the way of love.[23]

This remarkable writing, however, has to be balanced – for most Muslims – by the necessity, as they see it, of Jesus foretelling

Muḥammad. If Jesus, as we have still to study, supplies Islam with its eschatological perception and goal, Muḥammad supplies the historical realism which is wanting in Jesus and precluded by his context. If Islamic traditions need to anticipate a Christ-style future, Jesus needed to anticipate a Muḥammad-style future, the one in eternal the other in temporal terms. The Gospel may have it right in the ultimate; the Qur'ān has it right in the concrete.

Khālid Muḥammad Khālid was, in any event, an ardent and rhetorical writer whom more sober, pedestrian ones suspect.[24] A more stolid, but still influential author was 'Abbās al-'Aqqād (1889–1964) whose *'Abqariyyat al-Masīḥ* (*The Genius of the Christ*,) was an important waymark in Muslim assessment of Jesus this century. His work enjoyed a wide, popular impact and belonged in a series on religious 'genius' which included Muḥammad, Gandhi and 'Umar, the second Caliph. 'Aqqād places Jesus firmly within the Islamic framework of the prophet–teacher tradition, which he explores in a study of contemporary Judaism and the social and political conditions of Jesus' time. He is interested in the contrast between Galilee and Judea in the narrative of the ministry and stresses the 'gentile', even 'Arab', character, as he sees it, of the former. The cosmopolitan quality of the 'nursery' of Jesus' movement around the lake, sharply differing from the enmity of the holy, capital city, 'Aqqād reads as a symbol of the central issue of the teaching ministry.

Here the Christian reader finds what is surely the most significant feature of 'Aqqād's Christology. He is deeply aware of a gathering opposition to Jesus. Such, indeed, is the occupational hazard of all prophets and one would expect a perceptive Muslim to be alert to it. Jesus, we can say, 'progresses' into ripeness. He does so by a pathway of obedience, by a struggle through uncertainty towards assurance. The disciples play a significant role. They and Jesus, as 'Aqqād sees them, begin in a temper of Jewish conservatism and arrive at a strong defiance of establishment. They start in popular Galilean terms and conclude in universal humanity.

The author here may be conflating the actualities of Jesus' ministry and the story of the Church. But, in a striking way, he does recognise a stern battle within the soul of Jesus as the cost of these developments. Jesus, he believes, had to wrestle with the meaning of despair and how God's will was to be understood in the context of adversity. He had to surrender despair itself to God that the answer, the rescue, might be God's alone. True security obtains only within the divine will. The way of faith is a drinking of the cup. 'Abbās al-'Aqqād, in line with his Quranic loyalty, 'takes the cup away,' in the rapture of Jesus to heaven.

Though Jesus 'encountered the most powerful opposition that a religion could encounter', the curtain of 'rapture' descends upon the drama and, after the cleansing of the Temple 'the role of history ends and the role of the creed begins'.[25]

Though respited from its climax in the Cross, the despair of Jesus within vocation stands as the most precious insight of *'Abqariyyat al-Masīḥ*. Though what is at issue between Jesus and the world is never brought, here, to the test of resurrection, 'Aqqād perceives clearly what the issue holds. Jesus called his hearers to a *metanoia*, to a new *qiblah*, away from orientation to self and Mammon, and round to the new *Sharī'ah* of the Beatitudes. It was urgent that society should hear and heed the 'woes' from Jesus against its follies and wrongs. Jesus' compassion for women, and all the disadvantaged, his ready affirmation of forgiveness, his ability to confound the hypocrites with answers, or questions, and his accent on inwardness, all indicate the virility of his character and the courage of his mission. In the evolution of both, in response to the context, 'Aqqād discerns a kind of *Hijrah* of Jesus into a universal gospel, in counteraction to the animosity he faced, just as Muḥammad's *Hijrah* opened new dimensions in defiance of the hostile Quraish.

vi

There is a similar concentration on adversity and misfortune in 'Abd al-Ḥamīd Jūdat al-Saḥḥār's study: *Al-Masīḥ 'Īsā ibn Maryam* ('Īsā the Christ, Son of Mary).[26] Writing in a very lyrical style, he prefaces all his fifty-six chapters with a verse from the Qur'ān.[27] He conflates the Quranic nativity narratives with the Gospels and links Christian faith in the Incarnation with the Satanic temptations in the wilderness which Jesus repudiates. Nevertheless he draws freely from the Gospels this faith bequeathed to trace the course of Jesus' ministry and his partnership with his disciples, not excluding the Gospel of John. It is a course which heads steadily into crisis. As Surah 30:41 has it: 'On land and sea corrupting evil has shown itself'. Jesus, however, pursues his teaching way unflinching. 'Hatred,' quotes Al-Saḥḥār from Surah 3:118, 'has become so evident in what they say and what lurks in their hearts is yet larger hate.' Recruiting Quranic echoes in this way for his narrative of Jesus, Al-Saḥḥār brings him to his Gethsemane, sees him resigning himself to his tribulations and yearning for another prophet (undoubtedly Muḥammad) who, in a future day, would be both dynamic and successful in confronting enemies of God such as he himself had not been able to overcome.

Thus Jesus is seen in Al-Saḥḥār's work as accepting that call of 3:55 ('O 'Īsā, I am causing you to die...'). The writer follows throughout the Passion story, though changing, in Jesus' prayers, the words 'the Father' and 'my Father' to *Allāh*.[28] In the climax Jesus walks unseen through the band of arresting soldiers and goes into hiding, while Judas (Iscariot), isolated there, is seized by the guards who suppose him to be Jesus. Judas is minded to resist and cry out to show them their error, but a vision of joy turns him instead to give himself up in atonement for his sin and as a ready response to a perceived vocation. Throughout the trial and condemnation and crucifixion, it is Judas who is here fitted into the record of the fidelity and yieldedness of Jesus. 'Today the men of evil were in manifest perversity' (Surah 19:38) is aligned with: '...they know not what they do'. Do we understand, though, the mis-identity about Judas, or the enormity in the Cross, in their 'doing what they know not'? Buoyed up with hope of the Messianic banquet with Jesus, Judas suffered death. Heaven did not intervene, because 'the crucified was not the apostle of God, nor was he the miracle-worker'.[29]

Meanwhile, Jesus lay concealed until Judas' crucifixion had allayed the anxieties of the authorities about the danger he posed to them. He emerged from hiding, visited Judas' tomb, greeted Mary Magdalene and came among the disciples as the Gospel narratives record. Finally he withdrew into the silence of the night and made an exit like that of Moses. He went to his Lord, the Lord who raised him to Himself. Al-Saḥḥār concludes:[30]

> Jesus departed. He did not establish truth on the earth. His enemies broke him. But the final one, the servant of God and His chosen, will not be weary nor will he be broken before he has set truth in the earth, and until the kingdom of God holds sway over this world. 'Īsā came finally into the heavy dark of night whence God raised him to power and glory and immortality.

vii

Al-Saḥḥār, in this portrayal of the blessed yet lonely and burdened Jesus, has many of the Muslim assessors on his side. Their traditions have it that Jesus, at his rapture to heaven, was clad in a patched and tattered garment. This so-called *muraqqa'ah* had as many as three hundred holes. Some mystics believed they emulated him by bedraggled clothes.[31] The 'Īsā of Al-Saḥḥār's version has not 'worn well' in this world and is denied even the courage to face his own destiny as his teaching shaped it and as the hostile world conspired to have it. The wounds he did not suffer in the flesh have made instead a patchwork of his garment or – to leave the analogy – an imperfection in his mission for which, however, the 'rapture' of the wearer duly compensates.

Not all Muslim writers, however, see Jesus' story this way. Fatḥī 'Uthmān published his *Ma'-al-Masīḥ fī-l-Anājīl al-Araba'ah* (*With the Christ in the Four Gospels*) in 1961.[32] Agreeing that the four Gospels were the closest, surest source for a knowledge of Jesus, he saw him essentially as a reformer of Judaism, a pioneer of a true ethical *Sharī'ah* to displace the formalism to which *Torah* had been reduced. There is a similar theme in Ismā'īl al-Fārūqī.[33] But Fatḥī 'Uthmān is not in commiseration about Jesus as Al-Saḥḥār tends to be. On the contrary, Jesus proclaimed in his historical context certain eternal principles and these are not assessable as 'failure' on circumstantial grounds. Jesus affected both his time and the future, not by revolutionary – or other – challenge to establishment but by the abiding integrity of religious values faithfully affirmed and served. 'Uthmān sees the ethics of the Gospels valid equally for Muslims as for Christians and in no way time-bound or superseded.

This kind of purely 'spiritual' achievement, however, though widely saluted by liberal Muslims, does not resolve the Islamic reservations springing from the need for 'manifest victory'. Have Christians read too much into too little in their credence of Jesus? 'Your so imaginative religion –' exclaimed the eighth-century Caliph 'Umar II writing to Leo III, 'why was it that Jesus and his disciples came naked into the world and returned the same?'[34] One twentieth-century Muslim academic declares himself confirmed in – if not converted into – Islam by none other than Dostoevsky! He has in mind those Jesus-like figures, Father Zossima in *The Brothers Karamazov* and Prince Myshkin in *The Idiot*, who are too good for this world. For these, Muḥammad Mujīb, former Vice-Chancellor of Jamia Millia Islamica in Delhi, wrote that the Sermon on the Mount was 'a vision of absolute values ... a dream, passionate and divine', but a 'road to self-realisation, too steep, too broken, too narrow'. He saw the road of Islam as more gradual, more on the gradient of spirit *and* nature. Nevertheless, 'the meaning of the Sermon on the Mount brings tears of prayer into my eyes now ... Because Christianity came to me through language, it stole into me as an intoxication'. This admiration came, via Dostoevsky, to rediscover the solid realism of the Qur'ān.[35]

Perhaps this overall view of Jesus is captured in a prayer attributed to him in the *Iḥyā'*[36] by Al-Ghazālī:

O God I have reached a point where I am unable to repel what I abhor or to accomplish what I hope. Things have passed into the hand of others. I have become a prey in my task. There is no poor man in a poorer state than I. O God, do not let my adversary gloat over me or my friend think evil of me. Do not allow my piety to be my calamity nor let this world be my maximum distress. Do not give me into the hand of those who will have no mercy on me, O Thou ever-living One, O Thou eternally abiding.

viii

This sounding of the Muslim awareness of Jesus, however cursory, leads us into two other areas before we come to the birth narratives and Christology. They are the Jesus role in the last things and the Sufi possession of this 'man of sorrows'. Both we have anticipated and it is only for purposes of exposition that we separate them out.

Khālid Muḥammad Khālid usefully represents the first, as earlier noted. The non-success of Jesus, despite – or perhaps because of – the nobility of his teaching, surely makes it natural that he should have foreseen and foretold the coming of the more ultimate 'kingdom of God' in and by Muḥammad. Equally, the cost-effectiveness of that prophethood (if we may so speak) requires a final dimension for which Islam, in turn, must look to Jesus. The success-criterion of Islam will be eternalised by the one whose purity in earthly context precluded his historical success.

That Jesus is available for this role follows from his being raptured to heaven, in contrast to the demise and burial of Muḥammad in Medina.[37] That the expansion of Islam into Christian territories in the early centuries afforded access to millenial traditions about Jesus is clear. However, such contact, of itself, with these sources about a Jesus-to-come does not suffice to explain his presence, or adoption, within Islam for this role. It stems from Islam's own need of millenial 'finality'. Precisely because Islam had a totally successful historical inauguration, and because that inauguration, by the same token, could not be made perpetual but, on the contrary, fell into rapid compromise as history sees it, a final future would be needed to make good in the end what had been 'the seal of the prophets' at the start. In his study of 'complaint and hope in medieval Islam', Franz Rosenthal[38] has the point well:

The times before Islam appeared on the scene were seen as unrelievedly evil. Those evil conditions were brought to an end by

> the divine revelation which came to Muḥammad and was to set things right once and for all. History did not fully cooperate in this grand scheme, as history has a way of doing. The process of transforming the time of Muḥammad's prophecy into a golden age thus appears to have had its origins already in the early days of Islam. Famous traditions of the Prophet state explicitly that a decline from the glorious days of Prophecy was to take place rapidly and inexorably within the next few generations... The world had peaked in the time of the Prophet and his generation and had gone downhill ever since... The world had seen its golden age in the time of Muḥammad and would never be the same again till its expected end.

There is something in the Arabic sense of the words *dunyā*, 'this world', and *dahr*, 'this age', which hint at this view of present history as a disappointment, given the ruling sense of a prophetic climax ever receding and, by its nature, not within present emulation. There might be various practical responses to this view of things – ascetic, political, philosophical. Piety in general lay hold on an 'Īsa-to-come as confronting and overcoming the *Dajjāl*, the 'antichrist' in whose person the recalcitrance of history to the divine *Sharī'ah* could be symbolised.

It seems clear that the main source of Muslim beliefs relating to Jesus and *Al-Dajjāl* came from traditional lore. However, there are Quranic passages which, according to how we read them, leave room for a relevance of Jesus *after* his 'rapture' to heaven. Surah 4:159 says that to a man the people of the Book will believe in him *before* his death. Since this 'death' is post-millenial the passage must refer to a faith in him, on their part, after his return. The invocation of 'peace upon him' in 19:33 must also mean a return to earth, if by 'rapture' Jesus is as yet 'alive'. A controversial passage in Surah 43:57–64[39] speaks of 'knowledge of the hour' between two explicit references to Jesus. Many commentators have taken the crucial pronoun about 'knowledge of the hour' to refer to Jesus also, in the sense that he is the clue to such 'knowledge'. Others, however, refer the pronoun to the Qur'ān and not to Jesus.

Certainly no detailed prospectus of the future place of Jesus could be had from these passages. It was Christian eschatology which supplied it in the context of the Islamic quest for finality. Given perfected truth in a consummate revelation, now always in receding retrospect, that future finality would be the operative actualisation of what Muslim history in itself had failed – though meant – to yield, in a failure bound up with 'the golden age' of the historical Muḥammad and his immediate caliphal heirs as something never since repeated. The clues to that actualisation would all be, properly, Quranic; but the agency, according to Tradition, would be that of Jesus. At his return from heaven, the great battle with 'the antichrist', *Al-Dajjāl*, would unfold. Jesus would confess and proclaim Islam, break all crosses, kill all swine, and so inaugurate millenial righteousness. Ultimately, after natural death, he would occupy the tomb prepared for him beside the Prophet and the first two Caliphs in Medina.[40]

There are numerous suggestions as to the origin of the term *Al-Dajjāl*. The root sense of the verb is 'to cover', or 'to smear', with the implication of concealing and defiling. Just as any coating covers the body so the lure of the antichrist covers the earth. Or the 'covering' may have to do with the vast array of his followers, caught in his deceptions across the face of the world. If the root is associated with 'gilding' then the element of deception is paramount. People are readily taken in by what they covet. *Al-Dajjāl*, in brief, is the personification of all that is evil. He is 'the father of lies' of the New Testament (John 8:44).

It is relevant to note that though *Al-Dajjāl* may be translated 'the antichrist', as the supreme adversary of God, the Arabic/Islamic term avoids to define that total enmity by reference to the Messianic achievement. As we have seen, *Al-Masīḥ* as a title for Jesus, is honorific not definitive. Antichrist is defeated eschatologically by Jesus as the agent, but by Islam in the event, and not by virtue of the Cross and of the love that redeems. The hope of history is the final triumph of the prophetic, as culminated in Muḥammad but assigned to his nearest predecessor. In terms of inter-faith converse there is an intriguing potential of gain and loss in this situation. We have a Jesus in emphatic, final espousal of Islam: we have a Muḥammad in ultimate accomplishment only through the agency of Jesus. Whatever either awaits, neither attains by the means their faiths assume. Jesus prevails, not through the Cross, Resurrection and grace, but with the Qur'ān. Muḥammad is final, not by *Jihād* and *Daulah*, but by heaven's Jesus. What this strange eventuality teaches us is not readily agreed.

ix

'Your so imaginative religion' and being 'naked in this world', reproachfully stated by 'Umar of Christians and Jesus, are no less apt as language about Sufism and the Sufis. Theirs was certainly an imaginative, even romantic, version of Islam and they eagerly coveted to be 'naked in the world', gladly dispossessed of wealth and luxury. Their literature and poetry through at least seven centuries has steady celebration of Jesus as exemplar and mentor of these aptitudes. Nowhere is Islamic awareness of Jesus more lively or more perceptive than in the Arabic, Persian, Turkish, and Urdu poems of the mystics of Islam. Sitting loosely by doctrinal contentiousness, they are free to aspire towards that soul-affection which first kindled the theology pundits dispute and which transcends what punditry can attain. The Jesus in Sufism kindles mutual recognition. Just as art yields back that from which it took its rise, so the poet-saint mirrors in his verses the image that has drawn him.

It is impossible to do justice to Sufi celebration of Jesus. It has some of the accents we have already studied in the moralists, like Al-Muḥāsibī, and in the chroniclers. We may well begin with the Quranic epithet for Jesus in 3:45 that he is among *al-muqarrabīn*, 'those who are brought near to God'. (cf. 56:11). For Sufis read in this descriptive the intimacy with God which Jesus exemplified in prayer and in compassion. Of all divine messengers he is the most complete example of a contemplative saint. It is this devotional union with the will of God which Christian faith, missing its esoteric quality, mistakenly interpreted into the doctrine of the Incarnation.[41] Jesus was, so to speak, a great Sufi personality. As a youth he left behind the external things of life and gave himself up to God, abstaining from food in order to worship, and refraining from 'the pride of the eyes'.[42]

It was easy for Sufis, musing in these terms, to draw on the Gospel narratives. The author just cited makes Matt. 19:12a to mean that Jesus was himself 'a eunuch from his mother's womb'. More natural examples lay in his practice of fasting, his long meditation and his call to renunciation. Such habits, of course, belong closely to Sufi disciplines of initiation. Such a (Muslim) initiate Shabastarī describes in his *Gulshān-i-Rāz*:[43]

> He obtains release from his own knowledge
> And, like the prophet Jesus, he becomes near to God.
> He gives up his existence utterly to be plundered
> And in the steps of the most pure he ascends

Loving, as they did in such context, the metaphor of intoxication for mystical ecstacy, some Sufi poets could neatly capture what they saw as Christian doctrinal faith by describing it as 'intoxication without having drunk'. Such faith pretends to the experience of insight with no real experience of the mystical union.[44] Wine, as a symbol of Sufi joy, explains why references to 'taverns' are so frequent in Muslim poetry.

The meaning should not be misread. The 'cupbearer' is the master of the discipline, not the barman of the inn. It is this which inspires Jalāl al-Dīn Rūmī to write in his *Mathnawī*: 'The house of 'Īsā was the banquet of men of heart. O afflicted one, quit not this door'.[45]

Rūmī continues with an evocative portrayal of the scene around Jesus in Galilee:

From all sides the people ever thronged,
Many blind and lame, halt and afflicted,
At the door of the house of 'Īsā at dawn,
That with his breath he might heal their ailments.
As soon as he had finished his orisons
That holy one would come forth at the third hour.
He pondered those impotent folk sitting,
Troop by troop, at his door in hope and expectation.
He spoke to them saying: 'O stricken ones,
The desires of you all have been granted by God,
Arise, walk without pain or affliction,
Acknowledge the mercy and beneficience of God.'
Then all, like camels whose feet are shackled,
When you loose their feet on the road,
Straightway rush in joy and delight to the halting place,
So did they run upon their feet at his command

In *The Hundred Letters* of the famous Sharafuddīn Manerī, a Bihārī master-Sufi of the fourteenth century, there are many allusions to the works and teachings of Jesus,[46] among them:

Jesus the prophet also said: 'A man cannot be reckoned among the host of angels in heaven and on earth, that is, those who have attained divine illumination, unless he be born again.'

Jesus said he could give sight to the blind and raise the dead, but he was powerless to help a fool.

Jesus always used to wear a woollen garment.

Jesus who never stayed in one place.

Jesus the crowning perfection of purity.

Jesus said: 'The world consists of three days. The first is the day that has passed, you can expect nothing from it now. As for tomorrow you do not know if you will survive until it comes. You are now in the third day: do not expect anything more than that.'

The ascetic note here is familiar enough, but Sufi celebrants of Jesus were interested in the theme of breath and wind, as well as wine. His 'never staying in one place' meant not merely a physical homelessness but the spontaneity of the spirit characteristic of the Quranic *Al-Khiḍr* and of Shams al-Dīn, the elusive saint in the story of Jalāl al-Dīn Rūmī[47] 'By the breath of Jesus' was a formula explaining attainment of enlightenment. This 'breath of 'Īsā,' said Rūmī, was 'not like very ordinary breath'.[48] Rather, it brought an infusion of the universal soul. Was not Jesus himself, in his earthly flesh, the fruit, in Mary, of the inbreathing spirit of annunciation? Such, too, was the new birth of which Jesus spoke in the Gospel. As Sufis cite them the disciples of Jesus often addressed him with the words: 'O Spirit of God'.[49]

Such usage at times enabled the poets in reflection on Jesus to ignore the sharp vetoes of the dogmatists on the forms of Christian theology. Thus Shams al-Dīn Ḥāfiẓ,[50] the most renowned of Persian poets (d. 1389), wrote:

> And if the Holy Ghost descend
> His comfort in these days to lend,
> To them that humbly wait on it,
> Theirs too the wondrous works can be
> That Jesus wrought in Galilee

while Ḥāṭif,[51] a poet of Isfahan in the eighteenth century, is found saying:

> In triple mirrors God, in endless love,
> Has His resplendent countenance displayed.
> Silk will not three things be, though it appears
> Sometimes as satin, damask, or brocade

For the most part, Sufi awareness of Jesus stays within the congenial themes of renunciation, the stages and states of the mystic way and the attainment of *tauḥīd*, the unitive goal of ecstacy.

What, it may be asked, of Jesus crucified, in Sufi poetry? In his *Mathnawī*, Rūmī, extolling the power of love to transform, to make 'a prison a rose-bower', and 'dregs taste like pure wine', adds that 'through love the stake becomes a throne', and 'through love the king becomes a slave'.[52] Apt as the words are, there is no evidence that he had Jesus' Cross in mind. One of his near contemporaries, Rukn al-Dīn Awḥādī, writes at length about the mystery of suffering and of Jesus as its epitome.[53]

> One day the Messiah was with his friends,
> His disciples, the repositories of his secrets.
> He made exposition to them on the subject of love,

Declared the matter openly and then concealed it.
In the midst of his discourse, his companions saw
He was weary, with tears streaming from his eyes.
So they asked him for a sign and proof of love.
He said: 'Tomorrow is the day of Abraham's fire.'
Upon the next day, when he proceeded to his task
And set his foot upon the plank of the gallows,
He said: 'If there be any man present here,
This surely is a sufficient proof of love.
Whoever turns his countenance to God
He must press his back against the Cross.
Until his body has been tied to the gallows
His soul cannot mount up to heaven

The reader notices here the interior preoccupations of the sufferer. His 'cross' is a proof of love and a release from the flesh. The 'four nails' which, the poet goes on, 'have been prescribed for the body' deliver the 'candle of the soul' to 'the candlestick of heaven'. The poem does not explore the actuality of the Cross and its well-springs in the evil of the world it faces and overcomes by the terms of that facing. Jesus served for the Sufis as a paragon of hope which, like other prophets with their appointed virtues, he brought to perfection.[54] Perhaps it is fair to say that the instinctive care of Sufism for its own goals disinclined it to reckon with the sharp realities of the New Testament crucifixion and its index to the human scene.

Manṣūr al-Ḥallāj (858–922), whose crucifixion at the hands of the 'Abbāsids bequeathed to Sufi Islam a Christ-resembling theme of poetry, drama and devotion, confirms the accents of Rukn al-Dīn Awḥādī's verses. For Al-Ḥallāj died more for the hiddenness of an esoteric wisdom he could not loyally divulge than for the preaching of a kingdom of grace that could not be hid.[55] His was, we might say, a Calvary of the esoteric. For all its mysterious appeal, it belongs with a Sufi view of the body, of suffering and of evil, hardly to be fitted into the history of the Gospels. So we look to Sufi poetry about Jesus for the evangelical themes of poverty, meekness and surrender, rather than for the evangelical transaction of pardon and peace.

X

Islamic poetry and the suffering Jesus come together significantly again in this century. Whether this is to be explained by some recession in esotericism among poets or by the intrusion of harsh and highly charged distress into Muslim experience in recent times, who shall say. Most bitter of all, the Palestinian tragedy had kindled a poetry of 'resistance' in which, perhaps inevitably, the figure of Jesus is drawn. Palestinianism is, of course, a shared experience between Muslim and Christian Arab. The common history of exile, dispersion, dispossession and injustice could readily make also common the symbolism of pain and travail central in the faith and the rite of one of the partners. There is also perhaps, sadly and perversely, the impulse to focus on Jesus because the same 'oppressors' can be emotionally identified. In some resistance poetry this stress on a 'crucified' land and people is more evident than reflection on the postures of the crucified Jesus.

This dimension of contemporary Muslim awareness of Jesus is not to be dismissed as merely political, or perverted and propagandist. There have been significant official Muslim statements countering and disowning the association of the Cross with current Islamic thought. Yet the association persists. For the confrontation with the actuality of Zionism and the depth of the Lebanese despair evoke an almost overwhelming sense of a history which sanity, hope and compassion cannot restore or repair – a drama of alienation and absurdity. Those themes, anyway, preoccupy much of contemporary Middle Eastern writing, interrogating the traditional Muslim assurance about identity and meaning.[56] Weighed down with the futilities and calamities of rejectionism and its anger, it is no strange thing that minds and poems should turn questioningly to the riddle of unrequited evil, yearn to unravel it and so to interrogate the Christ.

In one of his quatrains addressed to 'my country', Maḥmūd Darwīsh, one of the most widely read poets of the time, cries: 'My love to you has brought me nothing save the wood of my cross. My country! How beautiful you are! Take my eyes, take my heart: O my love, take.' He entitles one edition of his verses *Awrāq al-Zaitūn* (*Leaves of the Olive*), and captures the pathos of his people's tribulation.[57]

Night is a hungry stalking wolf
Trailing the stranger howsoever he goes.
Night's horizons fill with phantoms.
The willow wood endlessly harbours the winds.
Mother! what are we in embryo
So that we die twice?
Once we die into life,
And at death once again we die.
Do you know what it is that fills me with tears?
That night I fell sick and disease wracked my body
Do you remember? he came here a fugitive
And never returned to his homeland?
Do you remember the evening he died,

A fugitive, unshrouded?
Wood of the willows will you remember
That the one they threw out neath your sorrowing shade,
As just some dead thing, was a man?
Do you remember that I too am a man?
Will you keep my corpse safe from marauding birds?
To whom have I written these 'leaves'
What postal courier bears them?
The way of the land and the sea and the far horizons
Is barred, and you, mother, my father,
My brothers and people and friends,
Perhaps you live, perhaps you are dead,
Perhaps you are like me with no place to be?
What is the value of man,
Without country, with no flag,
Bereft of identity,
What is the value of man?

In Darwīsh the anger is powerful and the defiance of adversity strong. With another prominent writer, the Egyptian, Ṣalāḥ 'Abd al-Ṣabūr (1931–1981) the sense of the world's wrongness deepens into a search beyond mere restoration. He describes his poesysing as a kind of 'crucifixion', and borrows from the Gospels the words *aqūlu lakum*: 'I say unto you'. Another collection has the title: *Ta'ammulāt fī Zaman Jarīḥ* (*Meditations in a Wounded Age*).[58] The cover of the former has, unmistakably, the thorn-crowned face of Jesus. One poem there has the title: 'The Shadow and the Cross', full of a Hamlet-like weariness with time and sex and society. There is no depth even to pain. For it is like oil on the outside of weariness. There is no savour in regret, for it only carries the burden for a moment and futility overtakes it, enveloping us from head to foot. We only bury in our regrets the corpses of thoughts and sorrows as in caves.

I am he who lives without dimension that means,
I am he who lives without reach that attains,
I am he who lives without grandeur to gain.
I am he who lives without shade ... without a cross.
Shade is a robber who steals happiness.
Whoever lives in his own shadow
Walks to the cross in the end.
His sorrow will crucify him

The unrelieved melancholy and despair of these verses must be the measure of an unnerving at work in current history which, for its own sake, makes a kinship between those who share its travail, and who note the symbols to which – however wearily – it gravitates. Evidently there are no cultures or faith-systems exempt from the shades of absurdity and *angst* of heart. If we incur a 'cross' in trusting the shadow we throw, in taking ourselves as real, in that very ending our beginning may lie, and the ultimate in despair be the door of faith. 'Lo, there am I, having traversed all my bewilderments up to this Golgotha,' writes a recent Persian poet, Aḥmad Shāmlū.[59] His positive identity with the healing, caring Christ kindles his writing as an incentive to the translation, in social and political terms, of the strenuous hopes of humankind.

xi

Whether as a paradigm of despair or as a warrant for faith the Cross of Jesus belongs in these ways, however uneasily, within Islam and Muslim perception. The study of the traditional issues about the death of Christ belongs to Chapter 6. Our final task in this chapter is to look, as promised, for those sources within Islam relating to the birth of Jesus and how they predispose the Muslim mind about him.

Tradition follows the Qur'ān in prizing the birth narratives of Surahs 3 and 19. Jesus as Ibn Maryam, 'son of Mary', constantly ensures her mention and her lively esteem. Popular belief in the immaculate conception of the Prophet of Islam and of his parents parallels that of Mary.[60] That Jesus was 'born of a virgin' and so, uniquely, a 'sign' – and necessarily a 'sign' with which his mother is linked – takes pride of place in Islamic possession of him and of her. Together they are preserved from the malice of Satan. Mary is celebrated among Muslims, not simply in that all prophethood must turn on being born and that, therefore, motherhood is the condition of all else, but in the larger, mystical, religious sense which gathers that basic truth and enshrines it in the supernatural.[61]

In the Gospels there is no evidence at all that the manner of the birth of Jesus played any part in the genesis, or the appeal, of his mission in Galilee. Nor is there any suggestion that it figured at all in the commendation of the Gospel in the initiation of the Church. The birth narratives came into their place in Matthew and Luke in the context of the realised faith in Jesus as master and Lord. It was that faith which gave them being, not they the faith. Thus the virgin birth of Jesus, in Christian orthodoxy, has always been *within* the larger, deeper, surer faith of the Incarnation. The latter can subsist without the former. For, otherwise, the former would have no *raison d'être*, either in fact or faith. That 'the Word was made flesh' is the controlling truth of faith. The means depend.

The fascinating situation in Islam is that virgin birth stands alone, does not serve, or effectuate, Incarnation, indeed, quite excludes it. Mary is understood as the virgin mother of the prophet 'Isā. She gives birth to him without human intervention in order that he and she may be 'signs' and that his prophethood as earlier noted in Chapter 2 may enter the world. The traditionalists have filled out the Quranic narratives in their details about the annunciation, the converse of Gabriel with Mary, the experiences of Mary from, and with, her babe. The Sufi theosophists, like Ibn 'Arabī (1172–1240) have developed from the Quranic sources a gnostic-style doctrine of a 'flesh' wholly spiritual and so incapable of being crucified.[62]

Deep veneration, then, of both simple devotional character and subtle philosophical theory, cherishes the person of Jesus among Muslims, because of the quality of his birth. There is, for Muslims, in whatever idiom of simplicity or sophistication, an exceptionality about Jesus, ranking him in uniqueness with Adam alone, whose genesis was likewise by the divine. *Kun fayakūn*, 'Be! and it is.' (Surah 3:47 and 3:59). 'This exceptional destiny of Jesus requires and receives exceptional sentiments.'[63]

There is, therefore, here what can properly be called a Christology, but in a profoundly different sense from the Christology in Christianity. Perhaps the difference can be expressed by saying that in the Islamic case it is a Christology *outside* theology, whereas in the Christian faith Christology is necessarily *inside* theology. Of course, in one sense nothing in Islam is outside theology, for all initiatives are from God and the exceptionality of Jesus is certainly by divine will, divine incidence and divine energy. However, by virtue of the monarchical theism of Islam, nothing that is believed about Jesus involves God or mediates His unstooping transcendence. The unique status of Jesus He permits, ordains and reveals, but God is not self-given. His glory, power and wisdom remain splendidly disengaged. They do not participate with humanity. A prophet may be virgin-born, but we cannot say: 'Emmanuel, God with us'.

Perhaps it is possible to understand the difference between a Christology within theology and one outside it, by recalling a medieval episode which, by its very crudity, takes us to the heart of faiths' disparities in this concern. It occurs in the memoirs of Usāmah ibn Munqidh, *Kitāb al-I'tibār*, written in the twelfth century.[64] He writes:

> I saw one of the Franks come to Amīr Mu'īn al-Dīn when he was in the Dome of the Rock and say to him: 'Do you want to see God as a child?' Mu'īn al-Dīn said: 'Yes!' The Frank walked ahead of us until

he showed us the picture of Mary with Christ (peace be upon him) as an infant in her lap. He then said: 'This is God as a child.' But God is far exalted above what infidels say about Him.

Indeed, He is, if that is what they, or 'Franks', say or said. The controversial tone of the conclusion of the story suggests that this was what Usāmah thought they said. Whether justified or not by what Christianity is held to say, it is certainly *not* what faith affirms. The words: 'seeing God as a child' do not exclude what they cannot mean and imply what they do not mean. On both counts they are false. As they stand they subject God to 'becoming', growth, contingency and change, and they speak all these exclusively, failing to say that all belong only *within* the eternal Being of God through His condescending to them within the meaning of all His being is in glory and in grace. The question should be: 'Do you want to see God in the self-disclosure of His greatness?' Then you may discern it in the fact that there was a birth, a child in a mother's arms. That birth will not signify its meaning, however, unless you follow it into a life, a service, a travail and a cross and understand it was for these, in the realism of grace, that a birth there had to be. The Incarnation is only about a babe because it is about a man: it only wonders at a Madonna because it kneels in a Gethsemane. These are what it means to say that Christology happens within theology. Virgin birth may mysteriously authenticate the Islamic 'Īsā for his prophetic role. But the resulting Christology is about him, not about God. In its different perception Christian faith reads the very being of God in the significance of Jesus, but it does so only because, as it believes, the significance of Jesus derives from the being of God. Usāmah was certainly right in his jealousy for the divine 'far exalted', and he rightly rejected what he read in the picture: but the picture was not rightly read.

xii

Usāmah and Amīr Mu'īn al-Dīn epitomise the Muslim centuries before and after the brief time in which the Latin Kingdom of Jerusalem had its icons in the Dome of the Rock. Iconography has long been the genius of eastern Christendom and iconoclasm the urgent duty of Islam. Old John of Damascus well advised seekers of the Christian meaning to gaze upon the icons, but those, like the Amīr, who too readily said 'Yes!' to the invitation arrived only at incredulity and passed instinctively from incredulity to scorn and to controversy. Iconoclasm and iconography have thus confronted each other, sadly unaware of how their ultimate intentions tallied and their enmities were conflicts of confusion. It was a matter of motherhood and *Magnificat* and how they might be related.

Does it matter? This question of Christology outside theology, or within it? This issue of an exceptionalising birth, 'Īsā or Emmanuel? This concern between a theology of transcendent immunity or transcendent love? Is it not all conceptual? A debate which insistent questions of life and society today must roundly ignore as irrelevant to the pressing claims of the real world?

Today and its relevances we leave to the concluding Chapter 11. If theology matters at all, its issues matter with it. No small part of their significance will be the patience to be learned in disentangling them. It is a patience which calls for the liveliest appreciation of Islamic perplexities about what the New Testament is. For Christianity is neither 'scriptural' nor 'political' in the ways that Muslims assume true religion should truly be. Muslim loyalty requires to test all else as anticipatory of Islam. Its criteria of such testing are all within its own authority. That, in a sense, is true of all faiths. They assess within their own dogmas. It is distinctively so in Islam, because of its reading of chronology and its instinct to believe that its historical expression is where religion properly culminates and embodies what religion is naturally required to be. Being prior in time, and in vital areas crucially distinctive, Christianity has been uniquely subjected to Islamic disavowals and disputings. The Christian task is still to learn how to respond. If postures of prejudice and rejection have been mutual, those of interpretation and discovery may become so also. The well-spring of Christian interpretation is the New Testament. Patience and discovery must begin there.

Notes

1 Aḥmad Shawqī, *Al-Shawqiyyāt* (Cairo, n.d.) Vol. 1, 2nd edn, p. 12, in *Great Events in the Nile Valley*. An alternative version, translated by A. J. Arberry will be found in his *Aspects of Islamic Civilization* (London, 1964), p. 367.

2 No war, or battle's sound,
Was heard the world around ...
The trumpet spake not to the armed throng ...
And kings sate still with awful eye,
As if they surely knew their sovran Lord was by

On the overthrow of idols at Jesus' birth, there is an intriguing parallel to Milton in the *Iḥyā' 'Ulūm al-Dīn* of Al-Ghazālī. In iii:28, he wrote: 'When Jesus was born the demons came to Satan and said: "The idols have been overturned." Satan said: "This is merely accidental: keep still." Then Satan flew till he had traversed both hemispheres. He found nothing. Then, afterwards, he found Jesus, son of Mary, already born, surrounded by angels. He went back to the demons and said: "A prophet was born yesterday: no woman ever conceived or bare a child when I was not present, save this one. Hope not, therefore, that idols will be worshipped after tonight."'

3 The blessing of peace on Jesus in 19:33 involves 'the day I was born, the day I die and the day I will be brought forth alive'. It follows the three great credal events about Jesus, 'born ... died ... rose again ...' and, like the Christian creeds, it comprehends the speaking, teaching Jesus within birth and death. Whatever the exegesis, at least the form of the peace-salutation is that of the Christian tradition.

4 The phrase is *Al-Fauz al-mubīn* (Surahs 6:16; 45:30). 'The great (*'aẓīm*) victory' occurs some fourteen times. Victory is wanting if it is not 'manifest', as being seen to be done is part of justice. This leaves open the question, very urgent in the things of the Spirit, of whether what is apparently so is always truly so and, conversely, of whether what *seems* defeat is actually defeatedness. Here as elsewhere the formula forgets the paradoxical.

5 The degree to which contemporary politics, stresses and tensions – not least vis-à-vis Zionism and Israel – affect Qur'ān reading and Muslim assessments of other faiths, is readily discernible and easy to understand. Scriptures are liable to be quarried on either side of political confrontation.

6 On *Taṣliyah* reference may be made to this author's *Muḥammad and the Christian* (London, 1984), pp. 55–65.

7 'Sobriety', here, is in the double sense of non-indulgence but also in the mystical sense of that ultimate wisdom which is on the further side of 'intoxication', i.e. ecstatic *fanā'*, the self restored to the self with individuation and all its illusions transcended.

8 Boris Pasternak (1890–1960) wrote in a letter on 2 May 1959: 'It was in the years 1910–12 more than at any other period of my life that I lived inside Christian thought. It was then that my originality's roots and principal bases were formed, together with my vision of things, of the world, and of life.' See R. Hingley, *Pasternak: A Biography* (London, 1983), p. 24. His haunting poem, 'Mary Magdalene ii', may have personal overtones relating to his mistress, Olga, who spent years in a concentration camp. Even so, the choice of the analogue abides in deeper significance.

For whom thy life, thy open arms?
For whom such agony, such power?
Are there so many souls to save
So many hamlets, rivers, woods?

Three days of agony shall pass,
Three days of frightful emptiness,
But with my faith I shall behold
The hour of Resurrection come

There are many other writers and artists who, despite their distance from credal Christology, are yet drawn powerfully towards the Christ-figure. William Faulkner, like Pasternak a Nobel-Prize-winner, is a familiar American example. Marc Chagall, among painters, invokes the Christian Passion from outside Christian faith. It may be that doctrinal concepts are responsible thus far for the absence of such perception, by and large, in Muslim literature – though, properly speaking, it is just such perception that doctrinal concepts exist to kindle. The concluding Chapter 11 will return to this theme.

9 This is the literal translation of James 1:22, the Greek being *poietai logou*. Acts 17:28 uses the word in respect of Athenian poets. 'Maker', or 'doer' is the more usual translation. The making of poems, however, is certainly included and in

conjunction with *logos* suggests that quality of obedience to 'law' in conduct whereby life expresses in discipline the theme of liberty, just as poetry does in the freedom which only the obligations of rhyme and rhythm allow.

10 See: Najm al-Dīn Rāzī, *Mirṣād al-'Ibād fī-l-Mabdā' ilā-l-Mu'ād* (*The Path of God's Servants from Origin to Return*), trans. Hamid Algar (New York, 1982), Persian Heritage Series, no. 35, p. 175.

11 For example see Alfred Guillaume, *The Traditions of Islam* (Oxford, 1924); James Robson, *Christ in Islam* (London, 1930); S.M. Zwemer, *The Moslem Christ* (London, 1912); Michel Hayek, *Le Christ de l'Islam* (Paris, 1959).

12 See Louis Massignon, *Revue des Études Islamiques* (1932), Cahier iv: 'Le Christ dans les Evangiles apres Al-Ghazālī.'

13 Rabbinic sources also attribute this sentiment to Jesus, cf. Rabbi Ya'qūb, c.200. For an estimate of the Muslim agrapha of Jesus see J. Jeremias, *Unknown Sayings of Jesus*, trans. R.H. Fuller (London, 1954), pp. 99–100.

14 *Ṭahārat al-Qulūb*, ('Purity of Heart') was a devotional manual of Islamic prayer and aspiration, in very numerous reprintings.

15 D.S. Margoliouth in *Expository Times*, vols 3 and 4, (Edinburgh, 1893–94), pp. 59f.

16 Fakhr al-Dīn al-Rāzī: *'Ilm al-Akhlāq*, trans. M.S.H. Ma'sumi (Islamabad, 1969), p. 190.

17 Margoliouth, *Expository Times*, vols 3 and 4, pp. 59ff., 107ff., 177ff., 503ff., 561ff.

18 Al-Muḥāsibī's *Kitāb al-Waṣāyā* was translated into English by Margaret Smith under the title: *An Early Mystic of Baghdad* (London, 1935).

19 An English translation from Al-Ya'qūbī's *Tārīkh* (edited by Houstma, vol. 1, pp. 74–89) by D.M. Donaldson will be found in *The MacDonald Presentation Volume* (Princeton, 1933), pp. 89–105. For a French text see: *IslamoChristiana* (Rome, 1977), vol. 3, pp. 65–84, by André Ferre: 'L'Historien Al-Ya'qūbī et Les Évangiles'.

20 'Alī Shari'atī: *On the Sociology of Islam*, trans. from the Persian by Hamid Algar (Berkeley, California, 1979), pp. 79 and 119.

21 Shari'atī, ibid., p. 172.

22 Margoliouth, *Expository Times*, vols 3 and 4, p. 504, *Iḥyā'* 4:120. This, of course, would make the recruit an old man among the youthful disciples. It may be that there is a reference to Barabbas, or to one of the two brigands crucified with Jesus whom some traditions associate with actual discipleship. Or Al-Ghazālī's point may simply be a further token of the other-worldliness of Jesus.

23 Khālid Muḥammad Khālid, *Ma'an 'alā-l-Ṭarīq* (Cairo, 1958). The quotation is from pp. 188–89.

24 For a discussion of his impact see *The Muslim World*, Vol. XLIV, 1954, nos. 3 and 4, pp. 236–52: 'A Cairo Debate on Islam'.

25 'Abbās al-'Aqqād, *'Abqariyyat al-Masīḥ* (Cairo, 1953).

26 'Abd al-Ḥamīd Jūdat al-Saḥḥār, *Al-Masīḥ 'Īsā ibn Maryam* (Cairo, n.d.).

27 Except chapters 23 and 25, where he uses, in the one case, a tradition, and in the other Isaiah 41:27: 'I will give to Jerusalem a bringer of good tidings'. In chapter 48 a verse from Psalm 2 about the conspiring nations is joined with the Qur'ān citation.

28 Ibid., p. 216ff.; also p. 253.

29 Ibid., p. 250.

30 Ibid., p. 256. The allusion, of course, is to Isaiah 42:1–4, the first of the Isaian 'Servant Songs', but the nature of the servant's staying power is altogether revised when read in this way.

31 See Michel Hayek, *Le Christ de l'Islam* (Paris, 1959), pp. 227–8.

32 Fatḥī 'Uthmān, *Ma' al-Masīḥ fī-l-Anājīl al-Araba'ah*, (Cairo, 1961; enlarged edn. 1967).

33 In, for example, his *Christian Ethics* (Montreal, 1967). Muḥammad Kāmil Ḥusain also held that 'the egocentric attitude of the sons of Israel made the mission of Christ a necessity'. (Private Paper.)

34 A translation of the Armenian version of this eighth century document by Arthur Jeffery will be found in the *Harvard Theological Review*, vol. 37, 1944, pp. 281–332. Whether the letters were in fact exchanged is debatable, but Leo III had spent his youth in North Syria, knew both Greek and Arabic and had long contact with Muslims, both martial and theological. 'Umar, for his part, was very ardent for Islam and when one of his tax officers deplored the number of Christians converting to Islam (because then they no longer paid the *jizyah* tax) 'Umar roundly informed him that God had not sent Muḥammad as a tax-collector but as a prophet. If the two protagonists did not correspond about their faiths, they certainly corresponded about politics. The charge that Christianity is an 'imaginative religion' has become frequent in modern Jewish studies also.

35 Muḥammad Mujīb in *The Student World*, 1959, no. 2, pp. 193ff., 'A Muslim View of Christianity'.

36 Al-Ghazālī, *Iḥyā' 'Ulūm al-Dīn*.
The strong other-worldliness of Jesus is central also to Najīb Maḥfūẓ' portrayal in *Awlād Ḥaratinā* (Beirut, 1967); Eng. trans. by Philip Stewart: *Children of Gebelawi* (London, 1981). Maḥfūẓ takes liberties with the Gospel story but his Rifa'ah, 'the gentle one' is a Jesus contrasting markedly with Moses and Muḥammad among divine messengers. An exorcist and healer, who marries a prostitute out of pure disinterested compassion and whose mission ends in failure, though he is 'beloved of God', Jesus, the carpenter's son, is ascetic but naive, harmless, easily duped and high-minded but evasive. He cannot understand why he incurs hatred when he has never hated. He is finally murdered by power-wielders who suspect he has designs against their *awqāf*, or endowments, and who are just uneasy with his odd threat to their assumptions. His body is exhumed after burial and it comes to be reputed that Gabalāwī (God) had reburied him in his own garden inside the walled mansion which is Najīb Maḥfūẓ' equivalent of divine *Qadr*.
There is much that is elusive in Maḥfūẓ' style and intentions. Kafka was among his mentors. However, the picture he offers of Jesus, for all its special pathos, accords broadly with the awareness we are studying. It is small consolation that Moses with his special peoplehood and Muḥammad with his vigilantes for God are both equally futile in the issue of their times. One's heart can then be with Jesus even if one's reason could not approve him nor, indeed, find any alternative to approve. See Kenneth Cragg, *The Pen and the Faith* (London, 1985), chap. 9.

37 Part of the impetus to the Ahmadiyyah Movement in Islam in the third quarter of the nineteenth century lay in this contrast between a Jesus, traditionally still to come after heavenly rapture, and a Muḥammad, his mission achieved, entombed in Medina. Mirzā Ghulām Aḥmad, the Movement's founder and first 'caliph', eliminated a Jesus-expectancy from Islam by interpreting the Quranic references to Jesus' death as already realised in his demise, not on the Cross (from which he was taken alive), but in old age in Kashmir after a long ministry in Asia. This, in his intention, effectively precluded the eschatological role assigned to Jesus in Tradition. It also, as Aḥmad saw it, relieved Islam of a possible, or actual, inferiority complex about the future under God.

38 Franz Rosenthal, 'Sweeter than Hope: Complaint and Hope' in *Medieval Islam* (Leiden, 1983), pp. 18–19. Rosenthal attributes to this attitude the general lack of appreciation in Islam for other civilizations, e.g. that of Greece, and also the disparagement of the pre-Islamic even in Arabia as total *jāhiliyyah*. Our concern here is with its implications for the final future.

39 See earlier, Chapter 2, pp. 17–18.

40 See Arthur Jeffery, 'The Descent of Jesus in Muslim Eschatology', in S.E. Johnson (ed.), *The Joy of Study* (New York, 1951), pp. 107–125. See also: S.L. Thrupp (ed.), *Millenial Dreams in Action* (The Hague, 1962), p. 218, and *The Muqaddimah of Ibn Khaldūn*, trans. F. Rosenthal (New York, 1958), Vol. 2, pp. 156–231.

41 So argues the fourteenth-century writer 'Abd al-Karīm al-Jīlī in *Al-Insān al-Kāmil* (Cairo, 1910). A French translation of extracts by Titus Burckhardt was published in Paris in 1974.

42 One source among many is Muḥammad 'Ārif Faḥmy, *Yasū'a al-Masīḥ wa-l-Imām 'Alī* (Cairo, n.d.), pp. 89–100.

43 E.H. Whinfield: *Masnavī-i-Ma'navī: Spiritual Couplets*, trans. and abridged (London, 1880), p. 34.

44 'Health to the people of the Christian monastery! How often were they intoxicated without having drunk thereof.' R.A. Nicholson's trans. of line 34 of Ibn al-Fāriḍ's wine ode, *Al-Khamriyyah*, in his *Studies in Islamic Mysticism* (Cambridge, 1921), p. 187.

45 E.H. Whinfield, *Masnavī-i-Ma'navī, Spiritual Couplets*, trans. and abridged (London, 1887), p. 116.

46 Sharafuddīn Manerī, *The Hundred Letters*, trans. with intro. and notes by Paul Jackson (London, 1980), pp. 33, 77, 355, 219, and 341. The 'woollen garment' is, of course, the familiar sign of the Sufi and perhaps the source of the name.

47 For Shams al-Dīn see *The Dīwān of Shams al-Dīn*, selected trans. R.A. Nicholson (Cambridge, 1952).

This Sufi wanderer was the means to Rumi's conversion and initiation in the mystic discipline. It is a story eminently exemplifying a soul-to-soul relationship.

48 There are occasions in Whinfield, *Masnavī*, pp. 75 and 239.

49 Cf. Michel Hayek, *loc. cit.*, pp. 155, 159 and 160, citing Sufi writings.

50 A.J. Arberry, *Hafiz* (Cambridge, 1947), p. 99.

51 Trans. by Norman Sharp

52 Whinfield, *Masnavī*, pp. 80–81.

53 In A.J. Arberry, *Classical Persian Literature* (London, 1958), pp. 307–8. Awḥadī was born in 1274. The reference to 'the day of Abraham's fire' is to that patriarch–prophet's persecution at the hands of idolaters whom his iconoclasm had aroused (Surah 29:24 and 21:69). Murderous hostility is the lot of prophets whoever they may be.

54 As for example in *Najm al-Dīn Rāzī* (*op. cit.*, p. 160), where, with Jesus as a sign of hope, Joseph figures sincerity, Job patience, Jacob sorrow, and Abraham friendship with God.

55 See the ardent presentation of Al-Ḥallāj in the scholarship of the great French Islamicist Louis Massignon who traced much in his own spirituality to this Islamic source. *La Passion d'al-Hallāj, Martyr Mystique de l'Islam* (Paris, 1922). On Massignon: Jean-Francois Six (ed.): *Louis Massignon* (L'Herne, Paris, 1982); G. Basetti-Sani: *Louis Massignon, Christian Ecumenist*, trans. from the Italian by A.H. Cutler (Chicago, 1974).

56 See *The Muslim World*, Vol. LXVIII, no. 2, April, 1978, J.R. King on 'The Theme of Alienation in Contemporary Middle Eastern Literature', pp. 111–31, with bibliography.

57 Maḥmūd Darwīsh: *Awrāq al-Zaitūn* (Beirut, n.d.), p. 142 and pp. 71–4.

58 The edition of *Aqūlu Lakum* referred to was published in Beirut in 1969. The poem quoted occurs on pp. 60–4. *Ta'ammulāt* was published in Beirut in 1971. 'Abd al-Ṣabūr's *Dīwān*, or Collected Works, appeared in 2 vols (Beirut, 1972).

59 Quoted from S.S. Soroudi in *The Muslim World*, Vol. LXIX, no. 4, Oct. 1979: 'On Jesus' Image in Modern Persian Poetry', p. 226.

60 For example, Yūsuf al-Nabahānī, of Damascus (d. 1932) in a popular manual of

devotions for the Prophet's *Maulid*, or birthday, extols 'Abdallah and Āminah, parents of the Prophet, and their parents, as immaculately pure ones and holds that no other children came to 'Abdallah and Āminah to share that unique begetting. Both died, the one soon after Muḥammad was conceived, the other in his childhood. That circumstance has a spiritual meaning.

61 See Victor Courtois, *Mary in Islam* (Calcutta, 1954).

62 Ibn 'Arabī, *Al-Futūḥāt al-Makkiyyah* (Cairo, n.d.), Vol. 1, pp. 134–46. It is noteworthy that some modern writers within Islam with esoteric stance, such as R. Guenon and F. Schuon, seem ready to allow a metaphysical sense to Jesus' 'sonship' which is acceptable to Islam. Thus S.H. Nasr writes that, while Islam firmly excludes Incarnation, 'doctrines such as the question of the nature of Christ or the Trinity can be understood metaphysically in such a way as to harmonise the two perspectives (i.e. the Islamic and the Christian)'. He adds, however, that the non-crucifixion of Jesus is 'the one irreducible fact separating Christianity and Islam, a fact which is in reality placed there providentially to prevent a mingling of the two religions' *Islamic Life and Thought* (London, 1981), pp. 209ff.

63 Ali Merad writing in *Revue de l'Occident Musulman et de la Mediterranée*, no. 2, 1968: 'Le Christ selon le Coran'.

64 *Kitāb al-I'tibār*, trans. Philip Hitti (Beirut, 1964), p. 164.

Chapter 4

A Muslim Reader and the New Testament

i

'Point to the Cross and say: "What a way to run the universe!"' It was a lively cynic speaking about the Gospels, with a totally sceptical, yet oddly discerning, mind. For the faith of the New Testament does hold that the eternal Creator meets us where we most need Him – in the reality of a suffering love, a love inseparably joined to sovereign power.

Given this theme, we might further say: 'Point to these Scriptures and say: "What a way to leave revelation!"' – so open to necessary scholarship, so linked in its recording with human memory, so involved in human custody and serving faith through its text only by becoming a text through the faith it served. The New Testament, as noted in Chapter 2, sets many potential – but in no way insurmountable – puzzles for the Muslim who comes to it. It is the hope of this chapter to examine and resolve these in what aims to be 'a Muslim Introduction to the Christian Scriptures'. An effort after one is long overdue. Underlying any such venture must be the sense – on which the New Testament so far turns – that scripture and meaning can only inhere together dependably, not arbitrarily, through the Holy Spirit. It must be remembered that belief in God, or a scripture, which we supposed to be absolute in the way mathematics is would have no religious value. In mathematics, we believe because we have no other option: we must. In the things of faith, we believe because we may and we ought. Assessing the New Testament, we must always keep in view what one author has well called 'the modesty of the Gospel'.[1] It is of such a sort as to await our recognition and deserve our faith, and this its quality dominates the form and feel of the Scriptures which are that faith's document and definition.

The Gospels and the Epistles which, with the linking Acts of the Apostles, comprise the New Testament clearly arise from, and are witness to, what they take to be the actual, real and historical situation of Jesus and the action within it by which he constituted the Gospel. They are the literary shape, and voice, of the faith to which that 'event' of Jesus gave rise. This character of theirs might well be described in the words of one of the writers who calls both himself and his readers to 'look intently to Jesus', whom he sees as 'the author and the perfecter of faith' (Hebrews 12:2).

'Looking intently towards Jesus' the Gospels certainly are. Their whole instinct is to relate back to the story from Galilee to the Cross and Resurrection, the history as they understand it to have been. The Epistles, or Letters, also – these steadily draw their moral bearings and spiritual impulse from the actuality of Jesus. They are, in effect, the working out within the new community of what a Christ's community should be. His personality and its meaning is their whole focus.[2] These are summed up in two unusual nouns: *archegos* and *teleiotes* (*auctor* and *consummator* in Latin). The first occurs only three times elsewhere in the New Testament, the second nowhere else, nor in the Septuagint.[3] In Hebrews 2:10 there is the same association of meanings. The Jesus to whom the Scriptures 'look' is the one in whose story 'faith originates', or 'is generated', or 'has its source'. The reference is primarily to the faithful obedience by which, as Chapter 5 will study, Jesus fulfilled the Messianic task, identifying it in the love that suffers, as suffering presented itself to him within the real encounter to which his faithful teaching led. That living course of a steadfast faith is what the four Gospels set themselves to depict. They are the story of a fidelity, its context, its cost and its necessity.

This living faith of Jesus generates the responsive faith of his disciples – the responsiveness by which the New Testament comes about as a literature confessing it. That faith of the disciples is distilled into the formal faith of the Church in what becomes finally the Creeds. The beginning of that prolonged event is within the Gospels, but not its completion, if completed we ever think it to be. It is this drawing out of a meaning which requires the second of the two words in Hebrews 12:2. Jesus himself brings his faithfulness through to its climax, as Chapter 6 aims to examine, but by so doing he may be said to perfect the faith of those who confess him as Messiah and Lord. *Teleiotes* means 'the one who ripens, or matures,' bringing what is potential into full being. He is the 'pioneer' who opens the way, drawing the past into its present and the present towards its future.

The term means, quite literally, 'the e-duca-tor' of faith, leading it out into fullness. Another way of describing this is to think of 'the extrapolator'. He projects the implications of what already *is* to reach what, because of them, must yet *come* to *be*. Christians believe that this is what Jesus did within the experience of his first followers and that it is the gathered significance of this experience, so mediated, which explains the very existence of the New Testament. It, therefore, explains also that time-lag between the event and its interpretation which, as we will see, is so crucial a matter in New Testament study. It also holds the secret of why that Scripture came, and could only come, in terms of such gathering apprehension and not as a celestial 'hand-down' in which revelation is already transcribed without the participation of ensuing experience.

It was said of the great artist Raphael that he was a painter 'only fully intelligible in the light of his fame'.[4] Jesus, as the Christ, is understood by the Church as the one who is truly to be known in his consequences in the world. That clue can only obtain, and be realised, in the sequel. Or, as Nietzsche wrote in quite another context: 'Deeds require time even after they are done, before they can be seen and heard'.[5] Such Christian apprehending of the Christ happened only in the active obedience to his 'faith', for – to use a nautical metaphor – 'only when the ship is in motion does it answer the helm'.[6] Both the motion and the helm are what the reader learns in the Gospels and the Epistles. Only a telling could possess the thing told. This is why all the New Testament is from 'interested parties'. We do not know about Jesus, except in the barest data sufficient to attest his life, and his suffering and his following, from 'neutral' or other than Christian sources. To be 'neutral' in this context would be not to know, just as to be disconnected from Muḥammad in the *Isnād* of Muslim Tradition would disqualify the *matn*, or substance.[7]

This does not mean that 'believing makes it so', or that because witnesses witnessed they were bound to be right. The search for historical actuality is central to New Testament integrity and has been long pursued, but it cannot be found in neglect of the ripening verdict to which Hebrews and the word *teleiotes* refer. One has to ask what should be understood and affirmed about Jesus for there to have been *these* consequences, this apprehending faith.

Before we embark on a summary study of the story of how *this* faith had *this* documentation, how Jesus came to be written into New Testament literature, it will be wise to remind ourselves of the need to appreciate how different the criteria are from those that are proper to the Qur'ān. There the text and the meaning are trusted as one. The Islamic Scripture is not *about* something more ultimate than itself. It is, itself, as Arabic script, *the* Scripture. *Waḥy*, or revelation-inspiration, in Islam is not understood as Muḥammad's enablement to express and communicate an apprehension of truth independent of – and so needing – a derivative literature. *Waḥy* is, instead, the delivery to him of the words and sentences in which truth is already housed. These are themselves the divine message, of which he can say: *Qāl Allāh*, 'God said'. In that divine *Qaul*, or speaking, God is held to have ensured the revelation by *not* leaving phrases and composition to the guided minds of authors, but by mediating in *Waḥy* the very syllables for its utterance, thus guaranteeing its verbal role in the conveyance of meaning. The latter, on this view, is too precious, too crucial and too imperative to have been left to a human authorship, however alert and inspired.

That the New Testament is *not* this way is altogether evident. But the wise Muslim will not take that situation as a deterrent, or as any ground for suspecting its scriptural status. He has to face, though in the opposite direction, the same necessity as the Christian who relates wisely to the Qur'ān, namely concede that he must come to terms with a contrasted understanding of what sacred writing ought to be. Both would be wrong to abandon the venture, or to disesteem the text, because it did not tally with their familiar idea. It is not that revelation, communally understood and received, is – by its form – to be invalidated: it is simply that it has to be differently understood in the form it has. All that follows in this chapter is in hope that such a readiness exists in the reader and can be fostered, in either direction, within both faiths.

ii

The whole New Testament is written in Greek, whereas Jesus himself spoke in Galilean Aramaic. The Hebrew Scriptures are its constant background and the mental home of its writers who were all Jews, except the evangelist Luke. Thus the New Testament as a document is, as it were, between languages and their cultures. Though the Hebrew and the Greek were deeply interpenetrating – as the great Septuagint, the Greek version of the Old Testament, signifies – they had widely differing vocabularies and the mentalities so housed. Thus the Christian Scripture 'translates' or 'intervenes' between two realms of language and it is well to keep this always in mind. Further, of course, it is rendered into more than a thousand different tongues, and into several versions of major languages like English.

This can be puzzling to Muslims accustomed to the stringently

Arabic quality of the Qur'ān and to the idea that it is authentically itself in no other tongue. Yet the diverse renderings of the New Testament's contents, and the need to compare and sense their nuances, can be very salutary. Those who have tried to de-Arabicise the Qur'ān (which is what translation is doing) know well how difficult it is to find elsewhere equivalents for *dhikr*, or *qadr*, or *qāri'ah*. So it is for New Testament translators of its rich and manifold terms. Sometimes the difficulty reaches back into the Aramaic original of the oral memory. Sometimes it concerns the flavour of the Greek itself and what the themes of Gospel and Epistle did with its classic words.

A few examples may be useful to point the reader's duty and opportunity in relating perceptively to whatever version he handles if he cannot return to the Greek itself. Many points that are at stake, for example, in familiar English renderings persist in the strongly Christian Arabic of Arabic New Testaments, so different in their lilt and feel from the Arabic Qur'ān. In Matt. 4:10, Jesus tells the tempter, Satan, to 'get behind' him. Here an underlying Aramaism has been misunderstood, so that it ought to read: 'Withdraw', or 'Away, let me see no more of you' (cf. Mark 8:33). Where the Greek of John 20:16 says that Mary 'turned herself' on hearing a voice speaking her name, a hidden Aramaism would read that she 'recognised' him. In Mark 9:33–37 and 10:15, the meaning is greatly clarified if it is realised that there is an Aramaic play on words, *talya* meaning both 'child' and 'servant', in a context where one is a parable of the other. The most fascinating Aramaism, however, has to do with the term *bar nasha*, or 'son of man' – a very odd expression when put into Greek. Is it just a synonym for 'any man', so that the saying 'nowhere to lay his head' simply means that humanity is homeless and restless? Or, as many scholars think, did Jesus use the term as if he were using the first person pronoun singular? In which case, why the circumlocution? Or does it belong to eschatology and the end-time?[8]

It is intriguing also, especially for Arabic speakers, to appreciate the Aramaic parallelism to be discerned in the speaking of Jesus. It is there in the rhythms of the Lord's Prayer and in such passages as Mark 8:17–18: 'How shall we liken the kingdom of God/or in what parable shall we set it forth?' Even via Greek and English one can detect it in such passages as Luke 6:27–29. Or note the balance in the sentence about a new patch on an old coat, when 'the fullness of the new tears away the weakness of the old' (Mark 2:21).[9]

The Aramaic hinterland apart, the Greek of the New Testament writers has a fine texture demanding to be savoured intelligently. Translation, as with the Qur'ān, has sometimes enfeebled or confused the sense. 'Mystery', for example, needs to be explored. *Musterion* was not something never found out. On the contrary, it is meant to be known; but it imposed its own conditions of commitment and humility.[10] It was 'initiates' who understood. Or there is *parrhesia* which occurs frequently as 'confidence', or 'boldness', or 'frankness', as a quality of the first Christians. The word denotes the right and vigour of the free citizen to speak his mind in the city assembly. Two rich terms denote 'patience' or 'steadfastness'. The one, *hupomone*, is akin to the *ṣabr* of the Qur'ān. It is constancy under strain, a refusal to succumb (cf. Surah 3:139 and 47:35). The other is *makrothumia*, the 'long-suffering' characteristic of God and to be emulated by believers. It is not merely a holding out but a non-retaliation, a bearing away of evil (cf. 2 Cor. 6:6 and 1 Peter 3:20).

Behind divine *makrothumia* is the whole implication of *diatheke*, the word for 'covenant'. *Suntheke* is not used, implying some contract between equals. *Diatheke* means a divine disposing, or ordering, a disposition of will or by will, within which humanity comes to stand. Descriptive of Jesus, and to characterise the Christian is the word *praotes*, from *praus*, 'gentleness' or 'meekness' (cf. Matt. 11:29 and 21:5; Gal. 5:23). Used also in the Beatitudes it has to do with the quiet strength in the resources of grace.

Examples of the wealth of New Testament vocabulary, lively and down-to-earth as its *koine* Greek was, are legion. The alert reader is on the watch for nuances the dull one misses. Thus in Luke 15:17, when the prodigal son recalls his father's house and resolves to return home and plead to be among the 'servants', he uses not the senior words that denoted those who had dignity and tenure (*diakonoi* and *douloi*) – he uses *misthioi*, the lowliest 'menials' paid by the hour. One needs to notice the tenses. Luke 6:36, for example, about being merciful 'as your Father in heaven is merciful' must be quite unthinkable, unless one appreciates here that the tenses or terms distinguish the imperfect effort (ours) and the eternal attribute (God's); or the imperfect again in Matt. 1:25, strongly implying that Mary and Joseph had normal marital relations after Jesus' birth. Then there are interesting plays on words like that in the Greek of Matt. 6:16 about pseudo-fasting people who 'disfigure their faces' in order to 'figure' as if they fasted, putting on a drawn face in putting on a feigned part.

iii

The exacting, yet also endearing, wealth of New Testament vocabulary has been experienced in the long and continuing task of

Christian translation in the effort to make the text available in all the languages of the earth.[11] The cares this obligation imposes prove occasions of riper awareness through the very necessity of inter-language search for equivalence. Some might be inclined to think that translating is meddling with inspiration. The play on words in Italian – *traduttore, traditore* (translator/traitor) – must always be in mind. Since inspiration is with a view to communication, and communication is readiest in mother tongues, the text must be brought into each of these, however awkward of reception their vocabularies and usages may seem initially to be.[12] Surmounting that awkwardness – if such it be – in fact serves meaning more ripely than if content never ventured out of its first form in the original language or if that original were assumed to have annexed the meaning and kept it singularly to itself.

Thus, for example, newly scripted languages, hitherto only oral, can be found to offer superb possibilities. 'Alms' can be had as 'gifts of love', or 'peace' be read as 'resting in the heart', or 'be not anxious' as 'do not let your mind worry you'. The terse and pithy wisdom of local proverbs anywhere will often be found to embody what a text intends and translation can sometimes be across the idiom rather than word-for-word. 'Calling at the door' might in some cultures be more intelligible than 'knocking at the door'. The needle does not need to have an 'eye'. An 'ear' might serve just as well.[13]

Conversely, the translator has to watch for points where a literal rendering would in fact falsify the meaning. 'Beating of the breast', in Biblical culture, is a sign of deep contrition and remorse. Elsewhere it is a gesture of pride and satisfaction with oneself. Among Shilluk people, to be large-hearted is not to be generously concerned for others: it is to be acquisitive and greedy so that one's heart is filled like a miser's with gains. In that idiom it is the small-hearted who are open to love because they have unselfish space within themselves. Whereas spitting is unseemly and repulsive for some societies, in others it conveys a blessing. 'Heaping coals of fire on the head' may well have no parallel as a usage where the translator wants to take its meaning. Or, central to all else, how do we read, and inter-change, the word that languages use for 'God'? Many tongues present great issues here both for Muslim and for Christian conviction. The Hopi Indians of North America are very close to the Biblical *Yahweh* and the Quranic *Allāh* with their term: 'The One who exists by his very existence'.[14] In all these ways, it is fair to say that to have the New Testament text in trust for others is a constant education in its possession. That 'meaning finds itself in words by finding words for itself' is a truth even of ordinary conversation and, more deeply, of any literature worthy of the name. It is what we must understand scripturally by 'inspiration' and the work of the Holy Spirit, in both the intent and the content of faith's document as entrusted to our study.

iv

Carrying forward from the foregoing a lively sense of what the Christian Scriptures purport to be, we take up a concise exploration of the formation of the gospel literature through the period of three to five decades between the events around which it centres and their recording from within their sequel. One crucial piece of history, namely, the siege and capture of Jerusalem by Titus, occurred within that time, with vital consequences for the whole Jewish body – political and religious – a small segment of which was directly involved in the new Christian movement. It is important to realise how relatively small the new 'sect' was which acknowledged the Messiahship of the crucified Jesus within the extensive world of Jewish dispersion and diversity. The Fall of Jerusalem, with the loss of the Temple and its worship, entailed a traumatic anguish in which Jewish identity struggled for its truth/security. Minor as it was in that whole tension and trauma, the Christian entity came to seem more and more either an irrelevance or a threat, jeopardising a properly Jewish present and future by its apolitical and implicitly divisive stance and its instinct – which soon became central – to see itself open to non-Jews. The reverberations of that crisis are clearly audible within the New Testament and must be appreciated in any study of the implications of the gap between the events and the recording of the Gospels.

A further vital dimension of that inter-period between happening and documenting was the sense of an immediate future. For any lived sequence the future is always 'immediate'. The Christian Church, in its growing awareness of how 'God was in Christ', was properly expectant about Christ. It lived in anticipation of *Parousia*, or 'presence'. The events of the Cross and the Resurrection, far from being 'an end' (in the sense of a 'finale' or 'terminus') emphatically had 'an end' (in the sense of a 'goal' and a 'purpose'). That completing of the redemption was naturally thought of within time's 'immediacy' as all life registers time's flow. It was only with the sense of time lapsed that non-immediate time entered the reckoning. That the work of redemption had a future tense the Church knew from the beginning. It was, necessarily, in waiting for it that they realised how it had to be awaited. They 'loved Christ's appearing', but came to understand that its meaning forward was a thing of present patience, that their faith was about both actuality and hope. This time-equation was the second significant factor within the period of New Testament recording of event. Chapter 5 notes how, during Jesus' ministry itself 'the kingdom' could only rightly be understood as already in hand and yet still ahead. The same was true for the apostles, as it had been when they were disciples, but with the difference made by the Cross and Resurrection.

A third broad factor to keep always in mind about the decades between Jesus in Galilee and Gospels in being as we now have them is the way in which the writing is, as it were, bifocal. It remembers, rehearses and composes with a fervent retrospect *to* Jesus but *from* the stresses of its own context. Among these were issues of new life in pagan society, of Jewish nervousness about 'Gentile' inclusion, of response to persecution and the Roman scene. The reader has, therefore, to have an eye for both angles when he comes to the Gospels.

For example, the familiar story in Luke 15:12–32 about the return to his father's house of the penitent son has an extended significance when we see the elder brother who will not share in the welcome against the background of the Jew/Gentile issue in the Church. Luke's concern with it is not only in its original import as a parable of repentance and grace but also as a paradigm of elder and younger, circumcised and uncircumcised, welcome and one within their Father's house. Similarly, several passages in Jesus' recorded preaching about unwillingness or unreadiness to hear had a sharper resonance in the given experience of the Church. The evident care of Matthew to present his story of Jesus with a conscious arrangement accentuating the pattern of a 'new law' from a 'mount', and the disciples as leading 'twelve tribes' within 'a new covenant' further illustrates a vision of a church-situation in his conception of the apostolic sequence to Jesus and his teaching.

Some studies have been tempted, riskily, to evaluate Gospel passages and sayings by reference to this Galilee/Church alignment. Their authors suggest that accents or nuances arguably uncongenial, which do however survive in an authorship which might have been expected not to let them remain, must therefore be held all the more authentic. Thus, when Jesus seemingly left non-Jews out of his reckoning, it must have been a very strong memory or it would not have persisted in the setting of a church then enlarging to include them.[15] Or, again, did the Church's interest in the fulfilment of prophecy tend to influence the choice, or placing, of narratives, showing such fulfilment? Was there, perhaps, even a collection of proof-texts circulating from which, for example, Matthew's frequent citations may have come, which affected his presentation? Could it even be that prophecies, in that way, were almost self-fulfilling, given the devotion in the Church to the sense of historic precedent informing Hebraic realisation of hope? If so, then the earlier Scriptures of the Hebrew Bible, via the Christian commitment to them, shaped the texture of the New Testament record as it was fashioned through the forming period.

It would seem that the worship of the Church through those recording decades also contributed to the growth of the Christian writings. The Hebraic context was familiar with liturgical reading of the Torah and appointed hours of prayer. The first Christians, in this same tradition, may have gathered the spoken memories of Jesus into liturgical 'lessons' alongside their ancient Scriptures. Some have detected such 'lectionary' form in the Gospels and even surmised a 'calendar' by which its sequences were listed.[16] While precision of this kind in such conjectures must be taken cautiously, there is no doubt that the Church's shaping of worship and its delineation of Jesus in its Scripture proceeded hand-in-hand. The old saying *Lex orandi*, *Lex credendi* might well be adapted to read *Vox orandi*, *vox scribendi*.[17]

The two come clearly together in one of the sweetest passages in the Gospels, namely Luke's narrative of the two disciples walking to Emmaus after the Resurrection. On the way is the exposition of the Messianic import of the prophets, 'Christ in all the scriptures' (24:27). At nightfall in the inn comes 'the breaking of the bread'. Luke is telling the story, as it were, within the framework of what was happening regularly in the life of the community of his readers whenever and wherever 'two or three were gathered together'. 'Word and sacrament' belonged in one. The second illuminated what the first enshrined. The sacramental mystery could be recognised because of the scriptural instruction. Luke, in effect, is mirroring the Church at worship in the window of the Jesus-story.

This is not, of course, to say that the Christian sequel to Jesus, in community, scripture and sacrament, determines what his story was: that story had its own historical quality and drama. It is to say that the sequel possesses it out of a communal practice and a communal understanding which believes the story as that without which neither sequel nor community would exist. The very phrase 'Where two or three are gathered in my name ...' with the promise '... there am I in their midst' (Matt. 18:20) reads like an assurance of Jesus' unfailing comradeship with disciples, but phrased in a form more suited to days when he was no longer present and church fellowships were scattered here and there in the Roman world. The context of Matt. 18:20 as a whole clearly presupposes the dispersed Christianity and the glorified

Lord. As will be clear further in Chapter 5, the implications of many of Jesus' parables relate to the early Church setting which has, in turn, entered into their telling. The historical point of departure, in Jesus, is always there; however, it is there not as mere archives would be but as the guiding and developing memory of the widening Church.

It is that widening which we must see, through and with the several factors just reviewed, as the ultimate factor in the years of gospel formation. The Fall of Jerusalem, the hope called *Parousia*, internal growth, liturgy and prophetic precedents all had their place. Housing them all, however, was the simple fact of expansion. Unaided by any external or political sanction - indeed shadowed and beset by many enmities - natal Christianity made its way into the world, from Jerusalem and Antioch and Damascus, reaching into territories quite unfamiliar with the locale of Jesus and with the scenes of his ministry. It was also moving out from the first generation with the lapsing years. On both counts of place and time there was an ever-enlarging need for recorded access to the knowledge of Christ. If, as we have been saying, there was a communal mediation of that knowledge as its channel, it was only so because there were expanding communities as its destination.

The times and place of gospel composition were the places and time of letter circulation. Those Epistles of the New Testament, to which we must come, or many of them, antedate the Gospels, but they are part of the same matrix. While epistles relate mainly to the spiritual and moral nurture of the Christian communities, the Gospels supply the generative story from which such nurture took its rise. When - through the passing of years - and where - through the change of locale - that story could no longer be safely (or only) oral, writing became mandatory, lest either time or place should forfeit it. The significant fact is that, through all the vicissitudes of changing date and place, its custodians never relinquished their founding memory, never cast their faith adrift from its moorings in Galilee, or took off into philosophical abstraction negligent of history. 'That which we have seen and heard, declare we ...' (1 John 1:3) was both their theme and their incentive. The Gospels are the result.

Before taking up, as much as brevity admits, a study of the processes of gospel composition as far as they can be discerned, there is one final observation about the foregoing. If, necessarily, church situations fold back into the telling of the history of Jesus, does this mean that the interests of faith have put at risk the interests of history? Having properly in mind the points already made, the answer must be 'No!' All history, anywhere, hinges on those two 'interests'. It has to do with what happened because of what what happened meant. Its necessary selectivity turns on faith about significance since, without some sense of meaning, recording of it would have no point and would simply not occur. Oblivion overtakes what does not, somehow, somewhere, avail enough to be memorialised.

If such is the case with any 'history', it is clearly so with the Gospels. They certainly give the data about Jesus according to the Christian memory. Indeed it is doubtful whether Jesus would have been substantially recalled at all in general history, apart from this Christian factor. Charismatic healers were familiar in Galilee and crucifixions were legion in Roman Palestine.[18] Apart from what his community of discipleship believed him to be – and grew by believing it – Jesus, too, might have had no memorial. Their indispensable testimony, while itself a new fact of history, recognised its historical responsibility to its acknowledged source and, in the Gospels, painstakingly undertook it. Those who, in recent times, have said that the fact of their faith is the only fact there was, or who imagine they can dissociate the believer altogether from the historian, have quite failed to reckon with how the very existence of the Gospels disproves them by offering the stranger a history. To be sure, it is not an unbelieving history which is offered. How could it be? But the commitment it confesses in believing it confesses as a narrative. It is hard to see how integrity could have it otherwise.

Questions remain open, within this confidence. There is no place here for infallibility. Such is not appropriate to religion or to faith. Confidence is the only right word to describe the claim that Christians make for the composition of their Scriptures. The brief details of such composition we must now take up.

V

It occupies the three or four decades through the middle of the first century of the Christian calendar. It builds itself from oral recollection, from preaching within community and to outsiders, from verbal instruction to new believers. It has to do with the dramatic realisation that, in Jesus – teaching, crucified and risen – the Messianic meaning has been defined and the Messianic action achieved. This is so dramatic – so decisively radical – a conviction that, for better assurance in a daunting world, predictive passages are pondered and invoked to shape and undergird the telling. The central theme is read and told against the background of the hope and the history it is believed to fulfil. The new life through *this* Jesus as *this* disconcerting

Christ interprets itself as a new 'exodus', liberating a new and open peoplehood intended for living doxology. The facts which enable them to identify the Messiah they possess in the Gospels as the clue to themselves.

Oral recollection, in this teaching, preaching situation, is what New Testament scholars try to recognise and analyse in what is known as 'form' study. This involves discerning, if possible, the original material, in its oral shape, on which Gospel composition drew as it proceeded. Mark is widely held to have been the first Gospel to reach final order and it seems clear that Matthew and Luke drew upon it extensively and, often, almost *verbatim*. There is, however, another body of sayings, referred to as 'Q', from which the writers draw and which many scholars hold to have been itself a written document, though no longer extant as such. 'Form study' tries, in this way, to discover the first 'units' of the traditions about Jesus and, hopefully, to trace the sequence of their incorporation into the text. There are, for example, occasions where a characteristic discourse of Jesus, such as those relating to the Sabbath, is set in a narrative turning on its observance. The parabolic 'form' is, of course, the most characteristic of all and 'form study' seeks to isolate the core of the parable from associated material which seems to derive from the local interests of the evangelist within the Church. For example, the parable of the wedding feast in Matt. 22:1–10 needs to be detached from what follows in verses 11–14 about the man who did not have a wedding garment. Since the guests had been brought in urgently from the streets (in the core theme of the parable) they could hardly have been expected to be rightly clad. 'Form study' would suggest that here the writer has conflated two quite separate meanings. Similarly verse 7 about the condign punishment of the recalcitrant invitees is hardly in place while the supper was on table awaiting the guests, apposite as it is 'between the lines' after the Fall of Jerusalem.

'Form study', in a further example, would suggest that the parable in Luke 16:1–12 has 'footnotes' from verses 8 to 12, on the part of the evangelist. Its central point – the one it is always important to identify and keep central in the reading of parables – has to do with an estate-manager who, threatened with dismissal for corruption, ingratiates himself with his boss's customers by adjusting their accounts to correct the hidden usury which he had negotiated with them.[19] The riders in the last five verses seem to be the further 'wisdom' of Luke or his sources, commenting on the story as it came from Jesus. The world is a place where many things are not entirely what they seem and the astuteness of the worldly-wise can be emulated in the contrasted interests of the godly.

Readers have need of care in studying 'forms' in order to discern, if they can, the ways in which the present text has been formulated from its springs in Jesus via the oral reporting and the editing within church situations. The chief merit of this area of Gospel scholarship is that, though its 'findings' may often be open, its active sense of the two elements in oral tradition, namely, 'then' (Jesus) and 'here' (the community) is proper and honest.

A further field of Gospel scholarship has to do with 'source study'. Whereas 'form study' is concerned with patterns of oral tradition and what may have happened to them *en route* to the text, 'source study' asks about material within the present Gospels which had separate shape and existence before it was incorporated into them. A prime example is the source, popularly labelled 'Q', on which all three Synoptic Gospels drew. They are called 'synoptic' because they present broadly the same 'synopsis' or portrayal, often in identical, or near identical, language, indicating cross-reference and inter-dependence. Which cited the other and which was prior is a matter of discussion. The strong majority opinion is that Mark antedates Matthew and Luke and that these are indebted to him, either directly or indirectly. If we are right in thinking of them as a parallel authorship, however, then the chronology of their mutual activity becomes less important. The verbal agreement – with minor changes – between all three, through long sequences of their contents, is too close to be a coincidence. It is not only shared tradition which underlies it but also shared literature.

This shared material may be called 'the triple tradition', in that it maintains the same order of events and employs closely comparable words. Matthew has about ninety per cent of Mark, and Luke has about fifty per cent, but each has material unique to his version, which occasions interruptions or deviations in Mark's sequence. This is largely drawn from 'Q' which Mark does not use, though in Luke's case it is augmented by passages (like the parables in Luke chapters 15, 16 and 18) which are Luke's alone. Luke, of course, is also unique in joining his Gospel significantly to the companion book of his authorship, the Acts of the Apostles (see Acts 1:1–2). John's Gospel serves to underline the close kinship of the other three by its own distinctive authorship and its interpretation of the same story. Scholars are liable to revise and review their conclusions over the minutiae of the debate about synoptic source study. New Testament scholarship is nothing if not meticulous and painstaking. However, reassuring as this is about integrity of faith, the reader whose studious range is necessarily modest need not be discouraged. Fascinating as the minutiae are, they do not affect – indeed they can only sustain – the broad structure of the Gospels as an event generating its literature and a literature emerging from an event. 'Source study' only investigates how.

With 'form and source study' there is also what has come to be known as redaction study – the noting, that is, as far as possible of the characteristic interests and emphases evident in the stance of the writers. What concerns can we detect in their selection of material and in the 'feel' they give to it in things both great and small? For example, Luke, as the only Greek to write in the New Testament, shows a great love of universal, human traits, in contrast to Matthew's strong accent on all things Jewish. Luke tells the parables that begin: 'A certain man ...' who could be any one at all. Yet, to balance this sense of the universal we find he has a deep love for Hebraic/Aramaic hymnology which he, and he alone, introduces into the narrative of Jesus' nativity and its antecedents in chapters 1 and 2.

Mark omits these and begins, with characteristic urgency, at Jesus' baptism and his Gospel is distinguished by the frequent word: 'immediately', which carries forward the urgent pace of his crowded pages. Another of his emphases is upon how uncomprehending the disciples were and how Jesus' Messianic identity was so far hidden from their minds. In somewhat different terms, it is easy to see how Matthew, in his 'redacting', or conscious authorship, loved to set Messiahship – for all its realism – in the framework of fulfilled prophecy which he steadily cites. There is no contradiction here, if one realises that the prophecies were opaque until the end of the story made them luminous, or they were themselves overlaid by contrasted expectations. Further, Matthew, when compared with Mark, sometimes leaves aside explanations he considers unnecessary or introduces others, often heightening the sense of Jesus' authority.

These three areas of study in the Gospels could be very amply illustrated. Our purpose with them now is simply to indicate how scholars see, and explore, the activity of Gospel composition in the interval between the history in place and the history in writing. 'Form study' takes the exploration closest to the tracing of oral tradition and teaching. 'Source study' weighs the material in which these came through into the Gospels, as it availed as quarry from which the evangelists shaped the conscious literary work where we can now register their characteristic presentations of Jesus.

Any alert Muslim, pondering the foregoing, is sure to ask himself, and so to ask the writer: Why four Gospels? Should there not be only one, given that the teaching of Jesus was all of one piece and, therefore, capable of a *verbatim* record after the example of the Qur'ān? Or, if four there need to be, why not forty-four? Once plurality of gospels is conceded need there be any limit?

The answer to the first question is implicit in all that has been said earlier about a gathering significance, anchored in events belonging to Jesus as the Christ but understood, and so literaturised (if the term may be allowed), in the sequel of faith. Given that understanding of the situation, it would be impossible for the literature about Jesus to be simply a text of speeches, and not also a portrayal of personal events. Any portrayal, needing and presupposing a context of recognition and discipleship, is arguably the better for being at least fourfold, the contributors complementing each other and reporting from within a range and partnership of comprehension and love. Their individual vision, belonging also with communal retrospect and spiritual possession, may fairly claim to depict the theme of each within the consensus of all in a way that makes accessible to study (as we have now briefly noted) the actual process of delineation.

As for the question: If four, why not forty-four? – it suffices to observe that the question in fact presented itself to the early Church.[20] There were, indeed, many Gospels. The reasons for *these* four, to the exclusion of the rest from canonical Scripture, engages us below when we look at the Canon of the New Testament. In part, the non-canonical Gospels belong with trends in interpretation which faith came to question and exclude. The Scriptures witness to faith and faith witnesses through Scriptures. It is that mutuality of doctrine and text which explains the acceptance of the Four Gospels we have and the status of those outside the New Testament which, while by no means negligible, lack a comparable dependability. Imagination is free to liken the four evangelists to the four winds, the four quarters of the compass, or the figures of lion, ox, man and eagle. These are simply metaphors for what may be prosaically stated by concluding that four suffices well.

vi

It is instructive to reflect on this whole story of Gospel formulation by relating it to the different pattern by which Qur'ān and Tradition came to belong in Islamic faith and society. The Qur'ān, of course, was understood as direct divine revelation, in Arabic script, to the Prophet and was collected as such during his prophethood and received canonical recension within a quarter century of his death. Faith understands and receives that recension as corresponding entirely with the Book in heaven. There is here no question of a communal mediation. The ongoing community has the revelation via audition contemporary with its incidence in *Tanzīl*. As we have seen, it is quite otherwise with the Gospels, for the reason that the revelation is the whole significance of the person of Jesus within Messianic vocation and achievement.

While, for that reason, the Gospel of Jesus may be likened to the Qur'ān in being the vital place and crux of revelation, it is capable, in other respects, of being usefully likened to Tradition in Islam. For there the personality of Muḥammad is given into the community of Muslims for oral and written possession and imitation. The comparison, however, is only a partial one and there are significant differences.

Tradition, in Islam, is made current by individuals in immediate proximity to the Prophet and/or to one another and continues in such individual reportage, in the chain of attestation, much longer than the period in which the Gospels came into being by the processes we have studied. The *isnād*, or attesting sequence of reporters, had this individual, not communal, character. Doubtless, the community was there to hear, to acknowledge and to cherish the reporting, and without community no currency would have been possible. Nevertheless, as the science of *Ḥadīth* criticism shows, with its biographies of reporters to prove their overlap and bespeak their honesty, the witness within the *Ḥadīth* was that of ear and sight, individually made and guaranteed in its passage from mouth to ear and mouth again. That guarantee-ing meant the far travels of would-be reporters seeking knowledge, i.e. *Ḥadīth*, 'though it were in China'.

That fascinating and prolonged activity has the same religious impulse as the composition of the Gospels. Although the latter have personal authors, they are writings by and through community. It was the corporate faith, emerging, apprehending and consolidating, which brought into being the record of its generating story in Jesus. By their nature and role in Islam the *aḥādīth* do not require 'form study' and have not been comparably subject to 'redaction' or literary composition. As for their 'source-study', it is fulfilled in the chain of *isnād* whose 'soundness' of itself suffices to justify the *matn*, or 'substance', of its witness. Minds accustomed to that view of things need patience to appreciate how the Gospels live and move in another idiom of fact and faith-possession. The one common feature within these contrasts is that the differing writings serve the single end of perpetuating for the faithful the memory of whence they came.

vii

A Muslim reader, fresh to the New Testament, may well be perplexed and dismayed by the several Epistles which form the other major segment of the Christian Scriptures. How can correspondence, from here to there, however wise or holy, be authentic 'revelation'? The concept of *Tanzīl* by which Islam lives cannot possibly admit of personal letters constituting 'God's word'. *Tanzīl* only comes down from heaven: epistles are horizontal, not vertical. Though oddly spatial, these terms express something irreconcilable with the Quranic norm of how God communicates.

Yet there they stand, those letters *of* Paul and Peter and John, letters *to* communities in Christ, to cities and the tiny churches among them, to individuals of standing and appointed 'elders'. By New Testament criteria such letters are eminently appropriate, in no way incongruous as 'revelation'. They belong within the life of the growing church. They educate new believers in the meaning and responsibility of their new discipleship. They are part of the world from within which the Gospels grew and were shaped into their present form. The recipients were the matrix where composition belonged, because they were the setting in which oral tradition circulated and awareness matured. Their growth in numbers and extending dispersion were precisely what made Gospels necessary.

Though both Gospels and Epistles are part of this same geography and story, they fulfil differing purposes. It is not the aim of the Letters to retell the events of Jesus. Gospel composition concurrently was doing that. While there are significant echoes of Jesus' teaching in them, the Epistles undertake the moral and spiritual education of the churches in the meaning of themselves as Christian. This involves the 'imitation' of Christ and presupposes the Gospel portraiture, interpreting its living translation into the stresses and tests of life in the wider world. What the Gospels were getting into focus as to Christhood according to Jesus the Epistles were applying to the character of the community. The two tasks make the two literatures, interdependent but distinctive. It is in the world of the Epistles that the Gospels come to birth: it is from the world of the Gospel that the Epistles teach the churches.

Examples of this inter-relation are numerous, quite apart from the actual quotations which serve to dissipate the notion – strangely held in some quarters – that Paul, for example, was disinterested in the Jesus of Galilee.[21] The whole argument of Rom. chapters 1 to 8 – highly doctrinal chapters – is followed directly (chapters 9 to 11 being a long parenthesis) by the practical: 'I beseech you, *therefore*, ... present your bodies a living sacrifice ...' (12:1). The rest of the Letter has to do, for the most part, with ethical and communal or pastoral teaching about conduct and order. Comparably the strong doctrinal summaries of Ephesians, Colossians and Philippians are each succeeded by directives for living. Or, if not succeeded, then prefaced, as in one of the greatest of all New Testament sequences in Phil. 2:4–11, which revolves around 'the mind of Christ', as the principle by which the Philippians are to be ruled in all their values and motives, *because* it is the principle at the heart of Messiahship in Jesus.

The First Letter of Peter, in the same way, intersperses what it tells about Christ with what it enjoins upon its readers. The two hinge on words like: 'Wherefore' (1:13, 2:2, 2:6,) or 'likewise' (4:1), linking Jesus' story with their conduct. 'Even as our Lord Jesus Christ has showed me,' says 2 Peter 1:14, echoing the claim in 1 Peter 5:1 about being 'a witness of the sufferings of Christ'. In either case, the point of the reference is the incentive from Jesus to true discipleship. To confess 'the good shepherd' is to be bound over to pastoral compassion and fidelity within the world that 'God so loved'.

This quality of the Epistles is the most telling evidence that they truly partner the Gospels in the Christian possession of Jesus and so present a common witness, the one historical and the other pastoral. The situation might be loosely likened to the twin nature of Islamic Tradition which at once rehearses Muḥammad's exemplariness and applies it in Muslim ethical norms. The paradigms differ with the difference between the Cross and the *Hijrah*, making for their respective moulds of response.

It is important to measure rightly this pastoral nature of early Christianity. Communities of the new faith – born out of preaching alone, surrounded by pagan idolatry or gnostic influence and susceptible to many temptations of flesh and spirit – needed wise nurture and patient care. The Epistles made these their goal. They brought the voice of leadership and maturity into the local groups of the faithful and helped to hold them to a loyal course. They transact unity via diversity. Their existence in the New Testament indicates how the one are many and the many one. The fact that they are sent bespeaks an apostolic concern which does not leave groups of believers to their own isolation but embraces them in a common love and in hope of a single quality of discipline. Yet these, as recipients, are evidently diverse and are treasured in their local idiosyncrasies, however fragile. It is hard to see how a pastoral scripture could have come into being, or a household of faith be identified to itself, in a more telling way.

The Muslim reader, ready to assess this unfamiliar scriptural phenomenon of a Christian cherishing, could well begin with the First Epistle to the Thessalonians, written about the year 50 C.E. and, therefore, the first surviving piece of Christian writing, antedating the present shape of any of the Gospels. At once he will find himself in the familiar theme of emancipation from idolatry – a salient feature throughout the New Testament.[22] 'You turned to God from idols to serve the living and true God', Paul tells his readers. How it happened is recorded in Acts 17:4, when Paul and his companions, on their second journey, came to Thessalonica in northern Greece. The church there, at the time of writing is evidently raw and new, immature and lively. The letter breathes great tenderness as well as high expectation. Paul recalls his visit, lifts their local needs and fears into the perspective of the wider church and of the whole Christ, and spells out what discipleship means in social peace and earnest zeal. He leaves them with no illusions about an easy path or escape from adversity, spiritual and physical, but his realism about their vocation is matched by his confidence in the resources of grace and the hope of their perseverance. The near horizon of Christ's 'presence' (*Parousia*) is there in 4:13–18, but is understood in the severely practical precepts and down-to-earth qualities of 5:12–22, which are followed by the characteristic benedictions of 5:23 and 5:28.

The reader can feel the 'primitive', warm quality of this Letter. In Romans, for example, written some seven years later, Paul's style has adapted to the deep apologia he there undertakes, in addressing what is in part a treatise to a major Christian community he had not yet himself visited and which he had not brought to birth. In Galatians he is passionately autobiographical in defending the liberty he understands in Christ from the yoke-makers of the circumcision. Philippians, too, is autobiographical but in a gentler tone. All Paul's theology, like his pastoral ministry, must be seen as – in his own words – 'obedience to the heavenly vision' (Acts 26:19). Such obedience could only be via a hospitable faith and in the open world.

How, it may be asked, are the Epistles supposed to serve us now, or to belong to the relevance of Scripture after their time and outside their *milieu*? It is a fair question. Letters as sharply local as these in their destinations and so intimately personal in their content might well be considered too specific to warrant the status their inclusion in the New Testament ensures. The answer is that they must be read and taken as affording precedents which can be translated for ongoing guidance elsewhere. There are many 'Corinthians' outside Corinth and 'Colossians' outside Colosse, if for either we read 'unruly partisans' and 'pretentious philosophisers'. The situations the apostles handled in these writings recur continually. The responses they exemplified and applied to them make all the better education of the future for being in the humdrum of events, as letters are, rather than in abstract dissertation. The education there and then may be apposite now and everywhere, given that it is wisely interpreted into every changing context. Is there not a like necessity in the documents of Islamic faith?

By the Epistles, then, the Scriptures stay close to the foibles of human nature and make even the vagaries of men yield nurture in the faith. What are some of these precedents which can illuminate issues of later time when read by their light? One of the most urgent was how the Corinthian Christians were to be liberated from their former pagan idolatry while still living in a pagan society. This is a central theme of the First Epistle to them. Idolatry was on every hand. One could not even make a rendezvous on a street with a friend without taking its pagan name upon one's lips. Meat in the markets was sold after killing rites which invoked some idol's name. If the Christian purchaser knew this and yet bought the meat 'offered to idols', did he thereby acknowledge the idol? His faith taught him that, anyway, the idol was a nonentity, for 'there is no god but God'. Therefore, the invocation of an idol name was, as one might say colloquially, 'neither here nor there', quite meaningless. To think the invocation might be significant would be to concede that the idol was 'real'.

However, there were 'weaker brothers' and outsiders for whom the fear, or fame, of the idol might still be very real. Pagan credulity certainly gives the nonentity-idol a very powerful suppositious meaning, as Muḥammad appreciated when striving hard to deliver the Quraish in Mecca from it. Is it not clear that the repudiation of idols is not merely a propositional matter of saying: 'they do not exist'? Their elimination means a patient weaning of the heart from the tyranny, or pseudo-comfort, of their 'existence' in the mind. We do not end *shirk* by merely saying, *Lā ilāha illā Allāh*, but by an inward liberation which cries, 'Whom *have* I in heaven but Thee?' So the Christian Corinthians had to reckon with the subtle, and often persistent, *trust* in false deities which, as Islam well knows, survives a formal denial of them, in the hearts of frail mortals still in the midst of their seeming power. Such in Corinth might well argue, from Christians ignoring 'idol meats' as deserving no taboo, that somehow by eating they were approving the deity concerned (which is what, for pagans, eating meant).

This, in turn, raised the vital question about Christian 'liberty'.

Were 'strong' Christians to eat freely because they denied idols and, therefore, regarded all meats the same, when, so doing, they *might* risk others being misled into thinking idolatry was, albeit indirectly, approved thereby? Ought their proper liberty of Christian conscience to take account of others' weakness and, for their sakes, *not* pursue its right to eat and, indeed, to disavow idols by so doing? Which had precedence – the weaker people's need or the enlightened brethren's exercise of mature faith? That area of the duty of some to others, of freedom to the fearful, has many implications in wider fields.

The whole matter can be studied in chapters 8 and 9 of the First Letter to the Corinthians. Such an issue, clearly, could not well be resolved in some remote 'decalogue' of 'thou shalt', 'thou shalt not...' but, more patiently within the give-and-take of a community in the throes of the problem, and by a gentle pastoral ministry of intimate concern. Equally clearly, the resolution of it sets a precedent capable of guiding other communities in other tensions over pagan, secular matters, and other conflicts between personal liberty and common good.

This is the way the Epistles work as Scripture. Their immediacy in no way disserves their universality, given the active acceptance of their quality. In the same Letters to Corinth came the perennial danger of partisanship, of people valuing, or evaluating, one leader over another and making sects. Paul reproves and guides them in this also (1 Cor. chapters 1–3). In so doing, he takes the opportunity to educate his readers in the nature of ministry (chapter 4). He tells them (chapters 12–14) that gifts of ministry are various and have to be discharged to the general good. This leads him into the celebrated hymn to love which occupies chapter 13 of 1 Corinthians.

Another educating precedent which belongs with these two Corinthian Letters and with Philippians also, has to do with the concerted act of almsgiving, by the dispersed churches on behalf of the poor in Jerusalem (see 1 Cor. chapter 16; 2 Cor. chapters 8 and 9; Phil. chapters 1 and 4). Brave words about the Jew/Gentile distinction being transcended in Christ, so that both were one, might have been dismissed as mere words without this tangible 'sacrament' of its reality in the *Zakāt*, or giving, which Paul concerted as a spontaneous gesture of unity across the gulf between Jew and non-Jew. It was because of this 'sacrament' and his desire to interpret it by conveying it in person to Jerusalem, that Paul forfeited his freedom, and became a prisoner. The offertory also helped to deepen and educate the awareness of the givers.

A precedent of a different order emerges from the Letter to the

Colossians. That city in Asia Minor, like many in the Graeco-Roman world, boasted many 'gnostics', who resembled tendencies later very evident in Islam. They were *illuminati*, who sought and found *gnosis*, or *'irfān*, not in the surface meaning of revelation or Scripture but, as they saw it, in an esoteric meaning, not known to the 'ordinary' reader but given to initiates on the condition of a discipline guided by a mentor. Such 'gnosticism' is well known across religious frontiers. It tends towards a neglect of 'orthodox' forms both of faith and symbol (if such have been reached). Where they are embryonic it seems to threaten them. Further it fosters an élitism and a trend to fantasy and pretension. In response in the Letter to the Colossians Paul argues for the true *gnosis* in Christ and warns his readers against gnostic philosophies, interpreting to them the *pleroma*, or 'fullness' to be noted later in Chapter 9. By his own lights, the gnostic was often found depreciating the body in a false asceticism, or fastidiously exaggerating ritual disciplines (cf. 2:8 and 2:16–23).

Though gnosticism had many diverse forms, something of the same order lies behind the sharp warnings of the First Epistle of John, where the church was endangered by ideas about the evil of the body which denied the physical reality of Jesus. Hence the firm insistence there of the reality of Jesus truly 'come in the flesh'. Scholars may feel that we need more light than the Epistles actually afford us on the whole complex phenomenon of esotericism which continued to beset the churches for some three centuries or more. If not exhaustive, at least the apostolic writings are precedent enough for the main issues at stake, namely, an intelligent faith, humility, a glad discipline of the body, and the constraining fellowship.

The word 'mystery' (*musterion*) which we find often in the Epistles (Rom. 16:25; 1 Cor. 2:7; Eph. 1:9, 3:3, 3:4 and 3:9, 6:19; Col. 1:26, 2:2, 4:3; 1 Tim. 3:9) is a fascinating index to how the faith borrowed vocabulary from its context in order both to differ and to be intelligible. *Musterion* was a very frequent term among the gnostics. Paul employs it to denote the 'secret' of experience in Christ, but insists that it is an open secret, in the sense that what was once 'hidden' is now revealed in Christ, and that its present knowledge turns on commitment and surrender. One cannot know the truth except by active trust and obedience; but, given such, it is freely open to all. Indeed, almost everywhere that 'mystery' is used 'knowledge' is affirmed.[23] It was in such ways that the apostles addressed themselves creatively to culture around them.

A further example might be cited in the strong accent of the Epistles on the creation, human nature and 'conscience'. Some readers have even discerned a Stoic dimension in Paul, perhaps reaching him through Seneca, in his concern for the due order of things. Natural relationships of family and sexual responsibility are enjoined in the *catechesis* or teaching office of the local churches (cf. Eph. 4:22–6:9). The axioms addressed to all areas of relationship - husbands, wives, children, masters, servants - lay down a pattern of peace, sanity, deference and grace. All is community-based, and comes within the sanction of corporate honour and the care of a social conscience. The repute of all is in the custody of each.

One strangely significant expression of this quality of New Testament ethics is the brief, private Letter to Philemon - strange because some would argue that its private topic makes it unfit for 'revelation' and significant because it illuminates how faith works within social structures. Onesimus, the subject of the letter, was a slave in the Christian household of Philemon, a leader of the church in Colosse. He had fled and eventually arrived in Rome where he had become a Christian through contact with Paul, then under house-arrest in the capital. Paul, though finding Onesimus a useful help and youthful companion, nonetheless urged Onesimus to return in penitence to Philemon, repaying what he had stolen to finance his wanderings. Paul wrote the letter for Onesimus to carry with him, commending him to Philemon and strongly implying (if this were necessary) that forgiveness and free acceptance must be his response. Legally, as a runaway Onesimus could be subject to dire penalty. Paul writes with a deft mixture of gentle entreaty and firm direction, and turns the episode into a warm parable of what grace in Christ can be for us all.

The precedent quality here is plain to see. The new relationship in the Gospel draws the sting of economic institutions. Paul does not campaign against the institution of slavery. He was a prisoner anyway and soon to be a martyr. But his reconciling Gospel effectively ends what slavery means between persons (if we can assume, as we surely must, that Philemon was ready for reconciliation).

It has to be remembered how few and scattered and politically powerless the Christian communities of these Epistles were. Not for three centuries would the faith be in 'corridors' of power, and only then because the Empire itself recruited it. Yet it was keenly aware that it 'wrestled with principalities and powers' - a phrase which stands for what current twentieth-century terminology would call white supremacy, *apartheid*, economic imperialism, nuclear blackmail, and the rest. The New Testament was neither truculent against the state, nor subservient where vital issues of Emperor-worship and idolatry were concerned.[24] It sought to be law-abiding, despite persecution and disdain for it in many quarters, but it held firmly to the prime rights of God. In all its postures, it saw itself 'between the times' and its great hope was 'the kingdom and patience of Jesus Christ'. The world was both passing away and also the steady arena of grace and a 'walking worthy of vocation'.

viii

Most significant of all in this world of the Epistles is the bid for a unity of *koinonia* (fellowship), a single community mastering and terminating the age-long distinction between Jew and Gentile. Within the few decades of these Letters it happened, tentatively but splendidly. Strains and tensions almost broke the achievement. Jewry drew back into its elect privacy with God, fearing for its identity especially after the Fall of Jerusalem and Hadrian's desolation. By the second century, the Church, against its deepest grain of undiscriminating *koinonia*, became almost entirely Gentile. The 'area' between Jewishness and the new faith tended to be tense with issues of circumcision, of alleged crypto-Christians and/or crypto-Jews coveted by both 'sides' and suspected by the fully committed either way. We see more of this tragedy in Chapter 9, as it bears closely on John's Gospel.

Despite all the pains and recriminations of this struggle and despite the failure to hold the splendid vision of a unity within which it did not matter who was Jew and who was Gentile because they were 'one in Christ', it is important to realise that the vision lived and worked, and that it arose directly and necessarily from the crucified Messiahship of Jesus. There are those today – in what they see as the interests of Jewish/Christian relationship – who are ready to maintain a two-covenant theory, making synagogue and church inherently separate or, at best, only parallel, so ignoring or forgetting the magnificent urge to oneness which the Epistles serve and celebrate.[25] 'There is neither Jew nor Greek, there is neither bond nor free, there is neither male nor female. For you are all one in Christ Jesus.'[26]

It is notable that, with the exception of the Epistle to Hebrews (which, as we see below, is a special case), there are no letters to 'races' or 'peoples' as such. The destinations are cities and the 'citizens' are not ethnically identified. This will for the world, indifferently to race or place, impartially as to culture, sex or speech, is the corollary of that enlargement of the Gospel *of* Jesus into the Gospel *about* Jesus which is the clue to the entire development we are studying, the New

Testament in its very making both as faith and literature. It is the interplay of the realisation that what had happened in Jesus belonged to the wide world, and that only in the wide world, unreservedly, could it keep faith with itself.

ix

How, it may be asked, were the Epistles written? Some, as we see in Galatians, had their origin in the immediate ardour of pastoral emotion. Others, like Romans and Ephesians, came as careful documentary tuition from writer to reader. The mind of Paul lies behind twelve that bear his name. It is important, however, to appreciate that where others are named in the greetings – Sosthenes, Timothy and Silvanus (see the opening verses of Corinthians, Philippians, Colossians and Philemon) – they were probably much more than associates or amanuenses and shared in the authorship. At a later point it was possible for authorship by disciples to take over altogether while still bearing an apostolic name. Outside the New Testament such writings are known as *Pseudepigrapha*, a term which does not imply dubiety but a relationship, like that within Islamic tradition and *isnād*, whereby what is subsequent 'leans', or relies, on what is prior and original, claiming to think the same thoughts. The three Letters to Timothy and Titus are held to be Pauline in this sense, because they reflect a later stage in the development of pastoral administration.[27]

Romans and Galatians are the two most evidently personal of the Pauline Letters, while Ephesians has no ascription at all, and would appear to be a circular letter, with a great metropolitan centre as addressee, but meant to be read elsewhere also. Colossians explicitly directs such wider use (4:16) and mentions a letter to Laodicea to be similarly shared. It is clear that many more apostolic letters circulated in the churches than have survived.

Aside from the Pauline Letters to churches, there are seven Letters bearing the name of the writer, namely, two ascribed to Peter, one each to James and Jude, and three to John. The second attributed to Peter and that to Jude have much in common with each other and with the Book of Revelation which, along with the special case of Hebrews, will be considered later. Those to John belong with the concerns of Chapter 9.

The Epistle of James could well hold strong fascination for a Muslim reader, coming as it does from the pen of a brother of Jesus and head of the Jerusalem Church. Many of its imaginative metaphors could be said to have a Quranic ring – the ships riding before the wind (3:4), wild beasts tamed by man (3:7), water sweet and water brackish (3:11), the early and latter rain fructifying the ground (5:7) and the scorching of the grass and the transitoriness of life (1:10–11). The reproach in 2:1–6 about preferential treatment to the rich with an instinct to despise the poor is very reminiscent of Surah 80 and the episode of Muḥammad and the blind man. James writes of caring for people 'in the way of God' (1:27); he rejoices in Abraham as *khalīl Allāh* (2:23); he rebukes *istikbār* (4:6) and commends *khushū'a* (4:10); his face is set against extortion (5:4); he singles out the patience of the prophets (5:10); and he lives by a deep sense of the ever-watchful vigilance of the divine Lord and judge (4:12, 5:9), unchanging and ever self-sufficing (*Al-Ṣamad*) (1:17).[28]

As we read him we are aware that James' world is very close to primitive Christian community. His may even be an earlier letter than 1 Thessalonians. There is no hint of the Jew/Gentile tensions which developed elsewhere. It is almost as if we are listening to Christian preaching at its simplest and most down-to-earth – forthright, vigorous, salted with lively metaphor and urgently ethical. It allows us to glimpse the solid qualities of the Gospel in the shaping of society and against its Jerusalem background the perennial task of the discipline and nurture of human personality in 'faith and works'.

The First Epistle of Peter, likewise, illuminates vividly the life, worship and discipline of the early Christian congregation, if we may assume that it embodies sermon material condensed into letter form and perhaps related to baptism and/or liturgy. Two features are conspicuous – the steady habit of deriving all guidance from the example of Jesus, and the fact of suffering as implicit in Christian vocation. These two come together, inasmuch as suffering for love's sake is the heart of the fact of Jesus himself (1:11, 2:19–25, 3:14–18, 4:1, 4:12–19, 5:10). Peter, no less than Paul, is a nurturer of faith and humility and gentleness. He carries forward into the new community deep legacies of thought and metaphor from the Judaic world (1:15, 1:24, 2:4–6, 3:6, 3:10–12, 3:20). He is equally at home in recollection of the words of Jesus (1:22, 2:12, 3:9, 3:14, 4:5, 4:7, 4:10, 5:2, 5:3, 5:6). From his pen we learn the rudiments of doxology and the beginning of formal Christian language of adoration incorporating the new dimensions of awareness of God, owed to Jesus and the Cross (4:11, 5:10). Like Paul, he has detailed directives for the church membership in their various obligations, within family and State (2:13–18, 3:1–8, 4:9, 5:5). His is one of the first recorded usages of the very term 'Christian', which, according to Acts 11:26, was coined by the pagan folk of the city of Antioch to denote a community which was neither simply Jewish nor simply Gentile, because it was comprised indifferently by both.

x

Of all the writings in the New Testament, the Epistle to Hebrews must seem opaque, at first encounter, to minds nurtured in Islam. It is, in any event, what Latins call *argumentum ad homines* – presenting a meaning in a form best calculated to convey it to the intended audience. As such, it demands careful perception from any modern reader, unfamiliar with its vocabulary of tabernacle, sacrifice, temple and offering. 'Priesthood', too, is a term almost anathema to Muslims; but, given patience, there is much to disentangle in this complex. In the age-long Biblical sense of 'the Holy', *Al-Quddūs*, there is much of the *Subḥāna wa Ta'āla* of the transcendence of God in the Qur'ān, in the unapproachability of God by mortal, sinful man. Hence the Judaic role of 'sacrifice' (*sacrificium*, or making holy) as that by which the human and the sinful might 'seek unto God', in a rite of penitence and hope, through a symbolism of access and forgiveness.

Such the Tabernacle in the wilderness, and its successor the Temple in Jerusalem, sought to be. It was believed to be divinely appointed under Moses, the great prophet-leader, and entrusted to his brother, Aaron, and the levitical officiants, who acted as the people's representatives. The Letter to Hebrews, within the growing Christian tradition, sees this levitical, Mosaic, pattern of things as foreshowing the redemptive significance of the obedience of Jesus in the drama of the Cross. The writer – only for the sake of those he is addressing with *their* preconcepts – aims to interpret how the death of Jesus opens our way to 'the mercy-seat' of God. Nigh impossible as it is, to fit the voluntary, actual human self-giving of Jesus, into a paradigm of animal sacrifice (since the two are so disparate), the Epistle endeavours to do so.

With that central aim, it invokes certain other arguments, one of which may well signify for Muslim readers. It has to do with Abraham, whose relationship with God antedated the wilderness and Moses, and therefore had priority over the levitical system. For that reason a mysterious figure named Melchisedec, to whom Abraham paid tithes as recorded in the Book of Genesis, possessed a sanctity acknowledged by Abraham by virtue of which – and of course by virtue of earlier time – Abraham related to God independently of the Mosaic law and ritual. Paul uses a similar theme about Abrahamic priority in his letter to the

Galatians. The Letter to the Hebrews reads this as pointing towards the distinction that the Christian tradition about Jesus makes between the Mosaic *cultus* and the inclusive grace of the Gospel which it believes Melchisedec, in his mysterious independence of Moses, foreshadows.

This Epistle, then, constitutes a commentary, for its immediate 'constituency' of mind, on the majestic symbol in which the Gospel says: 'The veil of the Temple was rent in twain' (Matt. 27:51; Luke 23:45). Its claim is that 'a new and living way is opened into the holiest', that recurring ritual sacrifices need no longer be offered, that ancient types have found their meaning, and that through Jesus and his obedience in suffering love the transcendent majesty of God receives the due adoration of forgiven man. Such is the meaning of 'priesthood', achieved once for all, now and ever, in Jesus as the Christ.

For all its deeply Hebraic idiom and theme, the Letter to Hebrews is graced with the finest Greek in the New Testament. We are uncertain to whom, precisely, it was sent, or where. Perhaps the recipients were a congregation, or even a small group of 'liberal' Jews, perhaps associated with an eloquent Jew named Apollos (Acts 18:24). What is certain is that they were in a dangerous time, probably around 66 C.E. in the persecution that followed the fire in Nero's Rome. Some of their leaders, we must infer from 13:7, had already suffered death. In this critical hour they were summoned, in the three superb closing chapters, to fortitude, fidelity and emulation of the great heroes of the past (chapters 11–13). There is something of a *Hijrah* in this appeal: 'Let us go forth unto him, outside the camp, bearing his reproach' (13:13). In all this theme of courage there is no violence, no inflicting – only the incurring – of wrong. It was a *Hijrah* of identity with a patient Christ and with the community of patience under adversity which he was steadily gathering to his name in the maelstrom of Roman society. We take even grimmer measure of this in the last book of the Christian Scriptures. It was not Joshua and his militarism that gave the people rest (4:8). As we saw earlier, 'the architect and captain of faith', as this writer believes, was Jesus, the shape of whose saving authority he presents in the distinctive analogies of his chosen field of reference. We can only speculate how he might have reconceived it for the Meccan/Medinan tradition of the 'sundry prophets' with whom he begins (1:1). For him both prophet and priest serve the glory and holiness of God, the one in the trust of the word, the other in the pattern of the symbol.

xi

The last book in the New Testament is known as The Revelation of (i.e. to) John the Theologian. The sharp differences in its Greek style have made most scholars sure that the 'John' who wrote it is not the 'John' to whom we owe the Gospel and the Epistles. The name was frequent enough. This John was a church 'brother' (1:9) in exile on the lonely island of Patmos in the Aegean Sea. The date is probably the time of the bitter persecution of the churches which occurred in the reign of Domitian in the final decade of the first century (96 C.E.). If, as some conjecture, the book was originally composed in Aramaic, the quality of its Greek might be explained by an over-literal translation.

Revelation belongs to a form of writing of which there were pre-Christian examples in books like The Apocalypse of Baruch and The Book of Enoch. 'Apocalypse', or 'unveiling', is the Greek for 'revelation'. It is a type of literature necessarily strange to the Qur'ān-reader. Though it has some affinities with Islamic tradition about *Al-Dajjāl*, or the antichrist (which is, of course, post-Quranic), it involves Messianic thoughts which the Qur'ān does not share. For the Qur'ān, 'Messiah' (*Al-Masīḥ*) is an honoured title of 'Īsā (Jesus), as prophet-messenger and 'word' of God. It does not denote the redemptive figure at the centre of hope and history, who is its meaning in the Hebraic and Christian vocabulary. It was from within the distinctive Jewish and Christian interpretations of 'Messiah' that 'apocalyptic' developed. In the broadest sense Messiahship was the answer properly to come from God to the predicament in which history oppressed and wearied man. In the Judaic case, the predicament was read as that of their own nation, by this time under Rome and bereft of Jerusalem. The Messiah must needs be a figure of power, a Maccabean style hero. Perhaps there would be two Messiahs – one kingly, one priestly. The bitterness of 'hope deferred' caused much Hebraic thinking to visualise the Messianic age as only coming when things had become utterly chronic. Were it to come prematurely, there would still be surviving evil to frustrate it.[29] The final realisation would have to be climactic, a supreme culmination, a totally inclusive encounter. For some believers, this meant reading all degenerative downward momentum in history as paradoxically to be endured as preparation for the 'unveiling' of the great and supernatural reversal when the Messianic day dawned through the storm-clouds and the Messianic deliverer appeared in overwhelming triumph. Such was Jewish apocalypse.

In Christian understanding, Messiah had already come in the

person of Jesus – teaching, crucified and risen. In him and in his Cross was the Messianic meaning, achieved and abiding; but history, read and lived by that faith, was still hostile, cruel and defiant. The world was both 'redeemed' and 'unredeemed'. *How* Messiah saves had been shown and accomplished in the suffering love of Christ and the Church lived in the emulation of that 'power and wisdom of God'. Clearly, that redemption had its future tense, through and beyond the present tribulation of the churches in its witness and service. This was Christian 'apocalypse'. The widespread persecution of the churches under the Romans took on the form, not simply of crushing adversity, but of a dark adversary 'against the Lord' and his 'anointed' servant, Jesus. Christians read their harsh sufferings as the index to a cosmic conflict between righteousness and wrong, between the Christ of God and the gathered *ẓulm* of the evil powers of society and state.

It is important to appreciate why this sense of things does not obtain within the Qur'ān, by reason of the absence of the Messianic dimension. That absence, in turn, is explained by the fact that Islam does not share the Judaic belief in ethnic exceptionality from which Judaic Messianism springs, as God's 'obligation' to *that* people and within *that* covenant. Nor does it share the Christian 'translation' of that Messianism into the universal dimension via Jesus and the Cross. In the Qur'ān the ultimacy of God – which is what Messianism means in concrete history – is seen and vindicated in the grand assize, the last judgement, *Yaum al-Dīn*, when divine vindication or retribution overtakes every soul of man and the balances are weighed. There are, it is true, parallels to 'apocalytic' in the vivid Quranic descriptions of the rolled-back heavens, the opened books, the melting earth, and the 'aweful' majesty of eternal *Qadr*. Those passages might serve to align a Muslim reader with the seals, the books, the clouds, the throne, in Revelation, but only within the otherwise decisive contrast of the differing theology of the 'whence' and 'whither' of judgement.

Nevertheless, one significant fact about the tribulation of the churches apocalyptically expressed in these Christian terms, will be readily admired by Muslims. The issue between Rome and the churches, the issue within the cosmic struggle, was idolatry. Persecution and martyrdom came by the refusal of the Christians to acknowledge the Emperor in the deifying formula: 'Caesar is Lord'. One need only say this, with ritual incense, once a year and be free otherwise to believe and worship whatever one willed, but the Christian could only say: 'The Lord, He is God alone'. His faith allowed no worship save the worship of God. Thus the issue between the Empire and the Christian community was the deeply Islamic one of *shirk*.

That demand for Emperor-worship, though crucial, was only one aspect of the context of stress and peril in which the churches lived at the time of John's writing. They felt themselves caught up in a truly cosmic crisis where 'Christ' and 'Anti-Christ' were confronting each other. They were 'companions in the kingdom and patience of Jesus' (1:9).[30] It is well to associate the Letters of Jude and 2 Peter in this same context. Verses 4–16 of Jude, which are repeated in 2 Peter chapter 2, are part of a tract against inner heresies, perhaps ensuing on the death of leaders (verse 17) and made all the more serious by the external dangers.[31] Jude calls for the same steadfastness, and evokes something of the same sense of jeopardy, as John's 'unveiling'.

As befits its theme, much of Revelation is written in a cryptic form. It uses a code language which readers could translate but censors not. The writer has a great way with numbers as symbols – seven churches, trumpets, seals, angels, bowls, four living creatures, four and twenty elders, and the mysterious 'six hundred and sixty-six'. In this he resembles earlier – and later – writers in the same tradition. There are, indeed, more than three hundred allusions to Ezekiel and Daniel and to Hebrew apocalyptic, and there are a number of snatches of triumphal music in which we can register an early hymnology of Christianity (e.g. 4:8, 11:15, 19:6).

Commentators have laboured to find explicit meaning for the subtle and interlocking symbolism. But, through and beyond their findings and debates, rings the essential message of the divine victory and the ultimacy of grace – themes splendidly caught in the magnificent phrase, 'the throne of God and of the Lamb' (22:3), meaning that transcendent sovereignty and self-expending love are one sublime authority. The historical background yields the prophetic vision of future victory, and both warrant the great *Allāhu akbar* of 19:6. Martyrs are celebrated in the assurance: 'Blessed are the dead who die in the Lord' (14:13). The 'great harlot' of faithlessness, of cosmic *kufr*, is destroyed and the blood of the saints is avenged, their fidelity vindicated. In a haunting variety of pictures and allusions, John in his island prison celebrates the anguish and the ecstasy of triumph. All could be said to be there at the outset in the superb vision of the living Lord in 1:10–20. Aptly the seven letters follow to a cluster of communities around Ephesus, 'the seven churches', exhorting to discipline, realism and hope.

Though some of the music or poetry comes from the songs of Jewish heroes, from Moses and the Maccabees, the Book of the Revelation has nothing to do with martyrs in the way of war, but only with martyrs in the path of peace, crying not on battlefields but beneath the altar. They are the protagonists, not of sufferings inflicted, but of long-suffering endured. The Satan who, in the counsels of creation (Surah 2:30 f.), disputed the divine intention in man – it is he, 'the accuser', who is here overthrown (12:10).[32] For 'by the spirit of prophecy' and 'by the testimony of Jesus' (19:10) the central imperative of all existence, 'Worship God', is fully and finally obeyed. The unveiling of that climax came to a solitary prisoner, immured on a rocky island, within sound of many waters. He told it with an eloquence and a verve which only that paradox could bestow. Like all Paul's letters, he too concludes the tumult of his scenes with the simplicity of the signature: 'The grace of our Lord Jesus Christ be with you all'.

xii

Joining Gospels and Epistles together, and recording some history of events within their common time, stands Acts of Apostles, the book of the New Testament it now remains to study. It is hardly '*the* acts of *the* apostles', since only Peter, James and John, with Stephen and Philip, have any extended mention in chapters 1 to 12, and thereafter it is Paul (with Barnabas, Silvanus and Luke) who fills the picture. There is much that church history enfolds outside this historian who, though he writes anonymously, is believed to be Luke the physician (Col. 4:14), author of the Gospel which bears his name and with which this book of Acts is always paired (Acts 1:1). Because his book is selective we must see his purpose as signifying, not exhausting, how things transpired. His direction (apart from 8:26–40, an episode taking a new disciple into Ethiopia, via Gaza), is all westward and he ends, inconclusively with Paul a prisoner in Rome under house-arrest. It is as if he wanted to symbolise a vital stage in 'the expanding circle of action',[33] by locating the great missionary apostle at the great capital of the western world. The church in Rome was already there, founded by unknown disciples. It was not of Paul's planting, but it was dearly within his sights as the way onward to 'the farthest parts', to which Luke knew the Gospel to be destined beyond Jerusalem, Judea and Samaria (1:8).

The sort of scholarship we noted earlier as expended on the text of the Gospels helps to elucidate the formation of Acts. Its structure is clearly designed to present both the steady mission of the Church from its Jerusalem origin, via Antioch, and also the spontaneous, but crucial, development by which the Jew/Gentile distinction was transcended in its outreach. Luke, in his opening address to Theophilus, his 'first' reader, stresses the continuity of the two books, about 'all that Jesus began to do' in the Galilean/Jerusalem ministry, and so 'continued to do' in the life and witness of the faithful. How that witness shaped itself, in the energy of its first launching (2:1–47), is told in Luke's digest of the early preaching. Its content and transmission must have involved some of the same patterns as those we noted in the Gospels – oral memory and liturgical and written sources. Such preaching as that in chapters 2–4, must often have been repeated within the Christian congregations. It is, we may say, almost another part of 'the Gospel according to Luke', maturing in the very genesis of the Church as the community of recognition, beginning articulately to possess – and thus to give – the faith about the risen Jesus through whom it lived.

The immediate audience is, at first, wholly Jewish. The preaching identifies in the crucified teacher the very Christ, who fulfils the ancient hope through that which apparently most surely disqualifies him, namely, the Cross. This revolutionary understanding of what it has taken for Messiah to be Messiah declares an open invitation to repentance and faith. It rejoices in the strange victory of suffering grace and assures the listeners – so close to the crisis in which they had participated – that evil leaves no ground for despair if they are ready to recognise themselves in its forgiving embrace. 'The promise is to you and to your children and to all that are afar off ...' (2:39).

That last phrase about the distant nations begins to be fulfilled in Luke's exposition by the intimations he gives in 8:4 and 11:20 of an apparently spontaneous initiative to include 'Greeks' also in the range of the Gospel. It is this development, on the part of nameless, ordinary disciples, which he later pursues in the narrative of Paul, its supreme symbol and genius. First there has to come the crucial narrative of Paul's conversion (see Chapter 8, below) and the intriguing experience of Peter with Cornelius. It is important to appreciate that, radical as these steps were in opening out the faith to 'the Gentiles', there were – and had long been – in the contemporary scene gestures of mutuality between Jews and Greeks and a willingness on the part of some Jews to soften the sharp rigours in distinction and to concede some common ties. What was new about the initiative Luke records was its focus around Jesus, crucified and risen and, for that reason, its welding of the diversity into new 'Christian' community.

Acts reflects that Jew/Greek intercourse in the context of the long narrative in chapters 6 and 7 of the martyrdom of Stephen. Coming into the history as one of the deacons appointed within the embryonic organisation of communal support in the Jerusalem church, Stephen in his zeal fell foul of the priestly caste, the rigorous Jews, *and* the

Hellenists. His offence, in the eyes of all, was no doubt his witness to Jesus as having accomplished Messiahship in terms utterly foreign both to Jewish orthodoxy and to 'Greek' wisdom. His defence is strongly Hebraic in its whole structure and content and undoubtedly figures in Luke's text from an earlier source which, in his presentation, he decided to incorporate. Its long survey of Hebraic history, broken off before it was complete, serves to reinforce the claim, familiar elsewhere in Luke and others, which links the wrong perpetrated against Jesus with the age-long exposure of all the prophets to calumny and rejection, in order to set the victory of redemptive love precisely where the evil is which love must overcome. Luke understands Stephen, in the very maul and bitterness of death's prelude, witnessing heroically to these central strands of Christian confession – prophecy vindicated, scriptural precedent fulfilled, and evil answered where it is most surely evident in its antipathy to Jesus. Luke sees Stephen's suffering, as the first martyr, essentially continuous with that of the Lord to whom he witnesses. It also prefaces the conversion of one, Saul – accessory to the crime – who is shortly to become Paul.

From this grim encounter, it is a respite from tragedy to turn to Luke's narrative (8:26–40) of the glad meeting of Philip with an important official from Ethiopia who was returning through the Gaza region to his native land after a pilgrimage to Jerusalem. Travelling in his chariot he is perusing the prophet Isaiah at the passage (chapter 53) which tells of the suffering servant of God. Philip rides with him and they discuss the meaning of the text. Once again, Luke makes occasion for his favourite theme, echoing the walk to Emmaus in his Gospel (24:13–35), and adducing the way in which the events about Jesus had fulfilled prophetic foreshowing. This is the only incident in his narrative of the first ventures of the faith into the world which is not northward and westward. It is the one intimation of its relevance to Africa and is left to do duty for all the absent detail about apostles, like Mark in Egypt, or Thomas – as tradition has it – finally in India. For reasons which must always remain conjectural, Luke the Greek contents himself with a symbolic story heading outward to the Mediterranean rather than eastward to the Arabian Sea and the Indian Ocean. However, the told story has to be read as the paradigm of the untold one, translated into the way the world differs from the Orontes to the Indus.

Peter, as well as Philip, has unexpected meetings and that with Cornelius – for all its charming simplicity as told in chapters 10 and 11 – is an important turning point in Luke's perspective. Peter finds himself in the coastal region of Palestine, on the shore at Jaffa, resting on the flat roof-top under an awning (we may suppose) in the heat of the day. Out on the sea (where they off-load on to lighters in the absence of a deep harbour) were the ships from afar, sharing in the famed commerce of that shore. Tyre, further to the north is graphically described by the prophet Ezekiel, as haven to 'all the ships of the sea with their mariners', and bearing a rich variety of cargoes. Their sails were the colourful product of Egypt's linen industry (Ezek. 27:3–9). It was these Peter saw in a troublesome dream as he dozed in the haze of heat. They seemed to him like sheets let down in front of him, carrying items of those gentile/foreign cargoes, food of non-Jews. A voice in his dream commanded him to make a meal of these non-kosher foods. Incensed in his spirit at the mischievous suggestion that he, Peter, could ever be party to such infraction of the strict dietary laws which symbolised his Jewish loyalty, he resolutely refused. But the command was repeated three times. While Peter was debating within himself what Satan this could be 'whispering in the bosom', there came a knock at the door, with the news that another man had been dreaming too, a Roman centurion stationed at Caesarea, and – as it was said – a devout man concerned to worship the One God. In his dream this soldier, Cornelius by name, had been directed to send for Peter from Jaffa, as one who could – and would – inform him further.

Peter was disconcerted and perplexed. A request to go into the house of a gentile was one to be shunned, but the strange coincidence of the two dreams puzzled him and gave him pause. He housed the messengers overnight and the next morning decided to go with them to Caesarea, wisely taking with him some companions from Jaffa, for better handling of a dubious venture. Doubtless on the way they aired their misgivings but, in them and above them, a logic was at work. Peter could hardly travel and then not arrive, nor arrive and not proceed to speak, so he found himself within the gentile's house and, indeed, awaited by a whole houseful of eager folk. His fisherman's realism, learned in the rough and tumble of Galilee, itself a region with gentiles around, told him he had better see the venture through. He told them simply the Gospel as he knew it, of Jesus as the Christ. The sequel dispelled all his fears. For there was an evident response of faith and enthusiasm which he could not gainsay. It was clear, beyond question, that 'God granted to gentiles also repentance unto life' (11:18). It was by such direct interhuman contact that the divine purpose of undivided community in Christ was achieved. Dreams had their place, but the gist was an inner obedience struggling against a traditional rejectionism. 'Table fellowship', as the Church called it, in the Christian Eucharist, or 'sacramental hospitality' each to the other, was the heart of the matter, just as avoidance of it, via the dietary laws, was the core of Jewish privacy. The vision did well to say: 'Rise, Peter ... eat'. His characteristic resistance: 'Not so, Lord ...' measures how deep the issue was.

It was, therefore, little wonder that the episode brought Peter under interrogation from the Church in Jerusalem. Luke then goes on to describe how this question of non-Jewish admission to the Church was resolved in the Council held in the Holy City (chapter 15), after subsequent occasions of gentile faith and baptism resulting from other, independent initiatives, notably in Antioch, had made the matter urgent of solution. It was in Antioch that outside observers, noting a fellowship neither Jewish nor gentile but both in one, coined the new and – to them – derisory name, *Christianoi* (11:26). The point was not whether gentiles were admissible to Christian faith, but whether they should first become Jews by undergoing circumcision and undertaking the keeping of the entire Judaic law. Was the Church, that is, to be understood as a Jewish sect essentially? Or was this Judaic 'sectarian' acknowledgement of Jesus as the suffering Christ veritably a communion unconditionally open to all, irrespective of race or culture or birth or language? The inspired answer of the Jerusalem Council was that the latter was the fact. The only conditions it laid down related to anti-idolatry, marital purity and two items of dietary hygiene (15:20, 15:29).

xiii

The vital ruling of the Council ensured that the new faith-community affirmed its inherent openness while seeking, on that condition, to reassure Judaic fears that somehow 'pearls were being wasted on swine', or that the sluice gates were being opened to all kinds of pagan excess. Its decision had become the more urgent because of the evolving story in and around Antioch and because of the first missionary journey of Paul and Barnabas into Asia Minor which, in fact, antedated the Jerusalem conclave. Luke's editorial strategy is to pass exclusively to Paul after intimating that gentile developments of which Paul was to be the great protagonist had been anticipated by Peter, and after briefly recording the martyrdom of James, son of Zebedee, brother of John, at the hand of Herod (12:2), and Peter's amazing escape from Herod's clutches. Thereafter, Luke's story follows entirely the travels and career of Paul, through two journeys, a return to Jerusalem, and a third journey towards Rome under arrest. The return to Jerusalem was on behalf of the offertory, from the scattered churches of his travels, to the poor of Jerusalem. Paul's experiences under arrest and his apologia before rulers allow Luke to keep the symbolic climax of Paul-in-Rome firmly in the setting of the transformation of Paul-in-Damascus. What the apostle called 'the heavenly vision' (26:19) inaugurates and explains all else.

Selective, as it is, of much more left to silence, it is a story of ripe heroism and steadfast tenacity. Though Luke comes early to a martyrdom and ends with a prisoner, there is no violence from the Church, no militarism, no threatening and no physical confrontation. The only swords in the story are those of Herod (12:2) and a frightened Roman gaoler (16:27). These are journeys of the defenceless, armed only with the shield of faith and the sword of the Spirit (cf. Eph. 6:16–17). Exposed as Paul and his companions are to mobs with stones, or even mobs with garlands, mistaking them for 'gods', (14:11–18), liable to ambushes and callous treatment, to contumely and scorn, they survive joyously and pursue their zealous way. It is true that the desperate dangers of Nero's last years are still ahead and Luke, as many believe, is at special pains to show that, by and large, Roman power can still do justly by evangelists. Such a reminder became grimly relevant when, as Revelation demonstrates, the Church came into dire confrontation with the imperial power. So we find Paul asserting his Roman citizenship, eliciting apology from unjust officials, and finally appealing to Caesar himself against the dilatoriness of governors in Jerusalem. There are scholars who have surmised that the long defence Paul makes before the tribunal of Felix and the hearing before Agrippa (24:10–21; also 26:1–23) may embody the content of a lawyer's brief for his defence as made in Rome before Caesar. Luke was a skilled – if amateur – historian, with a careful mind for detail and personal access to both material and experience germane to his record.

That is most obviously true of the passages (16:10–17, 20:5–21:17, chapters 27 and 28) in which he uses the personal pronoun 'We', with the clear implication that he is a fellow-traveller, and diarist, of the events at Troas and Philippi and en route later to Jerusalem. Reading the intervening passages in which Luke reverts to 'he' and 'they' (i.e. 16:16–20:4, 21:18–27:1), it is not difficult to understand that these refer to journeys and episodes, or court appearances of Paul, in which Luke was not personally involved. From Troas to Philippi, from Philippi via Ephesus up to Jerusalem, and lastly from Jerusalem on to Rome, are the segments of the story in which Luke was attending on Paul. It would seem that the friendship began in Troas, about the year 50 C.E. may have originated in Paul consulting Luke, a practising physician in that city, about wounds earlier incurred from batterings received from stoning mobs in previous journeys.

While Luke leaves many points to tantalising silence, not least what finally happened to Paul in Rome, he follows a clear strategy in his presentation. He traces from Jerusalem, through Judea and Samaria, the thrust of the Gospel as the vehicle of the grace of the risen Jesus, fulfilling the meaning of his ministry and death, in the continuing and widening fact of his community. The mother-city, Jerusalem, stages the faith forward from a new daughter-mother, Antioch. From Troas, their faith-children extend into Europe and reach to Rome. The circuit is 'Jerusalem round about to Illyricum' (Rom. 15:19), fulfilling the Gospel, and Spain is there just below the horizon. In his narrative, Luke enables us to overhear the preaching of this Church before a variety of audiences. In 13:26–41, Paul is before a Jewish audience in the synagogue of Antioch in Pisidia where his message echoes many of the themes of Stephen's last sermon. In 14:15–18, he is calming an excited throng of pagan *mushrikīn*, credulously mistaking him for an embodiment of Mercury and Barnabas, his companion, for Jupiter. It may be that this is the incident occurring in the Qur'ān.[34] In 17:22–31, we find Paul in Athens addressing a sophisticated audience on the Areopagus and taking his text from a wayside inscription ascribing worship to 'a god unknown'. In what we may justly feel to be thoroughly Quranic terms, he reproaches the idolatrous illusions, relates natural phenomena wholly to the providing hand of *Allāh al-Razzāq*, *al-Wahhāb*, and invites his listeners to read the *āyāt* of nature rightly and turn from fables and idols to the living Lord. When he reaches the heart of his message about Jesus, the Athenians cut him short and dismiss his warning of the resurrection and the judgement. It could almost be a band of the Quraish.

In Acts 20:17–35 comes one of the most moving of all Paul's discourses, this time not to a pagan congregation but to a group of elders of the church at Ephesus, whom he called to meet him at the port of Miletus when he was en route to Jerusalem, and imprisonment, carrying that significant act of *ṣadaqāt* from the dispersion to the holy city. His farewell to these local leaders breathes the warm pastoral quality of all Paul's exertions on behalf of the communities he founded. Speaking from an impending sense of peril ahead, he gives them a charge from within his own travail of mind and spirit for the true expression of Christ to the world. His words tell of unstinted labour, spiritual travail and personal integrity. There is no clearer or more graphic picture of the essence of New Testament Christianity, in form and ethos, than this passage.

It was at Ephesus, at an earlier juncture that there occurred a scene capable of ready comparison with the issue in pre-*Hijrah* between Muḥammad and the Quraish. The pagan Meccans saw Muḥammad's message as a threat to their vested interest in idols and idolatrous pilgrimage and so, in turn, to the prestige of their city. Hence their vigorous opposition, defending both their traditions and themselves. Likewise the Ephesians, worshippers of Diana their goddess, sensed a threat in Paul's Gospel of the One God. The silversmiths in particular, who made silver shrines of Diana, realised that if Paul's Gospel recruited believers, their craft, trade and livelihood would all be at risk. So they made a riot, crying: 'Great is Diana of the Ephesians', or *Diana akbar*. Their suspicion was correct, for many did repudiate the goddess and turn to the Lord. Only with much difficulty did the town clerk of Ephesus succeed in quieting the mob and securing Paul and his companions from lynching (19:18–41).

xiv

One final intriguing point remains about this book of Acts. Why did Luke end as he did? Why did he not narrate the deaths of Peter and Paul? Why does he end around the date 62 C.E. when, presumably, he knew the dark sequel and (?) was writing after it? Did he intend some further text? Or was it that he meant his ending to be symbolic? His final Greek word, *akolutos* ('without hindrance'), has a stirring note. It is, of course, ironical. Paul is under house-arrest, a prisoner with a grave case pending before the Emperor. Yet, paradoxically, he is free to receive hearers – the runaway slave, Onesimus, among them – and to preach his message. He is 'an ambassador in bonds', but, incongruous as this may be, it is a parable of the faith itself, speaking out of hardship about grace, out of adversity about peace, out of suffering about forgiveness. His sense of destiny is buoyed up by retrospect over his many adventures, not least that long and perilous voyage from Crete to Malta which Luke, who shared it, tells with graphic detail and nautical knowledge (27). All those vicissitudes served to reinforce Paul's confidence that, however the trial might eventuate, it would be his prize to stand before Caesar, where his defence in court would be also his story of Christ's grace. A Hebrew, speaking Greek, his words would surely be translated into Latin. There, using the languages of the inscription on the Cross of Jesus, interpreter and Emperor would stand face-to-face. Deprived as we are of that scene by Luke's silence, he has at least served us by his story to hold it in the imagination of the mind.

XV

There remain two literary questions in this venture at New Testament introduction relating to Muslim perplexities and assumptions. The one is the nature of the Canon of Scripture: the other is the documentary quality of the text. A clear understanding of both is necessary to an intelligent readership.

The twenty-seven books which make up the New Testament comprise what is known as the Canon, from the Greek word (*regula* in Latin) meaning, either a carpenter's measuring rod, or a scribe's list. Their presence in the Canon signifies their acceptance within the Church as forming a body of Scripture to which reference can be made for authenticity of doctrine. Its formation occupied more than three centuries, though most of the books were received as canonical by the early second century, and question remained about only six or seven, whose inclusion was finalised much later. That fact should not be understood as disquieting or curious, when the nature of the Canon is rightly appreciated. The four Gospels established themselves early, together with some thirteen Epistles of Paul and Acts. They did so, not by formal conciliar action, which did not come till 363 AD in the Eastern Church and 495 AD in the Western, but rather by consensus, or *ijmā*', from below via usage and gathering tradition.

There were two factors in the context. The one was the precedent of Old Testament Canon, which enjoyed general agreement by about the time of Jesus. The Church took it as it was in the Septuagint, out of deference to a sense of continuity and in perpetuation of the practice of Torah reading in the synagogue. Christian worship, no less, treasured and rehearsed these earlier 'oracles of God', but – and this was the second factor – it was instinctive that, within the same worship and in the self-awareness of the new community, the sayings of Jesus and the teaching of his apostles should dominate the mind and the meetings of the faithful. The same pastoral and spiritual factors which operated, as we have seen, to bring the Christian Scriptures into being, operated equally to require and promote their official recognition and usage as such.

This naturally took time and involved process, prior to consensus, across the wide dispersion of the churches. Some localities were especially fond of particular writings or had distinctive connection with their genesis. After the time of the immediate apostles, there was a steady growth of writings, pseudepigraphic 'Gospels' and Letters, which needed to be assessed. Some of these belonged with two forces at work in the second century and beyond, namely, partisans of gnosticism and Montanism. These groups developed secret writings with esoteric elements calculated to distort a growing 'orthodoxy' or they challenged apostolic sufficiency by claiming inner wisdom newly minted by themselves. Both sources of division needed to be stemmed and this necessity stimulated the need for, and the authority of, a recognised *corpus*.

But recognition took time. It received a particularly strong challenge from an important 'heresiarch' named Marcion, who rejected the Old Testament and repudiated all in the embryonic Canon of the New Testament except portions of Luke, and ten letters of Paul. The main test applied against such deviation, and others of lesser import, was that of apostolic authorship and so of pristine 'orthodoxy'. As we have seen earlier, 'apostolicity' need not rigorously require actual penmanship but rather dependable attribution to one of the apostles or their close associates. Muslims familiar with the prerequisites of authentic *isnād* in Tradition will readily recognise what was meant. 'Apostolicity' and 'orthodoxy' naturally tended to be mutually defining, with the latter something itself 'on the way', by the measure of the former. Throughout there was a deep desire to conserve the loved origins, to walk in the way of the faithful and to ensure to the world the Christian credentials. These ends interacted, within the worshipping and self-educating community.

In the process distinctions were made – which belonged also with the indecision as long as it obtained – as to writings proper for public reading and writings valuable for study. Both might be 'scripture', but only the former 'Canon', in view of the fact that public liturgical reading was a major aspect both of 'orthodoxy' and of education in faith. Border-line books, at one time or another, were the Epistle of James, 2 and 3 John, 2 Peter, Jude, Hebrews and Revelation. These, for example, were the 'absentees' from Origen's list. Irenaeus, at the end of the second century, excluded only 3 John and 2 Peter, but included *The Shepherd of Hermas* which, along with the *Didache*, was from time to time a candidate for inclusion.

The first conciliar decision on this gathering *ijmā'* of many decades and churches, deriving from the roots, did not come until 363 AD at Ephesus, to be followed by an Easter Letter from Athanasius, Bishop of Alexandria, dated 367 AD, in which the present Canon is listed. Rome followed suit much later. The long process should not be thought of as if the churches *endowed* the writings with their status, making them the 'creature' of the churches' will. On the contrary, the churches recognised as inherent in them the authority they possessed. Both writings and churches were the interacting and derivative consequence of the primary fact of Christ, the one institutional and corporate, the other documentary.[35]

xvi

Our second concluding concern has to do with the quality of the actual text, within the Canon and possessed by the faithful in the sort of scholarship which we have studied earlier, exploring form and source and redaction. Those three presume the prior establishment of the text itself, though – to a degree – they also assist it. That establishing of the text is often known as 'textual criticism', 'criticism', here, being decision about variant readings, not a passing of judgement on content. The task of decision by New Testament scholarship on the text has been largely completed and it is unlikely that any textual discovery will produce any new reading of serious relevance or with better claim to be the original than existing texts.

Before we can appreciate how variant readings arose and how scholarship can best resolve them, the papyri and the codices must be noted. Needless to say, all of them long antedate Islam, making impossible any distortion consciously contrived to respond to it. The earliest papyri, often fragmentary, come from the turn of the first century. There are four codices, the earliest being the Codex Vaticanus, of the early fourth century containing most of the New Testament. The Codex Sinaiticus also has some of the Greek Fathers. The Alexandrian is slightly later, while Codices Bezae belong to the fifth or sixth centuries. These are the major manuscripts, sometimes known as majuscules, to distinguish them from the near three thousand minuscules, because they use wholly capital letters, whereas minuscules employ both large and small. As well as some ninety papyrii, and around 270 majuscules, there are nearly three thousand lectionary pieces of the New Testament, preserved in liturgical documents.

It is the very wealth of this material which makes the task of textual scholarship so exacting and rewarding. In addition to these mainly Greek materials, there are numerous translations, of great antiquity, into languages like Syriac, Coptic, Latin, Armenian, Slavonic and Gothic, where the translator may have had Greek texts older than those we now possess. Careful study of these renderings may enable the resolution of problems remaining between variants about which, otherwise, it would be harder to adjudicate.

Yet another important field for textual scholarship is the writings of the Church Fathers in the early centuries. In their exegesis and theology, they quoted extensively and from manuscripts which have not survived. Or the way they interpreted what they found may illuminate what a reading is more likely to be. In all these ways the meticulous establishment of the text, with the critical apparatus now in use by students, carries us back to within a century of the history itself, even though the four major codices in their manuscript form date four centuries on. There is no ancient literature for which so rich a source material exists nor for which so assiduous a scholarship avails.

Assiduous and painstaking it had to be. There were strenuous duties involved. Many of the oldest papyri are in delicate physical preservation, or highly fragmentary, and difficult to decipher. The earliest of them with some majuscules, had no inter-word spaces, nor punctuation, nor breathing marks, nor accents. Though the 'probability' of readings is far, far less than is the case with Old Testament Hebrew (for Greek does have written vowels), there were, nevertheless formidable difficulties in actually deciphering what the text said. An example might be drawn from the Arabic of the Qur'ān which originally contained no diacritical pointing. In Surah 2:30 did God announce that He was setting 'a deputy' in the earth, or 'a creature'? In modern Arabic there is a single point difference between *khalīfah* and *khalīqah*, between *fā* and *qaf*. When no points were there, how should it be read? The variant anyway was hidden. Conceptually, it would make no difference to the fact of man, as being creature placed by God within creation. But it would mean a vast difference about his status under God, with all its rich implications about responsibility and 'dominion' and being 'on behalf of God' over the natural order.

Much, then, in all scriptures, can turn on what is actually set down for the eye or what the eye takes to be set down. In ancient manuscripts, most of all sacred ones, with all their fragility in time, and their taxing linguistic occasion for obscurity, reading rightly is no light task. Nor was it, for the long and patient, but very human, sequence of scribes who laboured, in scattered centres beyond mutual reach, to reproduce the texts. As these multiplied, often on none too robust materials, and through all the vicissitudes to which mortal man is prone, it is understandable that, highly treasured as the texts were, they should suffer verbal changes, slips of eyesight, repetition of words, omission of letters, or insertion of what were meant as marginal notes by an earlier copyist. Some emendations were due to scribes collating with citations known to them in different form, or perhaps choosing a preference for theological reasons.

In modern times, and since the availability in the seventeenth century of Sinaiticus and Vaticanus to western scholars and, more recently, of Codices Bezae, long labour has been expended in textual comparison, the refining of a critical apparatus, and the establishment of a recognised text. A German scholar, Tischendorf, who published in 1872 a critical text of Sinaiticus, and two English scholars, Westcott and Hort, with their Greek Testament *textus receptus* of 1882, have been leaders in this enterprise. Their work continues, in other hands, alert to whatever manuscripts may come to light, as study proceeds.

These textual labours mean much more than noting differences between readings, or taking a majority test. It cannot be assumed that what is later is less to be preferred. For its copy-source may be earlier still. Contextual considerations help to a decision, on the basis of intrinsic probability, arguable from an author's style or the point he is making. Study may gauge a particular scribe's idiosyncrasies and keep them in view in making decisions. If they are found liable to simplify (as scribes often are) one may suspect a simplification and prefer a more difficult reading. Often a shorter is to be preferred to a longer variant. Less often a scholar may conjecture his own variant where puzzlement persists.

Complex and fastidious as this whole science of textual study is, and vital as it is for the will to scriptural integrity both of scholarship and faith, its actual effect on the detailed character and witness of the New Testament could well be likened to loving brush-strokes on a finished portrait. It has been calculated that significant variations amount to about one-thousandth part of the whole, or twenty lines of the entire text of the New Testament.

A few examples may be useful. Does 1 Peter 2:24 say that Jesus bore our sins 'on the tree' (i.e. the Cross) or 'right up to the tree'? The second 'as far as' would more likely suggest a graphic touch of the eye-witness who followed 'afar off', but either is true. Was Barabbas in the text of Matt. 27:16–17 actually called 'Jesus-Barabbas', in which case the contrast with 'Jesus called the Christ' would be the more arresting? Was John the Baptist, in Mark 1:6, clothed with 'a camel's skin', or with 'a coat of camel's hair'? Does 1 John 4:19 say 'We love Him, because He first loved us', or 'We love God because ...' (Sinaiticus), or simply 'We love, because ...' (Alexandrian where the verb has no object)? Again, all are true. Should we read 'Seek first His Kingdom...' or '...the kingdom of God ...' in Matthew 6:33? In 1 John 5:8 there is what textual study almost certainly identifies as a scribe's interpolation echoing what stands in verse 7.

It will be seen that such textual decisions, important as they are for the will to exactitude, have no import for theology or history. A deeper example may perhaps afford us a conviction with which to leave this long venture in New Testament introduction. It occurs in a familiar text in Rom. 8:28, long taken to read, in English: 'All things work together for good to those who love God. ...' What is now clear is that the verb 'to work' has, in fact, God for subject whereby translation should read 'In everything God works for good with those who love Him. ...' Perhaps we may believe that this has been so in the long vicissitudes through which, via evangelists, believers, scribes, copyists and scholars, the New Testament literature gives dependable access to Jesus and how he was the Christ, and to the genesis and life of the community which believed itself constituted and chartered by his recognition.[36]

Notes

1 Basil Willey, *Samuel Taylor Coleridge* (London, 1972), p. 149.

2 'Focus' is very much what the Greek verb implies, with its meaning of 'looking away from all else', so being undistracted and intent.

3 The Septuagint, often referred to by the symbol LXX, was the Greek version of the Old Testament, recourse to which often greatly assists New Testament scholars in reading usages, and examining quotations from the Hebrew as there rendered. The LXX was, of course, the great token of the rich interpenetration of the Hebrew and Greek worlds of thought and language in the time of Jesus and the apostles. It was completed in the second century, BC. The order of the books differs from that of the original Hebrew and it includes the apocryphal books. New Testament writers often quoted from it rather than from the Hebrew text.

4 *Raphael: the Life and the Legacy* (London: B.B.C., 1983), p. 201.

5 In: *The Joyful Wisdom*, vol. 10, *Collected Works*, trans. T. Common (New York, 1964), Sect. 125, pp. 167–69.

6 An observation much loved by Bishop Joe Fison. See: F. W. Dillistone, *Life of Bishop Fison* (London, 1983).

7 'Criticism' of Islamic *Ḥadīth* has turned, not primarily on the substance (*matn*) of the tradition – i.e. Is it in character? Does it ring true? Did the Prophet have the sentiments it suggests? and like questions – but rather, is the *isnād* strong? The strength of *isnād* turns on the verifiable 'overlap' of linked witnesses, on their credibility (for which biographies of them were necessary), and on their proven connection with the first 'companion' at the head of the 'chain'.

8 On Aramaic issues in general, see: Matthew Black, *An Aramaic Approach to the Gospels and Acts* (Oxford, 1967); and C. F. Burney, *The Aramaic Origin of the Fourth Gospel* (Oxford, 1922). The play on the word *talya* in Mark 9:35–36, if taken along with Mark 10:15, could be very illuminating for the Muslim's 'problem' over Jesus being only and always 'servant' and, therefore, never 'son'. For the two are synonymous. The 'child' whom Jesus set in the midst in 9:36 is not only a type of simplicity of heart and humility but also what 'servants' are to be in their relationship to vocation. The servant is 'received', acknowledged as such, for his Lord's sake, just as a child is as God's clear entrustment. Surah 4:142 affirms that 'Messiah will never scorn to be a servant', clearly assuming, there, the type of 'sonship' – i.e. that of pampered status – which would be incompatible with service. In the Gospel, and throughout the New Testament, Jesus as 'son' and 'servant' is only either in the meaning of each. He has a 'service' which only 'sonship' can bring, a 'sonship' which only 'service' fulfils and enjoys.

9 See, further: C. F. Burney, *The Poetry of our Lord* (Oxford, 1925). Martin Buber once remarked: 'If a man has a gift of listening, he can hear the voice of Jesus himself speaking in the late accounts of the Gospels.' David Flusser, *Jesus*, trans. R. Walls (New York, 1969).

10 There was some danger in this 'borrowing', lest the Christian meaning should be confused with that 'initiation' by which the mystery cults transacted their esoteric style of 'knowledge'. But, without venture, no theology can communicate and the 'risk', appropriately handled and watched, can become the means of understanding. So here there is no spiritual experience without commitment: it is 'he that seeks who finds'.

11 See, for example, the expert publications of the United Bible Societies, for the guidance of Biblical translation, often into languages only reduced to writing by the translators themselves. See also: Eugene A. Nida, *The Theory and Practice of Translation* (Leiden, 1969); *Bible Translation: an Analysis of Principles and Procedures*, rev. edn (London, 1961); *Language Structure and Translation* (Stanford, 1975).

12 One very able Christian versed in Hindi writes, nevertheless, 'In Hindi, I have to say what I can, not what I want', meaning not any incompetence but the sheer lack of terms and vocabulary to serve what he means. Muslim translators of the Qur'ān have strongly sensed the same problem when wrestling with its Arabic and the incapacity of other languages adequately to 'take' it.

13 The 'knocking' metaphor in Rev. 3:20 is very close to Surah 47:24, which asks of unbelievers why they 'do not reflect on the Qur'ān' or can it be that 'hearts have locks upon them'? It just happens that in Matt. 19:24, Mark 10:25 and Luke 18:25, and in the Hebraic/Greek idiom, needles prefer to have eyes.

14 Eugene A. Nida is a useful source of such examples in several writings, e.g. *God's Word in Man's Languages* (New York, 1952); *Meaning across Cultures* (New York, 1981).

15 This reasoning does not commend itself to many scholars. For it implies less loyalty to its traditions than the Church in fact brought and it ignores how elements which, by a counter argument, must be seen as very congenial to the expanding faith, are embedded deeply in the scriptural sources. One marked example of the Jewish focus of Jesus' ministry is the passage in Matt. 15:22–28, and Mark 7:24–30, relating to the woman from Phoenicia, whose daughter Jesus healed. It occurred in the context of a journey outside Jesus' normal area of ministry in search of quiet and withdrawal. There were urgent reasons against a wide extension of his field of preaching. Its confinement then was in the interests of its enlargement later when the vital Messianic task had been attained and the Church was born. Yet even prior to that stage there are many indications of Jesus' accessibility to, and concern for, both gentiles and wayward Jews (the two have much in common from the angle of Judaic rigorism). In the immediate instance, it is notable that Jesus acceded to the woman's plea, so that his initial check to her hopes, if not an intended test of faith, certainly had that effect – a test she triumphantly passed with a quality of spirit that transcended ethnic distinctions.

16 See, for example: Philip Carrington, *The Primitive Christian Calendar* (1940), *A Study in the Making of the Markan Gospel* (Cambridge, 1952); and *According to Mark* (Cambridge, 1960).

17 It has long been acknowledged that what decides our praying decides our believing. (*Lex*) The voice of our praying (what the heart says as distinct from what the mind thinks) through the liturgy and its devotional readings, becomes, we may say, the voice of our Scripture in those same hearts. Is not *Tajwīd*, or loving recital, in Islam the due form of Qur'ān-possession by the community and the person?

18 On *charisma*, see for example: Geza Vermes, *Jesus the Jew* (London, 1973). There

are very few references to Jesus in the Jewish *Talmud* and those there are – in the bitterness of first-century attitudes – are sharply hostile. He was the illegitimate son of a soldier named Panthera. In Egypt he learned the magic which was the basis of his 'miracles'. He was legally executed and his body stolen by his disciples, who invented the story of his resurrection. His teaching made him a traitor to Israel. Judeo-Christians are characterised in the same way.

19 This 'hidden usury' seems the likeliest way to explain the story's meaning and moral and was probably more than half suspected by the hearers. Jewish Law firmly prohibited usury (*ribā'*) or any sort of loan from Jew to Jew. Money should change hands only in purchasing or giving. There were many provisions to prevent circumvention, such as a subsequent 'gift' after money had been surreptitiously 'lent', to serve as 'interest'.

What probably happened in the parable was that the 'lord' (whom we will call 'A') had through the steward agreed that a 'buyer' ('B') would contract to pay later for goods acquired on credit worth, let us say, 100 units. That bond exchanged, A would immediately buy the goods back from B for 90 units. B thus had his 90 units cash to function as the loan he sought, while A had his goods back and 100 units cash to be repaid, making 10 units effectively 'interest'. A had thus contrived the 'loan' he wanted to make, and which B sought, with a fictitious transaction as the means to satisfying both. In Jesus' story the steward could, at one and the same time, ingratiate himself with the debtor, and yet do his lord no wrong save to deprive him of interest which was illegal anyway. The moral of the story is to commend the steward's resourcefulness in an evasive world as a spur to the quite different, but often sadly wanting, liveliness of the servants of the kingdom of heaven.

20 See: Oscar Cullmann, 'The Plurality of the Gospels as a Theological Problem in Antiquity,' in *The Early Church*, ed. A. J. G. Higgins (London, 1956), pp. 39–54. Cullmann points out that there is no polemical *animus* against other evangelists in any of the four Gospels. There were solid reasons why 'reduction' to one should, in fact, have stayed at four, such as apostolic authority and the different areas of 'circulation'. As the concept of the 'Canon' developed it resisted plurality without requiring singularity.

21 Useful documentation of Paul's citations from Jesus will be found in: D. J. Dungan, *The Sayings of Jesus in the Churches of Paul* (Oxford, 1971); and W. D. Davies, *Paul and Rabbinic Judaism* (London, 1948), pp. 136–46, who remarks: 'Paul is steeped in the mind and words of his Lord.' See also: D. C. Allison, 'The Pauline Epistles and the Synoptic Gospels, the Pattern of the Parallels', in *New Testament Studies*, vol. 28, no. 1, 1982, pp. 1–32. See also: C. H. Dodd, 'The Primitive Catechism and the Sayings of Jesus', *More New Testament Studies*, (Manchester, 1968), pp. 11–29.

22 See below in respect of Ephesus and Diana. The last appeal of one of the latest writings (1 John 5:21) is: 'Keep yourselves from idols'. The writer is well aware that there are many more 'idols' than the literal ones of wood or stone. Throughout the New Testament, from Mary's song, *Magnificat*, or *Takbīr*, to the end runs the steady theme of how 'God is all in all', the only and unrivalled Lord of the worlds.

23 Unlike the popular modern sense of 'mystery', for which 'mystery' ends when a clue is found or the 'secret' is brought into the open. For the New Testament, *musterion* is both 'known' (by the believer) and yet perpetually to be wondered at and inquired into. See also note 10 above.

24 See: Oscar Cullmann, *The State in the New Testament* (New York, 1956).

25 Among exponents of the two-covenant view which disavows the New Testament vision – and achievement of Jew/Gentile unity, are, on the Jewish side: Franz Rosenzweig, *The Star of Redemption*, trans. W. H. Hallo (New York, 1970). On the Christian side see James Parkes, *The Foundations of Judaism and Christianity*

(London, 1960), *Prelude to Dialogue* (London, 1969), and *Voyages of Discoveries*, (London, 1969); see also: A. R. Eckardt, *Elder and Younger Brothers* (New York, 1967); Reinhold Niebuhr, *Pious and Secular America* (New York, 1958).

The doctrine is attacked by Jacob Taubes in *Arguments and Doctrines: A Reader in Jewish Thinking in the Aftermath of the Holocaust*, ed. A. A. Cohen (New York, 1970), and also bitterly by Eliezer Berkovits, in *Disputation and Dialogue: Readings in Jewish/Christian Encounter*, ed. F. E. Talmage (New York, 1975), pp. 284–95. See also: E. Rosenstock-Huessy, *Judaism despite Christianity, Letters on Christianity and Judaism Between E. Rosenstock-Huessy and Franz Rosenzweig* (Alabama, 1969).

26 Gal. 3:28. 'There is ...' here does not, of course, mean that distinctions do not exist ('male and female' happily persist). It means that the distinctions are not relevant: for Christian purposes they do not avail as distinctions as to the openness of faith.

Comparably the Creed affirms, about the Incarnation, that it was 'for us men ...' i.e. 'for us humans', not: 'for us Jews and Gentiles', 'us blacks and whites', 'us east and west'. Though such statements affirm 'oneness' they are still interested in distinction even within inclusion. 'For us humans' transcends it altogether.

27 When on strong ground of content, these Letters are held to represent a somewhat later stage in church development, the question arises about the very personal matters involving Paul himself, especially 2 Tim. 4:9–21. Two solutions may be suggested. Personal notes may be part of an early fragment-letter attached to the later draft; or it is possible to think of the whole letter as a conscious literary art, as both discourse and reminiscence, so that Paul's example of patient suffering and final steadfastness reinforces what his disciple is teaching the flock who hold their great protagonist in so high a love. They are not 'invented', but rather 'presented', details as from the great apostle. See: Robert Falconer, *The Pastoral Epistles* (Oxford, 1937); and P. N. Harrison, *The Problem of the Pastoral Epistles* (Oxford, 1921).

For our later interest in scribal points, it is interesting to note that the Greek word in 2 Tim. 4:13 for 'cloak', may be written either *phailones* or *phainoles*, the 'l' and 'n' interchanging. Cf. Arabic *ḥamada* and *madaḥa*.

28 All these notes are, plainly, in strong affinity with the Qur'ān.

29 Hence the doctrine, frequent in the thought of Martin Buber, Arthur Cohen, and many others in recent Judaism, that Messiah never comes in order that he may always be awaited. Realised Messiahship is a contradiction in terms. To identify and 'have' the Messiah is premature romanticism. 'The Jew,' remarks Arthur Cohen, 'is an expert in unfulfilled time.' *The Myth of the Judeo-Christian Tradition* (New York, 1970), p. xx.

30 'Companion' is a significant word, with its Latin source *cum pane*, 'with bread'. Table-fellowship in the Eucharist was the infraction of the laws as to appropriate common eating within Jewry.

31 2 Peter was most doubtful of inclusion in the process of the formation of the Canon, of all New Testament writings.

32 The title of Satan (*Al-Shaiṭān al-Rajīm*) as 'accuser' is a common Judeo/Christian/Islamic tradition. As indicated in Surah 2:30 f. Satan's disavowal of God's will and wisdom is over the authority – we might say the 'experiment' – of man as *khalīfah* in the creation. The other angels at first demur and express surprise and disbelief at the divine announcement of man's dignity. But they all submit, except *Iblīs*. It then becomes the set policy of *Iblīs* so to disorient, deceive and seduce the creature-man that he (*Iblīs*) may be then able to say to God: 'I told you so! Your design in man was foolish!' It is important to see that Satan's activity as the 'accuser', 'the discrediter', is a defiance of God over the issue about man.

It thus becomes the task of man to disavow the disavower, to repudiate the repudiator, and so to 'justify' God's wisdom in the *amānah* man has received as to give the lie for ever to the liar, Satan. This is the theme of history.

Hence, of course, the stoning ceremonies in the *Ḥajj*, when pebbles are thrown against the pillars that bear Satan's name. Stoning has always been a powerful symbol of the utmost rejection and enmity (Cf. Psalm 8).

33 The phrase comes from *Henry Martyn: Journals and Letters of*, ed. Samuel Wilberforce (London, 1837), vol. 2, p. 45.

34 See Chapter 8 and Surah 36:13–25.

35 See further: A. Souter, *Text and Canon of the New Testament*, rev. edn (London, 1954); B. F. Westcott, *A General Survey of the Canon of the New Testament*, 4th edn (London, 1876).

36 See, further: F. G. Kenyon, *Handbook to the Textual Criticism of the New Testament* (London, 1912); A. T. Robertson, *An Introduction to Textual Criticism of the New Testament*. In *The Gentile Bias and Other Essays* (Leiden, 1980), K. W. Clark writes on 'The Theological Relevance of Textual Variation in Current Criticism of the Greek N.T.' (pp. 104–119). He stresses variants and minimal changes and pleads for a lively sense of how significant they can be as some index to the course of thought within the Church. However, apart from emendations whose tendentious character (like those of Marcion) is evident, the examples he cites are not deeply significant. John 6:5 may read: 'Where can we buy bread', or 'where can they buy bread?' In Luke 15:24, '... they began to be merry', may become '... and the father became joyous'. Luke 24:26 may read 'kingdom' instead of 'glory' as that which Christ entered.

In another paper, 'Textual Criticism and Doctrine', (*Ibid.*, pp. 90–103), Prof. Clark instances, e.g., 1 Cor. 13:3, where '... though I give my body to be burned', may need to be read: '... though I give my body in order to boast' (*kauthesomai* displaced by *kauchesomai*). Should 1 Cor. 6:20 read, simply, 'Glorify God in your body'? Or should it continue, '... and in your spirit, both of which are God's'? Many will wonder whether anything critical is here at stake, since the one does not exclude the other and both speak true, but no one should dispute Prof. Clark's conclusion: 'It is the great responsibility of textual criticism to refine the N.T. text toward an ever-increasing purity. It must lay the foundation on which alone doctrinal interpretation of the N.T. may be soundly based' (p. 103).

Chapter 5

Jesus as the Christ

i

In his celebrated poem, *The Garden of Truth*, the twelfth-century Persian poet, Sanā'ī, writes of the robe of Jesus, which, according to tradition, was all of a single colour, symbolising holiness and integrity. John, too, in his Gospel records that the robe was 'without seam, woven from the top throughout' (19:23).[1] 'Like Jesus,' says Sanā'ī, 'Let thy robe one colour be.' Only a detail and conjectural but, with John's observation to sustain it, it may serve well to take us into the theme of this chapter, which is the active ministry of Jesus as presented in the New Testament. 'Jesus in his History' we might have entitled the chapter, had not that title implied those debates about the relation between the story and the telling, between historian and theologian in the writing, which have been reviewed in Chapter 4. 'Jesus in His Work and Person' might have been another title, with the interplay of significance between who and how he was. 'Jesus as the Christ' seems best suited to gather history, work and personality into their single clue, namely how Jesus constituted what the Christ must be in the reality, both as history and as faith, of Christhood made good.

The central theme of that reality was 'the kingdom of God', or – as it was often phrased – 'the kingdom of heaven'. The kingdom was inseparably linked with the hope of Messiah. Kingdom and Messiah, in their mutual action, belonged deeply and mysteriously within everything that Jesus was and said and did. Theirs was the integrity woven like the robe throughout. Theirs, too, if Sanā'ī is right, was its single colour, unlike the garish 'coat of many colours' with which a doting Jacob decked his favoured Joseph.

The integrity within the garment of events in no way means that these were less than crowded, lively and dramatic. The sheer pace of the Gospels, especially that by Mark, is urgent and keen. The setting, both in Galilee and Jerusalem, was often seething with unrest. The country was occupied territory, alive with rumour and burning with nationalist fervour. There was intrigue and cunning, political and religious, on all sides and a population liable to wild enthusiasms, when not lapsing into stolid apathy or immersed in private hardship and distress. Youth movement as it was, the ministry of Jesus belonged with the open air, with the freshness of spring, and the uplands and lake shores of the northern hills. The Gospels present a human panorama of fascinating diversity with a vividness that is intense, and all in a situation of bewildering complexity. Yet the unity of the theme of kingdom and Messiah which they weave around the central figure, which truly the central figure wears, is unmistakable.

It is this unity, within all that else might confuse or sidetrack the reader, which this chapter aims to identify and portray in the framework earlier discussed of the New Testament documentation. It is a unity of kingdom and Messiah which requires to be studied under five elements belonging with, and emerging from, each other. They are: teaching, healing, communing, resolving and suffering. The last will bring us to the threshold of Chapter 6, to 'Gethsemane and Beyond'. The suffering dimension which finally emerges decisively is present by implication all the time.[2] It is the growing theme of the resolving which is borne in upon Jesus in the context of his teaching and healing. These are steadily sustained by communion with 'the Father' on Jesus' part, a communion which becomes increasingly preoccupied with the prospect of suffering and death. A counterpart of that prayer dimension in the personality of Jesus is his communing with his disciples, his *anṣāru ila-Allāh* as the Qur'ān calls them (Surah 3:52).[3] The role they played in the experience and travail of Jesus has often been overlooked in presentation of his personality and mission.[4] His deep communion with the One he called 'my Father and your Father' did not preclude the fullest human intimacy with the men he chose. Rather, it was a communion which moved with a close earthly partnership, frail and often uncomprehending as that discipleship was. The education of the disciples – so uneven in the story, so triumphant in the sequel – was a central element in the ministry of Jesus.

To trace, through resolving and communing, the climax of the ministry of Jesus into suffering is to have his perspective on the deepest of all religious issues, namely the sort of 'victories' proper to truth, the dimension of what must be acknowledged as ultimate in our reckoning with history. It is important to see that the sense of a suffering vocation on the part of Jesus – in which Christianity once for all read its decisive clue to God – was no martyr-cult, no morbid death-wish, no apocalyptic gamble. It arose squarely out of the gathering hostility and rejection which accompanied Jesus' course as teacher and healer. His pathway led by its own inner quality into confrontation with the vested interests, the prejudice, the human perversities which it challenged and whose self-securing enmities it aroused.

In the idiom distinctive to Jerusalem which was their stronghold, those enmities paralleled situations familiar enough in all prophetic history and certainly recognisable to any student of the experience of Muḥammad in the sharply contrasted setting of Mecca in the years before the *Hijrah*. In this human world the tragic situation was, and is, the occupational hazard of all prophetic calling. What was distinctive about Jesus was not the fact of that dimension, but rather its intensity, the entail of the drama around it, and - most of all - the reading, by Jesus, of the Messianic clue within it.

ii

Our confidence, then, is that we can truly 'see Jesus' (to borrow the form of the Greeks' inquiry in John 12:21) in both Islamic and New Testament perspective, if we follow this sequence of teaching, healing, resolving, communing and suffering, and if we see them as an integral whole. Strangely, the Apostles' Creed in Christian liturgy embraces the first four in no more than a comma between: 'born of the Virgin Mary, suffered under Pontius Pilate'. Could it be - in the words of the Turkish poet, Özdemir Asaf[5] - that

> He was born, they shed tears of joy.
> He died, they shed tears of sorrow.
> He lived in between: this they never thought of

Hardly. The word 'suffered', within the Creed's brevity, comprehends all, if we see the climax, otherwise inexplicable, arising only and altogether out of antecedents in word and deed, as those antecedents engaged with their environment and were always prospectively identified with their final fulfilment in the Cross. Is there not a sense in which all history, as story, awaits its ending? For it is only the outcome which determines what is relevant and significant in the past which led to it. As we have seen earlier, the evangelists have not escaped this 'sense of an ending' which all narrative writing undergoes. In their case, however, it is an ending which comprehends all else. Jesus suffered as he taught, taught as he suffered, and both in compassionate action for man and resolute obedience to God. 'His garment was without seam, woven from the top throughout.'

iii

In this fivefold study the Gospels, as assessed in Chapter 4, are our source. In the main, it is recognised that they are the only source there is. According to Joachim Jeremias, the apocryphal Gospel of Thomas yields perhaps fifty extra-canonical sayings of Jesus. None of these, or others attested elsewhere, materially alter either the corpus, or the accents, of the teaching of Jesus as both New Testament Gospels and the Epistles present it.[6]

It was clear earlier how their report is mediated through the corporate mind of the early Church. The Gospels are not archives: they witness; but they offer the witness of a community concerned to write them, not a community cutting loose from its moorings in a master's words.[7] It is a community which clearly shows itself desiring, by this very authorship, to be under the authority of what it believes to be its origins in Jesus and his teaching. That authority is within the recognition, just as the receiving is from the authority. Whether it be the Qur'ān or the New Testament (in very different incidence), we have to trust this mutuality of document and faith, if revelatory history is to be possessed.

There is hardly a theme in the teaching of Jesus which the later experience of the Church does not illuminate. The immediate teaching situation in Galilee or beyond of Jesus himself has to be seen across the comprehending, and writing, situation of the Christian communities in their dispersion. We have to align these scattered, often lonely and hard-pressed, groups across the Roman world with the first hearers who knew Jesus as a local presence. There is a double resonance to sayings like 'Take up your cross and follow me', or the assurance 'He that receives you receives me. ...' There are immediate meanings in the primary context of Jesus' preaching, and there are continuing meanings within the new bearings of the wider Church. For the latter, the guiding principle is 'that which we have seen, and heard, and handled of the word of life' (1 John 1:1).

This dual vision of the Gospels, analysed in Chapter 4, means that the documentary mediation of Jesus' teaching has happened in experience of living by its light, as that light was understood in the community of its sequel. Central to both the teaching and the institution was the theme of the kingdom and the Messiah. The kingdom of God, or of heaven, is this urgent, immediate, decisive reality of grace at work in the world, coming with compassionate power into human situations, demanding response.

The sinner is aroused to the truth about himself and drawn towards deliverance, on the radical condition of honesty and action. The presence of the kingdom, in the terms of its claim (for in another sense it is 'absent' until it is received), confronts the self-satisfied, rewrites their congenial values and allows them no neutrality. Jesus' message of the kingdom is not *about* something external to himself of which he merely *tells*. It is something he announces as operative through him, warranted as real and present by virtue of his ministry as its sign and its energy.

In those parables – for example, in Luke chapter 15 about the lost sheep, the lost silver and the lost son, where Jesus responds to criticism of *his* own open attitude to 'sinners' (15:2) – his ground is in what, he affirms, *God* does. His own hospitality to evildoers for the sake of their becoming righteous he identifies as reciprocal to the 'joy in heaven' over their repentance. He proceeds by an inherent authority out of a sure confidence in the eternal wisdom and the capacity to speak in its name. There is a relevance of Jesus *in himself* to the word he brings from which all formulated theology *about him* later came to be derived. The note of 'But I say to you ...' – which we hear so often in the Gospels' account of Jesus' discourse and which was so contrasted with characteristic citations of authority by the Scribes – is to be understood, not as some external arbitrary assertiveness, but as the authentic assurance in Jesus of the kingdom's reality *within* his sense of mission.

This New Testament awareness of truth *in* Jesus and not simply *from* him, of 'the Word' that he is rather than the words that he *brings*, not only gives rise to the later theology: it is central to the Gospel narrative. It needs to be understood for what it is, given the different concept of 'prophethood' upon which Islam and the Qur'ān proceed.

'Prophet' is certainly a term which the Gospels readily and proudly apply to Jesus in the context of his ministry. The crowds hailing his entry into Jerusalem shout, possessively: 'This is Jesus the prophet of Nazareth of Galilee' (Matt. 21:11). That 'a great prophet has risen up among us' (Luke 7:16) is the verdict of the people on another occasion. Jesus himself confirmed the term when, in reference to his reception by local sceptics, he observed that 'a prophet is not without honour, except in his own country' (Matt. 13:57). Yet, authentic as the title was, it was transcended in a larger significance not adequately denoted if the 'prophetic' has to do simply with a verbal task, the passing on of a message.

To borrow here the Qur'ān's term, *al-balāgh*, or 'communication', one has to move beyond the bare delivery of words into what the whole 'person' of the messenger signifies. Does not this happen, to a degree in Islam itself where the rise of Tradition and the inclusive role of Muḥammad within Muslim devotion demonstrate the deep import of personhood alongside the spoken *balāgh*? Truth via a spokesman deepens into truth in personhood. It is very much so with the greatest of the Hebrew prophets, notably Amos, Hosea and Jeremiah. The impact belongs more ultimately with the man saying it than with the thing said. It is as if 'prophecy' necessitates and enlists, indeed becomes, 'biography'.

While Islam, with its strong sense of *waḥy*, or revelation-inspiration, as a language bestowal, has – despite strong instinct for Muḥammad's biographical significance – found this perspective suspect and uncongenial, in the Christian understanding of Jesus it is paramount. In the New Testament, 'truth-through-personality' is not, as in Islamic tradition, a secondary, ancillary, vehicle of revelation – it is crucial and definitive.[8] What, in retrospect, moved John to say 'the Word was made flesh and dwelt among us' (John 1:14) only formulates the situation, from the outset, for all the evangelists, namely, the intimate relation, as they depict it, between the actuality *of* the kingdom and its actuality *in* Jesus.

> Jesus came into Galilee, preaching the gospel of the kingdom and saying: 'The time is fulfilled, and the kingdom of God is at hand: repent and believe the gospel'. (Mark 1:14–15)

The kingdom is present in the form and thrust of its announcement as 'good news' (the core meaning of 'gospel', or 'happy tidings'). It is present in the accents and enablings of Jesus' teaching, standing as these do in divine commission and divine communion. Through these the kingdom summons its hearers to liberation and love and confronts the forces of evil and of pride. Jesus' conviction about God energises and informs all that he says to men. Jesus takes as real and dynamic a forgiving Father who welcomes the penitent, whose mercy embraces all seekers, whose love searches for them, and whose compassion moves through all created things. Heaven's rain, Jesus says, waters alike the just and the unjust (Matt. 5:45). God's sovereign justice sifts through all hypocrisy and judges all vain religion. These *are* the dimensions of the kingdom in the immediacy of its challenge to human *ẓulm*, or wrong, in every form and in the claim of its benediction on the allegiance of all.

The immediacy or radical urgency of Jesus' words must not be mistaken, as by some scholars, for 'apocalypticism', or belief in a dire winding up of the world in cataclysm. There are so many indications that the kingdom was central and intrusive into daily living, not because doomsday would come tomorrow, but because the liberating kingdom was waiting here and now. Its radical grace was a present joy, knocking at the doors of the slow of heart or sceptical of will. Jesus' language was not that of 'futurists' who withdrew from home and market and farm to purify themselves by isolation while awaiting the divine intervention which would rescue them privately from the world's calamity.[9] When he spoke of men's entrustment with the world 'for a long season' – if such it should prove (Matt. 25:19; Luke 20:9) – it was that his hearers might learn to invest themselves in common life, understood as a delegation of authority (*khilāfah*) in an existence which was, indeed, prospective towards eternity but had presently within it the drama of decision.

Jesus was not impatient with legalism and the minutiae of the Scribes because the kingdom was so imminent that these became irrelevant. He did not urge to reconciliation with one's enemies because the advent of final apocalypse was near enough to submerge all human business. He did not invite his hearers to leave the plough and follow the disciples who had left their fishing, for the reason that time was about to run out on them all. It was that they might be heralds of the kingdom.

There *are* imminent notès, to be sure, in Jesus' preaching. In every situation the horizon is always close at hand, receding as the voyager proceeds. To imprison Jesus' affirmation of the kingdom of God in mere time-criteria, however, is to ignore the steady emphasis on patience in his ethical teaching and to scout the positive dimensions of reconciliation with neighbours, peace within oneself through confidence in God, and a compassion not to be overridden by scruples of the law. It would be a travesty of the Jesus whom the Gospels describe – not to say also a falsification of all that his Church became – to assert that Jesus either taught or suffered on behalf of a kingdom of God understood as other than patient, redemptive, resourceful, compassionate and lowly. These its attributes were beyond the range of what arbitrarily intervenes, as sheer apocalypse does, and reverses all time at a stroke. Immediate indeed the kingdom was as he proclaimed it, but its immediacy was not of the calendar: it was in its moral crisis. The kingdom neither waved a wand nor pressed a final button. Its charter was the Beatitudes and its sign was the Cross.

iv

The benedictions in Matthew 5:1–12, with which the evangelist opens his record of the teaching of Jesus, are the clearest token of the immediacy of the kingdom as an experience of grace within the heart and of its patient, personal working within society. Woes and imprecations were a familiar part of rabbinic discourse and, as we note in studying Jesus' anger in the present context, they were not absent from the Gospel. The deep positives which the Beatitudes declare are the measure of how we should read all else in the story of Jesus. They are the criteria his own vocation expressed and his inward decisions of ministry translated into deed. The veneration for Jesus on which all Islam prides itself can learn what it venerates in weighing the import of these verses. They are the surest clue, not only to his achievement as the Christ, but to the *fiṭrah*, or 'nature', of the kingdom in the human heart.

> Blessed are the poor in spirit, for theirs is the kingdom of heaven.
> Blessed are they that mourn, for they shall be comforted.
> Blessed are the meek, for they shall inherit the earth.
> Blessed are those who hunger and thirst after righteousness, for they shall be filled.
> Blessed are the merciful, for they shall obtain mercy.
> Blessed are the pure in heart, for they shall see God.
> Blessed are the peacemakers, for they shall be called the children of God.
> Blessed are they that are persecuted for righteousness' sake, for theirs is the kingdom of heaven.

A Quranic-style *tadabbur* here, or careful pondering, is at once aware of several arresting facts. The statements have to do with fact and not with promise. Their truth is by their paradox, for they plainly reverse all normal expectation and run counter to common assumption. If the world were doomed to imminent demise there would be neither place nor proof for these virtues. They invite as well as describe. Readers aloud are often at fault about where the emphasis should fall and tend to place it heavily on 'they' and 'theirs' (as if there were any others who could have the predicate), or else on the 'shall' (as if the essence of the matter was mere futurity arousing doubt, and not spiritual logic excluding it). The stress properly belongs on the main verb in the final clause. The balance of Aramaic parallelism must be kept in mind in the firm equivalence of the two parts of the sentence.

Further, what is noteworthy about those pronouns and the nouns they serve is their sheer 'democracy'. The hearers, to be sure, were Galileans and, being Jews, were accustomed to cherishing distinctiveness, finding reassurance in *not* being 'gentiles'. But what they hear, takes no account of such sentiments – has no racial, ethnic, cultural or other conditions. The descriptives are open to all: their benediction has no pre-conditions that turn on birth or breeding or peoplehood. Direct address naming the immediate audience comes only in verse 11 and then, characteristically, only in the context of suffering wrongfully inflicted on them. The Beatitudes cannot be circumstantially limited to time, place, condition, or context.

The blessedness, moreover, as well as being 'democratic', is joyously 'human' in a further sense. Not only is it open to any. It is also *within* the earthly scene. The Qur'ān-reader, as with all Semitic tradition, is familiar with the divine blessedness. *Tabāraka Allāh* occurs some nine times: 'Blessed be God ...' or 'Blessed be He who. ...' This divine blessedness is also attributed to figures like 'the people of the house', or Noah, or to the Qur'ān, or to Mecca as 'a blessed place' (Surahs 11:73, 11:48, 6:92, 21:50, 3:96). In the Beatitudes, however, benediction comes upon all who – in their ordinariness – answer the description.[10]

The alert Qur'ān-reader will appreciate this open human blessedness by noting the echo of Matt. 5:5 in Surah 21:105: 'As for the earth, We have written in the psalms, following the reminder, that it is the inheritance of My righteous servants'.[11] That rare coincidence of phrasing, between Psalm, Gospel and Qur'ān, leaves us with how to comprehend the 'inheritance' of the earth, and Jesus' identifying 'the righteous' with 'the meek'. The second word belongs with his own characterisation in Matt. 11:29: 'I am meek and lowly in heart. ...' The word (*praus* in Greek) means one who makes no claim, who – having rights – nonetheless waives them. It denotes an absorption of evil, rather than its requital in retaliation. 'Do not resist evil' (Matt. 5:39) does not imply that wrong is never to be opposed, but rather that evil is not allowed to involve us in its resentments. Instead, for example, of the *lex talionis* (the *right* to exact one's rights) by which the evil comes round full circle and persists in retaliatory being, 'the meek' stay (arrest) it in themselves and thereby purge the situation of its enmity. In so doing, they take the context into creative renewal and cause the goodness of the earth to be repossessed, whereas the contrary stance confirms its evil, serves its cynicism, sides with its contentiousness and justifies its despair.[12] Only in the redemptiveness of which meekness is the nerve and fibre is the earth held in righteous trust.

It is clear how all the Beatitudes can be read within the motivations behind the ministry of Jesus being reviewed in this chapter. It is also clear how they re-echo through the teaching and practice of the apostolic Church. Indeed, the movement of Jesus into his Messianic pattern exemplifies what every benediction means. It is in the context of this exposition that we can safely leave their detailed meaning, not to say also living exegesis.

V

It is useful, and instructive, to pass from the Beatitudes into what was earlier remarked about the 'anger' of Jesus. For the Sermon on the Mount – as the whole discourse in Matthew chapters 5 to 7 is usually called – quickly passes to contrasts in practice and to radical reproach of a variety of evils, notably hypocrisy, anxiety and pride. What are we to say of the sternness of Jesus here, and even more sharply in the 'woes' or denunciations as, for example, in Matthew chapter 23? Do they contradict the quality required in the Beatitudes? or do they, rather, help to illuminate what these entail? Surely the latter. The meekness, the mercy, the purity, the peace, the spiritual hunger they affirm as blest are not withdrawn, or neutral, or timid, or aloof. On the contrary, they immerse their *dramatis personae* more vitally, more strenuously, than could happen in their absence, in the tensions and toils and testings of the world.

There is actually very little about 'sin' (by that term) in the Gospel.[13] The indignation of Jesus is directed against what distorts and corrupts the humanity intended in creation and meant in the kingdom. Hypocrisy is the crucial offender – the misrepresentation of God in oppressive ritual, the exploitation of the needy or the powerless by religious sanction, the blindness of bigotry, or the suppression of the human meaning in the institutional order. These were the constant features of society against which Jesus' parables and sayings were directed. His criticism of evil did not simply denounce and reproach: it searched its meaning in order to sharpen the focus and deepen the categories. His severity reflected the ambition of grace. The crux of evil was its sheer travesty of the good, whether *qua* law, or kin, or rite, or sabbath, or the body, or sex, or bread, or one's neighbour.

His passion of rightness under God, inwardly authentic, was the militancy of the kingdom of God – a kingdom which would, and could, make its way only in terms of its own nature and not via those coercive forms of word or action which only proceed by conforming in temper or in act to the evils they fight. This more ultimate militancy incurs greater strains and sterner claims on hope and zeal, for the reason that it engages with evil more radically measured and perceived.

In Mark 7:20–23 there are listed, by Jesus, thirteen evils which, he says, come from within the heart and 'defile the person'. The last of these 'evil intentions' is *aphrosune*, or 'folly', the antonym of the treasured Greek virtue of *sophrosune*, or 'being of sound mind'. *Aphrosune* might well be likened to the *jāhiliyyah* of pre-Islam. The terms are close, each having the meaning of wilful ignoring of truth. *Jāhiliyyah*, when it is institutionalised in traditional Muslim historiography, is liable to be taken as characterising a society to its discredit but without incisive diagnosis of its inner and ethical quality. Wrong is then only attributed and not explored. The *jāhiliyyah* which Jesus encountered and the Gospels depict had a different idiom from the *jāhiliyyah* of the Quraish six centuries later. Confronting a highly religious establishment and continuing to the end in exclusively religious confrontation of it, Jesus necessarily engaged essentially with the inward factors, as proud religion abetted and concealed them more subtly than the crude paganism and idolatry which plagued Muḥammad's Mecca.

The first word in Mark's list of human *ẓulm* is very close to the concern of Islamic *niyyah*. The *dialogismoi kakoi* are 'the evil intentions', the musings and reasonings of the mind which motivate to wrong, and so destroy inward truth, or *niyyah*. After the brutal antisocial sins, the passage goes on to *pleoneziai* (pl.) which, elsewhere Paul links to idolatry. It means 'avarice', or an insatiable possessiveness which covets and greedily acquires. Its fellow is (in literal Greek) 'the evil eye' (*ophthalmos poneros*), the 'envy' which Muslim ethic solidly accuses as the menace of society. Underlying them all is the *uperephania*, the 'pride' which, like the *istikbār* and *istighnā'* of the Qur'ān, holds all but itself in contempt. It rides with that *blasphemia* (lit. 'blasphemy') which reveres neither God nor man in a common repudiation of both.

Gospel and Qur'ān are, here, very close together in their ethical emphasis on the inter-relation of things divine and things human. In transgression against our fellow-man, God is denied: in denying common humanity we transgress against God. It is in their understanding of how this quality of evil is overcome that Gospel and Qur'ān diverge. The issue between them here can be said to underlie all the decisions by which Jesus responded to the manifestations of evil which – in people and in structures – his ministry encountered. The questions to do with the surmounting and saving of evil being so contrasted makes all the more important the convergence we can find in its ethical measure. The law which can identify and reproach the sins listed in Mark chapter 3, and the force which can do battle against establishments accused of them, are not factors – however prestigious – which suffice for their salvation. There is a sense in which law, as such, cannot always identify their presence, while compulsion may find itself conniving with them. It was just such a sense of the non-finality of law and politics which took Jesus, via the clear evidence of his teaching experience, into his Messianic decision.

vi

One feature of discussion about the impact of Jesus' teaching which has arisen sharply in Judeo/Christian thinking, and in which Quranic study is also involved, centres around the parties concerned in the context and in the exchanges to which both the Beatitudes and the strictures belonged. 'The Scribes and Pharisees' have been the butt of much deep criticism and it is true that they tend to be always the representatives of what has to be condemned. The role, the quality, and the vicissitudes of Pharisaism have occupied much historical research and revision of traditional assumption in the recent past and the situation is complex.[14] It is right, and necessary, to avoid any cavalier and insensitive judgement which misses either their merits or their aspirations. It was never a crude legalism which was at issue, either in Galilee or, later, with Paul. The Pharisees themselves were well able to appreciate and reprove the features to which all 'zeal for the Lord' is prone and for which Jesus chastened all his hearers. It was a 'righteousness exceeding (not dismissing) that of the Scribes and Pharisees' (Matt. 5:20) for which he called. To be critically meticulous about the Torah became reprehensible only when it obscured or impeded the weightier matters of liberty, integrity and compassion.

There has been some tendency within recent Muslim thinking to sharpen the edge of Jesus' encounter with the Jewish establishment and to think of him exclusively as the accuser of his own people.[15] There has been the same temptation for some Christians. Either way it has provoked, as have other factors, a lively and scholarly Jewish concern for Jesus as a Jew.[16] A careful discernment here calls for the realisation that it was not people, groups, label-bearers, or identities, as such, that were Jesus' theme, but rather the attitudes, the actions and the choices that they exemplified. As with the Cross, so with the teaching. It was not *who* but *what*, or only *who* because of *what*. Certainly no intelligent hearer of the famous parable in Luke 18:9–14, about the two men who went up into the Temple to pray could well register its meaning by saying: 'O God, I thank thee that I am not as this Pharisee'. The parable is readily convertible into the postures of a hypocritical penitent, beating his breast and saying 'I come humbly into thy house, I stand afar off, I beat my breast', and then, looking sidelong in the Pharisee's direction, '... not like him....' For there can be a sinister self-congratulation in the attitudes of repentance.[17] The transparent simplicity of Jesus' story has a double edge. He did not exonerate all the rest of the world in having serious *ad-hoc* and *in-situ* contention with 'the Pharisees'. It happened that it was they who were around, but in the immediacy of Jesus' teaching there was nothing exclusive to them in all that was at stake.[18] This has to be remembered both when they are pilloried and where they are vindicated.

vii

Care to reckon duly with the teaching of Jesus has a further duty in respect of its implications for society at large and the political order in particular. It is a duty which can well be broached by noting that the Beatitudes, which we have studied in Matthew, while reduced to four in Luke (6:20–23), are also changed from the third person into direct speech in Luke: 'Blessed are you, the poor.' Does this contradict what was earlier said about their 'democracy'? Does the omission of 'in spirit' suggest a more explicit active meaning? Could it imply a case for Jesus as a partisan of the economically deprived? If we cannot claim him as an activist, do we have to say that his message stopped short of its own implications in being only 'verbal'? Also, if Jesus did not carry a passion about the poor into open political action, was the reason only circumstantial, having to do with the massive dominance of the Roman order?

Nowhere was his 'programme' more cogently or dramatically enunciated than in the synagogue at Nazareth when he cited Isaiah (61:1–2) taking to himself in personal commission its theme of deliverance, emancipation, healing and grace, for the poor, the sick, the broken, the captives, the blind and the bruised. But the operative verb, thrice repeated, was 'to preach'. Liberation, it may be urged, does not happen by verbalism. Yet, all is set in terms of 'the Spirit of the Lord is upon me. ...'

We must leave till later, under the theme of 'resolving', Jesus' decision in the public scene. Certainly he did not invite zealots into a discipleship they had to share with publicans if their zealotry was all they had to bring. We must read 'You poor, you hungry now, you sorrowing folk ...' in Luke's version of the Sermon, not as to a seedbed of visionary revolution but consistently with Matthew's, making the disciples exemplary of the character their vocation was summoned to create within their hearers.

The Muslim instinct, as we saw in Chapter 3, has often been to explain the uncompulsiveness of Jesus' Gospel as a privation, contrasted with the forthrightness of the *Hijrah*. He was as he was, on this view, because the situation allowed him no other option. Rome was irreducible. The forces against liberation and the rights of the poor were such as to make all such enterprise doomed from the start. The argument is externally impressive, although the Maccabees had left a telling precedent and it is possible to argue that a charisma like that of Jesus, popularly employed, could have given Pilate more to do than wash his hands and Caiaphas more to do than pervert Judas.

Such conjectures aside, the case against the argument within the teaching of Jesus is overwhelming. The compassion that can engender revolutions is certainly there, but it is aware of the sheer futurism, fantasy, or cruelty that can overtake them and of measures of the human situation and its redemption which will always be beyond their reach. With Jesus there is an immediate reality to the kingdom, in its present tense of peace through penitence and grace through faith. Its hope-dimension does not turn upon an eventuation yet to be contrived, but upon the reality of what already is, within the heart and, through the heart, expressively within society. This does not make it negligent of present wrong, or complacent about injustices and evil deeds. But its militancy centres on the person, on the transformation which releases the rich from their possessions, the poor from their non-possession, and both for their recruitment to the way of the Gospel. The story of the rich lawyer (Matt. 19:16–22; Luke 18:18–23) tells it all – that the crisis of discipleship consists in an obedience of which Jesus is the master, the world the setting and the will the crux. That story leaves the decision open. Its terms are not in doubt. On both counts this is the nature of the Gospel, requiring categorically but taking only by consent.

viii

We cannot leave the teaching ministry of Jesus without reference to its temper of authority. The evangelists frequently remark on this quality about him.[19] Whereas the rabbis, and those with 'academic' or 'ecclesiastical' standing, prefaced all their dicta, carefully and cautiously, with proper citation, Jesus simply grounded his words in some inherent right to say them. Their authentic character belonged with their content, so that neither he, nor they, needed extraneous support from outside their truth and his teaching ministry. At times when Jesus imitated the traditional teachers' style it was either to bring a point into their recognition or to draw the contrast. 'You have heard it said ... but I say to you' was then his formula. 'Amen, amen, I say to you ...' was his frequent usage, clothing what followed in the authority of one of the Names of God, the *Amen*.

Matthew, in particular, responds to this element in his picture of Jesus by deliberately organising his account around the image of Moses on Sinai as the great lawgiver and Jesus 'going up into the mountain' to 'legislate' the new law of the kingdom (5:1). In the same context he clearly relishes the parallel between the twelve tribes of Israel and the twelve disciples symbolising a new peoplehood and its progenitors. He is careful, however, to record Jesus' exclusion of all things pretentious or congratulatory in this status (Matt. 19:28, 20:20–29). In respect of the harsh realities of vocation, it is enough for disciples that they be as their lord. This was the paradox within Jesus' authority itself. Its note of unequivocal conviction and assurance had precisely to do with its frequent departure from assumed, and therefore credible, norms. To counter so decisively the many familiar estimates and attitudes of society – about election, or birth, or ritual, or divine favour, or wisdom – was, by the same token, to rely upon an authority exempt from, and resolute against, the rulings which sustained them. Of no teacher, in his teaching, was this more tellingly so than in the case of Jesus.

Yet, disconcerting as his authority was to those who clung, as in their own context did the Quraish, to 'what the fathers' held (Surah 31:21), there was nothing arbitrary about its confidence. The decisive note in Jesus' teaching belonged with the inherent quality of its content. This is evident in that most characteristic form – the parable. Because of the ruling in Surah 3:7 of the Qur'ān about *mutashābihāt*, or 'similitudes', being liable to misreading at the hands of the shifty, Muslims have often been wary of them and have preferred the 'categorical' statement. Yet the Qur'ān itself is full of imagery and metaphor.[20] Teaching in the human field is hardly feasible without them. The Gospel parables have their categorical quality but communicate it by recruiting the intelligent recognition of the hearer. It is in this invitation they make to shared perception, their habit of evoking – rather than imposing – an assent to truth, which is the essence of their purpose and the ground of their effectiveness.

They begin, for example, with an appeal like 'What man of you ...' and thus first enlist a sympathy and an acknowledgement of what is to follow by virtue of an immediate familiarity with what carries the meaning, as stories and analogies are designed to do. Jesus drew upon a wide range of down-to-earth imagery from the fields, farms and fisheries of Galilee. One can even detect in the lost ornamental silver coin, or the patch on a garment, or the leaven in the loaf, scenes from the home in Nazareth in the youth of Jesus. Runaway sons, squandering an inheritance, were scarcely foreign to Capernaum gossip, nor the nuisance of weeds among the wheat, nor the hot malice which might sow them there. Everybody knew Safad, 'the city set on a hill', or the beacons letting their light shine from the hilltops to announce the appearance of the new moon when solemnities began. The salt which was employed in the Temple sacrifices might also have been strewn on the altar steps lest the priests should slip, and the second was more likely when it had 'lost its saltness' (Matt. 5:13; Mark 9:49–50).

Alongside these images of daily life and local lore were the parables Jesus drew from the long Hebraic prophetic tradition, about vineyards, marriage feasts, keystones, broken reeds and smoking wicks. In controversy, he would draw on common instinct, as about healing on the sabbath, or even on a sense of the ludicrous, as in the question about seven brothers, successively deceased husbands of the same woman who finally herself died (Matt. 22:23–32). Or the artfulness of loaded questions put to him could be deftly turned by its exposure, leaving the conclusion to the listeners' own lights (Matt. 22:15–22 on tax-payment and 21:23–27 on the baptism of John). All that made the teaching of Jesus in these ways accessible to his immediate hearers still avails for his Muslim audience today along with all the centuries elsewhere, given that – as then so now – there is a mind and a will 'very attentive to hear him' (Luke 19:48, where the Greek word is akin to the Arabic *mu'allaqah*, the English 'hanging upon ...').

Other aspects of the teaching ministry of Jesus will best emerge in later study. The role of the parabolic leads us naturally to the dimension of healing as the second broad import of the whole.

ix

There has long been a tradition, both in Islam and Christian theology, and in the converse between them, to see in sheer miracle an argument for, an evidence of, the divine. In Muslim faith, it is the miracle, or *i'jāz*, of the Book as a celestially mediated syllabic sequence on the lips of a completely illiterate Muḥammad. In much Christian reception of the New Testament history, the divine has been identified in the otherwise inexplicable marvel of things that happened, and happened in order to betoken the arbitrary divine status of Jesus and to be so taken as the manifestation of omnipotent omniscience.

Aside from how such a posture of belief does violence to the very nature of the Incarnation in which Christians believe, in respect of Jesus, as authentically human, there is the clear fact that it runs counter to the situation in the Gospel history itself. There the occasions of healing and compassion, with the one puzzling exception of the withering fig tree (Mark 11:21),[21] all have to do with genuine suffering, emergency and need. None of them are merely demonstrative, or contrived to impress, or intended for idle admiration and astonishment. They belong essentially to ministry and compassion. In this they are quite unlike the stories which occur in apocryphal writing about purely fortuitous 'miracles', such as the making of clay birds that flew. It is important to see the healing activity of Jesus as all of one piece with his teaching, underlining the liberating meaning of the kingdom of God and bringing home its implications for newness of life. Also many occasions of what the evangelists call 'his mighty works' came when Jesus was being challenged in his doctrine. It was this which, either before or after, in anticipation or corroboration, they illuminated. Such was their purpose.

That 'his mighty works' were not miracle for miracle's sake is evident from the way in which Mark, in particular, stresses Jesus' habit of secrecy, or at least non-publicity, lest he should have unwanted credulity as response. Those being healed would be taken aside from the crowd: they would be enjoined to say nothing to anyone (unless in the case of leprosy it were the priestly authorities), even the restored demoniac in Geresa, who so yearned to stay with Jesus, was sent home to his own. Of course, Jesus could not be hidden. These precautions were overborne by celebrity and celebration. The blind newly sighted, the lame walking and the lepers cleansed can hardly be silenced or concealed. Nevertheless, Jesus' will to avoid mere adulation or crowd enthusiasm did something to dampen popular ardour and preclude the distracting, distorting following which would otherwise have clogged his course.

There was a frequent, explicit reproach also for those who followed because they sought the benefits. All the Gospels record these occasions. Compassion for its own sufficient reason, response for need's own sake – these were the hallmarks of Jesus' ministry, whether with hungry crowds or private sufferers. That policy was implicit, too, in his reaction to the temptations to be studied later. John, in particular, underlines it when he very deliberately presents 'mighty works' as 'signs', and reads parables in deeds – all within the conscious artistry of his presentation. In so doing, he is only carrying to a further degree the sense of New Testament history.

Yet, such is the fascination of 'miracle' that this sense of the kingdom-in-sign is often ignored and an idea of extraneous 'marvel' preferred. A recent Turkish poet, Can Yücel, is one among many. He writes[22] of a vision he has of Jesus by the sea (Galilee understood) and goes on:

> As he entered my dream I said to myself: 'Now,
> Is he going to challenge nature again?' ...
> As you know the prophet's is also a craft
> ... a science, an art.
> At first occasion, he must push forward his ware,
> So that the demand increases, the market widens.
> What is Christ's craft? Miracles, of course.

Yücel adds that human fish no longer swallow the hook of miracles, 'the bane of dialectical materialism' having passed into the sea. But the demand which increased in the narrative of Jesus is precisely the demand he curbed and refused. If at first 'the market widened', in the end it contracted altogether while the real issues – which works of mercy might exemplify but not of themselves resolve – were otherwise joined in the Cross.

It is important, therefore, to comprehend Jesus' healing 'signs' consistently within his Incarnation, his human situation and his total mission. That there is mystery wherever there is charisma is clear. But throughout there is an emphasis on the recipient's faith where personal deliverance comes, and the prelude to the healing is the evocation of such faith. 'Will you be made whole?' (e.g. John 5:6) was not a question *about* the future but *to* the self. There, and in several other stories about infirmity and recovery, it was in the avenue of kindled, inward, confidence that the new health came, and not by some arbitrary bestowal from behind. It is fair to say that the event was participatory, disciples also (when they were so oriented, as they were not always) as well as 'subjects' being involved.

Such faith was active, however despairingly, when the 'signs' in Jesus' ministry concerned not the sick but the bereaved. The narrative of the raising of Lazarus in John chapter 11 moves tensely with the hopes and fears of the sisters which Jesus is depicted as distressfully sharing in the bonds of the home at Bethany. When the briefest of summaries in Surah 5:109 – about Jesus healing the blind and the leper and bringing forth the dead – is filled out from the graphic pens in the Gospels, Muslim readers can more readily appreciate how the 'sign'-quality the Surah stresses can be read and has been read by generations of Christian faith.

Sickness, blindness, paralysis, the physical wasting of disease, demonism and death itself are all analogues of the blight of evil, despair, spiritual atrophy and chronic sinfulness. It is not that there is a necessary correlation between sickness and sin. That facile notion is ruled out in John 9:2–3. It is, rather, that the transforming power of the kingdom of God in personal life resembles the recovery of new physical health. The story of the paralysed man let down through the roof in the house where Jesus was preaching (Matt. 9:2–8; Mark 2:3–12; Luke 5:18–26) brings together the cure and the forgiveness, as being both of comparable difficulty and comparable benediction. We are to understand, not that sin occasions the palsy, but that the one liberation dramatises the other. There would seem to be an identical meaning in Luke's story (13:11–16) of the cripple to whom Jesus referred as 'imprisoned by Satan these eighteen years' and whom he healed on the Sabbath. The tyranny of a crippled physical condition symbolises the bondage in which evil holds the human soul. The power that masters the one avails against the other, and the 'sign' is clear.

Ironically, it was in part the very works of Jesus which occasioned the final encounter with 'establishment'. The authorities at least read them for the 'signs' they were and resisted their significance. It was not simply that the works of mercy generated popular enthusiasm and might have become – had Jesus so connived – a spur to politically inconvenient unrest. In official reckoning those considerations were present; but, more vitally, the 'mighty works' carried implications, as interpreted by the words and attitudes of Jesus, which the religious hierarchy could not concede. As we must see shortly, Jesus concentrated into the Palm Sunday entry to Jerusalem a whole, pent-up and long-deferred popular expression of celebration and gratitude. On his part, this was strangely out of character. Yet that Galilean procession – for such it was – comprised many of the lame, the blind, the dumb, the sick and the demoniacs of Jesus' ministry, now exulting in their new health and faculties and sanity. Charles Wesley's familiar hymn captures that occasion of corporate demonstration, strangely now allowed by Jesus and witnessing to 'the healing kingdom'.[23]

> Hear him ye deaf, his praise ye dumb,
> Your loosened tongues employ,
> Ye blind, behold your Saviour come,
> And leap, ye lame, for joy.

There is something highly paradoxical in the fact that the procession of acclaim was the journey into crisis. The event five days before the passion gathered into one final, inclusive 'sign' the entire significance of Jesus' teaching and healing activity. It was also an index to what he had resolved about things Messianic. On which count, our study must return to it. The decision came through his 'communing' intimately with his disciples, and more intimately still with the One he called 'my Father'.

x

> O Caesarea Philippi: to accept condemnation of the Way as its fulfilment, its definition ...

Dag Hammarskjöld's diary-of-the-heart has many Biblical echoes.[24] As Secretary General of the United Nations, (1953–61) he was a deeply articulate Christian in being a protagonist for peace; but why 'Caesarea Philippi' in this entry from 1949? His reference was to the pivotal mid-career event in the life of Jesus, read by Hammarskjöld as a symbol of all supreme, ethical decisions that test with tribulation our human integrity.

Caesarea Philippi – not to be confused with Caesarea on the Mediterranean coast – was far to the north of Galilee at the foot of Mount Hermon, in the territory of Philip the Tetrarch, who had named it in honour of Augustus Caesar. It was the location of one of Herod's Temples and, from earlier pagan associations with the Greek god, Pan, was also named Paneas – a name which survives in today's Banias.[25] Jesus' presence there with his disciples marked his only journey, in active years, outside the borders of Palestine and Decapolis. It came at a point which the evangelists see as marking a crisis in the sequence of events. It was a deliberate withdrawal from the Galilean scene, with its urgent crowds and claims.

Matthew (16:13–20) has the fullest account of what transpired. The significance will be with us to the end of the story. The immediate bearing on our exposition here is its witness to the inner counsel of Jesus with his disciples in the context of the developing situation. Despite the authority and content of Jesus' teaching, and his deeds of liberating compassion – or strangely because of these – a rising tide of hostility was unmistakable. Ominous shadows lay across the path ahead. Jesus knew himself faced with hard decisions about the way he should take and these involved the very understanding of Messiahship. After Caesarea Philippi the reader of the Gospels perceives how the pattern changes. The sense of a suffering climax becomes sharper and, in its light – or shadow – the education of the disciples becomes more central, within the still public ministry. It does so precisely because what they have now to learn about impending tragedy is the most disconcerting mystery of all.

Communion between master and men, then, at Caesarea Philippi opens for us a clear window into the habit of Jesus. We read it as a crucial instance of what was always instinctive to him. The disciples, truly, were called 'that they might be with him', and not simply that he 'might send them out to preach' (Mark 3:14). They were not casual associates or mere subalterns: they were genuine companions. It is in their trauma that we have to study the supreme and ultimate significance of Jesus, as discerned in the sequel of which they were the apostolic means. The questions Jesus put to them, in withdrawal at Caesarea Philippi, were not leading questions, asked rhetorically, with answers already known. They were a genuine reference to the disciples of the burden of Jesus' own wrestling with vocation. 'Whom do people say that I am?' How should we take the reaction we have kindled? Does Messiahship have to be outwardly acknowledged before it can be inwardly confirmed? Are its patterns to be rightly read in acclaim or in being despised? What does public confusion require of inward conviction and fidelity? What has ministry meant, thus far, and what does that meaning demand of us now? 'Whom do they say that I am?'

In the travail of that question Jesus is the more urgent to know '... but whom do you say that I am?' What light have you on the pattern and the policy? How do you read what has happened since everything began there at Capernaum? Who but the disciples were best qualified to weigh events and point their moral? Or, if they were too dull to give their verdict, their incomprehension would not end the issue: it would be another element in its urgency. If – however ambiguously – they reached one, their recognition would carry both them and Jesus into new liabilities about what they had affirmed. The more eager and assured their instincts in response, the more imperative their education into its implications. Jesus was in the role, with them, of a teacher feeling – for his own sake and for theirs – after assurance about a meaning registered, and so, in turn, pursuing its further logic. All serious education is this way, and there are times when the teacher learns with the learners – if not the lesson he imparts, then at least the struggle of imparting it.

This is how we must read those deep exchanges, so tersely summarised in the Gospel. 'Whom do you say that I am? Simon Peter, answering said: "You are the Christ, the Son of the living God."' 'From that time onward,' the Gospel goes on to say, Jesus 'began to show to his disciples how he ... must suffer.' From Caesarea Philippi the new and final dimension takes over. The mountain retreat was a watershed of the whole story. The Qur'ān is right in describing the disciples as Jesus' 'helpers on behalf of God'. The disciples, alike in their partial perception and in their loving inter-action with Jesus, enabled him in the Messianic course. It is true that they were all he had, but – in the real world of the Incarnation – they were all he needed, men in whose company, comprehending or uncomprehending, his vocation could take shape.

What came to a climax between Jesus and the twelve at Caesarea Philippi was, of course, a steady feature from the beginning. The call of the disciples figures prominently in every Gospel. There is ground for thinking that Peter's house in Capernaum was the first headquarters of the Christian movement.[26] The comradeship there launched was close and lively. The Gospels are frank and honest about the human qualities of the disciples, their ineptness and proneness to misunderstanding. It is these which provide a foil by which so much about Jesus comes to be known. What we are here calling his 'communing' with them is where our education via the text moves, as it were, with theirs.

Nowhere can we reach what this participation meant, he with them, and they with him, more readily than in the request they made about learning to pray. His response gave them what is universally called 'the Lord's Prayer'. It was and is, equally, 'the disciples' prayer' because they had it from Jesus (Luke 11:1–4; Matt. 6:9–15). Luke says that they made their request 'when Jesus was praying in a certain place', meaning, no doubt, that the impulse was generated by their sense of what 'praying' meant to him. Accordingly, the Lord's Prayer can serve us here to understudy Jesus' communion with the disciples. It has the further benefit of leading us into his own communion with 'the Father'.

xi

The first three petitions, like the rest of the prayer, are Aramaic in form and temper. At once it must be understood that they are not aspirations that have human addressees in mind, as if an intense Semitic idiom were miscued as some exhortation to human arbiters. On the contrary, the hallowing of the divine Name, the incidence of the divine kingdom and the 'happening' of the divine will are here in plea for God's fulfilment. This is the clear sense of the Aramaic passive voice. The sanctifying of the Name, with the kingdom and the will which 'parallelise' it, are what we ask that God will 'let be' here and now. There is a dynamic immediacy about the English 'hallowed be . . .', 'come', and 'be done', not, as it were, an indirect appeal *to* us but a passionate yearning *in* us, in direct appeal to God. Missing this idiom, there has been some Muslim commentary dismissing the prayer as pointless, on the ground that, anyway, the divine Name *is* holy, and the will of God is so inevitably 'done' that it is superfluous to pray that it may be done. Holy, to be sure, but with a holiness needing to be realised among us in the obedience of the kingdom. 'Actualised', indeed, but only in the arena of history and the heart. 'Speedily and soon' was the phrase the Judaic *Kaddish* prayer used in the clauses which the Lord's Prayer echoes here from the synagogue worship.

That Judaic prayer included a clear reference to 'Israel' which the Lord's Prayer significantly omits. Its yearning for the Name, the kingdom and the will is indifferently for all people, 'as in heaven, so on earth'. These are no longer confined to 'Hear, O Israel. . . .' The Lord's Prayer, in this way, moves within the 'democracy' we earlier noted in the Beatitudes. It looks universally for the saving action of God and breathes the immediacy about the kingdom which we learned from Jesus' first days of ministry. 'Give us today the bread of the coming [day]' pursues the same theme. For though it *may* doubtless be taken – as by long generations of Christian devotion – as a simple plea for sustenance and a sure dependence, it certainly has a primary meaning about 'the kingdom'. All turns on the sense of the Greek word *epiousios* which is usually rendered 'daily', though 'this day', or 'today', is there in the rest of the clause. *Epiousios* occurs nowhere else in the New Testament and nowhere in the whole of Greek literature. It is clear that it has a sense of the future, but to ask for 'our future bread' today is hardly intelligible. It has been suggested that 'our bread of the morrow' might be meant – in line, perhaps, with the manna in the wilderness, gathered in the evening (Numbers 11:9). But something more than 'tomorrow' is intended, more indeed than literal 'bread'. Jesus often referred to his task as a 'bread' he had to eat. His 'meat', or 'food', was to do the will of his Father. One day an admirer said: 'Blessed is he who will eat bread in the kingdom of God' (Luke 14:15). In response to him, Jesus told the parable of the great supper which many invitees refused. The speaker was doubtless referring to the Messianic banquet, the feast which would inaugurate and celebrate the Messianic victory, as popular concept had it.

This, in the context, not of celebration but of toil and commitment, seems to be the likeliest meaning of *ton arton epiousion*, 'the bread of the coming [one]'. The prayer here is within the early clauses about Name, kingdom and will, and in paraphrase would read, 'Let us have here and now the bread of the Messiah to be', the one whose task and expectation will be our daily food. For this 'manna' would not fall artlessly from heaven to feed a restive people. It would come in the strenuous service of the kingdom which was already ('today') at grips with the world and recruiting its ardent servants.

One token of their quality was the will to forgive and be forgiven. The next clause has the Aramaic 'debts' rather than 'sins'. It does not mean that our forgivingness towards others is the measure of God's forgiving us. It means that we cannot receive forgiveness except in a readiness to practise forgiving relationships to others. This was affirmed in the parable of the two servants (Matt. 18:23–35).

The last two clauses of the Lord's Prayer before the final ascription must be held very closely together. The word *peirasmos* is very close to the Quranic *fitnah* minus political overtones. It means 'trial' in the double sense of 'tribulation' and so 'temptation'. Just as the perils of following Muḥammad through Quraishī 'persecution' 'tried' or 'tested' the quality of the 'emigrants', or *muhājirūn*, so the tribulations of the Messianic task would sift and try disciples. Hence the petition: 'Do not bring us where trial/temptation will master us but set us free from evil' (or 'from the evil one'). God would not 'lead us' into pride, lust, greed, envy, sloth, or whatever else belongs with the familiar meaning of 'temptation' as our private and corporate proneness to wrong. At a deeper level still, the prayer concerns participation in the radical encounter of the Messianic redemption with the Satanic principle. Just as the Satanic aims to give the lie to the whole divine enterprise of creation and humanity, so the Messianic is set to give the lie to the liar, to 'silence the accuser', and vindicate in righteousness and grace the very sovereignty of God. That our human share in this encounter might be occasion of *fitnah*, or critical sifting of heart and will, is no mystery, but all apprehension about our frailty has to be gathered immediately into the will for deliverance.

Thus the communion of Jesus with his disciples, of which the Lord's Prayer is so vital an index, is instinct with hope, consecration and a vivid realism. As a careful scholar[27] of the parables and prayers of Jesus has it:

> The disciples, ... utter this word 'Today', even now, even here, already on this day give us the bread of life. Jesus grants to them as the children of God the privilege of stretching forth their hands to grasp the glory of the consummation, to fetch it down, to believe it down, to pray it down, right into their poor lives, even now, even here, today.

How fitting, then, that the Lord's Prayer should conclude, in Matthew's version, with the ascription: 'For Thine is the kingdom, the power and the glory'. The whole is in those three realities, presently, actively, dynamically at work within the Messianic role of Jesus and so, in turn, the lodestar of his disciples.

xii

It is clear from the Gospels that the communing of Jesus with his disciples was all the time informed by his own inner communion with the One he taught them to name as 'our Father'. 'My Father' was no less steadily and ardently his own usage. It is from this deep personal surrender that we must understand the Christian meaning of divine 'Sonship', so often misinterpreted and scouted by Islamic preconceptions. The vital decisions of Jesus to which the whole logic of his ministry leads are seen in the New Testament as flowing from his communion with God. What happens is an alignment of wills, whereby what Jesus sees to be the intention of the Father becomes, in the given situation, the readiness of the Son. That mutuality between a divine purpose, intensely realised by Jesus as vocation, and a human fulfilment of it, wrought out in travail, characterises all the praying of Jesus and inspired the Church to formulate, in Christology, the faith which recognised its meaning. A theology of the prayers of Jesus concerns us in Chapter 7.

Here our need is to enter, as best we may, into the immediate context of that alignment of the will of Jesus with the will of 'his Father'. He had stood in the synagogue in Nazareth reading the passage in Isaiah (verses to which he deliberately turned: Luke 4:16–21; Isaiah 61:1–2) acknowledging that 'the Spirit of the Lord is upon me'. Consistently, whether in the ordinary or the critical, that sense of vocation moved him and moved with him through all vicissitudes. Prayer was its inner counsel. All the Gospels record Jesus' habit of withdrawal and devotion, on occasions of healing, in the besetting presence of the crowds, over the choice of disciples, in their commissioning and their education. His life of prayer was in fact their most eloquent school. Its most characteristic word was the Aramaic *Abba*, a tender (in some usage almost an affectionate) term, quite unlike the stern, austere language often preferred by Semitic instincts for an unnameable Lordship or, rather, an unpronouncable Name (Mark 14:36).

It was in the concreteness of what he faced in ministry that the praying of Jesus had its themes and in the praying that his ministry found its resources. His praying, we have to say, was 'incarnational'. Its sphere was the receiving and the doing of the will of God in Messianic action: its burden was the shaping of that action in the inner spirit and in the outer world. How else should Jesus sustain his conflict with authority? How else was he to face those popular misconceptions of what Messianic purposes involved, beguiling as they might otherwise have been? How else should he surmount those anxious fears of Jewry for survival, fears which lay behind so much of their rigorism about sabbaths and minutiae of the law? How else was he to bear with the tensions and frailties among the disciples he had chosen? How else transcend the enmities of his own Nazarene townsfolk and acquaintance? In all these situations 'hallowed be Thy Name' was a costly aspiration; and 'Thy kingdom come ...' a strenuous calling. 'Thy will be done' did not mean 'Thy will be suffered' in passive acquiescence: it meant 'Thy will be accomplished in active devotion'.

So it was that Jesus' life of prayer was in no way merely exemplary. Example it assuredly was, but only because in it Jesus lived his Messianic vocation. As we must see, in passing to the last of our four themes of his ministry, it was the ground of all his 'resolving'. 'The cup which my Father has given me' was how he read what awaited him (John 18:11; cf. Mark 10:39, 14:36), just as all contradiction to that sense of things constituted for him either a denial or a disowning of his Sonship.

xiii

'Jesus as the Christ' is our theme. What we are set to understand, in the remainder of this chapter, is how Jesus came to Gethsemane, the garden of prayer which was the garden of his final arrest. Unmistakable in all the Gospels is this movement into tragedy – or what is 'tragedy' by every outward reckoning. They could all be well described as a prelude of teaching and ministry, in preface to a climax of suffering. What emerges from the prelude and preface is hardening hostility. What is to be made of that hostility becomes the burning issue Jesus faces. How he resolves it is what makes him 'the Christ'.

The factors in the rejectionism are clear enough. They revolve around questions of authority, the Sabbath, forgiveness of sins, the kingdom of God and its ways, the inner self-consciousness of Jesus and his 'good news' as that kingdom's sign and pivot. In all these issues Jesus is disputed and resisted. How is this obduracy to be read? What should he make of this failure to understand? It is a failure of his own people. It is 'his own who received him not' (John 1:11). These rejectors are 'masters in Israel', mentors who might be assumed to comprehend things Messianic vital to Jesus. Such acceptance as there is comes largely from 'the vulgar throng', enthusiastic, maybe, but also effervescent and motivated more by works of mercy than by comprehension of spiritual priorities. On every count of corporate custody of authentic Torah heritage, Jesus is – it harshly seems – solidly disapproved.

There *is* a sense, however disparate the context, in which this must be seen as a very 'Muḥammadan' dilemma. How is that which is 'in the name of God' to respond to that which disallows 'the God of *this* Name', the message and the bearer in the Name? How is that which believes itself to be *fī sabīl Illāh*, 'in the way of God', to meet that which defies the belief? How is the servant rightly 'on behalf of God' when both his credentials and his *credenda*, his calling and his call, are disavowed?

It is, of course, possible for him to desist and so betray, to resist and so confuse the things at stake. In no way can he dissociate what he experiences as done to him from what he perceives as done in perverse response – or, rather, non-responsive obduracy – to God. It would not be wise to do more than note the parallel. In this respect Mecca and Jerusalem, the Quraishī and the Sadducean enmity, are not dissimilar.

Our business here is only with how Jesus responds to the darkening scene which Caesarea Philippi registers and the sequence confirms. Desisting in the face of threats and danger is never a loyal option. Messiah may not abnegate or adjust his message to evade its hostile reception. On the contrary, in the Gospels, Jesus deliberately and strongly seeks out Jerusalem, the citadel and shrine of the forces and prejudices which disown him. There is no evasion here. Galilee might have accommodated a healing and a teaching service for years ahead, given its cosmopolitan character and its local feeling, but 'it cannot be that a prophet perish out of Jerusalem' (Mark 11:33). It seems clear that, for Jesus, 'going up to Jerusalem' and 'the Son of Man must suffer' were in fact one destiny (Luke 18:31, and other passages). We can read Jesus' 'resolving' on the very map of his country.

It follows what reverence may call 'the map in the mind'. The pain and travail of Jesus, in Messianic awareness, came from the sheer strain and contention of alternative Messiahships as these obtained within popular emotion and were sadly present in the confused loyalty of the disciples. Their diversity turned on *who* Messiah was to save and *from what* he was to save them. Given that the Messianic hope had its first context in Jewish national consciousness, it could well be assumed that *for* Jewry *from* Rome was obviously the answer. But there might be more subtle interpretation, depending on whether a 'royal' or a 'priestly' Messiah was anticipated – or possibly a combination of both. Further to perplex the question was whether Messiah would be personal at all, or whether some communal or corporate identity was in view, perhaps Jewry itself suitably perfected in a worthy self-redemption, either by an apocalyptic 'remnant' or by an accomplished Torah-integrity.

There was also the question, weighing with Jesus, as to how circumstantial history was to be read in Messianic perspective. Was evil destined necessarily to worsen into the (so-called) 'Messianic woes' so that the final victory would not be had against a partial crisis leaving a still-defiant, residual wrong, but would be veritably achieved against the ultimate and worst? If so, how was the complete reach of evil to be identified and Messiah not be premature? How should the intervening time be spent – in passive waiting, in tacit stolidity, or in feverish expectation? Jesus had said that 'the kingdom of heaven was at hand'. How did he understand its proximity, its presence, when the tokens of its reality here and now in his own ministry, were being received with such concerted antipathy? How was that antipathy to be taken into its stride as the promised kingdom in the given terms?

It is urgent for us to see these questions within the travail of Jesus and as the theme of his inner Sonship, belonging inescapably as they did to what he knew as 'the will of my Father.' The clue, it is here believed, lay for him in certain precedents crucial to Biblical prophecy, from which he would seem to have drawn his conviction of what 'the mind of God' entailed – that mind to which his own must loyally conform. Had he not reproached Peter's attempt at Caesarea Philippi to dissuade him from such thoughts by telling Peter: 'You do not think like God thinks'? (Matt. 16:23). Was it the figure of the mysterious suffering servant in whom Jesus identified 'the mind of God' as the key to Jesus' own vocation as the reality of ministry and rejection seemed inexorably to be shaping it? Before reaching that conclusion, it is wise to study Jesus' sojourn in the desert of Judea which the evangelists place at the outset of his calling, for it is no less a clue at the end for two evident reasons. Its issues were present from first to last, and the way in which they were resolved throughout in fact left no other alternative than the pattern of 'the suffering servant'.

xiv

There is in Mark 1:12–13 the briefest reference to what are usually called Jesus' 'temptations' in the desert. Fuller narratives occur in

Matt. 4:1–11 and Luke 3:2–17, with the second and third 'temptations' in reverse order. It is clear from both themes of the tempter and of Jesus' response that these had to do, not with what we normally mean by 'temptations' in the personal context, but with the Messianic task, its content and its way. Any study must keep in mind the Quranic, and Biblical, role of Satan as 'the accuser' of man, God's creature and trustee, and so as 'the accuser' of God whose wisdom and grace underlie the creation and its human custody. Satan's objective was, and is, so to inveigle man into wrong motives and false-mindedness about God's sovereignty as to be able, as Satan, to discredit the whole divine design in man and so, by implication, the essential Lordship of God. Nowhere did such Satanism have more crucial encounter than in the desert with Jesus.[28]

The narrative in Matthew chapter 4 and Luke chapter 3 would, of course, have no point or credibility in the absence of those features of the kingdom, in teaching and healing, which we have studied in Jesus earlier. These Satan astutely formulated in terms of his identity. 'If you are the son of God ...' inviting Jesus to patterns of Messianic fulfilment by this formula (it can have no other connotation in this context) which would, arguably, accomplish what 'the Father' had in mind in Jesus as His filial executant.

The alternatives were three. 'Turning stones into bread' would suggest a Messiahship of sheer economic plenty, providing effectively, but exclusively, for material need. We detect the point of the temptation – as in each case – by noting the terms in which it was rejected. 'Man does live by bread', indeed; but 'not by bread alone'. Events like the feeding of the five thousand might demonstrate a proper care for the hungry but, repeated constantly, would not suffice the deeper hunger of the human spirit. The notion of 'stones into bread' might also have concerned Jesus' own survival in a time of fasting and privation, especially if the sight of the flat stones, strewn around in the desert sun, had suggested the idea of perpetual miracle because they resembled loaves. Jesus, even in the fasting time, had 'meat to eat' which Satan knew not of – the meat of the doing of God's will.

Pure spectacle was the nub of the second temptation. The figure descending unscathed from the pinnacle of the Temple into the crowded outer court would certainly awe and astonish the volatile folk there into prompt credulity. Was not the 'son of man' supposed to ride upon clouds of power? Did not Satan, this time – stirred by Jesus' example – find a scripture for his purpose, quoting Psalm 91 with a significant omission?[29] Credulity is never faith. Nor does human salvation ever hinge on crude impression, on mere surprise that leaves the inner self unprobed and untransformed. Eschatological intrusion is not the patient way of grace. Messiah must not force the hand of God by contriving a situation in which He must intervene on dictated terms. Was it precisely this which Judas had in view, confronting both God and Jesus by the arrest in Gethsemane with a situation so desperate that, without decisive action (such as neither had yet taken) all would be lost? Were the scoffers at the crucifixion not offering the same temptation? 'Come down from the cross ...' (Matt. 27:40) – an even more dramatic inducement to 'faith', of a sort, than descending from the Temple height?

These are not 'the ways of God'. Nor is He to be put to the test in such terms, as Jesus insisted in reply to Satan. The things of the Spirit can only be served and fulfilled in the ways of the Spirit. Satan's third option to Messiah follows. It is the option for power. Satan has Jesus visualise political empire with its compelling short cuts to the goal and, because of these, its inevitable compromise with evil, with brutality and force. The supremely Islamic principle with which Jesus refuses this temptation – 'You shall worship the Lord your God and Him only shall you serve' – excludes the option of a *Hijrah*, a shift, a diversion into force and, therefore, away from the quiet strength of truth and the sure fidelities of love. There *are* 'the kingdoms of this world' – to be sure – but Messiahship is *in* them not *of* them. Those kingdoms are nationalist, competitive, exclusivist, political and coercive. As such they leave areas of life, reaches of humanity and depths of need outside both their range and their capacity, and even their achievements generate their contradiction. At the very centre of Jesus' reading of his destiny, in the sort of world the reception of his ministry disclosed, was the perception that the Messianic task and the political arm were not compatible.

It is interesting to ponder where the narrative of the desert temptations originated. In Jesus' solitude there was no recording witness: there were no disciples overhearing. Whence then did the evangelists have the event and its themes? Must its presence in their record not be explained by the steady recurrence of these arguable options within the sequence of the ministry and so in the exchanges of its comradeship? For recurrent they certainly were, right to the Cross itself, as we have seen. So it was a sure instinct which inspired Matthew and Luke to set their significance, as a clue, at the very outset of Jesus' work, following his baptism as its inauguration.

For the decisions there determined were steadily sustained as situations unfolded requiring them anew by sharpening into climax all that was at stake. The logic, there implied, as to what required to be rejected had to be resolutely followed in the living sequence of events. In truth, the pattern of mind narrated in the desert victory of Jesus over Satan anticipated how Messianic action must be shaped. But the fulfilment of the pattern in the action was a travail of spirit to the end. It was one thing to weigh and refuse the false options: another to achieve the true one.

XV

How should we understand the inner springs of Jesus' mind and will in this decision? Where did the 'resolving' we are studying derive its warrant? How was it authentic? The orthodox answer would take us to the divinity of Jesus. For here is that in which the divinity of Jesus consists; but faith must penetrate what that doctrine means. It claims that in the fashion of the Messiahship of Jesus we have a living disclosure of what we must ascribe to God in a living fulfilment we ascribe to Jesus. The theology here concerns us in Chapter 7. In the history here we identify the wisdom of God in the mind of Jesus, the grace of God in the love of Jesus. It is Messiahship in which they meet. For Messiahship is where God locates His saving responsibility to human history and where Jesus achieves the human counterpart of a responsibly divine saving.

There were Biblical precedents from which Jesus, in his ministry, could draw inspiration for his Messianic guidance. There were other 'crises' of encounter between truth and evil, where suffering grace had emerged as the only final factor in decision. To find the Gospel story inclusive and definitive is not to see it in total unrelation to the content of all history. Quite the contrary: it epitomises in a declarative climax what may be recognised in part elsewhere throughout the human story.

For Jesus, in the Judaic tradition, those precedents were in the prophets, and most compellingly in 'the suffering servant' of chapters 42, 51 and 53 of Isaiah. The biography of the prophet Jeremiah needs to be associated closely with the meaning of this strange, elusive figure of 'the servant'. The service of truth, in the evil world, entails travail, suffering and peril. Enmity is the reward of the truthful. The bearer of the word takes in his own person the rejection of his message. Issues are joined in which he has no option but to suffer, to bear and to endure and to forgive. By his fidelity he ensures that truth survives and mercy abides. The evil society is not left without witness against itself. These meanings become, as it were, biography. They emerge in their costly way in the very fabric of personal grief and tragedy. They are spoken in pain. The personal anguish they exact intensifies their moral force. Society is blessed in spite of itself. There are some who learn in retrospect to consider the suffering prophet and acknowledge that 'with his stripes we are healed'.

There is textual evidence in the Gospels that this was the precedent which we may say minded Jesus to read his suffering situation by this light and to identify in 'the suffering servant' the secret of Messiah. This was a quite revolutionary decision. The precedent was in no way operative in Messianic terms. The Messianic was normally assumed to be triumphalist.[30] What Jesus saw as its very secret should be seen, otherwise, as its complete negation. The early Church certainly lived by this conviction as to Jesus. It would be altogether odd to think it original to them and not to him. They were called 'Christians' only because he had been, this way, the Christ and because his being so had become decisive for their faith in God.

Words and haunting imagery from Isaiah chapter 53 can be detected in the language of Jesus in anticipating the Cross. 'He was despised and we esteemed him not' (53:3) and 'rejected by men' are echoed directly in Mark 8:31, the first of the three occasions in Mark and parallel passages where Jesus tells his disciples of the hostility ahead. 'We thought nothing of him, and so shunned and disallowed him' is the sense of the Isaian passage, almost exactly reproduced in the Greek of the Gospel. According to Luke 9:51, Jesus 'set his face to go to Jerusalem'. Isaiah 50:7 says the same about the servant, 'like a flint'. The servant had been Jesus' mentor at the outset in the Nazareth synagogue. It would seem that he continued so to the end. There is no mistaking the parallel sense of a context of enmity, a vocation of travail and a climax of grief. It is, of course, possible to attribute the alignment of Gospel narrative and prophetic precedent to the evangelists as if, somehow, the precedents determined the story. But could they, as it were, be self-fulfilling without a living self – the self of Jesus – to fulfil them? Are we to suppose the precedents dormant until the historians arrive? Is it they who make them the clue to the story – a story about a hero who was not their pioneer? The role of the evangelists was responsive, not original. Theirs it was, in respect of Jesus, to be like the perceptive contemporaries of 'the suffering servant' who 'saw of the travail of his soul', learned in him the price of redemption and knew in themselves 'the fruit of his redemption'.

xvi

The dramatic event of Jesus' entry into Jerusalem, earlier noted as a climax of celebration, was also the clearest index to his Messianic decision. It was not only that Galilean pilgrims to Jerusalem were applauding his healing benediction in their lives. It was also that the capital city was receiving a deliberate challenge in the enactment of an old, prophetic vision of a king in meekness (Zechariah 9:9–10) coming in peace and liberation. In both vision and event there was enigma and a calculated spur to a questioning awareness about the very nature of 'salvation'. Some modern studies have puzzled over Jesus' meaning and read into it their own predilections. It has been seen, in fact, as a zealot-style bid for power which sadly miscarried, or as an appeal to apocalyptic intervention. Puzzlement cannot be resolved by taking the entry to the city in isolation from the meaning of Caesarea Philippi and its sequel. Viewed in that whole context, as we have surveyed it, it seems intelligible to believe that Jesus was bringing to a head the opposition he had long experienced and doing so in the heart and symbol of its source and passion, and – further – in the idiom of gentleness and peace by which his response would be defined. It was not a suicidal forcing of the hand of his rejectors. It was a statement of the issue which had never been concealed and which must duly come to climax.

The cleansing of the Temple certainly pointedly stated it further. For the Temple was the citadel where the whole question of God, and Jewishness, and grace, and law – with all the human themes that lived in these – was posed. It was cleansing Jesus sought, retrieval from *ḍalāl* or deviation, and for honest and inclusive benediction. What else but the Messianic goal were these? The Temple commerce was a symptom of the inner wrong. It was by the reality in the court, not the fantasy from the pinnacle, that Messiahship would realise vocation. To the bemused or indignant authorities it seemed no more than a gesture, crude and parlous. Gesture, merely, it seemed also by the evening of the day when the excited crowds had all dispersed and Jesus and his disciples were again, almost secretively, in Bethany.

xvii

Study of the story of Jesus before Gethsemane and a reading of the Messianic principle at its heart have one other clue to ponder. It has, as many think, a place in the Qur'ān, and it generated the central act of Christian worship. On the evening before his arrest, Jesus and his disciples gathered in an 'upper room' somewhere in Jerusalem. There, in all the associations of the Passover, he broke and blessed bread and, with thanksgiving, poured wine, and they shared the first 'Holy Communion'. It was the clearest commentary on how he understood the immediate situation – the gathered enmity, the impending sentence to death, commemorated here in the framework of the ancient 'exodus' and its 'salvation'.

Surah 5 of the Qur'ān is entitled *Al-Mā'idah* (The Table), from the reference in verse 113 in which the disciples request 'a table from heaven' which is to be 'a festival for the first and the last of them . . . and a sign'. The whole passage could be associated with the manna in the wilderness, or with occasions on which Jesus fed the crowds. But the emphases in the context on 'a festival', on continuity through the generations, rest, solace and confirmation as to the truth of Jesus, all seem to fit the occasion of 'this last supper' in Jerusalem. That it is Jesus, in the Gospel, who initiates it – not the disciples who request it (as in Surah 5) – need not tell against this view, since we may assume implicit desire in the disciples also. 'That we may know that you have dealt truly with us [*ṣadaqtanā*] and may be among the witnesses thereto', on the lips of the disciples, surely fits the Gospel context.

It might be urged against this that the Quranic Jesus is not finally a victim – the theme we take up in the next chapter. On any count he was certainly in a situation in which he was meant to be a victim, in the intention of the enmity even then laying plans against him. There is nothing unfitting in the Quranic Jesus presiding at this *mā'idah* of communion with his disciples and of solace to their hearts. As Surah 3:56 has it, God – in all the portents of the hour – was 'bringing him to a dying' (*Innī mutawaffīka*).

In the Gospels the significance of 'the table' on the eve of the Passion is clear. Here is Messiah's bread, in the sense of the Lord's Prayer. As in the Gospels, so in the sacrament – the climax belongs in suffering. Just as the narrative, and all it contains, leads on into the pain of rejection, so the bread and wine – broken and outpoured – represent what the acceptance of that suffering means in fellowship and faith – how the Cross is at the heart of a divine forgiveness, how the bearing of the enmity becomes life for the world. 'This is my body,' Jesus says, 'this is my blood.' 'Make this your own, in remembrance of me.'

It was not that Jesus *needed* some device to obviate oblivion: he was unforgettable. Devices, anyway, do not themselves survive forgetfulness if there is no will to recollection. The bread and the wine did not have to do with *whether* Jesus would be remembered. Resurrection itself lay ahead and by it his unfailing presence. Partaking had to do, not with whether, but with *how* – not with the fact of memory but with the manner. *How* we hold in mind is always vital. Here we understand that Jesus was legislating, in a rite of great depth and intimacy, for the perennial interpretation of his Messiahship. He was giving his disciples, and beyond them the centuries, the authentic clue by which to know and to make him known (Surah 5:113). It lay in the mystery of the love that suffers – the love which takes the evil situation its own truth has incurred and reads in that taking the divine mind – and in the active meaning of Sonship to the Father (thus fulfilled) masters the evil and achieves a forgiveness to which all are called. There was a psalm refrain traditional to the Passover ritual: 'This is the Lord's doing and it is marvellous in our eyes' (Psalm 118:23).

The final focus of interpretation, then, as we have it from Jesus himself in 'the upper room', was not on rehearsal of teaching, or recitation of wisdom, or commemoration of healing, or celebration of family links, or congratulatory peoplehood. The focus of finality was his 'obedience unto death' understood as the Messianic secret in which the deepest reach of human need and the surest quality of divine grace would come to meeting. All that Christians mean by their faith *in* Jesus, in the form of their faith *about* him, intends and enshrines this confession of his Christhood, and of that Christhood as the active – and disconcerting – disclosure of the very sovereignty of God.

xviii

We come only in conclusion to the birth of Jesus, which has so large a place in the Qur'ān. To be sure, without birth, there is nothing. The condition of all else in this world is a mother's womb. So it is right that Mary (*Maryam*) should have so large a place in both Muslim and Christian veneration. Her significance, in either case – if differently – is relational. Mary, in the Gospel, stands near the Cross and has her anguish too; but Jesus is upon it, Jesus only. All that devotion has built around the person of the Virgin stands finally and authentically within the redeeming significance we have been tracing of Jesus as the Christ.

Nowhere is that Christhood more superbly celebrated, in all its paradox, than in the hymn which Luke has preserved in his Gospel (1:46–55), the song of Mary, the *Magnificat*. Its familiar Latin name among Christians (from the first word in the Latin text) is precisely that *kabbirhu takbīran*, 'make him greatly great' which we find in Surah 17:111. The meaning, of course, in either case is not conferring, but celebrating, the greatness of God. It will be a congenial and

Islamic thing to explore what *Magnificat* means. We will find that it corroborates most tellingly all that we have been comprehending through this study of Jesus and his story.

It is fair to ask how Luke came by the song and why he set it in the prelude to his Gospel. Clearly no tape-recorders invaded Mary's privacy on her visit to the godly Elisabeth in the hill country of Judea. Did Luke have it years later in recollection from Mary? Would she remember in old age the very words she used in her near ecstacy? Or should we assume that Luke is exercising a very reverent authorship and conveying a deep reading of Jesus' birth, on the lips of Mary? Scholarship is reasonably certain that he is employing sources already existing and giving them a meaning all his own – that he is, to these sources, what Shakespeare was to Hamlet, namely, a new interpreter, at once creative and indebted.

Plainly, *Magnificat*, like the *Benedictus* and the *Nunc Dimittis*, in Luke's prelude are very Hebraic in their idiom and style. Luke, of course, was a Greek, the only non-Jew writing in the New Testament. There are many echoes in *Magnificat* of Hebrew poetry celebrating the birth of Samuel (1 Samuel 2:1–11) and David's song before the Ark (1 Chronicles chapter 16). More surprisingly, there are parallels with the songs of the Maccabean warriors, those redoubtable freedom-fighters of the second century before Christ, either steeling their hearts before battle or exulting in victory after battle. It is these parallels which underscore the strange paradox of Mary's (Luke's?) use of them. How were 'the mighty humbled' while Herod the tyrant reigned? How were 'the hungry filled with good' when oppression stalked the land? How were 'the proud scattered in their conceits' when Herod was poised at any time to murder innocents in Bethlehem or wherever brute suspicion identified a threat to vested interest? Such exultation made sense when, for example, Mattathyahu (Mattathias, a Maccabee), or 'rod of Yahweh', had smitten the enemies of God and Israel. How, though, should it fit the birth of the Messiah, of the Messiah Jesus was to be?

To ask that question is further to ask why Luke, in his authorship, adapted these warrior songs in which mothers exulted in Maccabean feats of arms, actual or prospective. Something of the gentleness of Hannah, Samuel's mother, was Mary's also. However, Mattathias could hardly be described as lowly or his mother as being of 'low estate'. Perhaps that phrase referred to the humil*iation* of Israel in the face of her enemies. Then why should Luke recruit it to express the humil*ity* of Mary?

The answer would seem to be in what is called 'prolepsis', namely, taking the future as something already present, celebrating as a sure prospect what is not yet an actual fact. History writing, of course, does this all the time. We can only write the past when we have come to know its future. Simeon holds a babe in arms and says: 'My eyes have seen your salvation, Lord' (Luke 2:30). So Luke has Mary rejoicing in the Messianic future, present in the near prospect of the babe here and now. She can celebrate that future in the past tense. 'He who is mighty has done for me great things. ...'[31]

The crucial thing, both for Mary's rejoicing spirit and for Luke's perceptive writing, is the terms of that 'might', the pattern of that victory. There is no more eloquent witness to the Messiahship of Jesus than the deliberate paradoxes of Mary's song. The 'imagination' of Mary's heart has to do, on one level, with the womb, the breast, the nursery and the laundry. These are the lowly necessities around the fact of birth – without which there would be no other fact. Through and beyond these, there is the lowliness of Galilee and Gethsemane as the 'filling of the hungry' and the dethroning of the proud. The 'great things' of divine majesty, at grips with human wrong, will be understood in wounded hands and pierced feet. The bread of the Messiah will be the body broken.

Such is the sublime, and effective, reversal of values we find happening in Jesus as the Christ – a ministry that dignifies the ordinary, that lifts up the humble, and a Cross that warrants rejoicing in 'God who is Saviour'. The birth of Jesus, read by these mother-lights, is presented by Luke as holding within itself the significance of all that would ensue. All that did ensue is read by those mother-lights. To understand Jesus as the Christ is 'to tell out the greatness of the Lord'.

Notes

1 Translation by Norman Sharp. Sanā'ī was an Afghan by birth. By language he is Persian. The couplet runs:

> The seven tinctured garment cast from thee.
> Like Jesus, let thy robe one colour be.

The thought throughout this chapter of 'the Christ' will be no matter of question for Muslims, thanks to the invariable Quranic usage about 'Īsā as *Al-Masīḥ*, i.e. 'the Christ'. Though English and Christian usage omits the definite article, it certainly intends its significance. That 'Jesus is Christ' means that 'Jesus is the Christ'. There are, however, strong reasons for reinserting 'the'. Its omission tends to obscure the fact that 'Christ' is a title, not a proper name. The Christian faith is that Jesus, in the entire 'event' this chapter traces, identified and achieved what

Christhood intends and demands. It is this which warrants, indeed requires, the phrase 'the Christ'. The early Church, we may say, ceased to need the article *Ho Xrištos* because they were so sure of its import. We do need it. That Islamic usage concurs is good, even though the Christian import of the term is not shared.

2 Present because of the issues, latent in the entire situation between Jesus and 'establishment', and because of the evident precedents of the prophetic past. ('O Jerusalem that kills the prophets ...', Matt. 23:37. Cf. Surah 2:87.) One may note the early anticipation which prompted Waraqah to warn Muḥammad, as Tradition has it, that hostility to his message would force him into exile. Since the obdurate world represented precisely what the measure of Messianic action had to be, Jesus took it cumulatively as the clue by which to understand Messiahship. Since his doing so is read, in Christianity, as the expression of his Sonship, it becomes in turn the clue to our understanding of God.

3 The sense of *anṣār*, as 'helpers', 'aiders to victory', will have been clear from Chapter 2.

4 The very fact of their obtuseness and frailty in crisis, which has no doubt contributed to a view of them as rather pathetic 'hangers-on', can be taken instead to indicate how far Jesus yearned for their comprehension and support. Occasions like that in Matt. 16:13–23, suggest that Jesus cherished their thoughts, interacting deeply with them in his own. This view, however, was obviously not shared by the Italian film-maker, Pier Paulo Pasolini, who depicts Jesus in his film on St Matthew's Gospel striding majestically, even magisterially, ahead of his uncomprehending disciples as one who hardly needed them.

5 Asaf, however, was not writing about Jesus. The lines will be found in: Talat Sait Halman, ed., *Contemporary Turkish Literature* (London, 1982), p. 232. The translation is by Yildiz Moran. Asaf, born 1923, died in 1981.

6 See Joachim Jeremias: *New Testament Theology I: The Proclamation of Jesus*, trans. John Bowden (London, 1971), and *Unknown Sayings of Jesus*, trans. R. H. Fuller (London, 1954). Jeremias (1900–79), of Gottingen, was a leading New Testament scholar and his work has close bearing on the Palestinian and Aramaic context against which Jesus' life and his sayings must be studied. According to R. F. Collins's *Introduction to the New Testament* (New York, 1983), p. 61, Jeremias' 'studies may yet prove to be the permanent legacy of the quest of the life of Jesus'.

7 The point is important to counter the view expressed, for example, by the philosopher, Ludwig Wittgenstein: 'The historical accounts in the Gospel might be, historically speaking, demonstrably false; yet the belief would lose nothing by this ... because historical proof is irrelevant to belief. This message [of the Gospel] is seized on by men believingly. *That* is the certainty characterizing this particular acceptance as true.' In G. H. Von Wright, *Culture and Value*, trans. P. Winch (Oxford, 1980), p. 32. Doubtless, as Wittgenstein goes on to say: 'Faith is what is needed by my heart, my soul, not by my speculative intelligence'. Surely, however, 'what is needed by the heart' is *in*, not careless of, the historical event. That is the conviction upon which we are proceeding here after the pattern of the New Testament itself, which fuses into one history and faith.

8 There are two related issues here, namely, does the 'prophetic' role consist adequately in 'word' alone, and does the 'prophetic' *per se* exhaust the divine revelatory 'concern' with the human world? By its understanding of the verbal status of the Qur'ān, Islam says 'Yes' to the first issue, though finding personal significance in Muḥammad and his *Sīrah* (or biography) in the lower status of Tradition. The Christian faith, in the meaning of the Incarnation, consummates the 'prophetic' factor in the import of the person of Jesus and makes revelation 'divine-autobiographical'. In so doing, it says 'No' to the second issue. It affirms a divine 'concern' for man and history which goes beyond instruction and direction

and exemplification into saving love and redemptive grace. This more costly 'concern' is in line with that, in both the Hebraic faith and in the Qur'ān, which informs all 'prophetic' vocation, namely a human agency in God's Name. It is in this way that the Gospels locate Jesus squarely within the 'prophetic' and yet depict him transcending it. The final chapter (24) of Luke expresses this clearly.

9 Albert Schweitzer, *The Quest of the Historical Jesus*, trans. W. Montgomery (New York, 1911; re-issued 1961), is the classic source of the thesis that the teaching of Jesus was essentially an 'interim-ethic' pending the imminent apocalypse. The theme can be had in popular form, for example, in Michael Grant, *Jesus* (London, 1977), where the kingdom of God is seen as so literally close at hand that there is no point in hating one's enemies! Citing verses he reads in this way, Grant says: 'The historian has to assume that he [Jesus] meant what he said and, in consequence, that he turned out to be wrong' (p. 20).

10 This 'democracy' of the Beatitudes can be found, in measure in *Pirke Aboth* and in the Zohar where, for example, makers of peace are extolled. Jewish particularist instinct was liable to read the several denominators – especially the last – as meant of 'the chosen people'. That category, for example, might determine the sense intended in 'my righteous servants'. See next note.

11 The verse occurs in Psalm 37:29. Cf. verse 11 of the same psalm.

12 Unless there is this 'meekness' even legitimate enmity to evil can itself become a real and culpable enmity to those with whom one identifies evil – often in potential self-righteousness or actual self-exoneration. Thus Eugene Ionesco observes: 'In detesting hatred, I become full of hatred myself and so play hatred's game.' *Notes and Counter-Notes*, trans. D. Watson (London, 1964), p. 164.

13 See, for example, C. Anderson Scott, *New Testament Ethics* (London, 1934), who counts only seven times in all (excluding duplicates) and then always in the setting of forgiveness (p. 27). He adds that the concern is not to denounce but to enlarge and deepen conceptions of 'sin'.

14 A pioneer work of reconception was R. T. Herford, *Pharisaism: Its Aims and Its Methods* (London, 1912). More recently: L. I. Finkelstein, *The Pharisees* (New York, 1962); John Bowker, *Jesus and the Pharisees* (Cambridge, 1973); and Gedalyahu Alon, *Jews, Judaism and the Classical World*, trans. I. Abrahams (Jerusalem, 1977), pp. 18–47. Also: A. Finkel, *The Pharisees and the Teacher of Nazareth* (Leiden, 1964); and J. Jeremias, *Jerusalem in the Time of Jesus*, trans. F. H. and C. H. Cave (London, 1969), pp. 246–67.

15 For example, Ismail R. al-Faruqi in his *Christian Ethics: A Historical and Systematic Analysis* (Montreal, 1967), in which he characterises the Judaic in the time of Jesus as 'racialist separatism and moral unworth' (p. 91). While stressing the universal implications of Jesus' ethic, Faruqi attributes to the evangelists' (esp. Matthew) Jewish prejudice or obduracy those emphases about Jesus' devotion to Torah and synagogue which the Gospels contain. As with many others, Faruqi's citation of the Gospels tends to be strongly determined, in its selectivity, by his predilections. It would appear that his view of the Judaic sense of 'election' and 'destiny' requires him to disallow – or to assign to Christian excess of devotion to things Judaic – those deep evidences of the Jewishness of Jesus which we need to read within (and not banish from) his real transcendence of it. This transcendence Faruqi has realised but interprets it as 'breaking the backbone of Jewish ethic' (p. 94). In so doing, he obscures how Jesus' radicalism was also fulfilment.

16 Notably, Geza Vermes, *Jesus the Jew: A Historian's Reading of the Gospels* (London, 1973).

17 Albert Camus, with his 'judge-penitent' and religion as 'a great laundering exercise', in *The Fall*, trans. Justin O'Brien (London, 1957).

18 The same reversal of significance which belongs in the parable in Luke chapter 18

about the two in the Temple may perhaps be paralleled – if we have imagination – in the great 'Quality of mercy' speech in Shakespeare's *The Merchant of Venice*. It is usually and rightly assumed that Shylock, the vengeful money-lender, the Jew, is being addressed in 'Portia's' plea for mercy. When the scene unfolds, however, and Shylock is left, broken, abject, by a legal technicality, Shakespeare surely means us to apply Portia's classic words to the baying, taunting, throng of 'gentiles' mercilessly oblivious of the deep, far-found tragedy of Shylock and his inner world with 'sufferance its badge'.

19 e.g. Matt. 7:29; Mark 1:22. 'Authority', also, was the crucial theme when confrontation happened with the 'authorities' (Matt. 21:23; Mark 11:28; Luke 20:2, etc.).

20 The wealth of Quranic imagery from both market and nature may be explored in this author's *The Event of the Qur'ān* (London, 1971), chaps. 5 and 6.

21 Though it was not yet the normal time of gathering figs, the incident may be explained by the fact that there were varieties of fig trees on which one's year's fruitage could be left, and so gathered, for two or three years following. Finding foliage only on such trees would be truly disappointing and not a cause of non-expectation, especially from a distance and on approach.

22 In Talat Sait Halman, ed., *Contemporary Turkish Literature*, trans. Murat Nejmet-Nejat (London, 1982), p. 439.

23 Charles Wesley, hymnwriter and partner with his brother John, was in the leadership of the Methodist Movement in the eighteenth century in England. He celebrated Palm Sunday in a gentler idiom than Dean Henry Milman whose hymn, 'Ride on, ride on in majesty', is one of the greatest in the language. The other significance of Jesus' entry into Jerusalem will concern us under 'resolving' later in this chapter.

24 Dag Hammarskjöld, *Markings*, trans. L. Sjöberg and W. H. Auden (London, 1964), p. 36.

25 The place has a shrine of Al-Khiḍr, the mysterious personality and wandering saint whom Tradition believes to be identified in Surah 18:65 f., 'one of God's servants' whom Moses encountered and in whose company Moses learned three strange lessons.

26 Simon's house is referred to in Matthew, Mark and Luke as a place where Jesus taught and the references to the healing, after fever, of Simon's mother-in-law has been taken to indicate that the headquarters of the movement may have been there. On New Testament personalities and locale, see Ronald Brownrigg, *Who's Who in the N.T.* (London, 1971).

27 J. Jeremias, *The Prayers of Jesus*, trans. J. Bowden and J. Reumann (London, 1967), p. 102.

28 Satan, in Surah 2:30 f., disputes the purpose and wisdom of God in setting the fickle creature, man, in custody of the created world and refuses to 'prostrate' to Adam, thus defying God. So, in the Biblical/Quranic 'myth' it becomes the goal of Satan, in history, so to discredit and deceive mankind that, thereby, he will demonstrate to God the folly of the human 'dominion'. So, in turn, it is the calling of man to give the liar to this liar, to disown the disowner, to frustrate the frustrator, and so, by obedience and holiness, 'vindicate' God. Cf. Ps. 8:2.

29 The omission was the clause 'to keep thee in all thy ways' (Ps. 91:11) which could not properly be dissociated from the assurance of the divine protection which Satan cited in inviting Jesus to throw himself down.

30 Either 'triumphalist' in a Maccabean sense, in nationalist Jewish victory, or in an apocalyptic sense after necessarily cataclysmic showdown with the evil world at its direst. According to J. H. Greenstone in *The Messianic Idea in Jewish History* (New

York, 1906), p. 78 f., it was Christian yearning which engendered the theory of the suffering Messiah, against the grain of Judaic 'realism'.

31 See Paul Winter, 'Magnificat and Benedictus: Maccabean Psalms' in *John Rylands Library Bulletin*, vol. 37, no. 1, Sept. 1954.

Chapter 6

Gethsemane and Beyond

i

That Jesus' teaching and ministry headed into a crisis of rejection and peril is nowhere in doubt. Galilee, the Beatitudes and the Sermon on the Mount, led towards Gethsemane, the garden of the agony. It is the sequel to that climax of hostility which is deeply in question between Christians and Muslims. What is at stake about it belongs with matters of history, but it also involves our ultimate understanding of God, our view of evil, of providence, of forgiveness and of divine power. So it is right to pursue our study, from the previous chapter, into 'Gethsemane and Beyond'. Was it rescue and rapture into heaven and God's vindication thereby? Or was it the Cross and the triumph of a love that truly suffered, the 'power and wisdom of God', reconciling the world?

The blind poet-philosopher, Abū-l-'Alā al-Ma'arī (973–1058 C.E.), one of Islam's greatest sceptics, was also a master of irony. The supreme irony, for him, was the Christian's conviction that crucifixion really happened to Jesus. How could it be, he asked, that one whom Christians believe to be 'divine' and 'son' to God should be ignominiously deserted by his 'father', and/or that God, his protector and Lord, should be worsted and defeated by a Jewish conspiracy? He found it both easy and congenial to make such an inconceivable belief the butt of his satire.

Whether in satire or perplexity, those points have always been central to the Islamic case against the credibility of the statement: '... crucified under Pontius Pilate'. The event which is the very fount and heart of Christianity is held by Muslims to be unhistorical and incredible. At least we all start from the fact of an intention to crucify. Abū-l-'Alā certainly did. Jesus, he wrote in the same passage, 'did not, out of pious devotion, shut his soul away in seclusion. On the contrary, as a wanderer, he went around walking the earth'.[1] So he was fair game for enemies and enmity. His preaching was public, his person accessible. His fidelity to God lay in steady, open discharge of his message to his time and place. In the face of gathering hostility, he was neither secretive nor evasive. Ready, at whatever cost, to let issues be joined between himself and his community, his 'vindication' (to use a Quranic term) would have to be either through and beyond suffering, or else by an intervention divinely ensuring it, suffering apart.

These alternatives – the only ones, short of blank futility and despair, such as all theism excludes – are alternatives about the nature of God and the vocation of his 'messengers', as well as about the facts of a situation in history. It is important to keep all the considerations together. We cannot here isolate the historian and the theologian from each other, and both – whether Muslim or Christian – begin from the undoubted fact that there was an intention to crucify. Jesus was a teacher whom his community sought to kill. We could not be at odds about the sequel if we were not at one about the situation. Nobody is doubting or denying among us that Jesus came into his Gethsemane. Was he raptured out of it into heavenly security? Or was his whole Gospel achieved by its costly acceptance?

Before turning to the decisive passages in the Qur'ān about Jesus' rejection and its sequel, it is vital to have this common ground understood – namely, a Jesus menacingly rejected by his context. This theme has been central in Chapter 5, reviewing the New Testament story. The Qur'ān constantly presents what perhaps we can call the occupational hazard of being a prophet. 'Some of them you said were liars, and some of them you put to death,' observes Surah 2:87. Was not Muḥammad himself reassured and fortified by the precedent of faithful predecessors who patiently bore contempt and intimidation? Jesus was among them, as the Qur'ān sees him and what it narrates about him at the close has to do with vindication, not immunity. There is nothing to vindicate where there is no calumny. Rescue would be pointless in the absence of menace.

It is, therefore, confusing and idle to say, as some Christians have said deploringly, 'the Qur'ān denies the crucifixion'. On the contrary, there are two vital senses in which it affirms it. For clarity's sake, divide 'crucifixion', as we must, into three elements: the will *to* it (on the part of perpetrators), the will *for* it (on the part of the sufferer), and the will *in* it (as it might be understood concerning God). The Cross, as an event that happened, would plainly be all three – that is, the act of men in wrong, the act of Jesus in love, and the act of God in grace. The Cross, as an event which was not allowed to happen, could still be nevertheless the first and second. That it was indeed the first and second would seem to be clear from the Qur'ān's own showing and *within* its own denial of its real and actual occurrence as a complete event. What the Qur'ān, and with it the whole corporate mind of Islam, denies is the third dimension, i.e. God's act. It is this which is totally precluded by every category of theology and faith. 'God was *not* in Christ reconciling the world to himself': he was with Jesus withdrawing him to heaven.

ii

That excluded element, however, crucial as it is in the Christian reckoning, does not eliminate the other two. Rather, it needs them for its own reading of the history. The will *to* crucifixion is intact. Otherwise, how could it be seen as thwarted? So we have to recognise and probe frankly the significance of the purpose to victimise Jesus. It is an important measure of what we think about our humanity, and about prophethood, its calling and its cost. There is no escaping the actuality of the Cross as an event intended and, being such, as an index to evil.

Given that intended situation, however, must we not also acknowledge a will *for* the cross in the soul of Jesus? The heavenly intervention which the Qur'ān affirms as happening was not, on Quranic ground, an eventuality present within the awareness of Jesus.[2] Faced with antagonism, Jesus, in both the Qur'ān and the Gospel, remains unflinching in loyalty to his mission. He draws towards the climax in readiness to face it. The Quranic dénouement is not within his sights. Even rescue, then, as a sudden, intervening reversal of danger, leaves us historically with a Jesus ready for suffering, with a real 'cross' as Jesus' act. Here, if anywhere, 'the readiness is all'. This means a Jesus, in the Qur'ān, very like the Jesus of the Gospels, even if the Quranic 'Īsā does not use this language: 'The cup which my Father has given me, shall I not drink it?' Unlooked for, and dramatic, rescue does not deprive us of such a quality in Jesus. Rather, it argues it. Otherwise, Jesus might have antecedently 'rescued' himself by compromise or abandonment of mission. In that event, Quranic 'rescue' would have been neither necessary nor appropriate.

The puzzling passage in Surah 3:55, where God's address to Jesus runs: 'O Jesus, I am causing you to die and will exalt you to Myself...', can well be read as the Qur'ān's clue to the inner experience of Jesus within that gathering sense of threat and rejection accompanying his ministry amid the vested interests and passions which he challenged. In his consciousness it must have seemed like an anticipation of death – death casting its shadow over his faithful course in God's Name. In that sense the inference is very close to the pattern of the Gospels. 'We are going up to Jerusalem and the Son of Man must suffer' (Mark 10:33). That Surah 3:55 has other interpretations we must see later, but they do not exclude this one, which is probably the most appropriate.

This will *for* the bearing of whatever a messenger's fidelity entails as being characteristic of Jesus in both Christian and Islamic perspectives is not, we must observe, some courting of martyrdom, some desire to precipitate divine action. Such a notion fits neither the Gospels nor the Qur'ān's '*I* [God] am causing you to die....' The occasion of suffering lies wholly in the setting: the will for it is entirely responsive to the claim of loyalty, within the situation, for God's sake. In all this Muslim and Christian are intelligently agreed. So it emerges that in the two important senses of the crucifixion as the purpose of men and as the self-giving of Jesus, the Qur'ān affirms it. Only because, for the Christian and his faith, the Cross is one whole actuality – men's act, Christ's act and God's act – is it necessary to say that the Qur'ān denies it. That 'denial' is, of course, radical and insistent. Yet it positively contains – or should we say retains – these two vital dimensions of its Christian significance.

The Quranic situation about Good Friday, then, is of an enmity disallowed its goal but not its intention, and of an anticipation of suffering spared its climax but not its testing and prelude. The purpose of enmity was halted in its tracks. The logic of the anticipation was miraculously reversed. There was no real death perpetrated, no actual dying required. It is these two negations which the Qur'ān presents as its own great positive view of the power and the wisdom of God. Our first duty is to explore the several interpretations of the pivotal passage on which negation rests, in order to elucidate, independently of any theological thinking, the Quranic account of what the event actually was, or was not, 'after Gethsemane'.

iii

That passage is in Surah 4:157–159. It comes in a context of accusation, on several counts, against the Jews, one of which is their assertion that 'they killed the Messiah, Jesus'. Some commentators have suggested that, while it is clearly denied that they did so, it is rather the alleged bravado, or boasting, behind the claim which is being reproached.[3] This view has been linked by some with the instinct to attribute all things to God, even when actually performed by evil men. On that score, 'killing the Messiah' would not be essentially a

Jewish deed but God's doing. Proponents of this reading link the passage with 5:17, which insists that 'if God wills to destroy the Messiah' no one can deny Him that power.

This predestinarian attribution of the crucifixion to God Himself in no way fits the thrust of the passage.

> ... the truth is they did not kill him, nor did they crucify him. They were under the illusion that they had. There is a lot of doubt about this matter among those who are at odds about it. They have no real knowledge but follow only surmise. Assuredly they did not kill him. On the contrary, God raised him to Himself.

Interpretation here may be said to be a question of pronouns and of one puzzling verb. Exploring it requires some simple technicalities of Arabic grammar. Pronouns, unless they are emphatic, are 'hidden' in the shape of their verbs. This is so with 'they did not kill ... they did not crucify....' The antecedent is certainly 'the Jews'. Since the hidden pronoun could, remotely, be some other agent, it has been suggested that the intention is to indicate a non-Jewish subject of the verb, probably 'the Romans' or, as just noted above, even 'God Himself'.[4] This makes havoc both of the Arabic construction and of the evident sense. If the context intended to substitute 'the Romans' it would surely have to say 'It was not they, the Jews, who killed him: it was the Romans'. There is no such construction here, nor could it tally, if there were, with the rest of the passage. We have no option but to read for 'they' 'the Jews'. We cannot escape the negation of crucifying by confusion as to the agent.

How then should the denial be understood? The answer brings us to the puzzling verb and to its own hidden pronoun. Some technicality is unavoidable here. *Shubbiha lahum* is here translated: '... they were under an illusion that they had' (i.e. 'crucified him'). That seems the most intelligent English, though there are many other turns of phrase, for example:

> Only a likeness of that was shown to them (Arberry)
>
> It only seemed to them as if it had been so (Asad)
>
> He was counterfeited for them (Bell)
>
> It appeared so unto them (Pickthall)
>
> So it was made to appear to them (Yusuf Ali)
>
> It was an illusion for them (Abd al-Latif)

The matter was made dubious to them (Muhammad Ali)

They thought they did (Dawood)

The verb is a passive, in the past tense, with the basic sense of 'to seem' made reflexive, i.e. 'made to seem', or 'to so appear'. There is a further derived sense (with which the rest of the passage is occupied), namely, 'to be obscure, or dubious'. The preposition with pronoun *lahum*, 'to them' suggests the translation 'they were under illusion that...' or, more clumsily, 'they were brought under the illusion that...' to get the reflexive force explicitly. The object of the preposition then becomes the subject of the English passive verb (passive via the preposition 'under the illusion').

What is the hidden subject pronoun of *shubbiha*? What was it within the illusion they were under? The two possibilities are 'he' and 'it'. Either 'he [i.e. Jesus] was ressembled to them', or 'it [crucifixion] was made to seem so to them'. On that hidden pronoun turns the decision whether we opt for a substitute sufferer, not the real Jesus, or whether we opt for an only 'apparent' crucifixion for Jesus himself? All exegesis turns on one or other of these alternatives and either of them has assumed confusing forms. The confusion is not only among the people in question in the passage and their conjectures: it is also very much among the commentators and their ingenuities. We have need to beware at all costs that Gethsemane does not just go out into controversy with only altercation under the olive trees.

Let us take the supposed-Jesus theory first. It has numerous forms in Islamic tradition. At some point at or after the arrest of Jesus another man was mistakenly seized and crucified in his stead while Jesus himself was raptured to heaven. The mistake in identity, on one view, was specifically caused by God, imparting to the substitute the exact features of 'the Messiah', so that the perpetrators were under the illusion that they had got their intended prey. The so-called Gospel of Barnabas, to be reviewed in Chapter 10, and Al-Saḥḥār, the author discussed in Chapter 3, identify the substitute as Judas Iscariot, thus condignly requited for his betrayal. Some suggest Simon of Cyrene, others a volunteer for the role sought from among the assembled disciples. We need not stay over these variants. The thought of Jesus' own assailant (named Titanus in some sources) or his betrayer, seized and crucified, makes a *bouleversement* attractive to certain casts of mind. In any event, there is a 'necessity' behind the thought, since a prophet is no true prophet if he is actually done to death. He must be rescued since otherwise he is discredited. The more melodramatic the issue the more total the vindication.

An actual 'likeness' cast upon another in a deliberate divine deception of evil men is not the only interpretation of *shubbiha* which takes the hidden pronoun to be personal, i.e. 'he' not 'it'. It could be a genuine mis-identity committed by the soldiers in the garden. Although this helps ethically it does not easily fit the Arabic of the passage where the negation, naturally read, is of the killing rather than of the victim supposed. It would, however, conduce to that later uncertainty as to the true facts which the following words indicate. All in all, it would seem wise to abandon the 'he' pronoun altogether as intended here and with it the whole unhappy notion of a substitute sufferer. It will surely help both Muslims and Christians, separately and together, if we can recognise the veritable, real and actual suffering identity of Jesus, in and through Gethsemane, and leave aside, once and for all, the belief that '*he* was ressembled to them'. That leaves us with the view that *shubbiha* refers to 'apparent' crucifixion, where it is not Jesus' involvement which is in doubt, but the manner and the point of it.

iv

To take this decision is in no way to terminate our problems. Let us consider first the way in which it may be factually alleged (as distinct from mysteriously alleged) that crucifixion was only apparent. It is the way adopted, among others, by the Aḥmadiyyah Movement.[5] On this showing, *mā qatalūhu*, 'they did not kill him', is quite literally true. On the actual cross, Jesus did not succumb. *Mā ṣalabūhu*, 'they did not crucify him', means that, while they actually nailed him to the Cross they did not cause him to die by so doing. For 'to crucify' has both these meanings. In normal, successful crucifixion, it is not necessary to distinguish between them. The nails and the agony do their work and have their grim climax in death by torture. It was not so, on this showing, in the case of Jesus. He was, indeed, thought to be dead and, supposedly a corpse, was taken down from the Cross, but life was still in him. This is held to be the 'apparentness' meant in Surah 4:157–159. Jesus revived in the tomb, rallied, drew vitality from his anointing, was spirited away eastward by the disciples and, as the Aḥmadiyyah believes, lived, taught and died at a great age in Kashmir.

This account of *shubbiha lahum* allows a 'natural' interpretation of those other Quranic verses which refer to the death of Jesus (3:55 and 19:33) which we have yet to review and which are puzzling otherwise.

But it runs into acute difficulty in respect of the following words: '...on the contrary, God raised him to Himself'. These align most naturally – as they have been assumed to do – with the view that Jesus escaped crucifixion and was there and then raptured to heaven. It would be odd indeed to insert between the two clauses a lengthened mortal story, an earthly sepulchre and resurrection at the last day. Moreover, the alleged Asian sojourn of Jesus requires the repudiation of all that is concrete in the Christian tradition – the emergence of the Church, the New Testament Scriptures, the Eucharist and the Canon. Taking Jesus into Asia may be read as a demur about the 'westward-ho' character of the New Testament record of expansion. It can hardly be credited as a total displacement of it, a radical rewriting of the sequel. Apostles, like Thomas, may well have carried their faith beyond the Indus River; but did they, or could they have done so, in these strangely different terms?[6]

There are other, more subtle, ways of handling the interpretation of the hidden pronoun in *shubbiha* as relating to a 'seeming' in the event, not a confusing of the person. These take us into a bewildering field of ideas about 'apparentness' and 'reality'. It is noteworthy that the verb *shubbiha* has the exact sense of *dokeo* (δοκέω) in Greek, the verb which gives name to the Docetics in the early Church – the people, that is, who understood the suffering of Jesus, even his very flesh also, as being only 'what seemed' and not 'what truly was'. It would be risky to relate the Quranic intention here to the Docetic influence, because of the long gap of centuries and the uncertainty of our knowledge about the survival of Docetism and its actual or potential impact in Muḥammad's context. Moreover, the underlying impulse to Christian Docetism lay through belief in, and theory of, the Incarnation and the desire to immunise 'divinity' from 'real' suffering and even from 'real' humanness, whereas the Islamic starting point throughout is a human Jesus, prophet and servant.

Nevertheless, there was, for the Qur'ān, a compelling reason – Christology apart – why Jesus should be preserved from ignominy and real death, namely, the credibility and authenticity of his prophetic role. If he were truly to have suffered and died, God must be understood to have deserted him and his whole status would thereby have been disowned. There are precedents, to be sure, in the Qur'ān of lesser messengers actually being martyred but, in the case of Jesus, as of Muḥammad, God their guardian, 'has the better of the schemers and plotters'. With Muḥammad there was 'manifest victory' in the open arena of the political and historical order. It was not so with Jesus.[7] Undestined as he was, in the world of Pilate and Caiaphas, to such evident success, there was all the more reason why his being *under* power as a victim, and not *in* power as a ruler, should eventuate in vindication. Perhaps it is fair to assume that the theme of the unreality of Jesus' suffering, so congenial to gnostics and the Manichees, should have found an echo in a Quranic verb and provide a theory by which commentators could understand it.

Is the clue, then, to assume that in some sense 'they were under an illusion' about crucifixion means that a *corpus phantasticum*[8] was what the crucifiers handled externally, while the true, veritable Jesus was no longer there within their clutches? The 'seeming', then, must be understood as a sort of charade. Or, Jesus dwelt essentially in an incorruptible body which was other than the apparent frame that could be crucified. Traces of these ideas occur in the Apocryphal New Testament[9] where, for example, in the *Acts of John* Jesus is said to have appeared to John on the Mount of Olives at the actual moment of crucifixion and assured him that it was all 'unreal'. Adoptionism, too, of which there are traces in the Qur'ān,[10] thought of Jesus residing only temporarily in an earthly body which, as the divine Christ, he might at any time vacate without any evident change. Humiliation and pain would be obvious circumstances in which, by this reckoning, to do so.[11]

In any or all of these ways, *shubbiha lahum* might be understood. Far removed as Islam is in its theology from originating these esoteric ideas, it could well have inherited them in the interests of its instincts away from the compromise humiliation implies for God's trusted servants. Further, in its own philosophical ventures or initiatives, Islam has generated mystical interpretations of prophethood which could readily accommodate esoteric attitudes to the exegesis of Jesus and his Cross. For example, Ibn 'Arabī (1172–1240 C.E.) one of the most famous, and elusive, of Muslim philosophers, commenting on Surah 4:156, ignores 'they did not kill him' altogether and goes at once to 'He raised him to Himself' and writes of the arrival in the fourth heaven of Jesus' spirit, 'which indicates the origin of his spirit', essentially distanced from the circumstances of the abandoned body in the physical order. Comparable readings of the meaning are natural to various forms of Sufism, and compatible too with some aspects of Shī'ah Islam with its doctrines of immaculate Imāms whose 'essence' is at once present in, and free of, corporeal, physical form, capable both of indwelling and transcending the bodily realm.

In this way, it is feasible to understand Surah 4 about the Cross in terms of 'everything goes out into mystery'. For example, Schuon[12] writes:

> When the Qur'ān appears to deny the death of Christ it can be understood to mean that in reality Jesus vanquished death, whereas the Jews believed they had killed the Christ in his very essence. Here the truth of the symbol prevails over the truth of the fact, in the sense that a spiritual negation takes the form of a material negation.

One might even, if coincidentally, link this with Hindu thinking on the unreality of the material order as being no more than appearance. 'The perpetrators,' writes Klaus Klostermaier, 'only saw *maya*, the body of Christ. They were ignorant of the real essence of Christ. Christ had not really died.'[13]

It would be wise not to attribute these esoteric interpretations at all widely among ordinary Muslims for many of whom they would be quite opaque and, if understood, suspect. But they do enable sensitive spirits to repudiate what they see as the crudity of identity divinely disguised. One such was Muḥammad Kāmil Ḥusain, who saw the *shubbiha* experience as a kind of veil, or curtain, run down between history and myth, between the world of fact and the world of symbol.[14] He wrote:

> The idea of a substitute for Christ is a very crude way of explaining the Quranic text. They had a lot to explain to the masses. No cultured Muslim believes in this nowadays. The text is taken to mean that the Jews thought they had killed Christ but God raised him unto Him in a way we can leave unexplained among the several mysteries which we have taken for granted on faith alone.

If 'they did not kill him ... it was an illusion they were under that they had' is rightly read as a negation of fact on behalf of a negation of significance, that the apparently tragic end was no end at all but a spiritual triumph, then clearly there is deep potential ground for Muslim/Christian meeting in such meaning. One might even find, in the 'seemingness' of the Cross, in reverent and careful sense, what Richard Crashaw[15] told in his poem of devotion:

> When on the Cross my King did bleed,
> Life *seemed* to die, death died indeed

More prosaically, this approach to the 'seeming' cross tallies with what the Surah says about the dubiety clinging to the event. That dubiety does not extend to the event itself. 'Assuredly they did not kill him,' insists the Qur'ān.[16] However, it did extend to the actors and narrators, then and later. Disguise, false identification, substitute-sufferer, presence and absence, appearance and reality – all these, whatever the exegesis, would tend to confusion, surmise, contention and debate, intensifying into partisanship, multiplying both curiosity and passion. Ordinary Muslims, believing themselves above this, see their Qur'ān as categorically terminating it. As we have seen, that conclusiveness is either itself debatable (substitution, etc.) or mysterious (the 'illusionists'). Either way, in the perspectives both of Christianity and Islam, an issue remains. It is surely best to acknowledge it frankly and to let it stand. Christianity lives by the confession of Jesus, veritably crucified and risen; Islam lives in the conviction that Jesus did not really die but was mysteriously received up into heaven. In respect of Surah 4:157–159, then, we differ about 'the nature of the fact', to borrow Schuon's phrase, because we also differ about 'the nature of the symbol'. Before coming to this, however, what – briefly – of other passages in the Qur'ān concerning the death of Jesus?

V

'Peace upon me the day I was born, the day I die, and the day of my being brought back alive', Surah 19:33 reports Jesus as saying. Zachariah invokes the same 'peace', in identical terms, upon his son John in 19:15. The most natural sense of the words would be resurrection after real death. Those in Islam who hold the 'illusionist' view of Surah 4:157–159, or who understand the rapture of a Jesus who escaped the Cross by substitution, must read his 'death' here in terms of the eschatological tradition noted in Chapter 3, when 'being brought back' (*uba'thu ḥayyan*) must mean a resurrection from the grave in Medina. For 'to be brought back' requires the burial which Christian orthodoxy, as we must see below, has always understood as credally vital. It cannot signify the rapture or exaltation which in the *shubbiha lahum* passage requires the negation of real or actual dying. It may be said to be strange to have to read 19:33 as having long, long centuries between its second and third events.

There remains the passage in 3:55, *Innī mutawaffīka*, addressed by God to Jesus. The verb, used only of God, almost invariably indicates death, as the culmination of life's reckoning, the finalising of mortal accountability. We have seen that it might well fit the inward experience of Jesus in 'the gathering storm' against his ministry. It might even comprehend the traditional 'rescue', given his unawareness that it was impending. Followed as it is, however, by 'I am raising you to Myself' (the verb used in 4:157 in different form), it is hard to see how it could relate to a deathless rapture or to a long delayed demise, whether in Kashmir or post-millenial, followed by resurrection from a grave deferred. There is an immediacy about the passage in 3:55 which seems, in all normal assessment, to require real dying and prompt resurrection – in other words, what the Christian faith affirms as the climax of the very real travail the phrase implies. This point was registered by the great exegete, Al-Baiḍāwī, who included among various possibilities of the passage the idea, opposed to the 'swoon' theory, that God did actually allow Jesus to die on the Cross and to remain dead for seven hours, prior to rapture into heaven. A real demise seems also to be required in 5:117, where the same root is used in the past tense, with an echo of John 17:12, by Jesus addressing God and saying: 'While I was among them (the disciples) they were my constant concern, but when You called me home it was You who were their guardian, watchful as You are over all things.'

Leaving, if inconclusively, the passages in the Qur'ān which directly pronounce on the sequel to Gethsemane, it will be wise to pursue our task by developing the clue of fact and symbol suggested by Frithjof Schuon. Christians, too, believe in Christ's 'Ascension', and it is clear they have something of the problem Muslims have about the imagery of 'assumption' into heaven and its relation to bodily personhood whether in, through, or without death. Indeed, Muḥammad Kāmil Ḥusain says of the curtain between the before and the after of Jesus' Quranic rapture that it corresponds to the New Testament 'Ascension', and that both represent the 'frontier' between time and eternity – a frontier not to be crossed either by the curious or the dogmatic. It is true that the New Testament, as in Phil. 2:9, conflates resurrection and ascension and sees them as one inclusive exaltation. But it steadily and repeatedly insists on a real and actual dying of Jesus and confirms this with '... and that he was buried' (e.g. 1 Cor. 15:4 where Paul is rehearsing the 'tradition' he received and handed on). This has passed, equally firmly, into the Christian Creeds: '... was crucified, dead and buried ...' and '... he suffered and was buried ...'

Why this emphasis? Would it not be possible for Christians to fall in with the Quranic assurance of the ultimate eminence, heavenly authenticity, vindication and authority of Jesus (denote it how we will) and leave in reverent mystery the precise detail of this sublime and blessed climax related to mortal flesh and blood, to wood and nails and oils of burial? Does not 1 Tim. 3:16 say: 'Great is the mystery of our religion'? Why not confess it so and let the matter stay?

vi

To some the suggestion may appeal. But much else appeals insistently against it. The reason why is that behind the question of history is the question of man and of God. If, despite the inconclusiveness we have reviewed, there is a Quranic consensus to say 'To Jesus at the Cross death did not happen', there is also an Islamic consensus to say, further, 'It need not happen, and, moreover, it should not happen'. It did not, historically, it need not redemptively, and it should not morally, happen to Jesus. Such is the threefold Muslim commentary against the firm Christian faith that it did, necessarily, and it ought – however disconcertingly – to happen.

The historical issue, historically taken, has been sufficiently studied in all the foregoing here and in Chapter 5. It is fair to say, however, that, for Muslims in this field, history was never just for historians. Perhaps it never is. Historians are always more than mere narrators, and events are never just bare facts. Islamic convictions about Jesus and the Cross have never simply been those of mere investigators dealing with evidence. They have been those of believers persuaded already by theology. It is these *à-priori* grounds of what is held as to history which must concern us now. Historicity is involved inextricably with the larger theme of what *ought* to be, what requires to be, and these are determined by how we think of God and how we perceive our humanity.

This is only another way of relating 'the nature of the symbol' to 'the nature of the fact'. What, then, for Christians, is the nature of the symbol in, for them, the fact of Jesus, 'crucified, dead and buried, raised the third day'? It is the Cross, fact and symbol, as the point or measure of what John, in his Gospel, calls 'the sin of the world' and Jesus acknowledged as its bearer. The real world of our humanity would not be truly 'symbolised' where the Cross was not a fact. The crucifying of Jesus takes the sounding line of honesty about ourselves down to the last, the lowest, fathom. There is, at the heart of Christian faith, that which will not let us superficialise our sense of human wrong. Mankind does go to *those* lengths in pursuit of its personal and collective interests, its distortion of its true being. If we are ever to be righted it can only be by realising how wrong we are. Salvation can only belong where the tragedy is. This is why the New Testament, and the Creeds, are committed to 'Christ crucified'.

One might interject: was it not argued earlier that the *will* to crucify, even when frustrated or diverted, sufficed to measure the wrong just as if it had been in fact accomplished? Indeed, but consider that frustration, whether eventuating by disguise, or error, or illusion. Does it not leave the guilty as they were - confused, angry, provoked, resentful, or baffled - probably all these - and, therefore, perverse still? They remain in the entail of their evil will, denied an objective but not disowning a wrong. In New Testament language, they are not 'loosed from their sin'. Forgiveness requires forgivingness, and there is none in a situation where the will for it is neither present in suffering nor sought in guilt-awareness.

Of course, it is well to forestall or circumvent evil by means of intervention, human or divine. Surah 22:40 observes that many places of worship would have been destroyed had not God countered the designs of evil men. This theme of necessary action for security and resistance to wrong is very familiar in Islam. Aḥmad Shawqī, for example, in his *Al-Shawqiyyāt*, is sure that evil can only be met by counteraction. Insisting that 'evil stops at nothing', he adds that Jesus himself, despite his goodness, would have been nailed to the Cross but for God's intervention'.[17] The Qur'ān is right (22:40) in seeing all faiths and cultures as one in this concern to ensure their safety.

The faith that came through Jesus' Cross in the New Testament does not see this security preoccupation as either the fact, or the symbol, of salvation. There are two reasons. First, in the real world immunity and security do not everywhere avail. There *is* tragedy. There *is* suffering which has to be vicariously 'taken' and its inflicters forgiven. Secondly - again in the real world - the element of evil in the resistance, though it may safeguard and defend effectively, does not positively redeem the evil it resists, nor of itself redeem the evil-doers. As we have seen, it may well arrest a situation: it does not deeply restore it. Its sequel may even be to complicate, or entrench, or perhaps, paradoxically, justify, the initial wrong it successfully, or dubiously, restrains.

So it is, that without denying the actualities of human 'relative evils', and the necessity of action in society by which the lesser may resist the greater, Christian faith believes that it needs, and has received, a fact and a symbol, inseparably, in Jesus crucified. In that fact and symbol the human tragedy is taken in its fullest measure, evil is vicariously borne, and being borne is borne away. The fact and symbol thereby constitute a sacrament of that one power by which, in the end and in the whole, all evil is redeemed. It is the power of the love that faces and undergoes the worst that we can do in sinfulness and for that very reason masters it without remainder and so accomplishes our forgiveness. This is how we understand what the New Testament sees as the necessity of the Cross, and Jesus tells his disciples: 'Ought not the Christ to have suffered these things?' (Luke 24:26) when, by every criterion of safety, prestige and popularity, he 'ought *not*'.

Any different fact, any lesser symbol, would not be – as Christianity sees it – the redeeming thing. Nor would it be a deep enough ground of hope and trust, nor adequate to the reality of evil. Nor on all these counts would it be appropriate for God. For, as will be explored more fully in Chapter 7, the matter of Jesus and the Cross takes us where we must all surely be ready to be taken, namely, into our understanding of God.

Nor should we let some reluctance here deter us – a reluctance to appear to be *requiring* things of God or subjecting the divine ways to our human thoughts. Is there not a sense, it will be asked, that we are forbidding liberty to God, if we say that His forgiveness must necessarily be through a pattern of suffering and that it cannot be without something like the Cross? Many in Islam have sensed this danger deeply and insisted, out of their confidence in divine competence, that His forgiveness of us is effortless and majestic, needing no saviourhood to enable Him. 'He only says "Be," and it is' (cf. Surah 3:59, of Adam's creation: his pardon is surely easier). May not our Christian sense that it is only through the suffering Christ that our pardon comes be, or seem to be, a limitation on God?

vii

It is right that this reluctance should suggest itself and come to mind, since the confidence in divine mercy is sound. But on reflection it surely melts away. It is clear that the redemptive action in Christ is truly the pattern of God's competence. Mercy, like justice and all else in God of which human experience is cognisant, is relational. Necessities are then within the order of things which God Himself has established within creation and in harmony with His own holiness and grace.[18] Shall we be wrong in believing that God meets and finds us at the rendezvous necessitated by our need as His creatures, that where we are in waywardness is where He restores us in mercy? Then the dimension of necessity arises within the nature of our humanness and the divine compassion is indeed under no constraint but its own free magnanimity.

Further, there is no escape, either way, from understanding God's ways with us under patterns of our own thought. Those who question the necessity of the Cross on the ground that forgiveness is effortless with God may be forbidding Him the will and power the Cross can measure. That He may not stoop to *that* compassion is no less a prohibition by dogma than to believe He will not forgive without it. Adamantly to exclude the Cross of Jesus from the wisdom of God is not truly to believe *Allāhu akbar*. It is, rather, to withhold from His greatness what may well be its greatest measure and sign. We *may* be wrong to hold that it is, but to exclude it essentially is to limit God no less – perhaps more – than to believe the principle of the Cross to be indispensable.

Many at this point will, of course, fall back on their respective revelation and take the issue dogmatically out of human reflection and initiative of mind. But, as long as we have disparate authorities turning on partially exclusive Scriptures we can only bring their contents and our loyalties into conversation by ventures of spirit and mutual interpretation.

The issue between us over the Cross as that which need not happen is often beset by the question of whether our human situation anyway is susceptible of such 'being-suffered-for' by another. Here we pass into the Islamic confidence, broadly speaking, that what need not happen *should* not happen. Shī'ah Islam has other thoughts here. But Sunnī Islam shrinks instinctively from the thought that any soul can be chargeable for what is not its own. Our evil doing is inalienable and belongs uniquely to each evil-doer separately accountable. The study of Paul in Chapter 8 will elucidate what is at stake here, while Chapter 7 will study more squarely the theme of redemption within the heart of God. Our present concern in Gethsemane, is with this deeply rooted Islamic hesitancy about seeing Jesus there – even allowing him there – as somehow bearing evil – evil of ours – and so serving our forgiveness. Such belief, it is said, is immoral. Jesus cannot have been a victim this way, not only because the Cross did not, and need not, happen but because on every count of divine power and moral meaning it should not happen.

The revulsion against 'shuffling the cards' of guilt, against false exoneration and incrimination, is proper and urgent. 'No man may deliver his brother ...', Psalm 49:7 (P.B.V.) assures us. The strong personalism of the Qur'ān about ethical responsibility is akin to the Gospel's. Our guilt, truly, is our own. But, in the words to be pondered in the chapter on Paul, we are 'in Adam'. We are part of a human solidarity in which the guilt of some persons becomes the pain of others. In the web of home, family, society and mankind, we are forever suffering *from* each other, *by* each other and *in* each other. While the guilt is inward and inalienable, the consequences are social. In wronging ourselves in what the Qur'ān calls *ẓulm al-nafs*, we also do evil against others and against God.

The crucial question about the evil, outward consequences of our inward sins and guilt is *how* they are taken by those they injure, grieve, wrong and violate. Do they not have to be so 'taken' that they are 'taken away'? There is no positive forgiveness in restraining though, as we have seen, this may be right and urgent. Retaliation, if that is the response, will, to be sure, repay the wrong, and 'get our own back' (as we say); but it will also sharpen the wrong done, keep it alive, accentuate it, even 'justify' it. Only 'taking' wrong forgivingly, takes it away. The wrong-doer has then no cause to perpetuate his enmity, no reason to despair of himself and no occasion to entrench himself in evil. On the contrary, there is in his neighbour's 'peace' that which closes the account, frees the spirit from enmity and hate, restores the broken community between the persons, and truly 'overcomes evil with good'. We cannot have it so, however, without knowing that a cost is borne, is readily and sacrificially paid, by the soul that wills forgiveness, whose 'peace' is active, compassionate and ready.

There is nothing 'immoral' here, no conspiracy against truth, no connivance about guilt. On the contrary, the will to forgive registers the nature of evil more utterly than any calculus of blame or condemnation because, while these only repudiate, love reconciles. If, in our frail and faltering human relationships, we see and know this redemptive principle, shall we faithlessly exclude it from the competence of God? 'Shall the creature surpass the Creator?' as the poet Browning asked.[19] Or shall we allow that 'God is greater than our heart'? It is clear in the Qur'ān (cf. 30.30) that there is *ẓulm* against God. His forgivingness will hardly be less adequate, less ready, less positive, than ours. Will the dimension of cost be any less vital because it is divine? The measure of the cost is the measure of the violation and everything, with God, is immeasurably greater.

viii

It is this conviction which lies behind the Christian faith that there is, as the central clue in history to the divine/human relationship, the fact and the symbol of the Cross. Thus it is possible to identify in what happens after Gethsemane the power and the wisdom of God in the reconciling of the world. If we can believe that the human will to crucify Jesus in the context we have studied constitutes a factual focus of the evil world we share, and if we can believe Jesus' will to 'take' that evil as he did, then in his forgivingness ('Father, forgive ...') we can rightly recognise the divine pattern of mercy and say that 'God was in Christ reconciling the world'. Our instinct to say that it need not, or it should not, happen will be reversed into the assurance that here we see into the heart of things and have reason to be glad. God becomes credible indeed in all that, as theists, we have believed Him to be – Creator, Lord of history and Lord of mercy.

'Beyond Gethsemane' has another point for us here. Suppose we allow Christians the conclusion they have reached, then the question persists: why the implied exclusiveness here? What, as so much Jewish thinking stresses,[20] are we to say about its seeming denial in the unredeemedness of the world today? Is it not all so long ago? Why should we see this redemptive principle (if see it we do) so exceptionally in Jesus and the Cross?

'Exceptionally' could be a misleading word. On the one hand, Christianity sees the Cross as a unique and definitive event, the sort of once-for-all inclusive fact which in its own idiom, Islam sees in the giving of the Qur'ān – something decisive by which all else is to be assessed and determined. On the other hand, the Cross, by its very quality, calls for emulation. It has to be taken up.[21] Those who know themselves redeemed by its power are called to become themselves redeemers through its secret. The world is, indeed, redeemed representatively and inclusively, but its redemption has to be continually practised in the same terms. 'What is lacking in the sufferings of Christ' (Col. 1:24) is not their efficacy but their imitation. The necessary reproduction of their reconciling pattern is truly enabled, as Christians believe, because they have truly happened once and for all, there and then. The fact is in the symbol and the symbol lives in the fact. The redeemedness of the world through Christ crucified is not a static romance but a vital order of grace. Its unredeemedness is not the evidence of misreading the Cross of Jesus but of the task of the Cross today. Contemporary redemption cannot emulate its charter except in the power of its once-for-all event.

It is in this way that Christianity wants to make its history and faith transparent for the comprehension of people in their religions or in their irreligion. To affirm the reality, the physical and theological reality, of the death of Jesus as the clue to redemption then, before and since, is – as Christians believe – truly to 'acknowledge God', 'God in Christ reconciling'. In doing so we are truly in the meaning of the Resurrection.

The difference between rescue and exaltation in Quranic terms and resurrection and exaltation in New Testament terms, is just this dimension of the love that suffers. The Gospels understand the risen Christ, not as a phantom, or a seeming, or a puzzle, but as the real and actual Lord, alive through his passion, he who 'was dead' and 'ever lives': as the Cross, so the Resurrection, in the same harmony of fact and symbol.

ix

We do not see the Resurrection as some inexplicable development somehow, in arbitrary terms, reversing the whole drama of Good Friday. It stands within the experience of salvation and explains it. Witness to it, on the part of the disciples, meant a complete transformation of the Messianic theme. Jesus died as a rejected Messiah and such a death should have been the end of his claim. That his shattered disciples were brought to the conviction of the truth of his claim because of such a death *is* the meaning of Resurrection. Easter is a statement of salvation through Jesus, grounded in what the New Testament presents as two inter-related facts and signs: 'he is not here, he is risen'.

The first fact/sign is a negative one: '... not here ...', the empty tomb. It had been occupied. That is the credal point, as we have seen, of '... and was buried'; but according to the Gospels it was found untenanted. While the simple fact of its empty state is nowhere highlighted in the apostolic preaching or in the Epistles, its 'not here', negative witness is important. The vacant sepulchre *could* be explained in terms of a stolen corpse, or a mistaken belief about which tomb it was, or by some other conceivable circumstance. In that event, however, it seems right to assume that the actual corpse of Jesus could, and would, have been produced by the authorities, bent on extinguishing the preaching of a risen Lord as obviously the most effective means of doing so, certainly far more conclusive than persecution. That this did not happen could be taken as confirming that only resurrection explained the vacant 'place where he was laid'.

Even so, the faith of the Resurrection does not stand in the circumstance of an empty place, i.e. in the failure of an effort at a detective solution to a riddle. Let us take the "not here" about the grave by the analogy of the artist's canvas and the artist's art. A landscape painting needs a canvas to carry it and pigments to enshrine it, but the landscape is not these. Chemical tests on the fabric would not give us the beauty. This resides and yet transcends. The fabric only carries the significance which is other than itself. This is why the Gospels pass to '... he is risen'. Otherwise, 'not here' could be a desolating and shattering mystery, as indeed it was to the disciples, until they encountered Jesus himself.

That experience, also, was both fact and sign. The fact was the realisation of forgiveness, of peace, of fulfilment and of the inclusive clue to God and themselves, in a suffering Messiah recognised in Jesus. The sign was themselves, what they became and the church community they discovered in the meaning of that recognition.

How this was so, particularly in the experience of Paul (Chapter 8) and in the witness of John in the Fourth Gospel (Chapter 9), will concern us below. It takes us first into the central Christian theological convictions to be explored in the next chapter.

Noting that the present chapter is ending, the reader may well be concluding that we have been too 'theological' already. 'Gethsemane and Beyond' surely requires a more factual treatment of events after Jesus was arrested there, the drama and reporting of his 'trial', and the grim nature of the verdict and its execution. The Gospels are graphic enough and any reader can repair to them. Historians – Christian, Jewish and others – take issue over points of detail. What they have between them about which to differ leaves compellingly intact the blessed paradox of majesty in shame and authority in humiliation which has held the Christian centuries in awe and grateful wonder recognising the wisdom of God. It would seem to be our best plan to have the 'trial' of Jesus – for reasons which will there be clear – in the care of Chapter 9 devoted to 'Jesus and John'.

Notes

1 See R. A. Nicholson, *Studies in Islamic Poetry* (Cambridge, 1921), pp. 170–71 and p. 130.

2 This is not to overlook the passage in Matt. 26:53, where Jesus rebukes Peter's hasty unsheathing of a sword, with the words: 'Thinkest thou that I cannot now pray to my Father and He shall presently give me more than twelve legions of angels?' Rather, the passage reinforces the case. Had such arbitrary 'rescue' been in Jesus' ken, it would have been more effective than Peter's blundering intervention. Jesus' repudiation of both shows that rescue was in no way a desired climax. In any event the incident of the sword occurs only at the last chapter of the crisis. That Jesus reached there by deliberate fidelity to vocation, excluding all disloyal escapism, is entirely clear from the whole shape and logic of the Gospels' narrative. That readiness is totally incompatible with either an expectation, or a 'policy', of evasion, personal or celestial.

3 The antecedent clauses in the lead-up to the pivotal words about claiming to have crucified Jesus would lend credence to this view. Al-Baiḍāwī, for example, suggests that in the dubiety over the identity of the 'crucified' some tried to brazen it out and still claim that they had 'killed' Jesus. Such insistence would be akin to their 'calumny against Mary', i.e. asserting something unthinkable (and, of course, untrue) for their own perverse pride.

4 See, for example, R. C. Zaehner in *Christianity and Other Religions* (New York, 1964), p. 105. Cf. the same author's *At Sundry Times* (London, 1958), pp. 195–217. The negation in the passage is of an event, not of one set of perpetrators with a view to accusing another set.

5 Founded in the last quarter of the nineteenth century by Mirzā Ghulām Aḥmad, who combined personal claims, in some sense, to 'prophethood', with strong anti-Christian animus which led him to counter belief in Jesus' resurrection with a claim that, like Muḥammad, he was in fact in an earthly grave. There may also have been a half-conscious desire to 'detach' Jesus from western 'possession', by bringing him as a preacher to India and honourably interring him, at a great age, in Kashmir.

6 The evidences were offered in Al-Hajj Khwaja Nazir Ahmad, *Jesus in Heaven on Earth* (Lahore, 1952). See review by George Johnston in *The Muslim World*, vol. XLII, no. 4, 1953, pp. 287–93.

7 It will have been evident from Chapters 3 and 5 why this is so and how it contrasts with Islam. For many Muslims the non-militancy of Jesus is seen as a privation, a circumstance of limitation (as compared with the concreteness of Muḥammad's achievement) arising from the irreducibility of the Roman power; but, since Jesus was in no position to challenge that power structure, he must not be left humiliated as its victim. Hence the rapture to heaven as his 'vindication'. The power success of Muḥammad, on this reckoning, becomes an index to his ultimacy as more 'final' than the faithful Jesus. More discerning Islamic study of the New Testament, however, sees that the pattern of Jesus was in no sense a necessity of circumstance, but a clear, deliberate and consistent set of his soul.

8 This term was frequent in the prolonged debates and controversies occasioned by Docetism as a widespread heresy of the early Christian centuries. The name (from the Greek verb *dokeo*, 'to be apparent' or 'to seem'), akin to *shubbiha*, denotes the idea that 'the flesh' of Jesus was somehow 'unreal', and that the divine could only seemingly be involved in the human and in the actual. Within the New Testament (for example, in Col. 2:8, 1 John 4:2–3, and 2 John Chapter 7), we find repudiation of this view as utterly incompatible with – indeed lethal to – the authentic Gospel. Nourished by Gnosticism, though, the heresy had a persistent currency. Irenaeus, for example, was at pains to insist that 'Christ performed his works not in appearance but in actual reality ... truly possessing flesh and blood ...' (*Adversos Haer*. V.1:2). Tertullian also, writing against Marcion, strenuously disavows the *corpus phantasticum* idea (*Adv. Marc*. III. 8:11 in *Patrologia Latinae*, II, 331–336).

9 In *The Apocalypse of Peter*, a gnostic text from Nag Hammadi 81:4–24, translated by J. Brashler, is the following:

> I saw him apparently being seized by them and I said: 'What am I seeing, Lord? Is it really you whom they take? And are you holding on to me? And are they hammering the feet and hands of another? Who is this one above the cross, who is glad and laughing?' The Saviour said to me: 'He whom you saw being glad and laughing above the cross is the living Jesus. But he whose hands and feet they are driving the nails in is his fleshly part, which is the substitute. They put to shame that which remained in his likeness. Look at him – and me.'

Some Coptic Gospel texts, however, like *The Gospel of Truth* do concede the reality of Jesus' death. *The Gospel of Peter* (V.10) interprets the silence of Jesus on the cross as of one who feels no pain. Eusebius, in his *Ecclesiastical History* (VI. 12:3–6), cites the *Gospel of Peter* in this sense and condemns it. The notion of the amusement of the 'real' Jesus above the cross at the outwitting of the perpetrators is denounced, among others, by Irenaeus who, in *Adv. Haer*. I.24:4, attributes a version of it to Basilides, a prominent gnostic. It may be relevant to note that the followers of Julius of Halicarnassus in the sixth century, called *Aphthartodoketai*, had missions in Syria, Persia and Iraq and, by 565, under Emperor Justinian became the mandatory teachers of the official doctrine as to Christ's body. Their name means that, being 'incorruptible', the body of Christ in their belief only *seemed* to have the natural qualities of human flesh and blood. It must remain a matter of surmise whether, and how far, these Christian issues around the Greek verb *dokeo* and its doctrinal currency are to be linked with the *shubbiha* of Surah 4:157.

10 Where the Qur'ān passes judgement on the Christian faith in the Incarnation of Jesus it uses the term *ittikhādh*, or the verb *ittakhadha*, which strictly means 'to adopt' or 'to take to oneself [with *waladan*] a son.' This properly understood is 'adoptionism', i.e. the doctrine that a human Jesus was 'elevated' into divinity and so, as it were, deified. The sense of the Christian faith is just the reverse of this, i.e. the coming into flesh, for sublimely divine purposes, of 'the Word from all eternity' *not* 'and was made, or accounted, God', *but* 'and was made man'. The Qur'ān does not reckon with the distinction. The fact remains that though it may intend to deny the second, what in terms it denies is only the first. We may assume that it intends to exclude both in its conviction that the divine ways with the human scene are limited to prophetic education, to messengerships in tuition of man. Cf. Surahs 17:11, 19:35, 19:92 and 39:4. The same term is used of pagans 'adopting' a deity.

11 So, for example, thought Cerinthus, one of the earliest Docetics in the first century, for whom Christ resided only temporarily in the body of Jesus and left it before the crucifixion, being incapable of bearing suffering. This doctrine may be the source of the idea of a substitute in Simon of Cyrene, doing duty for the ghost-like immateriality of the 'real' Christ in the drama of death. See B. Hagglund, *A History of Theology*, trans. G. J. Lund (London, 1968), p. 80.

12 F. Schuon, *Comprendre L'Islam* (Paris, 1961), pp. 27–8. (Translated by D. Matheson, London, 1963.)

13 Klaus Klostermaier, *Hindu and Christian in Vrindaban* (London, 1969), p. 54.

14 Muḥammad Kāmil Ḥusain, *City of Wrong*, trans. Kenneth Cragg (Amsterdam, 1958), p. 222.

15 Richard Crashaw, *Poetical Works of Richard Crashaw and Quarles' Emblems* (Edinburgh, 1857), p. 146.

16 The emphasis on *yaqīnan*, 'assuredly', is taken in some quarters as simply insisting that, whatever the surmises and debatings, the central fact is the negation of any real crucifixion in respect of Jesus. *Both* the notion that it happened *and* the copious argumentation can be terminated together.

17 Aḥmad Shawqī, *Al-Shawqiyyāt* (Cairo, 1948), vol. 1, p. 242.

18 There is, of course, an almost insuperable Islamic counter-necessity to repudiate such 'necessity' in respect of God and, therefore, a complete unreadiness to take the issue *into* the divine nature where, as argued here, it ceases to require the counter-necessity that excludes it. Either way, it is important to see that the Muslim view also puts God 'under necessity' (albeit on behalf of His majesty and immunity). Islam is found forbidding things to God, by its own lights, just as Christianity is found attributing them. All turns on how we conceive of His transcendence and its quality, not on whether or not we are unwarrantably submitting Him to 'limitation'.

19 Robert Browning, *Poetical Works* (Oxford, 1940 edn), 'Saul', p. 231.

20 The writings of Elie Wiesel are an eloquent case in point with their powerful intimation of Jewish tragedy. Earlier this century Leo Baeck described the Christians as sheer 'romantics' by virtue of their 'witness' that Messiah had 'come' and that the world was 'redeemed'. How can such belief be other than romantic given what one writer called 'the bloody body of our people' and 'the unredeemedness of the world'? 'Judaism ...' wrote Leo Baeck, 'does not pretend to bring heaven to earth', implying that Christianity does so 'pretend'. See his *The Essence of Judaism*, trans. W. Kaufmann (Philadelphia, 1948), p. 13.

21 As Jesus affirms in the Gospels. His saying (Matt. 10:38, 16:24; Mark 8:34, 10:21; Luke 9:23, 14:27) is the more remarkable in that, as a metaphor prior to Jesus' own

crucifixion, it could only be heard as a most stark suggestion. Heard after the Cross itself it could only mean the call to proceed in all evil situations by those same criteria of decision that had brought Jesus to Gethsemane. 'Romanticism' seems then the last thing to allege against such a focus of identity and obedience.

Chapter 7

The Decisive Faith: 'God in Christ'

i

'This is why My people will know My Name. On that day they will understand that it is I who say: "Behold, I am here."' So run the prophet's words in Isaiah 52:6. He was looking forward to a decisive experience in which, and from which, there would be an assured knowledge of God rooted in the confidence that it was God Himself who had imparted it. We need not stay here over what he had in mind, nor over where and when – or whether – his expectation came to pass. We simply borrow his clear insistence that his hope turns on three factors. First, it has to do with an eventfulness there, actually in history – a story which will be told and cherished in experience. Secondly, that story – lived through and treasured – pre-supposes a community, 'My people', among whom and about whom it happens. Thirdly, that 'happenedness', with the knowledge it brings, is God's own doing, since, on every count, it takes God to reveal God. If we are authentically to know Him we must know the revelation to be His.

Christian faith in God, as the New Testament defines it, has exactly these three characteristics. It is bound up with the 'story' of Jesus – teacher, healer, master, sufferer, Messiah-redeemer – which we have now traced. Of that history it understands God saying: 'Behold, I am here.' 'It is I who say.' Its understanding the story so, is the corporate mind and conviction of a community which owes its very existence to that reading of its source in Christ. Its entire theology moving, through and beyond the New Testament, into mature confession, stands altogether in the assurance that 'all – history, meaning, community, faith – is of God, who has reconciled us to Himself by Jesus Christ' (2 Cor. 5:18).

Our duty in this chapter is to explore this faith as to 'God in Christ', to relate it carefully to Islamic concerns and to understand the interaction between the crucial history, the perceiving community and the divine credentials taken to be God-given. It is right to stress that all three Semitic faiths incorporate the sense of history in their clues about God and, comparably, believe that those clues are divinely underwritten. This is very evident in the Judaic tradition of exodus and exile, of covenant at Sinai and of kingship in David. In different terms there is for Muslims the incidence of divinely attested truth in and through the prophethood of Muḥammad. Muḥammad constitutes the point of 'association' within Islam between God and the human world, the context in which men experience God's ways and God's mercy. For example, Surah 3:31: 'Say: "If you love God, follow me; God will love you and forgive you your evil doings. For God is forgiving and merciful."' Here divine mercy and forgiveness 'coincide' (we might almost say) with love to Muḥammad by the Muslim, and the 'juncture' of the two is affirmed in a divinely decreed statement: 'Say.'

Christian faith, again in its different way, believes in 'association' between human experience – and so knowledge – of God at the distinctive rendezvous of Jesus in his actuality as the Christ. When Paul, in 2 Cor. 5:19 tells his Corinthian readers that 'God was in Christ reconciling the world to Himself . . .', he means that what transpired in Jesus' ministry and suffering transcribes the very love of God. The event arouses the recognition of faith and the faith recognises what the event really was. We will need to study later why Christianity distinctively centres its clue-history in a Cross, that is, in an inclusive encounter of love with evil. That has to do with how doctrines about God cannot be separated from realism about man. For the moment, however, given the wide disparities between the focal point of revelation in Islam and Christianity, the factor of historical 'association' is uncannily similar. John 16:27 has Jesus saying: 'The Father Himself loves you because you have loved me and have believed that I came forth from God'. That could readily be aligned with Surah 3:31, just quoted, as also might Matt. 10:40: 'He that receives me receives Him that sent me,' where Jesus links his own reception by his disciples with their relation to God. The setting, to be sure, is different – even contrasted – but the principle of communal knowledge of the divine via a sphere which is index to it is identical.

That the index must bear the divine imprint is vital to its proper credence. Just as what is not divine must not be so regarded, what *is* authentically divine must be faithfully acknowledged. One must never bring worship to the wrong object, but one must never withhold it from the right one. The problem, of course, is rightly to identify the only one truly worshipable. Some Muslims have translated *Lā ilāha illa-Allāh*, as 'Not God unless God', to be read as a warning that a true worship must always discriminate against a false. This was what Islam in its very essence was set to do. The Christian claims a similar vigilance. The proof that Christian theology has never abandoned it is evident in the fact that its acknowledgement of 'God in Christ' relies on the warrant, as it believes, of God Himself. It is not, therefore, acting irresponsibly or without credentials. The crucial question is what the credentials are and how we know them to be such. The issue, then, between Islamic and Christian theology is not that about acknowledging God rightly, which we both seek to do. It is about how, and by what criteria, He is rightly recognised. What we both need here is not recrimination about our theologies but patience about their frames of reference.

A significant refrain in the Qur'ān about the pagans may help us in this context. Surahs 6:91, 22:74 and 39:67 say that 'they did not reckon God a right reckoning' (*Mā qadarū Allāha ḥaqqa qadrihi*). 'They did not esteem God with a true esteeming.' We might paraphrase the meaning by saying: 'They did not realise God's reality'. Mysticism, Islamic or otherwise, might read that verdict in a highly elusive sense having to do with persistence in the illusion of separateness and failure to enter the unitive state in which the self is lost (*al-fanā'*) in the all-embracing One. (*Al-Ḥaqq* is often read in that sense by Sufism.) The Qur'ān does not mean the words that way. The contexts have to do with idolatry, with disbelief of the Prophet and with unconcern about final judgement. The 'realisation' of God here is squarely within the Semitic tradition of living encounter where God as Lord and man as *'abd* are meant. It relates to a cosmos understood as the Creator's world and to the creature summoned to the Creator's will. It brings together transcendence and conscience. The reckoning with God it demands is conceptual, certainly, but only because it is existential, moral and religious. The submission it requires – and which the pagan fails either to appreciate or to bring – turns upon a right awareness of who God is. A right awareness, both in the mind and in the will, is the purpose of the prophetic mission or *Risālah*.

In the Qur'ān that mission imparts the right awareness – for those who will heed – through the word uttered, the divine *Kalimah*, or speech, the *Hudā*, or guidance, mediated by *Tanzīl* upon Muḥammad, rehearsed anew and recorded and memorised by his followers as the touchstone of their *islām* and of God's will. Thanks to that Qur'ān, and to the attendant religious constraints of Islam, a 'right reckoning with God' is institutionalised for human fulfilment as *muslim* to Him. This, we can fairly say, is theism in the imperative mood. The being of God is to command and the being of man is to be commanded. *Ḥaqqa qadrihi*, 'the truth of His disposing', 'the reality of His authority', comes home to man in revelation as claim, in knowledge as obedience. Such knowledge on our part of God, via revelation, yields a right theology but only for the sake of, and in the setting of, a right submission. It is in no sense merely discursive, to intrigue the imagination or to exercise the mind. It is a theology to exhort, to discipline, to enjoin and to regulate existence. The Qur'ān is not addressed to curiosity but to action.

Ḥaqqa qadrihi, 'the reality of His worth', means for Christians a different, though by no means unrelated, sense of God. The imperative dimension is certainly present, but it belongs in what, keeping grammatical terms, we might call the divine 'indicative'. We are called, as Christians believe, in Christ, not only to such knowledge of God's nature as His will may indicate, but to a knowledge of His will through a disclosure of His nature. The nature/will distinction must not be pressed too far, since neither can be within our knowing without the other. Nevertheless there is a cherished priority in the Christian scheme of faith for who God is as the ground of what and why God wills. There is the indicative of faith which warrants us to say that 'God is love' (1 John 4:16).

In line with this distinction between the ways in which faith should identify what is a true 'measure' of God (i.e. *ḥaqqa qadrihi*), the Christian also sees the agency by which the right 'identity' is known (i.e. revelation) in terms different from those of Islam. For Islam the instrument is the messenger, Muḥammad as spokesman and mouthpiece. He brings the word which is the Book. His role in bringing it means that he is also significant in himself. That significance, as example and mentor, *Ḥadīth*, or Tradition, in Islam acknowledges and perpetuates. This personal element is not within the *Waḥy*, or revelatory event, except as its voice. It is the Book, the Qur'ān, which alone constitutes the revelatory fact.

In the New Testament, by contrast, Jesus is understood not only as bringing a teaching – as indeed he did – but as himself personifying what God reveals. He is not only an 'emissary' but the personality in and through whom God is known. As explored in Chapter 4 this means a different status for the Christian Scriptures. Whereas in Islam the Qur'ān is the very 'text' of divine truth, the New Testament is the access to the Christ-expression of God. The Scripture has its being by derivation from the prior and primary reality of 'the Word made flesh'. All that we have studied in Chapter 5 of 'Jesus in his Story' gathers into this conviction and, in Christian faith, is read as the event in which God is known within our humanity. Here, in Jesus as the Christ, is how and where 'people know God's Name', the place where they believe they hear God say: 'Behold, I am here'. This is what is meant by Paul in the verse quoted in Chapter 1: 'The love of Christ decides us' (2 Cor. 5:14). He means it makes up our minds about God, leaves us no option but to confess that here in the Christ-event is *ḥaqqa qadrihi*, the index in our history to the reality of God.

Our duty then is to explore what that decision meant and the constraints by which it would not, and could not, be evaded. This will be the surest way to mediate it to those – Jews, Muslims and others – for whom it seems puzzling and repellent.[1]

ii

The first necessity is to insist that it was a decision by monotheists within monotheism. It was made and maintained by those who were by all their deepest traditions confessors of the faith that 'the Lord our God the Lord is One'. When they made room in their theology for what they believed to be the theological significance of Jesus, they were tenacious of their faith in the divine unity. To see in the development of their theology the circumstances of Emperor worship in the Roman tradition, or Graeco-Roman mythology and pagan superstition, is to ignore how strenuously the formulation of the faith resisted and repudiated these patterns. That repudiation is the clearest demonstration of the decisive monotheism within which, not counter to which, the Christian credal definition emerged.

The concern throughout was not whether God is One, but how. It was a concern very close to issues always latent, if not always articulate, in the other faiths of theism, Jewish and Muslim. To read the Christian search, because of Jesus, for authentic statement of how 'God is One' as disloyal to that truth is altogether to misread.

A second vital aspect is that what was decisive for theology with the first Christians and their heirs was precisely their sense of what was decisive about the Messiah. They came to their conviction about 'God in Christ' because they acknowledged the 'Christ in Jesus' and in 'Jesus crucified'. This was indeed a revolutionary conviction. The fact of the Cross ought to have been, on every count of traditional assumption, Jewish or otherwise, the conclusive *dis*proof of any Messianic claim or relevance. As the mockers at the Cross implied, a Messiah who cannot even 'save himself' can obviously save no one else. Had not Peter insisted 'This shall never be to thee' at Caesarea

Philippi? (Matt. 16:22). A crucified Messiah was unthinkable. Either word excluded the other. Disciples, like pawns, might be expendable but not the king. Perhaps this, in his horror, was what Peter meant.

After the Resurrection, here was Peter with his comrades, affirming the nails of crucifixion to be the very insignia of Messiahship. In a sense that affirmation *is* the Resurrection, as well as the sequel to it. Chapter 6 has explored some of the reasons, in God and in man, why that conviction came about, joining suffering and Messiah in one. Chapter 8 on Paul will probe others. In the context of this chapter our concern is with the assurance as definitive of Christianity. It is the reason why Christianity is rightly so named. We have been careful in Chapter 5 to appreciate why the 'politics' and perhaps the 'tactics' of which we must be aware in the situation in the Gospels leave issues about the use and range, there, of the term 'Messiah'. The phrase 'the kingdom of heaven' is more prominent, while 'the Son of Man' is at times enigmatic. Yet there is no question that Christian faith consists in that understanding of the Messianic task and meaning seen as fulfilled in Jesus crucified and risen. It consists, therefore, in the understanding of God drawn from, because expressed in, such Messiahship. For the Messianic, however diversely, had always been understood as what must be awaited, and expected, from God, in consistency with His divine nature and in adequate response to the human situation, as the Creator's responsibility.[2] In academic language, and as noted in Chapter 3, Christology is within theology, and theology must be about Christology. Detractors might call the new faith 'the sect of the Nazarenes' (Acts 24:5) deprecatingly removing it from Messianic significance. Its own firm conviction was that 'God has made this same Jesus ... crucified both Lord and Christ' (Acts 2:36). Hence the name of 'Christian'.

iii

To understand the name and its bearers is to trace a threefold movement which we can only do here in a summary form. There was the movement into faith, the movement into community and the movement into confession, or towards the Creeds. The three belong together and bind the sequences in one. The earlier phases we have already followed in studying the emergence of the New Testament writings, for they are bound up with them. The faith came into being as the way in which the whole story of Jesus was read and, by their conviction, rightly read. The first faith *in* Jesus as master and teacher became the ripe faith *about* Jesus as Saviour and Lord. Faith's reading of the story was warranted by the story itself. There is of necessity a certain circularity here. It is events which generate their interpretation: it is interpretation which tells what events were. This is especially crucial where event and interpretation enshrine religion.

The word 'Lord' is our best clue to how faith schools itself into creed. As a title it contains the whole development within itself. 'Jesus is Lord' (*Iesous Kurios*) (1 Cor. 12:4) is the earliest form of Christian confession. The word could be used in the most ordinary form of courtesy, like the English 'Sir'. Through a whole ascending range of meaning it could also describe the very sovereignty of God. It is that final, ultimate sense which it acquires - appropriately disciplined - when credally used of 'one Lord Jesus Christ by whom are all things ...' (1 Cor. 8:6). Paul here is firmly repudiating all pluralism and idolatry. He is worlds away from that instinct to deify which was characteristic of Greek and Roman usage of *Kurios* and which some have wrongly supposed made the term *Kurios* the verbal trap through which faith about Jesus was unwittingly, or deliberately, paganised - or, if not paganised, de-Semiticised.

On the contrary, the word *Kurios* applied to Jesus gathered into one the first devotion of *disciples* to him, and the new sense of his Messianic significance which made them his *apostles*, and the belief that this Messiahship required to be confessed as divine because it could not otherwise be truly told and because its telling demanded to be fitted into the unity of God in Whom they unswervingly believed. The very range of the term *Kurios* allowed of this credal growth of meaning but did not prompt it. What inspired it was the reverent interpretation of the real dimensions of Christian experience.

The movement into faith was by the same token a movement into community. The sense that 'God was in Christ ...' broke through the *apartheid* of Jew and Gentile and forged them into a single humanity. Hence the new name of 'Christian' necessary to denote a community which brought into one identities usually most stubbornly interested in not being confused. Thus the deepening confession of Jesus as Lord enlisted the cultural diversity of those who confessed him, but never at the expense of the Hebraic norm that 'God is One'. The *Logos* language to be studied in Chapter 9 was the most fertile of these cross-cultural resources but there were several others.

Why, the Muslim must ask, should the conviction that Jesus was Messiah - and even, as Messiah, in some sense also 'Lord' - require those Christians to say further that as Messiah and Lord he was somehow also 'divine'? It is clear that, Christians apart, the Messiah in all the sundry concepts - whether kingly, priestly, prophetic or corporate – was always and only 'servant to God'. This was emphatically the Islamic view as noted in Surah 4:171 in Chapter 2. Could it be that Christians have been misguided? Hardly.

The point is that those earlier anticipations of Messiahship were left behind in the actual Messianic fact of Jesus. The divine status of his Messiahship belongs with the transformed vision of the Messianic task as Jesus fulfilled it into history. Then we can see, in the terms of Surah 4:171 a 'servant' who is necessarily and actually 'servant-son'. Prior to Jesus Messianic hope had been seen as political domination, national liberation, or Jewish utopia – all of them feasibly *human* goals. Such hope, indeed, was always in God but the achievement under God would be political and tactical, a matter of leadership and human determination. Jesus, as Christianity understood and followed him, read what it meant to be the Christ in terms of the love that suffers and opened out its range as 'the saving of the world'. It was that radically deeper, altogether wider, Messianic meaning, accomplished in Jesus, which justified and required the interpretation of its status and its agency as 'divine'. The sphere of action was the human sphere but now, evidently, the competence was divine. This is what Paul meant by affirming that 'God was in Christ ...'

That early Christian confession might be explained as if the apostles had borrowed from its different context the sense of Isaiah's words in 25:9: 'This is the Lord: we have waited for Him, we will be glad and rejoice in His salvation'. Their experience of 'salvation' through Jesus warranted their confession of 'God in Christ'. They were saying 'This is the Lord' in respect of all they had come to know in Jesus – teaching, healing, loving, dying and risen again. In their sense of 'salvation' they did not say 'We have waited for *it*.' They said 'We have waited for Him'. In all that history God was the One they had known. In that knowing it was necessary to make room for the significance of Jesus in their understanding of God. It was right to do so because only in God could the significance be explained.

Such was the meaning of the striking words in 1 Cor. 3:23, where Paul writes: 'Christ is God's'. All Christian theology is in that possessive and a whole sequence of unnamed nouns could be pondered – God's action, God's enterprise, God's policy, God's doing and so God's revelation. To say 'Jesus is God the Son' is to say the same in terms philosophers call ontological. So real and so great is the Christ according to Jesus that recognition means worship. The faith which takes it in confesses God in His grace and truth. So it was that in the ancient *Te Deum Laudamus* (so like the *Fātiḥah* in its grammar)[3] Christian hymnology moved readily from: 'We praise Thee, O God

...' to 'Thou art the king of glory, O Christ ...' Christians see the Messianic task as great enough to be, and need to be, God's doing, and they see God as great enough to be the doer. All subsequent credal formulation was designed to bear that witness, to shield it from misapprehension and to commend it, without distortion, to the time to come. It was hammered out in much physical adversity and communal danger and with all the human frailties of mind and heart. The conviction was that the Messianic reality in Jesus – the hope of which had always involved God in history – had proved in truth to be a divine presence both for what it undertook and in the actual undertaking.

iv

The language of Sonship, so sadly misconstrued by the other Semitic theisms, was the metaphor which was meant to carry this meaning. The divine love to the world fulfilled itself in that which most perfectly expressed it, namely grace doing what grace must, via a crucified Messiah. Where the Qur'ān uses the language of 'sending', and of 'mission' in the prophetic sense of *risālah* (language which the Gospels also frequently employ), New Testament theology uses the language of 'begetting' alongside that of 'sending'. The two belong together. They have to do with a divine relationship to the human situation arising essentially from the divine nature – the nature to rule, to care and to respond, in other words, to *be* God or, as the Creed has it, to be 'very God'.

The central source of 'Sonship' language and its sufficient warrant are within the story of Jesus as reviewed in Chapter 5. Perhaps, to avoid the pitfalls of 'Son' and 'Sonship' as Muslims incur them, we have to coin another term, appropriately non-physical, and speak of 'filiality'.[4] It is, to be sure, a sadly abstract term for that warm communion with God we have traced in Jesus' ministry. It is clear that all his decisions and accents came from that sense of God as 'Father', and His will as calling for a 'Son's' obedience. 'My Father and your Father,' he said to his disciples (John 20:17). 'Abba, Father' (the Aramaic is a term of deep endearment) were the words characteristically on his lips both in the day-to-day and in the final crisis of Gethsemane (Mark 14:36). 'The cup my Father has given me' was his way of interpreting the vocation to suffer (John 18:11). The most treasured words from the Cross were: 'Father, forgive ...' and 'Father, into thy hands ...' (Luke 23:34, 23:45). 'Father' was the simple address to preface the most representative of prayers (Matt. 6:9; Luke 11:2). This active sonship of Jesus was the living actuality in the story before it became the credal confession of the disciples about him. In the same way, Christology is first the art of being the Christ before it is the formulation of what being the Christ warrants us to say in doctrine. What Christology is saying is that the very idea of God involves the relationship to mankind which we can identify in Jesus as the Christ. Without these dimensions of grace in the overcoming of wrong the sovereignty in which Muslims too believe would be, for Christians, less than ultimate, less than final. At the end of Book 8:4 of his *Iḥya' 'Ulūm al-Dīn*, Al-Ghazālī quotes the tradition: 'I am unable to praise You. You are as You have praised Yourself.'[5] That is very much the Christian meaning about 'God in Christ'.

Nevertheless, it remains largely opaque to the generations of Islam. So it is urgent to think through the reservations which preoccupy Muslims. It would seem that there are five, though the implications overlap.

First, does not this Christian faith somehow unwarrantably and improperly 'compromise' God? Is not our paramount duty, in the subtleties of idolatry, to refuse resolutely all that might even unintentionally violate divine transcendence 'above all that they (i.e. the idolaters) associate'? The Christian agrees. Indeed his New Testament is among the most inclusive liquidators of idolatry in all history, whether the idols of the nation or of the market-place. The divine transcendence which the idolater degrades and which the true theist is set to assert, is far from being a divine dissociation from mankind. It is important to realise that what Christians affirm about 'God in Christ' is continuous with aspects of faith which Muslims, and Christians, together hold. It is continuous with their common faith in creation, for creation means the Creator/creature relationship. Only in that situation can transcendence be acknowledged. The Creator has a stake in the creature. This cannot be a 'compromise' of God, since His was the authority that 'let it be'.

Further, together we hold that this Creator/creature relationship means law and revelation, guidance and reminder, command and submission. These 'charter' the created order under God and give man his mandate to be human as *khalīfah*, having dominion over nature. We do not 'compromise' God by believing vitally in His 'interest' in ourselves as custodians who are law-directed and commissioned for submission. That divine 'interest' in us is embodied and enjoined in prophethood and proceeds within the given structures of *al-Dīn 'inda-Allāh* (Surah 3:19), 'religion according to God', through that *fiṭrah*, or 'human, religious nature' according to which God 'fashioned humanity' (Surah 30:30).[6] Only if these 'compromise' God could the faith as to Christ also 'compromise' Him, for that faith only carries forward into its own perspectives that divine 'interest' in man which creation, law and prophethood express. It sees these as prospectively one with what happens in Jesus. It would say, if we are to talk of 'compromise' at all, that the absence, not the fact, of what it finds in Jesus, would be the ultimately compromising thing. It might indicate a Creator no longer vitally concerned with man, no longer consistently patient with creation.

V

Yet the thought persists: should we not immunise God from the sort of human criteria that are here in mind? Could we not sincerely believe in creation and yet allow that claims on what God ought to be and do, based on our human stance, are inappropriate and, if pressed, somehow irreverent? Did not Isaiah 55:8 remind us that God's thoughts are not our thoughts? God must be freed altogether from *our* criteria, which Christians are so prone to apply, and free for His own counsel, however arbitrary, as Islam instinctively assumes. Christian theology is too much an 'anthropology', seeing God in terms of human wistfulness, implying criteria which we have no right to imply. 'Is it any pleasure to the Almighty that thou art righteous,' one of Job's friends inquired (Job 22:3) and the answer he certainly had in mind was: 'No'. There have been many, on Islamic grounds, who have located divine sovereignty precisely in such total unpredictability, such moral unaccountability, on the part of God.[7] The issue haunts Gethsemane, as Chapter 6 discovered.

Christians do well to face the onus of this view. Do we have God too much 'in our own image'? Mystery and enigma certainly belong with all theology. But if we are 'made in the image of God' then perhaps the reciprocal 'image of man' cannot be excluded from what may be discerned about God. 'My thoughts are not your thoughts' in no way means there is nothing commensurate. For we have nothing *but* our thoughts, with or without revelation. God's thoughts are *not* ours in the length of their generosity, the reach of their magnanimity – as the context in Isaiah chapter 55 makes plain about the rain and the snow from heaven (cf. Jesus in Matt. 5:45). That God transcends our capacity for truth and love is evident. Yet our capacity can hardly not be an index to His. Can we ever begin to adore what we cannot stay to admire?

So perhaps we can conclude that we meet God's demands on us for worship, obedience and love, precisely at that point where our 'demands' reach toward Him for justice, mercy, forgiveness and love. If so, then Jesus could well be seen as the point where the mutual expectations meet and are transacted. If 'demands' in this context seems a rash word, must we not also question claims on us which have to do with righteousness, compassion, reverence and peace? All, to be sure, must be within *ḥaqqa qadrihi*, already studied. Who is to say that a 'right measure' of God's due should exclude the right to be realistically and expectantly invoked by man His creature?

Many efforts have been made in all our theisms to reserve to God what we have judged should be reserved and to leave room for an infinite majesty beyond all our reckoning. There have been Hebraic distinctions between *Yahweh* and His *Shechinah* or 'glory', and His 'wisdom', so that by these usages (or hypostases) He Himself might be immune from human proximity. Similarly, some Christian mystics like Meister Eckhart have distinguished the inaccessible, inconceivable 'Godhead' from the 'God' of worshipable concept and aspiration. Then our deepest duty to 'Godhead' may be 'taking leave of God'.[8] Islamic theology, for its part, has long been minded to reserve the Divine Names (*Al-Asmā' al-Ḥusnā*) from human association by the doctrine of *Al-Mukhālafah* and *bilā tashbīh*[9]. That is a necessary check to a theology unmindful of the problems of language and analogy. There *are* many situations in which it is urgent to say with the Qur'ān: 'Praise is God's, the Lord of the throne, beyond all that they describe' (21:22; cf. 23:91, 37:159, 37:180, 43:82).

We do no justice to that unutterable transcendence, however, if we plead it to negate what *is* given in revelation. Surpassing mystery is one thing, total enigma would be another. As Deuteronomy 29:29 has it: 'The secret things belong to the Lord our God: but those things which have been revealed belong to us and to our children for ever, that we may do all the words of this law.' There could be no obeying a wholly elusive Lordship. A negative theology, as some have called it (the need to 'deny' our concepts as the only way of reserving them from error or presumption), may have its point, but faith does not allow us to imply that what we believe is cancelled by what we cannot penetrate. Deepened, vastly enlarged and purified it may well be – but annulled? Surely not. For then all our theology would be mere language games, a sort of futile make-belief, or even mock-belief. To find *only* enigma in God is to find only jest in the universe. Revelation becomes a sorry joke if its claims are no more than a tantalising stance, an 'as-if' which derides us when it most enjoins. 'We have not created the heaven and the earth and all they hold together as if We jested' (Surah 21:16, 44:37). We must not equate the frailty of language with the futility of faith.

vi

As a related issue, have we not in the foregoing put God under necessity? If transcendence is not in entire transcendent isolation but, as argued, 'involved' by creation, law and prophethood in the human situation, does not that somehow 'subject' God to human factors? If so, what has become of omnipotence? If, again as argued, we read that 'involvement' as having the quality of suffering and compassion present in Christ, have we not even further subjected the divine? Can we ever use the word 'ought' in respect of God and His ways with men? If we do, we may seem to imply some external source of such constraints and so deny the real sovereignty of God. These are important considerations, not least for the Islamic mind with its insistent care for the divine Lordship.

The fear that we may be 'necessitating' things of God is dispelled when we realise that the 'constraints' – as we must call them – of justice and love are within His own nature. His being characterised by them is His entire freedom. So when we use 'ought' about God we do so by the warrant of His being essentially righteous and merciful. Indeed, in a paradoxical sort of way, the denial of this situation would itself be *our* pretentious limitation on God, our 'necessitating' that He must be understood as arbitrary and despotic, or that He must be denied the liberty for the kind of loving initiative which Christians identify in Christ and attribute to God as 'Father'. What they call the Incarnation may not have happened as a matter of fact, but, as noted in Chapter 6, we have no right to exclude it from the divine competence. Nor could we so exclude it without being involved in the same sort of implied 'limitation' of God with which Muslims are minded to accuse those who hold that 'the Word truly was made flesh'. Either way, we must 'let God be God', and His counsels His own. If we theists are exercised about *not* thinking of God in 'necessary' terms, this will apply alike to those whose theology thinks the 'necessity' to be transcendent immunity and those whose theology takes it to be a transcendent role within human pathos and tragedy.

Nor will the latter entirely lack arguable support from the Qur'ān. Surah 6:12, for example, declares that 'God has prescribed [written] for Himself mercy', while in 36:30, 'O the pity of it about My servants', has been interpreted as indicating a divine pathos over mankind.[10] It must be recognised that *lau shā'a Allāh*, 'had God so willed', broods over many situations that should dearly have been otherwise; for example, 'Had He so willed He had guided you all together' (16:9). Even so the earlier part of the same verse, *Wa 'alā Allāhi qaṣda-l-sabīl*

('It is incumbent on God to point out the way') has been taken by some commentators to sustain the concept of *luṭf wājib*, or 'necessary' solicitude for mankind. This reading insists that the sending of the prophets was not an act of sovereign will that could have been otherwise. It was an act of divine benevolence God was obliged to perform. The concept of divine justice requires requital of evil, compensation for innocence, and what is salutary for man.[11]

Human considerations, then, cannot be alien to the heart of God. Were they to be so, prophethood, as well as Incarnation, would have to go. Surah 21:23 warns us that 'He [God] is not to be questioned about His acts'. It does so in the context of the obdurate folly of idolaters. It is 'they', the verse continues, 'who will be interrogated'. The note of praise throughout the passage, the chorus of creation in acknowledgement of 'the Lord of the throne', turn the tables on the pagans on whom the onus lies for their obtuseness. We need not read the verse as excluding all intelligent wrestling with theology in a setting so rich in incentives to worship, and – unlike the idolaters – to worship aright.

That God does as He pleases leaves *how* He pleases an open question which only by His leave can theology resolve. Perhaps it is well, in this context, to consider the element of judgement and the grand assize which are so characteristic a dimension of the Quranic view of God and in imagination the most potent aspect, for Muslims, of His entire sovereignty. Final judgement necessarily involves criteria applied by God juridically. These can hardly be understood as irrelevant inwardly and divinely. The certainty of judgement seems to require the necessity of righteousness. Can the divinely judgemental be the divinely inconsistent? The very concept of judgement is denied if the criteria are arbitrary. The necessities of justice are the necessities of the Judge.

Further, it often seems to the Christian mind in tutelage to the New Testament, that law and judgement point beyond themselves. To see God only and severely as Judge is to depersonalise all relationships with Him. The 'legal' dimension must be tempered throughout by the meanings of grace, with acceptance, forgiveness and compassion taking up the thwarted goals of law and precept and transforming the calculus of merit into the uncoercive ways of mercy.

In sum, perhaps what we have to do is to revise our understanding of what *can* be meant by omnipotence. 'The ability to do anything' would be a vacuous and foolish definition – a definition which could soon be shown foolish by the fable of the Rabbis about a God who could create a stone so weighty as to be unable to lift it.[12] Omnipotence is not constituted by irresistible coercion or by untrammelled might.

To be divine it has to be compatible with love. It must be the capacity to stand unrivalled in the end, to outdo without remainder all that might defy or defeat its purposes or undo its consistency. Never in contradiction with itself, it out-masters all contradiction. Omnipotence is the spiritual counterpart of the sublime truth that 'God is One'.

vii

If Christians hold that *this* omnipotence is to be acknowledged in the things concerning Jesus and the Cross, are they not, nevertheless, still somehow 'deifiers'? Do we not have to face the charge that Christology really involves itself in *Shirk*? The possibility appals Muslims. Yet the anxiety and the puzzlement are readily dispelled if we explore patiently what Christology is *not*, what *Shirk* is, and what is *not Shirk*. Since such patience has deeply Islamic concerns in view it will be wise to bring it.

What Christians mean by 'God in Christ' is not adoptionism. This, as earlier noted, was a misreading which the early Church itself resisted and rejected. But it is a way of thinking which, in rebuking Christians, the Qur'ān itself has frequently in view. Its rejection of Christology is in fact a rejection of adoptionism which Christians also repudiate. The critical phrase here is *ittikhādh*, or 'the taking up' of a son by adoption. Thus 17:111: 'Say: "Praise to God who took not up a son"', a sentiment repeated in the passage about the birth of Jesus in 19:35, 19:92, and 25:2 *et al*. It is the verb used in 2:54 reproaching the people of Israel for 'taking to themselves' as a deity the golden calf, and in sundry other verses that reproach acts of 'adoption' of idols or patrons in the sin of pluralism.

The usage has to do with a cult habit by which what is merely human or physical is given the status of deity and erected into a focus of worship. The direction, so to speak, is 'upward', from mundane to celestial. The whole meaning of the Christian recognition of Christ is totally contrasted. It has to do with the condescension of God in love to mankind. Deification in *ittikhādh* is all human and chronically misguided. In *tanāzul* the initiative is all God's and blessedly compassionate. The Qur'ān uses the latter root in respect of the angels (19:64) and, more significantly, in relation to the *Amr*, or divine *fiat*, 'descending between the seven heavens and the earth'. The Christian usage enlarges the divine relationship to history to embrace not only creation and the sustaining of the Prophet but the grace that enlightens and redeems in the shape of human personality.

When later the New Testament speaks of the 'exaltation' of Jesus as, for example, in the credal passage in Phil. chapter 2, earlier noted in Chapter 2, this is no way corresponds to *ittikhādh*. It is reciprocal to the achievement of salvation which the Scripture sees accomplished in the *tanāzul* of 'God in Christ'. 'He that ascended is he that descended,' says the writer in Eph. 4:8–10, using, as all thought must, the spatial language which avails for analogy of the relationship between God and the world, eternity and time.[13]

To speak of *tanāzul* in whatever sense and to whatever degree is to believe, as Islam emphatically does, in divine relation to humanity. It is this which must always discipline what we say about *Shirk*, the cardinal sin of 'association' with God. What it means is plural worship, the alienating of what alone is divine to what is not, as idolatry does in all its forms. What *Shirk* does *not* mean is that its repudiation forbids us to recognise divine 'signs' in nature and all the manifold 'association' that exists between Creator and creature, between Lord and servant. That is why 'association', in one sense, is an unhappy translation. That '*Shirk* is great wrong' (31:13) is one truth; that *Ḥamd* and *Shukr* (praise and gratefulness) are great duty, is another. The 'associations' of God with mankind, in mercy, compassion, revelation, law, justice, refuge and authority are many and sure. These tokens of God's relation to us are precious and should evoke our worship of Him alone. In strenuously avoiding to be deceived by them into idolatry, we must not fail to register the bond they constitute between God and ourselves, as the Qur'ān repeatedly insists in its summons to a true sense of the sacrament of all our experience.[14] Seen in this light, there is no trace of *Shirk* in the Christian acknowledgement of Jesus as the Christ, no basis for the suspicion that Christians are 'deifiers' of Jesus. Rather, their conviction that their worship of God must duly incorporate the significance they found in him must be seen as firmly within the Islamic principle of the due and undivided recognition of the divine.

That clear exclusion of 'deification' is reinforced by the faith that what happened historically in Jesus had eternal antecedence. Theologians speak of 'the pre-existent Christ'. They do not thereby jeopardise the real humanness of Jesus. The instinct behind this faith is akin to that which led Muslims to affirm the 'uncreatedness' of the Qur'ān. That of which we say it is 'of God' cannot well be thought of as 'innovative' or a new departure. It comes into history, necessarily, at a time, but if it is 'of God', it comes from beyond time. Hence the belief of Muslims in the eternity of the Qur'ān. How that belief squares with its actual earthly incidence is contained, but not explained, in the concept of *Tanzīl*, or 'sending down'. Comparably, the mystery of how the earthly Jesus is the eternal Word is contained, but not explained, in the meaning of 'Incarnation'. There was a similar instinct in Judaism to attribute pre-existence to those elements, like Torah, wisdom, or the Temple, which were crucial in the mediation of the knowledge or activity of God.

Linking Jesus in time with the Christ in eternity in this way in the Christian tradition had also another purpose, besides excluding 'innovation' in God's ways. It symbolised the integral bond between creation and Incarnation. The principle of order expressed in the created world found its complement in the principle of redemption realised in Christ. It is John (see Chapter 9) who especially develops this theme in his Prologue. A parallel, if not in part his inspiration, can be found in Prov. 8:22–31, where 'wisdom' says: 'The Lord possessed me in the beginning of his way, before his works of old ... and my delight was with the sons of men.'

viii

However, may not the suspicion still lurk in minds taught by Islam that, somehow, the divine Unity is at risk in this faith about Jesus as the Incarnate Word? Be reassured. The Christian significance of Jesus is thoroughly within the Islamic concern for genuine theism and the entire sovereignty of God. Indeed, it could be said this sovereignty is most deeply evident in fact, and confessed in faith, by the Christian's theism. In the words of one Muslim writer:[15]

> It will be a very vacant concept of *Tauḥīd* to think that this Unity is the negation and rejection of idols only. It is the negation of all ultimacy to anything but God.

Are we not right in saying that, to be effective, any such negation must be redemptive? The *lā* of negation in the *Shahādah* ('there is *no* god but ...') does not only have to do with pagan pluralising of gods. It has to do with giving the lie to all that defies the divine rule. Beyond the literal idols, and more heinous, are the evils of human pretension and sin. These are the crucial violators of the unity of God and so the most inclusive issue for His sovereignty. How is the 'No!' of the *Shahādah* to be truly said against them and God then truly confessed in a single and undeviated worship?

For the Christian the answer requires what we have in Jesus as the

Christ. Law, education, warning and exhortation do not suffice. Divine Unity itself presupposes something more resourceful, more realist and more radical than these, if we are to come in our humanity to a relationship in which we are truly God's and He is truly Lord. This is why, by New Testament criteria, the unity of God entails the actual, historical affirmation of His sovereignty made in that drama of divine concern for man which happens in the personality and passion of Jesus as the Christ. If we can have this in true perspective, terms and definitions like 'Sonship', 'Trinity', 'Logos', or 'Divinity', will take care of themselves, within the larger theme of God Himself.

It can then be seen that the Christian significance of Jesus is firmly within the Islamic conviction that God is One. Far from being some aberration which has deserted the Islamic instinct for *Tauḥīd*, it proceeds from those resources of divine power which, otherwise, would not be fully measured against the realities of the human situation evident, not only in our idols but in ourselves.

There is a verbal point here which may be useful. Other religions, especially in Asia, have been puzzled and pained by what they see as the singularity of the Christ in Jesus. Why 'the only begotten'? If we are to think of 'incarnation', why not repeatedly? Muslims are unlikely to be troubled this way. They will rather see the question as underlining the dangers of the idea in the first place and in the singular. 'Let God,' they will say, 'be God', and none else. Christianity, however, being under pressure in this way from Hindus, for example, has an interesting relevance for Islam. That 'only begotten' phrase should be read as 'one-ly'. The English 'only' has that sense. If we are to say that 'God was in Christ' we are saying that he is not partially so, or fractionally so. On any ground of unity these are impossible notions. The redemptive principle which was exemplified in Jesus may, and must, be blessedly repeated endlessly, in Socratic, Gandhian, or Martin-Luther-King terms. Such reproduction was its purpose as we recognised in Chapter 6. But the definitive, heavenly commissioned, incarnation of the pattern, in a once-for-all disclosure of its nature and its cost, could not be other than as singular as God is. It is seldom realised how close in this way is the Christian doctrine of '*the* Word made flesh' to the Islamic passion for the divine Unity. Both are in line with Zechariah 14:9: 'In that day there shall be one Lord and His name one.' If 'His Name' is written in Jesus as time and place allow then Jesus is within *Tauḥīd*.

Can we theists – Muslims and Christians – somehow think ourselves outside the instincts of our faith where these are dismissive or negligent of the other? To do so means to be patient with differing criteria. Those of the Christian were well phrased by Gregory of Nyssa in the fourth century.[16]

> That the omnipotence of God's nature should have had strength to descend to the lowliness of humanity furnishes a more manifest proof of power. ... It is not the vastness of the heavens and the bright shining of the constellations, the order of the universe, and the unbroken administration over all existence, that so manifestly displays the transcendent power of God as the condescension to the weakness of our nature, in the way the sublimity is seen in lowliness and yet the loftiness descends not.

Christianity opts so crucially for Jesus as the indicative from God because it reads within the event of Jesus and its climax in the Cross the authentic clue to the human relevance of God which is the crux of faith and of theology. It finds in the Christ-event the epitome of the issues at the heart of human experience. It sees them both illuminated and resolved in the power and wisdom there present. That it takes its meaning from a tragic measure of the world is only the other side of its confidence in creation's purpose of joy and liberation. That measure and that purpose are its surest confession of the Lordship of God. It takes 'the life of Jesus as the great historic act of God's love for man ... the characteristic and effective act of the eternal Son.'[17]

It rejoices that this resulting faith is entrusted, not to an infallible text or a private people, but precariously to a fellowship of ordinary human frailty and universal openness. Even where it parts from fellow theisms it belongs with them in their confidence in the great and continuing Original, God Himself. Its distinctiveness lies in the resourcefulness by which the great Original fulfils Himself, where Jesus is the index and the sign.

Notes

1 To speak, as we do here, of 'decision' in theology is to be close to a deep issue which obtains also in idolatry. In one sense the reality of God has nothing to do with our decision. He is. He is, whether anyone so affirms or not, but He exists for us only when *we* choose whether we will exist *for* Him, in authentic creaturehood and love. On that choice depends the question whether God *exists* as worshipped and obeyed. Clearly, it is the same with the idolater. He gives effective being to a nonentity by the fact that he avows its claim, submits to its 'reality' and worships its image.

In this way the very meaning of the term 'God' is 'God *for* man'. As Luther had it, faith and God belong together. All the predicates of God are what we let them be. Being Who He is, we realise that it is of Himself that He wills to be, operatively, only on the ground of our acknowledgement of that He is and who He is. This is the situation which needs to be in mind throughout this chapter on 'Decision for God', which cannot be other than 'decision about God'.

2 There are bewildering diversities of Messianic understanding; see for example: Gershom Scholem, *The Messianic Idea in Judaism* (London, 1971); Joseph Klausner, *The Messianic Idea in Israel, from its Beginning to the Completion of the Mishnah* (London, 1956). Perhaps it is fair to see in the Messianic hope the necessary corollary of any real faith in God in history. Christianity made central an act of faith in Messiah Jesus *within* its Judaic faith in God and believed them to be one inwardly consistent faith.

3 *Iyyāka na'budu*, in the *Fātiḥah*, 'Thee it is we worship', has the same emphatic pronoun as the Latin: *Te Deum*, 'Thee it is, being God, we worship. ...'

4 The term, though rare, does occur in the Oxford Dictionary, meaning 'the state of being son-like'. Cold as Latinisms often are, it may serve to exclude the confusions which arise for those who will read 'sonship' only as physical.

5 Abū Ḥāmid al-Ghazālī: *Iḥyā' 'Ulūm al-Dīn*, Book 8:4, quoting a tradition at the conclusion of the section.

6 Surah 30:30 is a very significant verse using verb and noun from the same root: *Fiṭrat Allāh allatī faṭara al-nāsa 'alaihā*: [lit.] 'the nature of God on which He natured mankind'. For some translators *fiṭrah* means 'faith' or 'religion' with the meaning that man is constitutionally fitted and apt for that relation to God which Islam embodies. *Homo religiosus* is *homo islamicus*. Either way man is inherently meant for a divine relatedness actualised in creation and law.

7 See, for example: R. C. Zaehner, 'Why Not Islam,' in *Religious Studies*, vol. 11 (London, 1975), pp. 167–79; and the same author's *Our Savage God* (London, 1971). For a response see this writer's 'How Not Islam', in *Religious Studies*, vol. 13, 1977, pp. 387–94.

8 A phrase of Meister Eckhart, used in the title of Don Cupitt's *Taking Leave of God* (London, 1980), in which there is a plea for the realisation that man is now fully 'autonomous' and that the sense of 'God' must be removed altogether from the external world (where man is now self-directing) and 'internalised' within the soul. This form of insistence on the Godhead/God distinction quite abandons traditional theism and approximates very closely to a Buddhist philosophy, though recognising the need for religious rituals.

9 *Al-Mukhālafah* means the necessary distinction to be made between the ostensible meaning of theological language and the feasible meaning, the latter being inaccessible to thought. *Bilā tashbīh* means 'without similarity implied'. Linked with *bilā kaif* ('without asking how') it admits of the use of language about God while reserving it from its normal import. In this way it is held possible to avoid what otherwise would be *shirk*, namely, causing God to share in human descriptives.

10 This is against the run of the old commentators. The late Dr Muḥammad al-Nuwaihī of Cairo read it in the sense of a divine yearning over the evil of human affairs. See *Religious Studies*, Vol. 13, 1977, p. 394.

11 These views were held, for example, by the Mu'tazilites in medieval Islam. See also Fakhr al-Dīn al-Rāzī, *Mafātīḥ al-Ghaib*, V:432.

According to the traditionalist, Al-Bukhārī, 'When He had completed creation, God wrote in the book that is kept by His side on the heavenly throne: "My compassion overcomes my wrath."' (On *Tauḥīd*, nos. 15, 22, 25 and 28). The issue of divine 'necessity' came of course to sharp focus over the phenomenon of unbelief. Cf. Jalāl al-Dīn Rūmī, *Mathnawī*, III, 1362 f., where the Prophet says that 'to be pleased with infidelity is an act of infidelity. But he has decreed also that the Muslim must be pleased with every divine ordainment. Now are not infidelity and hypocrisy God's ordainment? If I am pleased with infidelity I shall be disobeying

God, and if I am not pleased that too will be wicked. How can I escape from this dilemma?' The reply came: 'Infidelity is the thing ordained, not the ordainment but the effect of the ordainment. I acquiesce in infidelity with respect to its being God's ordainment, not in respect of its being our rebellion and wickedness. In respect of the ordainment infidelity is not infidelity. Do not call God infidel!' To such obtuseness are they led who may not allow a veritable freedom to man. Jalāl al-Dīn Rūmī goes on oddly to comment on God's ordaining what contravenes His own law by observing that 'the ugliness of the script is not the ugliness of the scribe'.

12 This is a very old fable designed to trap the response either way. The important thing is to see that whatever omnipotence is understood to mean it is not outside relationship. 'Almighty' cannot be read as 'all-compulsive'.

13 The difference between *ittikhādh* and *tanāzul*, between human deification and divine condescension into our human condition, is more than a terminological distinction. It is clear that, though the Qur'ān may intend to exclude 'Incarnation', what it actually excludes is adoptionism. See Chapter 6, note 10.

14 See this writer's *The Mind of the Qur'ān* (London, 1973), Chapter 9, 'The Sacramental Earth'.

15 S. Vahiduddin, *Studies in Islam*, Indian Institute of Islamic Studies, vol. XVI, no. 2, 1979, p. 75.

16 Gregory of Nyssa, *Oratio Catechetica Magna*, p. 24.

17 Oliver C. Quick, *Christian Belief and Modern Questions* (London, 1923), p. 57.

Chapter 8

Paul and the Qur'ān

i

May it be that we have in the Qur'ān an episode from the Acts of the Apostles? It is an intriguing conjecture. The Muslim commentators are sure that the reference is to disciples of Jesus. The reception the preachers had is certainly reminiscent of the experience of Paul and Barnabas, at Iconium, related in Acts 14:5. The passage is in Surah 36:13–25. It reads that Muḥammad was directed to use in parable for his hearers the story of

> the town to whose people the messengers came on their errand. There were two whom We [God] sent among them but they rejected them as liars. So We sent a third to give further weight to their message. 'We are messengers to you,' they said. To which the people responded: 'You are just mortals like ourselves. Moreover the Merciful has revealed nothing. You are nothing but liars.' To which they answered: 'Our Lord knows that we are truly His messengers to you. Our one responsibility is to bring you the message clear as it is.' The people said: 'For our part the auguries bode no good from you. Quit! or else we'll certainly stone you: it will be dire punishment you'll get at our hands!' To which they replied: 'The auguries you get from your birds are what you go by. What if this has been your call [from God] to remember? But you are people who go wantonly your own way.'
>
> Then from the farthest part of the town there came a man running who said: 'My people, follow the messengers. Follow those who ask no reward from you: they are rightly guided. My one resolve is to serve the One Who gave me being, the One to Whom is our returning, all of us. Shall I take gods other than Him? Their intercession could avail me nothing, nor could they deliver me, if the Merciful Himself wills my affliction. Were I to do so I would be

plainly deluded and wrong. Apostles, my faith is in your Lord. Townsmen, listen to me.'

It would seem from the sequel that the courageous new believer was martyred for his faith as the Surah continues with the invitation: 'Enter Paradise'.

Pagan antagonism, the threat of stoning and entrenched prejudice, certainly attended the path of the two Apostles on their journey through Asia Minor. Like many other possible 'parallels' in the Qur'ān with histories outside it, the echoes are often distant and the reference at best approximate. The margins of the passage speak with some confidence of Antioch as the city in question and the two unnamed envoys as Christian witnesses. The third man who came running (cf. Surah 28:19, where a similar figure accosts Moses) has been named as Ḥabīb, a carpenter.[1] We must remember that Surah 36 presents the story only as a 'parable', and its first relevance must be to Muḥammad's own context when he preached in Mecca (to which the Surah is assigned). However, it may allow us to indulge the surmise that Paul the Apostle has place, if only obliquely, in the Scripture of Islam, and in partnership with a colleague, as we always find him in the Acts – whether Barnabas, Silas, Silvanus, or Luke, all of them looking for no reward for their fidelity.

That possibility is the more welcome inasmuch as many Muslim writers this century see Paul as the villain of the piece in what is to them the misdirection of the faith from Jesus into the Christological faith about him. For example, the noted Indian Muslim, Sayyid Amīr 'Alī wrote: 'To Paul, Jew by birth, Greek by education, is due the present divergence between Islam and Christianity.'[2] But for Paul, he suggests, the incubus of Christology and of atonement doctrine would never have come upon the simple message of Jesus as prophet and 'Christianity' would have been in prefatory line with Islam. A number of Arabic authors make a comparable case, among them Aḥmad Shalabī, in *Muqāranat al-Adyān: Al-Masīḥiyyah* (The Comparison of Religions: Christianity,) where he has Paul, Luke and John fashion the Christian faith in deviation from the 'Christianity' original to Jesus.[3]

Such opinions, of course, are not confined to Muslims. Rebuttal of them is not the direct concern of this chapter. On the basic issue we let Chapter 7 stand. Rather the aim here is a double one. It is to review certain aspects of Paul which fill out the New Testament presentation of Jesus. These at the same time can be seen to illuminate areas of the Qur'ān at points where historic Christian faith has seemed peculiarly dubious or opaque to Muslims.

It is ironical that the alleged 'westerniser' of Jesus had his spiritual birthplace in Damascus, later the celebrated capital of the first Islamic Empire, and that he took his birthright into meditation in Arabia (Galatians 1:17). Certainly the essentials of his conversion were thoroughly 'eastern' in character and the whole impulse of his later travels sprang from them. Paul's westward reach of mission was made in Damascus. It is important for the clarity of things Christian to Muslim minds that we have his dramatic experience in right perspective.

ii

The drama of the climax should not conceal from us the deep and growing logic in the antecedents.[4] Paul had Greek nurture in Tarsus, his city of origin – then a splendid harbour on the River Cnidus – and he enjoyed Roman citizenship. But his whole heritage was that of the rigorous Pharisee, meticulous about the Jewish Law, devoted to the synagogue and tenacious of everything Judaic and the Messianic hope. His Hebrew name, Sha'ūl, 'asked [of God]', expressed his sense of destiny and the obligation to discharge it. When the despised followers of Jesus began publicising their scandalous conviction that their crucified Master was in truth the Messiah, Saul found it utterly abhorrent. Whatever his own personal interpretation of the Jewish Messianic theme among the many current – of which we cannot be sure – the idea of anyone fulfilling it by virtue of having suffered crucifixion was anathema. Death on a cross was itself the clearest possible disproof, for it branded the sufferer as accursed. At this point Saul was incapable of the radical distinction between the fact of such a death and the manner of it or of the possibility that the one might retrieve and transform the other. 'Cursed is every one that hangs on a tree,' sufficed him (Gal. 3:13 citing Deuteronomy 21:23). So the 'Christians' finding 'Messiah' in Jesus crucified, were damnable deceivers, fit only to be harried into silence and, if they persisted, into death. All Saul's pride of birth, zeal of religion, jealousy for Israel and impetuous will, fuelled his enmity to Jesus and his passion for the Christ-image he determined to rescue from Jesus' deluded and dangerous followers. That they were capable of the patient serenity he witnessed at the stoning of the first martyr Stephen only intensified his hostility.

Armed with mandate from higher authority the zealous militant set out for Damascus where the new faith had already brought its noxious message. The Book of Acts tells the story of the sequel three times, twice in Saul's own words (Acts 9:1–22, 22:3–21, 26:9–20). It might be wondered why the author is so generous of space when there are so many other incidents in the first life of the Church we need eagerly to know which he leaves to silence. He is justified inasmuch as Saul's is the conversion to define conversion, the very gist of that recognition by which Christians are made. This is not to say that its suddenness is necessarily characteristic of the birth of faith within the soul; rather that its inner theme is vital. That theme was Jesus as the Christ, central as it was to Jesus' ministry, and central now to what changed Saul in his tracks. His very vehemence has to be seen as the sign of a man resisting a possibility he cannot otherwise suppress – the conviction that the Christians might be right! Apparently sudden changes of heart are often this way, only seeming to be dramatic because obstinacy has refused the gathering logic within them which a final crisis only brings to climax.

This truth of the matter is graphically present in the metaphor of the pricks: 'It is hard ... to kick against the pricks,' said the voice within the vision. The beast he rode was the parable of himself refusing to be goaded against his own stubbornness. He could no longer drive either it, or himself, further on the angry course of enmity to Jesus and his witnesses. The voice said: 'I am Jesus whom you are persecuting.' It did *not* say: 'I am Christ!' A voice from heaven so identified would have been no reason for halting him, or any other pious Jew. Rather it would have spurred him on, as a proof of congratulation, both meant and welcomed. Was not the Christ supposed to be 'riding on the clouds of power'? The voice said: 'I am Jesus ...' *Where* the voice came from denoted Messianic power and right; *who* the voice identified joined them unmistakably with the crucified sufferer, still being harried by Saul in the persons of his people, whom Jesus thus acknowledged as his own.

This, the significance of the voice and the vision, was the transforming truth which turned Saul into Paul – Jesus as the Messiah of God and Messiah by virtue of his sorrows. 'Jesus Christ Lord', that was the meaning, and that became the favourite formula of all Paul's writing. The words might come in any order: 'our Lord Jesus Christ', 'Christ Jesus my Lord'. It mattered little. There was Jesus the person in his ministry, there was the office in his passion, and there was the Lordship in his victory – each the secret of the other.

It is important to understand that Paul's subsequent mission to and beyond Jewry 'into all the world' belongs with this Messianic secret realised in Jesus. The narrative always links immediately with his conversion his impulse into the world. The two are truly one. A

Messiahship of much popular, or official, character ensuring Jewish triumph over Rome would never have embraced a universal relevance. Nor would a political Messiah after the mind of the Zealots; nor again a visionary Messiah awaited in circles like Qumran. In disavowing all these, a Messiah of suffering love, Messiah according to Jesus, could incorporate any into grace without badge of birth or exclusion of culture. In the language of John's Gospel, it was in being 'lifted up' (that is, in suffering) that Christ would 'draw all mankind' to himself (John 12:32–33).[5] This was how the arch-enemy was to become the arch-apostle. An early touch of this inclusiveness came in the visit of Ananias to Saul in Damascus with the simple greeting: 'Brother Saul' (Acts 9:17). Not all the Church was so immediately trustful, but without benefit of Ananias' dream they had good reason to be circumspect.

Saul became Paul, then, in the terms that ever since have been the core of Christian experience – Jesus, crucified, Messiah – just as he himself received it from those who had been the means to its transmission to him by having suffered at his hands. The trauma left Paul prostrate for some days, as well it might. It is not easy to plot the exact course of subsequent events from the two sources we have, that is, in Acts and in Paul's own letter to Galatians. In the latter he tells of a sojourn in Arabia. There is no certainty about the area he means. (Even Sinai is located in Arabia in Gal. 4:25.) It could hardly have been deep into Najd or further still into the peninsula. The probability is that he spent some time south of Damascus, perhaps not any great distance from the city itself, or around Petra in the territory of the Nabataeans.

iii

Even if only on the fringes, it is well to let that eastern world envelop him awhile in our mind's eye. It is assumed by most writers that he went to ponder rather than to preach. There was much to be rethought. Things Messianic were so central, and now they had been revolutionised. How much, prior to persecuting his 'sect', had Paul known about Jesus himself? Clearly there was much background to overtake. The process of re-orientation took him early to Jerusalem where he spent fifteen days with Peter. The purpose, surely, was to compare notes with a leading disciple and particularly to ascertain from him all the intimate antecedents of that Messiahship that stemmed from Jesus' ministry and how that ministry had come to its climax in the Cross. Paul needed to know Gethsemane and who was better equipped than Peter to interpret its dark and desperate story?

There is in some quarters a strange notion that Paul, because he did not write a Gospel, was somehow uninterested in the Jesus of Galilee, the Jesus of the first disciples. So bent was he, these interpreters suggest, on the Christ of glory and on the Gentile world, that he left Nazareth and the Jewish Jesus far behind in indifference. A little reflection sees how misconceived this notion is.[6] It is often based on a misreading of a passage in which Paul writes to the Corinthians (2 Cor. 5:16) about 'not knowing Christ according to the flesh', which some take to mean 'not caring about knowing Jesus in his lifetime'. But the context plainly disallows any such reading. Paul is speaking about not conceiving of the Christ 'according to worldly notions of how he would, or should, be' – precisely those political, nationalist ideas which Paul's vision had negated. He is in no way disowning any desire for knowledge of Jesus in his ministry, though whether – coming and going between Tarsus and Jerusalem – he had ever physically encountered Jesus we cannot say. Certainly he had not shared, as Peter and the others had shared, the companionship of Jesus from the beginnings in Galilee. This it was vital for him to learn. Hence the long colloquy with Peter – a consultation all the more impressive since, when he writes of it, Paul is stressing how, thanks to the inaugural vision, he does not lack authority of his own and goes, therefore, to Peter to learn, not to get 'accredited'.[7]

We certainly find the image of Jesus and echoes of Galilee coming from time to time in Paul's letters. How could it be otherwise when he is teaching Christian conduct? One cannot reflect well on Paul's great hymn of the portraiture of love in the famous chapter 13 of 1 Corinthians and imagine that Paul is disinterested in the Jesus who seems to be the person there depicted.

What else passed between Paul and Peter, in their historic rendezvous, we can only conjecture. It was the lively inspiration of Barnabas which drew him into active participation with the Church in Antioch and soon afterwards Paul was launched on the long sequence of travels, preaching and pastoral care of the churches he or others had founded in the northern Mediterranean lands. The Gospel he brought was the one he had received, not some new departure of his own (1 Cor. 15:3 and 11:23). Its content and its confidence we have explored already in Chapter 7. The purpose of his many letters we have studied in Chapter 4 in explaining the way in which Christian nurture proceeded under apostolic guidance and was enshrined in Scriptures. What calls now for investigation is the thought of Paul, within the New Testament, in areas which have occasioned difficulty for Muslims and perhaps contributed to their strong reservations about everything

Pauline. In fact, as we shall see, Paul has some important things in common with the Qur'ān and in all the points concerned he has close links with Jesus. To show how this is so may help to correct those definitions of 'Christianity' which either exclude Paul from them entirely or assign them to him alone as a misleader.

iv

It is fitting to begin with Paul's sense of the Gospel's intention to embrace all mankind. He was the great architect of the Gentile mission, the inclusion of non-Jews in the Messianic grace of Jesus. This sprang, as we have seen, from the meaning of his own conversion. It was in no way just a rebound from his sense of being rejected by his own community. Indeed that rejection arose in large measure from his prior concern for Gentiles and confirmed him in his instinct to give them priority also in his efforts. But these were never to the exclusion of Jewish loves and hopes – witness his passionate statement in Rom. chapters 9–11.

So natural has it become to think of the Church as universal and inclusive that it is hard to appreciate what a vast revolution was involved. The Jew/Gentile distinction was the most insistent division known to history. The two worlds, of course, mingled culturally in Paul's time and produced Hellenised Jews and Judaised Greeks, but these contacts and fusions did not diminish or transcend the utter exceptionality of Jewishness, rooted in the covenant of Sinai, sealed in circumcision and solemnised in Temple and synagogue. Theologically, Jews remained 'a people dwelling apart', cherishing an unshared and inalienable relationship with God.

It was this which Paul, and others, in the beginning of the Church knew themselves called to transcend as members of a new fellowship where Jews and Gentiles equally and without advantage or disadvantage belonged together. The word 'Christian' was itself coined to denote this new community (Acts 11:26) by the citizens of Antioch who meant it as a gibe. They had done so before Paul came there, to describe a group, the Christ-people, who were neither Jews nor Gentiles exclusively. The name was well coined and soon became, precisely for that reason, a usage associated with pain and ridicule (see Acts 26:28 and 1 Peter 4:16). The new people gratefully inherited the Jewish sense of being meant for an instrument of God's purposes but no longer saw such instrumentality as limited by birth and nationality. Faith was now its only condition – a condition open to all.

When he came to write his mature thinking on this new openness in

Christ – as he did particularly in his letters to Corinth and to Rome – Paul became fond of the expression 'in Adam', which he joined with a parallel phrase 'in Christ'. We have seen in Chapter 7 what the faith meant by 'God in Christ'. What of 'man in Christ'? The answer has first to understand mankind 'in Adam'. The Qur'ān can help us take Paul's point.

In Surah 5:32 occurs a passage about manslaughter following the story of Cain's murder of his brother Abel. It reads:

> On that account We [God] ordained for the children of Israel that whoever slays a human being other than in retaliation for a manslaughter or for some heinous crime in the land shall be as if he had slain mankind as a whole. And whoever saves a life it shall be as if he had saved all humanity.

The opening of Surah 4 calls upon humanity to recognise with awe the living Creator 'who created you from one living soul'. Paul's word that all are 'in Adam' is precisely this emphasis. A Tractate in the Mishnah,[8] *Sanhedrin*, provides an apt commentary.

> A single man was created in the world to teach that if any man has caused a single soul to perish Scripture imputes it to him as though he had caused a whole world to perish: and if any man saves alive a single soul Scripture imputes it to him as though he had saved alive a whole world.
>
> Again, but a single man was created for the sake of peace among mankind, that none should say to his fellow 'My father was greater than your father ...' Everyone must say: 'For my sake was the world created.'

Each is thus in solidarity with all. Physical, ethnic, cultural and religious distinctions within humanity do not override a common humanness: they belong within it. To kill or to save a single individual is to deny or to retrieve humanity itself. Each is in all and all in each. Surah 5:32 is decreed to the Jews as the 'earliest enunciation'. This does not 'detract from the universal validity'.[9]

Such is the significance of Adam, the progenitor who 'contains' and symbolises us all. To think of him as a temporal 'ancestor' is natural to our time-and-sequence condition of mind. The vital truth is not that of heritage from the primeval but participation in the human. If we take Adam as a private person then, in the words of 2 Baruch 54, he is not the cause save of his own soul's doing. If we take him as representative, then 'each of us has been [and is] the Adam of his own soul'.

Hence Paul's adaption of this truth in his phrase, so vital to his thought, 'in Adam'. He is not at all espousing those curious notions many have attributed to him of rigid 'heredity' going back to 'original' man by which we are allegedly condemned for sins we never did or have to conclude some inherent flaw in the original creation. Adam, for him, is this participation by our own will in the common human condition – the reproducing within us of Adam's humanity in a paradox of pride and frailty. To see this will save us from a lot of futile and misdirected controversy about how sin, in any other way than this, could be said to be 'original'. If we do think of ancestry and genealogy it can only rightly be because that is physically the way by which we were ushered into our own Adamic being.

V

It is wise here to refer to another crucial Quranic passage which has often been made the ground of a vigorous rejection of New Testament thought about man. Surah 30:30 speaks of 'the nature of God on which He constituted man'. Some take the word *fiṭrah* (nature) to mean the 'religion' (Islam) for which man was meant. More generally, it is taken, with the cognate verb in the verse, to mean something like the Biblical 'image of God' in which man was 'made' – the divine intention for humanity in the wholly, good initiative in his creation.

Paul and the rest of the New Testament share that conviction. 'Every creation of God is good' says the First Letter to Timothy 4:4. Man's positive destiny is not in question. Rather it is taken in all seriousness – a seriousness which does not minimise the degree to which human perversity in fact seems to defy that goodness. It is precisely when we believe most passionately in the human meaning as blessedly willed by God for good that we must realise how actively its good is thwarted or denied and realise, further, that what counters it cannot well be seen merely as circumstance or accident, but has to be laid at the door of an inward bent of human selfhood. External factors may well connive with inward evil: they do not of themselves explain it. We do not understand the divine intention for us if we do not appreciate its accusation against us. At least, so it was for Paul with his understanding of himself 'in Adam'. It means, not some hopeless pessimism but a realism, an honesty, about how we cannot isolate or exonerate ourselves from humanity. In John Donne's oft-quoted words, we are 'involved in mankind'. We share relationships which implicate us in wrongs from which we cannot claim to be exempt. What we might otherwise be minded to see as our private selves have to be set in a universal frame of reference – so Surah 5:32; so Paul.

In his sense of the human condition Paul is evidently closely in line with the teaching of Jesus. Behind all its personal meaning as his own synonym, the phrase 'Son of Man' in Jesus' usage reflected the common identity of all things human, the single mortal birth of all mankind. The parables, particularly those in Luke, speak of these in simple clarity. The prodigal son is anywhere and everywhere. Pharisee and publican can be translated into any idiom and 'God be merciful to me, a sinner' utters a universal prayer. Our solidarity, as Jesus saw it, is taught in external nature where God's sun rises indiscriminately on all, in society where the bundle of life holds us all in debts and claims, and in grace where privilege possesses no priorities. Jesus, too, was no less emphatic about what his apostles later called 'the exceeding sinfulness of sin'. He taught a liability about ourselves and for our brethren in which there could be no shuffling or subterfuge but only a true repentance and a steady responsibility. With the background of Chapter 5 we can go along with Paul in no fear that Jesus will call us from his realism.

Our best plan in doing so will be to keep in view how this human solidarity makes for dimensions of human evil which a purely individual view of relationships is likely to overlook. As we must see later, the Qur'ān in general presents a very personalistic picture of wrong-doing. It lays stress on private acts and choices and personal accounting before the great Assize. But the evil of structures, of states and society, of collectives and institutions is no less, and often much greater, as the realm to burden conscience. When motives of personal selfishness become corporate, or find excuse in the expediency to which things political and economic readily appeal, then the collective selfishness intensifies the wrong.

This truth of things was seen very forcibly in Muḥammad Kāmil Ḥusain's study of the motives lying behind the will to the crucifixion of Jesus.[10] Even highly 'religious' forms of power and 'interest', as he saw them, override individual conscience and draw false sanction for their crimes from appeal to collective security. This led him to a deep scepticism about the amenability of public 'causes' to the moral restraints and standards that might weigh with private people. Paul's name for these structures of vested interest, in the idiom of his day, was 'principalities and powers' – personifications almost, as he saw them, of 'establishments' becoming a law unto themselves.[11]

It is this feature of his thought which stirs reflection on the frequent emphasis of the Qur'ān on the individual aspects of human evil. These are usually to the fore, with the paramount sense of personal liability in the Judgement Day and the stress – to which we will shortly come – on the inalienable nature of human guilt. 'God does not call any soul to account except for what is its own.' [12] In terms of guilt this is a vital truth, as is that crucial Quranic commentary on evil-doing and evil-doers: 'It was their own selves they wronged'. [13] One of the deepest tragedies of sin is what it does inwardly to the culprit – the warped mind, the forfeited dignity, the distorted will, the blighted life, the whole nemesis of 'wrong within'. The Qur'ān's teaching on *Ẓulm al-nafs* (the self-its-own-enemy) has strong reinforcement from its sense of history and certainly from Biblical sources with which, in this area, it is one.

This authentic sense of the inwardness of evil, however, need not blind us to the wrong in which others are caught as sufferers because of the evil that men do. There are few occasions of 'self-wronging' which are not also a wronging of others. That it should be so is part of the human solidarity and 'the single soul' vision of Surah 5:32. What defiles a human (the evil-doer) defiles humanity: what destroys a human (the sufferer) destroys mankind. The guilt, to be sure, is truly privatised and attaches inalienably to the doer, as the Qur'ān insists. The consequences, sadly, are not privatised. They belong in and through the whole, or at least the 'others' caught in the entail of the deeds.

The Qur'ān, of course, knows this well. It has a lively concern, for example, with the sufferings of the prophets, with what they are called upon to bear from the hardness of the heart, the obduracy, the perversity, of those to whom they are sent, who reward them with calumny, intimidation, wounds, and even death. Examples of this are numerous throughout the Qur'ān.

So it is important to proceed from the plain fact of suffering *in* situations to suffering *for* the people who create them. Whether the sequence is significantly made depends on the sufferers concerned, but it is there. One cannot ever undergo evil without being involved in the issue of forgiveness. The suffering links them. It is shaped by the one and so faced with the option of the other. We cannot identify guilt and be absolved from reaction. To see this is to come very close to Paul's central doctrine of grace and 'justification', which we must try to explore within our Quranic concern.

vi

What is 'reaction' to be? The guilt is there, with the party to the wrong-doing. Let us leave that where it belongs, in *Ẓulm al-nafs* and in retribution. But the parties to the consequences – what of them? What they have to bear must not be left to seem 'appropriate' (Job's problem), nor left to indifference as fit to be ignored, condoned, or forgotten. There has to be 'vindication', lest the wronged party – the victim – should seem to be deserted by society's values or by God's concern. We have noted in the narrative about Jesus in Chapter 6 the Qur'ān's theme of *Taṭhīr*, 'cleansing' almost, whereby the suffering teacher is upheld, rescued from all the implications which malice might otherwise read into his story in libellous ill-will. Shī'ah Muslims have the same intense feeling about Ḥusain. Innocence must not be suffocated: tragedy must not be compounded by confusion as to rights and wrongs. God is the *Muṭahhir*, the Vindicator of His servants.[14] Were it otherwise, 'the foundations would be destroyed and what would the righteous do?' (Psalm 11:3). The Resurrection has precisely this significance in Christianity.

The unity of thought here between Qur'ān and New Testament conceals a basic distinction also. The suffering prophet, the right-dealing victim, is justified. That is vital. But can it conceivably happen or be achieved, in a way that includes the evil-doer? Not, of course, with any 'justification' of his wrongdoing – that way lies chaos, and worse – but his inclusion in the final issue of the whole? In Job's case vindication is from the false implications possibly drawn (as by his 'friends') from the evil of natural calamity. Though the Book of Job is sublime, that is relatively simple. What of 'vindication' where the evil is human sin and wrong – not 'natural' but moral? Qur'ān-style vindication leaves the sinful doer(s) out, if not in outer darkness. The wrong-bearers are shown to be right – their innocence affirmed, their persons exalted – but what of the wrong-doers? Is there a way to their inclusion, on proper grounds, in some new thing? Can a right dissociation of the sufferers from any implied guilt read into consequences have within it also a right dissociation (liberation) of the wrong-doers from the actual guilt at work in the very deeds?

To discover how the answer can be 'Yes!' while keeping the Qur'ān's perspectives in mind, we must take note of an intriguing use of Scripture in which Paul deliberately 'turns' a quotation into a different significance. Writing to the Romans (1:17) and to the Galatians (3:11), he cites the prophet Habakkuk (2:4): 'The just shall live by his faith'. When he was assured by God in these words, Habakkuk was in the very situation we have just been considering. He was oppressed and puzzled by the evil of heathen powers. Why is the world the way it is, with good overborne and evil seemingly triumphant? Why is he left, though God's loyal servant, in dismay and darkness?

The answer he receives is that he must continue in his integrity, trusting God's wisdom and mercy. In so doing he will 'live', and he will save the situation. By such fidelity the 'righteous' endure and the issue, however long delayed, is their 'vindication'. To such loyalty God pledges 'justification'.

Thus far Habakkuk. Paul adapts the sense. He is writing about sinful man. The context is not heathen empires but wrong in the soul. By 'faith' he means not so much 'fidelity' (though that will follow) but 'trust in' God's action. That action, however, is not a future pledge vindicating the fidelity, but a present fact justifying the sinner, who is brought to 'righteousness' by the realisation of what another (Jesus) has suffered for him on God's behalf.

This is where Paul finds the significance of the Cross, as we have studied it in Chapters 6 and 7. In Jesus crucified he saw, not simply a suffering *in* an evil situation, but a suffering *for* the wrong-doers who made that situation – wrong-doers with whom, for Paul and the Christian, we are *all* to be identified (this being the meaning of repentance). 'Suffering *in*' is there anyway: 'suffering *for*' is the act of the sufferer and his quality – 'Father, forgive them for they know not what they do.' To see this act for what it is and to acknowledge it inclusive of oneself is to receive forgiveness, to be made 'righteous'. That 'righteousness' is the double reality of a forgiveness received *and* of a will, so generated, to live righteously out of gratitude and love.

Paul's 'just' or 'righteous' man in the adapted quotation (unlike Habakkuk's) was not initially so. He becomes so through the fact of his 'faith' in the sufferer – for him. It is important to remember throughout that Biblical thought about 'righteousness' is never some Platonic, abstract 'state' of virtue. It is always a 'rightingness' (on God's part) and a 'rightedness' (for mankind's part). The meaning is always active, not passive – actual not mental. The suffering, exemplified in Jesus, which achieves it, is not understood merely as an endurance until requital but positively as a spiritual force which avails to bring into rightness those who acknowledge its grace. It is this secret which contrasts sharply with the frequent Quranic accent on suffering as calling for a tenacity which holds out for retaliation and feels itself 'justified' only when it is requited by the wrong-doer's punishment or defeat.[15] This does not include the perpetrators in the 'righting' of the situation. If they are only 'defeated' there remains a sense in which their evil is still in the mastery (over them).

The other way – the way of 'justification' – is what Paul and the Christian Gospel mean by 'vicarious' suffering – suffering 'on behalf of' others, 'the just for the unjust' 'to bring us to God' (1 Peter 3:18).

Habakkuk's calling was a patient suffering *for* the truth, for justice under adversity: that of Jesus was *for* these *and* for the evildoers themselves.

vii

Here it is necessary to take up a point anticipated earlier. It relates to the Qur'ān's strong emphasis on personal liability and what it sees as the impossibility of burden-bearing for others. 'No burden bearer bears any other burden but its own', says Surah 6:164 (*lā taziru wāziratun wizra ukhrā*) – a saying repeated in 17:15, 35:18, 39:7 and 53:38.[16] In respect of guilt, indeed yes! But, otherwise, this cannot be true absolutely and surely the Qur'ān does not mean it to be taken so. There *is* burden-bearing for others; there *is* vicarious pain. The bundle of life ensures that. Our mothers at our very birth bore for us in bearing us. Prophets have borne the burden of their mission and suffered at the hands of obdurate peoples. It is urgent not to let a proper stress on the things that cannot be shared obscure an urgent sense of the things that must be. Paul himself, in Galatians, has the distinction neatly. In chapter 6:5 he says that 'every man shall bear his own burden'; in 6:2 he directs: 'Bear ye one another's burdens.' His Greek tells the clue to the distinction the English conceals. The first is the soldier's knapsack which, clearly, is not rightly to be fobbed off on to another. He has his own. The second is the weight of that which, like the atmosphere (the word yields the term 'barometer') weighs upon us all – frailty, fear, trouble, distress, adversity. These in any meaning of compassion must be shared. Family is the primary institution of this mutuality, but society is meant to be another. Both are expressly seen so, in the Qur'ān, where duty to parents, care for wards, compassion for wayfarers, obligations in ownership, are all steadily enjoined. The question of questions, of course, is whether God also 'bears the burdens' of mankind.

All the foregoing about man's being 'righted' through the suffering by which 'God in Christ' is the 'justifier' leads us into the large theme of the law, where again the Qur'ān and Paul have a field in common. That Islam is totally committed to divine *Sharī'ah*, or revealed law, is well known. Like Judaism, it could be said of it that law is more central, broadly speaking, than theology, and knowledge of the divine will and our obedience more crucial than knowledge of the divine nature and our experience. Worship, in Islam, even though phrased in the divine Names,[17] is concerned with God's sovereignty over our wills, rather than – except within Sufism – His fellowship with our spirits.

Paul, likewise, was reared in profound reverence for the divine claims on the true Jew embodied in the Torah and the Covenant. So, with care, we can bring together the Qur'ān and his letters in all that has to do with man's submission to God. Paul's controversy with the traditional attitude to Torah was a direct consequence of his conversion and a central feature of his thought. Briefly it can be set out as follows. He had throughout an intense sense of the purpose, the end or objective, of the Torah, which was righteousness – man's due responsiveness to God. It was this which he saw grace accomplishing but by a different route. The forgiven soul, the 'justified' person – in the sense just studied – lived, out of debt and out of love, the relationship with God and with fellow mankind which the law envisaged. In grace, the law had its 'end', but grace achieved it just where Torah failed of its own objective.

Why did it fail? In part because, when it was piously obeyed, it generated a pride and a self-satisfaction, even a censoriousness of others (who stayed sinners), which vitiated its goodness and soured its honesty. Merit was lost in conscious meritoriousness. What might be right in form was wrong in heart. There was no goodness which pride in it could not compromise. Even when outwardly 'successful' within the character of a person, law was still frustrated of its real goal as long as that goal was understood to be 'a pure heart'.

When, by contrast, the law actually failed – as it mostly did – to attain such goodness it was frustrated in another way. It had to become punitive, or go on exhorting. Either way, its real end remained unfulfilled. It could offer nothing to the prodigal, or the publican, or the prostitute, or the renegade, except reproach and censure. 'Requiring that which is past', it could hardly offer new beginnings. Judgement, interim or eschatological, might uphold it, but, by the same token, confirmed its non-success as far as the law-breakers were concerned. This was the nub of Jesus' own quarrel with it – careful as he was for its claims – in offering a new start to prodigals, publicans and prostitutes, to the scandal of the stricter Pharisees.

Paul was one with him in this awareness. Further, Paul realised from his own experience, like Augustine, Luther, Wesley and multitudes after him, that in a curious sense the law actually provokes man to wrong-doing. Such is our waywardness, our *'iṣyān* (49:7), our 'rebelliousness'. This is what he tells his friends in Rome. There is a fascination in the forbidden thing; as Augustine observes, he picked the fruit he stole only out of will to be a thief.[18]

This does not free us to conclude that law and commandment have no claim. Quite the contrary, the enjoined and the forbidden (to use

Islamic terms) retain their entire authority over us and under God. The law will not tolerate to be repudiated. That is benediction. For to be without law would be to be without meaning, without destiny. But *how* is its intention to be realised? Not, it would seem, merely as command and prohibition. We are such that these may well stimulate us into flouting them (Rom. 7:7–15).

Out of his own biography Paul knew this truth of his psyche and it was anguish to him. 'The good that I would I do not, and the evil that I would not that I do.' 'Who shall deliver me?' he cries. His trouble is not ignorance: he knows only too well. The law fails him in the perversity of his own will. He comes to realise that the right relationship with God, which the Torah came to teach, he reaches in fact only through grace. Grace can afford new beginnings, can free the past, can liberate from merit. Grace leaves no place for corrupting pride and gains the Torah's ends by going beyond the law's means.

Within the New Testament history of the Church Paul's controversy with the law is not to be attributed – as has been the case in some quarters – to misunderstanding, to 'sour grapes', to confusing the law with legalism, or to gaining converts on the cheap, 'offering a reduced rate to entice [pagan] customers'.[19] It sprang directly from his earnest, devout Jewish practice of the Torah and the lesson his rigorous behaviour taught him. He may have been a pioneer, but his experience has a universal ring. Perhaps it was his honesty and force of personality which made him its protagonist in a crucial chapter in the genesis of Christianity.

All this is of evident relevance to Muslims and has kinship in the Qur'ān, where the capacity for human defiance of divine claims is clear enough in the harsh lot at men's hands of the divine prophets. A passage in Surah 7:146 comes close to Pauline thinking on how the very presence of God's claim excites a human will to its denial.

> 'They see every sign but believe them not and though they have before their eyes the path of right conduct they do not take it for themselves, and though they see the way of false delusion they go it – all of which is because they have belied Our signs and turned to them a blind eye.'[20]

There is also in the Quranic meaning of the *Jāhiliyyah*, to which we come shortly within the theme of idolatry, something of this dimension of willed rebellion which is more than ignorance and is, rather, a deliberate 'ignoring' in the heart.

viii

Perhaps it is here that we can best notice another correlation between Paul and the Qur'ān, namely, their common interest in the significance of Abraham. Abraham as 'unifier' of Christian, Muslim and Jewish loyalties, is a rich and fascinating topic. [21] Suffice it here to appreciate how both the Qur'ān and Paul in Galatians and Romans centre a case on Abraham because he antedates Moses. Moses, of course, represents Sinai and Torah. Abraham exemplifies a relationship with God which precedes that of the law. His was a personal covenant founded on the free promise of God, in which Paul saw a precedent for that grace which he believed to be ours 'in Christ', something that was Abraham's not by legal 'works' but by God's good gift. Similarly, in the Qur'ān Abraham is the exemplar of a 'friendship' with God (*khalīl Allāh*) (4:125), and his 'submission' to the divine will in the Meccan 'station of prayer' (2:123–125) and in union with Ishmael in its building has been seen by some as the very origin of the term *islām*.[22] Either way, the Abrahamic is seen as a precedent for that which in Paul's case the Gospel has come to be and in Muḥammad's case *islām* has always been. The kindred point is a priority over the Mosaic implications of Sinai, though it is to be noted that in respect of the Qur'ān and Abraham this priority supersedes 'Christianity' also, as well as Judaism.

These affinities between Paul and the Qur'ān over Abraham may seem slight in relation to the deep disparities they possess. With Abraham as the iconoclast, the breaker of idols, we can see clearer kinship still. It is true that the Biblical Abraham is much more the founder of a 'seed' (where Paul encountered sharp problems) than the destroyer of idolatry. Nevertheless, the New Testament, and Paul's role within it, are vigorously and successfully involved in a most vital Quranic concern – the relinquishing of idols and the emancipation of idolaters. It is surprising that this feature has not been more explored in Muslim/Christian encounters of mind. The Gospel in the early Church, it is fair to say, was history's most thorough and far-reaching dethronement of idols. Any thoughtful Muslim should find himself much at home with Paul in his dethroning of the gods.

ix

First he should realise the oppressive prevalence of idolatry throughout the world into which, westward, the Christian faith went. Greek philosophy had not been able to subjugate the follies of Greek religion. Roman Emperors were deified. With the names of pagan deities, oaths were sworn, soldiers regimented, streets called, temples revered, plays staged and a hundred acts of daily life transacted. Christianity, it is true, had some allies. The Stoics saw the human race as one, meant for relationship with God, and the Epicureans rejected superstition. Paul borrowed some of their ideas, according to Acts 17:16–34, when he addressed the Athenians on the Areopagus in their debating hall. He saw the populace in a state of *deisidaimonia*, having 'gods many and lords many' (1 Cor. 8:5). He told them and all his audiences that these assumed deities were nonentities (Acts 19:26; 1 Cor. 8:5; Gal. 4:8). His words were more than disavowal: they brought lively abandonment of vain worships. At Ephesus there was a bonfire of idolatrous books and a 'vested interest' riot by the Diana-making silversmiths anxious for their trade (Acts 19:1–28). Fifty thousand *arguria* went up in smoke on that occasion.

Less spectacular but more important was the steady education of the new Christians into the moral obligations of their new-found faith in the One Lord. 'You turned to God from idols,' Paul told the Thessalonian Christians, in what is the earliest surviving piece of Christian writing; but to what end? '... to serve the living and the true God ...' (1 Thess. 1:10). Those descriptives, *Al-Ḥayy* and *Al-Ḥaqq*, are frequent in the Qur'ān. Freedom *from* idolatry, on this reckoning had to become a freedom *for* those patterns of holiness, compassion and love which belonged to the God of a single worship. In Col. 3:5 at the end of a catalogue of evil ways, Paul sees as idolatry what he calls *pleoneziai*, and calls upon his readers for its utter banishment from their heart and their ways. Jesus, too, according to Mark 7:22, included it among 'the things that defile a man'. It means an insatiable will to possess and to dominate, the idolatry of goods and power, of the self acquisitively set on the throne of its own claims and demands.

This, and not superstitious idols, is the ultimate idolatry, and it is much more hard than they to disown and dethrone. It cannot be dislodged, like Abraham's wood and stone images, with axe and hammer, and then consumed, as he did those, with cleansing fire. It takes for its putting away something like that quiet, steady nurture into love for God and man, that patient transforming of the selfish into the serving spirit, which were the burden of the apostolic ministry by which Paul and his partners strived to make monotheism real in a chronically pagan world. Has it then no relevance to the Qur'ān, for which monotheism made real was the ruling passion?

Among those inner evils listed by Jesus as 'defiling man' was *aphrosune*, another striking New Testament word. It means folly, the opposite of that *sophrosune*, or sound-mindedness which elsewhere the Epistles extol, the mind whose thoughts are 'right'. This *aphrosune*, it is fair to say, is close to the Islamic concept of *Jāhiliyyah* mentioned earlier. 'The times of ignorance' before Islam were, in measure ignorant because they still lacked the final revelation.[23] More than ignorance is meant, however, in both the Quranic and the New Testament terms. There is about both a certain wilfulness, a moral obtuseness which refuses to acknowledge truth and be guided by it.[24] Here we meet again, in both contexts, that same fact of human insubordination which we found before in discussing the law and the complex it arouses in our psyche, even generating its own frustration by our wills. There is no unifying of the human world under a divine sovereignty unless this will in us to resist is turned to 'wisdom' and to 'grace'. If Paul had survived to be contemporary with nascent Islam, he would have understood the dilemma posed by *Jāhiliyyah*. It would have reinforced all he had taught and practised in his apostleship. He would have found it mirrored in his own conflicts with a disorderly will. His soul biography in Romans chapter 7 might have proved a key to Muḥammad's patient confrontation with Meccans in pre-Hijrah years.

x

We come, finally, after this long review of Quranic and Pauline perspectives on our being 'in Adam', to what Paul meant by his well-loved phrase 'in Christ'. The parallel between two figures is evident. To be 'in Adam' is to be 'involved in mankind', in all the meanings of community, spiritual calling, moral decision, wrong and pardon, suffering and being suffered for, obligation to law and consciousness of sin which we have considered. Adam is the image of us all – creatures of time and sense and soul.

What, then, is it to be 'in Christ?' He is seen by Paul as the inaugurator of a new community to which we have access freely by faith, the community of response to those acts of grace on the part of 'God in Christ' which bring it into being. 'Christ', here, is more than a teacher accepted or a prophet heeded. None of the inner evils which Jesus reproved – and Paul after him – can be countered or excluded merely by a written law. Paul saw 'in Christ' the focal point of a divine event which avails to bring us to rightness with God through the love that receives us in forgiveness and grace.

Our response incorporates us into 'fellowship one with another' in that common experience and so constitutes a divine society, a new people of God, inheriting the vocation of the old one to be God's servant in history but no longer confining it to a single ethnic identity. Paul believed he experienced within that society all that he had earlier known of solidarity in his Jewish nationhood but now opened out inclusively and no longer requiring those reservations of mind which belonged with traditional Jewry. This peoplehood derived its cohesion from the divine grace of which Jesus as the Christ had been the crux and so demanded to take his name for its own. Just as the natural order was humanity one in Adam, so the redeemed order was humanity potentially one in Christ. To make the potential actual was the heartbeat of his life, but he knew, from within that it turned on personal faith from each and all. To persuade this, to gain it and to evoke it was the constant spur of his efforts, so that he described all his vicissitudes, even his very prison chains, as being 'in Christ'. The term is hardly ever out of his mind, whether he is greeting friends, counselling people, planning journeys, writing letters, celebrating fellowship, or exercising authority.

Thus his sense of being 'in Christ' was a highly vigorous, active impulse throbbing through all things. It was also a deeply mystical experience.[25] Jesus came to be for him a presence dwelling with, and within, him on whom all the ardour of his soul was centred. 'Christ in you, the hope of glory,' he told his Colossian friends (Col. 1:27). In that 'love of Christ' transcending knowledge was to be experienced the very 'fulness of God' (Eph. 3:19). Not seldom he risked drawing vocabulary from the 'Gnosticism' familiar to many of his readers – the notion of *gnosis* through the initiation of an élite into esoteric mystery forbidden to the many and abstracted from the world of common day and active history. Though borrowing some of its terms, Paul strenuously resisted its studied élitism and its flight from actuality. His Christ-love was an open invitation to which all might respond and attain and was always firmly linked to the particulars both of Jesus' story in Galilee/Jerusalem and of his ordinary lovers, be they in Corinth, Rome, or Philippi.

The ecstacy which Gnostics hoped to find through their theosophy Paul experienced in his inward cherishing of the crucified Lord. The key which pagan mysticism sought to find into the mysteries of the cosmos Paul took to be his own in Jesus. Christ was for him the cosmic secret in that what had happened in the Gospel, there in Palestine, interpreted the purpose of what had happened in creation. 'The light which shined out of darkness', he wrote, meaning the 'Let there be light' of Genesis/creation, 'has shined in our hearts'; but where and to what end? 'To give the light of the knowledge of the glory of God,' he went on, 'in the face of Jesus Christ' (2 Cor. 4:6). What a face is to a human person, namely, the place of recognition, Jesus is to God. It was in this way, in Jesus as the Christ, that Paul saw the ultimate fulfilled significance of the ancient Jewish blessing of Aaron: 'May the Lord lift upon you the light of His face' (Num. 6:24–26).

Paul's employment of mystical terms, which are certainly paralleled in many areas of Islamic Sufism ('light', 'face', 'secret', 'knowledge', 'fullness', and the rest), should not mislead us into thinking that he also shared the notion of *fanā*' (to take the Sufi term), the will, that is, to abate all 'desire', and so extinguish personal identity in some undifferentiated whole. He might from time to time know himself taken out of himself in mystical wonder. He seems to be referring to such an experience in 2 Cor. 12:1–5, but always his rapture returned him to the living scene and to the real Cross. 'Desire', which some mystics seek to abate into nothingness or total apathy of will, was for him the driving urge of all his activity. It was a desire centred on Christ. 'To me,' he wrote 'to live is Christ' (Phil. 1:21). The ecstacies which grace might allow him in the rigours of his pilgrimage were always fuel to the fire of his ventures and his efforts.

The surest index to Paul's Christ-mysticism in both its cosmic and intimate meaning is in his letters as a Church leader and especially Galatians, Philippians and Colossians. It may help to a long overdue interest in them from among Muslims if we conclude with a phrase from the Naqshabandī manual of Sufi devotion, an invocation of God by 'the name that is written on the leaves of the olive'. We cannot be certain what the meaning is. We can be certain that it would have taken Paul at once to Gethsemane. 'The name that was written on the leaves of the olive' was the name translated into human history by the suffering Christhood of Jesus decided there under the trees of the garden.

In the Qur'ān, the olive, it would seem, stands pictorially for Jerusalem; so many traditionalists and commentators understand the opening of Surah 95, the 'fig' in the same verse standing for Damascus. The olive, which yields fruit for food, oil for light and healing, and pulp to fertilise the ground, is celebrated in the Qur'ān most honourably.[26] If Paul's journeys were to be plotted on a map showing the distribution of the olive east and north of the Mediterranean shores they would be found to share the same lands. This might be only sentiment. What mattered for Paul was what had come to pass by the Mount of Olives where, as he put it, 'the Son of God loved me and gave himself for me' (Gal. 2:20) and where the commission of the Church into the world had begun.

'It pleased God,' he wrote in the same letter, 'to reveal His Son in me. ...' What could he have meant? 'His Son in me ...'? Was it not that he had discovered all that could be meant in the 'Fatherhood' of God by virtue of what had happened in Jesus and that this discovery had been the interior shaping of his whole mind and self?

The end was gratitude. 'Thanks be to God for His unspeakable gift,' summed up all (2 Cor. 9:15) – Jesus, faith, ministry, community, the oneness in God and the oneness with man, the experience 'in Adam' seen through the experience 'in Christ'. Careful readers of the Qur'ān will know that, there too, gratitude is the hallmark of faith.[27]

Notes

1 Al-Baiḍāwī, the great exegete of the seventh Muslim century, says that the town was Antioch and that the two messengers were John (Yaḥya) and Paul (Būlos) and that the third was Simon (Shim'ūn). He says that Jesus sent them, that the townspeople were idolaters, that Ḥabīb the carpenter was keeping sheep when he met the apostles and that he asked them for a sign. They responded by anointing a sick boy who recovered. Ḥabīb believed and the news spread, causing the two to be brought before the King. He imprisoned them when they challenged the gods in the Name of Him who gave being to all. They subsequently raised to life a young man who had been dead seven days who described his *post-mortem* journey through seven valleys. Ḥabīb's preconversion carpentry was for the idols of the town

2 Syed Amīr 'Alī in 'Christianity from Islamic Standpoint,' *Hibbert Journal*, vol. iv. 2, 1906, p. 247. See also his *The Spirit of Islam*, rev. edn, (London, 1922), p. xxxviii f.

3 Aḥmad Shalabī: *Muqāranat al-Adyān: Al-Masiḥiyyah* (Cairo, n.d.). His case is the very familiar one that if Jesus' message were freed from the 'development' of it into what the Gospels present after the lapse of years it would be found to tally fully with the Qur'ān's account of 'Īsā.

4 The conversion of 'Umar in the early story of Muḥammad's mission is sometimes seen as a parallel. 'Umar, later to be the Second Caliph, was initially an inveterate opponent of the Prophet's mission. After a dramatic crisis all the impetuous ardour of his hostility fired his new discipleship.

5 The passage in John 12:32 is set by the evangelist in the context of the visit of the inquiring Greeks present at the Jerusalem festival. The import is very clear: response to the Gentile world opens out from the Cross. 'Drawing all men ...' means not a universally successful salvation but a universally accessible one.

6 One notable example is Michael Grant, *Jesus* (London, 1977), p. 178. He writes:

> Paul showed a startling lack of concern for the occurrences of Jesus' life and career. Whether he had any knowledge of them at all we often cannot say for certain. But in any case they scarcely interested him.

He goes further curiously to suggest (p. 199) that this alleged indifference even gave 'encouragement' to the Docetic view that 'Jesus never came into the world "in the flesh" but only seemed to'. Strange comment indeed for the apostle who always insisted so ardently on the reality of Jesus in deed and word, in life and in death. Michael Grant altogether ignores Paul's long visit to Peter, observing (p. 233) 'He made no attempt to get in touch with those who had known Jesus', adding:

> The happenings which Paul proclaimed to be decisive had not occurred during Jesus' life at all but at the moment of his death and after it, since it was not until the Resurrection that Paul believed Jesus to have been 'declared the Son of God' (Rom. 1:4).

Those decisive events, however, were inseparable from their antecedents in the ministry from Galilee onwards, and it was by the light of these that Paul interpreted his Gospel of the Resurrection.

There is incidentally an intriguing reference to Paul's contact with the original 'Jesus people' in Acts 21:16 in the person of Mnason, 'an old disciple'. It would be odd if he were the only one through all those long journeys.

7 For examples, and further discussion, see this writer's *Paul and Peter: Meeting in Jerusalem* (London, 1980).

8 *The Mishnah*, trans. Herbert Danby (Oxford, 1938), p. 388, in the Tractate, Sanhedrin 4, 5. Some versions have the words 'from Israel' following each occurrence of the words '... a single soul'.

9 The comment *ad loc.* of Muhammad Asad, *The Message of the Qur'ān*, translated and explained, Dar al-Andalus (Gibraltar, 1980), p. 147.

10 *Op. cit.* Chapter 6, note 14. In his later work, *The Hallowed Valley* (Cairo, 1968), Eng. trans. by the present writer (Cairo, 1977). Kāmil Ḥusain writes: 'The effect of individual purity on the refining of the relations between man and the community is less than its influence within the person himself. As for its impact on the inter-relationship of communities – that is a frail thing and hardly to be depended on' (p. 26).

11 The phrase occurs in Paul's writings in Eph. 3:10 and 6:12, Col. 1:16 and 2:15, and Romans 8:38. It must be read within his cosmogony, his cosmic world-view; but the sense of all the passages corresponds very closely with what we would now call 'structures' and 'institutions' of society, 'forces' evidently operative in historical processes and the 'daimonism' in all these by which they tend to self-absolutising, to tyranny, to rejection of all reference outside their own 'interests', making 'eternal vigilance' against them a necessity of liberty, not to say of compassion.

12 Surah 2:286. Cf. 2:233 (passive: 'no soul shall be charged etc.' and 6:152, 7:32 and 23:62: 'We do not charge any soul etc ...' with God as the subject. The word *wasa'* here means the soul's due accountability, its capacity for blame arising from its liability for deeds done.

13 The Arabic *Fa kāna anfusahum yaẓlamūn* is a very frequent usage. Verb, noun, and agent from the root *ẓ l m* are an important Quranic theme. The core meaning of *ẓalama* is 'to do wrong by', 'not to treat according to due'. One can do violence to God, as *Shirk* does (31:13: 'Truly *Shirk* is great wrong'), or to fellow man or, most often, to one's own self. Thus man is capable of being his own worst enemy, acting wilfully against his true meaning, as pagans and unbelievers do. See Chap. 6 Note for Muḥammad Kāmil Ḥusain's use of this concept as applied to the 'crime' of Good Friday in *Ẓulm* against Jesus. See also his article: 'The Meaning of *Ẓulm* in the Qur'ān', *The Muslim World*, vol. 49, July 1959, pp. 196–212.

14 The verb is used in address to Jesus according to 3:56 when he is told he is being brought into the suffering of death. Cf. Chapter 6 earlier. In 33:33, in a verse precious to the Shī'ah the noun is applied to the people of Muḥammad's household and is the basis of the belief in their 'immaculate' quality, being cleared from all calumny to have a holy immunity from evil. Vindication also obtains for the denizens of heaven, (cf. 3:15) in contrast to the lusts which capture the worldly in this world). Note also the descriptive in 9:108 of the godly in the mosque.

15 The root term here is *ṣabr*, the capacity for 'patience' in the sense of holding out against wrong done. 'God is with the *ṣābirīn*, the patient ones' (2:153). 'Counsel

each other to be steadfast' (103:3). *Ṣabr* is often linked with prayer (*Ṣalāt*) (2:45, 2:153) and with God's faithful promise (40:55 and 40:77). Restitution and reversal of fortune are often in view where the term occurs.

16 Verb, noun and object here are all from a single root, making 'echoing' translation difficult. 'No liable one is made liable outside his own liability', or: 'the only account anyone has to render is to account for himself'.

17 These are *Al-Asmā' al-Ḥusnā*, 'the beautiful Names' recited with the rosary (*Sibḥah*) and central to Islamic theology (Surah 59:24 and 17:110). Their use may be said to 'denote' God for purposes of praise and devotion, but not to 'define' God for purposes of 'description'. They had to be used, said the classical theologians, without inquiring 'how' they could signify (*bilā kaif*).

18 *Confessions of Saint Augustine*, 2:6.

19 The Jewish writer, Samuel Sandmel in his *The Genius of Paul*, (New York, 1958), pp. 28–29, writes: 'It is not his [Paul's] Christian convictions which raise the Law as a problem for him, but rather it is his problem with the Law that brings him ultimately to his Christian convictions ... We quite frequently encounter the view that his nullification of the Law of Moses was the concession which ... he made to gain converts among the pagans: to rephrase this vulgarly that Paul was offering a reduced rate to entice customers.' In respect of Jewish Christians there was, of course, no 'nullification'. The central question was whether it was required of Gentile believers that they become observing Jews.

Other Jewish writers, however, like Hans Joachim Schoeps, have taken the view, which Sandmel rejects, that Paul's view of the Torah in its ritual demands, as a yoke improper to Gentile Christians, did arise from his lowering of the fees for monotheism.

20 Surah 7:146 in fact refers to Jews obdurate against Moses. It applies appropriately to the less favoured pagan Meccans who, prior to Muḥammad, did not have a prophetic word addressed to them directly.

21 See Youakim Moubarak, *Abraham dans Le Coran* (Paris, 1958); Louis Massignon, *Les Trois Prières d'Abraham* (Paris, 1935); C.C. Torrey, *The Jewish Foundation of Islam* (New York, 1933); Kenneth Cragg, *The Privilege of Man* (London, 1968), chapter 3.

22 For example, C.C. Torrey (see note 21 above), citing Surah 22:78 where God 'named you Muslims [men and women] as being the community of your father Abraham'. Cf. Abraham's prayer in 2:128.

23 It is true, however, that piety tended to paint the pre-Islamic period in darker colours than is warranted by the evidence of pre-Islamic poetry, of the role of the *Ḥanīfs* as seeking monotheists and perhaps Muḥammad's own inspiration, and of Mecca's own increasing prosperity under Hāshim, Muḥammad's great-grandfather.

24 The very word 'acknowledge' has something of this point in it, meaning 'to allow into knowledge', implying a conscious ability to exclude if one so wills. None are so blind as those who will not see.

25 The term 'mysticism' is perhaps too wide to apply without care to Paul, since it may cover things anathema to him, just as his activism and doctrinal assurance would be anathema to many 'mystics'. For a classic study of a less cautious use, see Albert Schweitzer, *The Mysticism of Paul the Apostle*, Eng. trans. W. Montgomery (London, 1911).

26 For a discussion of all the passages in the Qur'ān bearing on the olive, see 'La Lampe el l'Olivier dans le Coran', by Clermont Ganneau in *Revue de l'Histoire des Religions*, vol. 81, 1920, pp. 213–50.

27 The Qur'ān makes a significant antithesis between *kufr* and *shukr*, unbelief and thankfulness. It may suggest that if *kufr* is the antonym of gratitude then, by 'unbelief' we must understand not so much the God we disbelieve but the God we essentially ignore. (See e.g. 27:40, 76:3, 31:12, 14:7, 2:152.)

Chapter 9

Jesus and John

i

Of all the New Testament documents to be interpreted to Islam the Gospel of John is the most demanding. It involves and intensifies those issues about revelation through personality, as distinct from revelation by decree, with all the consequences for revelation as record, which we studied in Chapter 4. All that must be said about the Fourth Gospel focuses and enlarges those themes. The reader has to be alert to the levels on which it must be understood and patient with the rewarding tasks of appreciation which it sets him. It clinches, in a strangely resolute yet tender exercise of mind, the basic witness of New Testament faith, namely, how the reality of God and the event of Jesus as the Christ belong together and must be mutually acknowledged. That it does this primarily in relation to the Greek world requires us to take it as representative of how the same God-and-Jesus theme may and must be undertaken by minds concerned with other cultures and mentalities for which the instincts of John's Hebraic roots and Greek reach are uncongenial. Among these the Islamic must surely have pride of place.

One of John's clue terms, illustrating his instinct to borrow and baptise others' terminology, was 'fullness'. It concludes his definitive Prologue (1:14, 1:16). Is there, following his example, a term in the Qur'ān which might suggest an apt point of departure – no more – into the complexities of communication between his meanings and Islam? Surah 2:138 suggests a possibility. 'Who is better than God,' it asks, 'at baptising', after a reference (in a word in the accusative without an antecedent verb) to: 'the baptism of God'.[1] *Ṣibghat Allāh* has a variety of renderings – 'God's dye', 'God's hue', 'God's savour,' 'God's colour', and 'God's religion'. – but 'baptism' seems the most satisfactory rendering. The root verb and noun have the idea of two factors, or entities, inter-penetrating, as fire in coals, or themes in conversing, or art in artists, or – more immediately in frequent usage of the term – colour in the fabric of a garment. In all these cases, 'something' enters into another 'something', which then provides its locale and its occasion precisely because it is 'fulfilled' or 'realised' by it. In a concrete sense the verb has to do with 'dipping', i.e. of a cloth into a vat of dye, or a launderer's tub, so acquiring a quality which inheres in its texture but is feasible only because the texture is there. It is this imagery which relates the crude meaning to the context of 'baptism', where symbolic immersion in ritual water, or historic passage through frontier waters, represents a new becoming.

The context in the Qur'ān has broadly to do with issues between Muslims and Jews and Christians, some of which when made explicit, lie behind the Gospel we are studying. Perhaps, then, 'baptism' as a rite becomes the sign of a particular religion, and the import of the passage is to assert the excellence of Islam as the 'religion' of God's own and final determination. In that case the meaning must be extended to embrace, in some sense, the prophetic agency by which God 'perfects religion' (cf. Surah 5:3) and so, in one focus, discloses the truth and creates its community. Islam, then, on both counts might be described as *Ṣibghat Allāh*, – the expression, in and for humanity, of what God humanly expresses in the strictly credal, codal and communal form to which Islam is committed.

Without pressing too far an isolated, and still perhaps enigmatic, passage, we may risk borrowing it to introduce John's theme of the *pleroma*, or 'fullness' which, he says, mankind perceives in the personality of Jesus. There is no mistaking how carefully and passionately he ties all back to the actual history of Jesus in Galilee and, even more vitally, in Jerusalem. It is a Gospel he writes, not a treatise or a philosophy. Yet he presents that history with deliberate artistry, with a high sense of symbolic drama, and with a creative interpretation of faith. This is the inter-penetrating reality which has for so long puzzled and intrigued his readers and given rise to so many confusing or confused verdicts about his intentions and his faith.[2] It is these we have to try to disentangle.

However – and maybe this is part of their secret – they are an 'inter-penetration' about a 'fullness' he sees as 'inter-penetrating'. He writes about Jesus as 'the Christ-event' and about 'the Christ-event' as the self-expression of God. He sees the human as the clue to the divine: he takes the divine to be the secret of the human and Jesus as the Christ the insignia of both. *Pleroma*, to the Greeks, was simply how lamps fulfil light and light engages lamps, how fire takes up fuel and fuel takes on fire, and how a face and a personality are mutually known. Such, arguably, would be John's *Ṣibghat Allāh*, his understanding of truth through personality, of God in Christ, of what he calls 'the flesh' and what he calls 'the Word' coming together so that a human story is the vehicle of divine presence in grace. There is a fabric, a drama, a story and a person/situation, and there is a reality infusing all, worthy to be recognised as that of God Himself, the love beyond and through all creation.

To ask: 'Who is better than God at baptising' is to know that there *are* divine initiatives concerned with authenticating truth to man and recruiting men to identify the truth, that it is appropriate to look for divine insignia within the world, to believe that a divine *imprimatur* might justify a faith – and be justified by it. All these, too, were John's convictions and are the reason why he writes his Gospel, takes on the confrontations he risks, creates vocabulary for its mediation and resolves the mind – first of his own community, and then of the wider Church – about the common faith. *Ṣibghat Allāh*, of course, cannot take us into all these. It was no more than a point of departure. As such, it has an uncanny affinity with John's central conviction that there is what we must call 'a divine definitive', that it is 'with men' and that it makes a faith/community.[3]

ii

Any introduction to his Gospel had better begin with an introduction to John. In the simplest of titles: 'Jesus and John', which John do we mean? Let us call him 'John the Evangelist of Ephesus'. The place, as we will see, is important. It might go without saying that we do *not* mean John the Baptist. The distinction between two Johns (Baptist and Evangelist) is clear enough, but there were several. The name anyway was common and there were those, like John Mark, who were not identified by their 'John' alone. Nowhere does the Fourth Gospel identify its writer as 'John'. It refers by name, but not frequently, to John, brother of James and son of Zebedee. It also refers, without a personal name, to 'the disciple whom Jesus loved' (13:23, 19:26, 20:2, 21:7, 21:20). In chapter 21 this disciple is listed among a group which also includes John the son of Zebedee, making it clear that they are two distinct persons. This final chapter of the Gospel is by a redactor (who may also have been called John) who added it as an epilogue, identifying 'the disciple whom Jesus loved' as the author of the Gospel which concludes at 20:31.[4] It seems likely that this disciple is the one also meant in references that speak simply of 'the other disciple,' in narratives like that of 20:2 f. which link this person with Peter as companion in particular incidents (18:15–16). Never assigned in the

Gospel a personal name, it is widely and confidently assumed that this 'disciple' is the writer of the Gospel and that he was, at the time of its composition, a loved and venerable figure in the Church (or churches) around the Asian capital of Ephesus, one of the most significant centres of early Christianity. It is clear, however, that – a Palestinian – he brought to his authorship an intimate personal experience with Jesus which he distilled into his writing as a witness to the events in the long retrospect of meditation and pastoral leadership which his weight of years allowed him. The tradition of the aged 'John' in Ephesus is firm and precious.

The whole stance of his Gospel, and much else in the record, suggests that this disciple-witness was a late recruit to Jesus and that his companionship belonged with the locale of Jerusalem. That he 'was known to the High Priest' (as the fisherman John Zebedee was hardly likely to have been except notoriously with Jesus and not as a person of any influence: 18:15) may mean that he belonged to the priestly class. His constant interaction with Peter at several points in the climax of Jesus' story has fascinating bearing on apostolic relationships in the subsequent Church. That he was outside the listed 'Twelve Disciples' named in Matthew, Mark and Luke does not diminish his authority as an eye-witness. Joseph of Arimathea and Nicodemus were also, it would seem, latecomers with significant relevance to Jesus without being numbered among the Twelve, and without impugning the Hebraic interest in twelve 'founder-figures' which Matthew especially stresses in his concern for precedents from older Israel.

If the writer's avoiding to identify himself with a personal name might be read as a token of self-effacing humility, must his 'signature' of 'whom Jesus loved' be taken, contrariwise, as pretentious pride? Hardly, if we read it as the summation of 'John's' deepest experience and the source of his insistent witness to the priority of love among his people. Certainly it was no exclusive label. He himself witnesses (13:1) to the inclusive and generous love of Jesus for them all. The phrase can be read as his tender way of identifying the experience which lay beneath his entire personality and his whole orientation in teaching and authorship. To sense that Christ's love was wholly his entailed no exclusion from it for the rest. There was no disciple who could not have described himself in the same terms. Why this John did so tells us why we have this Gospel at his hand.

His Jerusalem connections and – if such it was – his late recruitment serve to explain some of the priorities as well as the main location of the Gospel. His clear Palestinian origin and his personal participation in the story's climax yielded their testimony to Jesus only out of the long retrospect and rumination of his years in Ephesus and out of the complexities of the Church-situation to which his thought and leadership responded. As reviewed in Chapter 4, the circumstances of the early decades of Christian dispersion conditioned the perspectives from which the Evangelists presented the Jesus-story and the Christ-event to which their criteria and their loyalties steadily returned. It was a continuing and an enlarging discipleship they were mediating from the bearings of the first. The continuity required a creative fidelity to the originating past; the enlarging required a careful response to the wider tensions and cultures of the world of their dispersion. John of Ephesus is the supreme exemplar of this double task. In fulfilling it, he developed Paul's theme about Christ as 'the power and wisdom of God', and the thought of the unknown author of the Epistle to the Hebrews, and he gave decisive shape to these convictions in the form he enshrined in his Gospel Prologue (1:1–18), so achieving what was to become the classic New Testament answer to Jesus' own question: 'Whom do men say that I am?' (Mark 8:27; Matt. 16:13; Luke 9:18). John would say that memory, experience, tension, reflection, exposure to the world, initiation – by all these – into Christ, alone enabled the answer, and that all these, by grace of God, had been fused into his biography and granted to his mind, in length of years, stresses of spirit and utter peace of heart. Throughout, from Jerusalem to Ephesus, from Gethsemane to the closing years of the first century, it was as a witness that he wrote and as a creative writer that he witnessed. Our study has to appreciate him on both counts.[5]

iii

In undertaking it we have to be alert on several fronts. It is our duty to take stock of why the Gospel by John of Ephesus has so sharp a confrontation with 'the Jews', and of what this does and does not mean. We have also to explore the reasons why the Gospel set itself so strongly against the Gnostic influences in the churches and yet had to establish its own authority against those who hesitated about it for the opposite reason.[6] These in turn require a careful awareness of what has been called 'the Johannine circle' – the church or churches in the Ephesus region which belonged with John, and their relationships with churches associated with Paul and Peter and their 'heirs', and with a variety of exponents of Christian/Jewish issues after the Fall of Jerusalem. John's deep sense of drama, his interest in Hebraic festivals as occasion for 'Christian' discourses, his weaving of interpretation into narrative, his design of consequential 'signs', his exposition of events through the prism of significance, his transvaluation of traditional values like 'Scripture', 'judgement', 'worship-rite' and 'holy place', his sense of irony and his reliance on key metaphors like 'light', 'life' and 'truth', – all these must command our notice even if we cannot well do justice to their impact for both faith and scholarship.[7]

Our best clue, having Islam and its predilections in mind, into a document of such crucial intensity, will be to centre ourselves on the theme of 'crisis' which runs through the whole Gospel. 'Now is the crisis of this world' (12:31) comes as a saying on the threshold of the last encounter of Jesus with the establishment of his day in Jerusalem. Encounter, in various accents, runs through the entire narrative and shapes many of its metaphors. 'There was a division among them because of him', we read (7:43, 9:16, 10:19). The blind man, like many of John's Ephesian friends, is thrown out of the synagogue. There is controversy over Messiahship, the Sabbath, and the interpretation of 'Scripture'. There is antipathy between 'light and darkness' (1:5, 3:19), between 'belief and unbelief' (12:37–43). At 13:1, the story pointedly withdraws into the inner circle of disciples, only to emerge dramatically into the final confrontation and the trial of Jesus which we decided in Chapter 6 to defer until we came to John. In a sense, Jesus is 'on trial' throughout the Gospel. What has been said of all the Gospels – namely, that they are Passion narratives with extended introduction – is most of all true about the Fourth Gospel. The whole is a gathering crisis, a judging or evaluating of society and a testing of the ultimates in religion and the human realm.

We will best keep faith with John, then, if we follow how, with this theme of crisis, he kept faith with Jesus. It is a very Islamic theme.[8] So many of the emphases of Jesus' teaching as prophet from Nazareth, as we reviewed them in Chapter 5, evoked this 'establishment' hostility. No reader of the Qur'ān can miss the occupational hazard of the prophet's calling and Jesus was no exception. That God's spokesmen should be maligned, resisted, threatened and disowned, by their spheres of human time and context, is entirely familiar to the Islamic sense of revelation. It was precisely out of his sense of what that confrontation implied in Jesus' case that John understood the facts, interpreted the teacher and witnessed to the meaning. His discipleship to Jesus took shape in the very terms of a crisis-situation, both comparable to and contrasted with that which Muḥammad knew, from which Islam draws its veneration of a teaching Jesus. That John's 'veneration' deepened into the convictions told in his Prologue was because he saw the 'prophetic' in Jesus as integral to the travail and the glory which only in Christology could he truly acknowledge.

There is a vivid scene in John's climax of the Jesus-story which captures in powerful symbol and fact the theme of 'the crisis of this world'. It is the scene in 18:28–40 where Jesus is arraigned before Pilate the Governor. The meaning turns graphically on the sense of a single word: 'king'. It is a crucial word for all that each of the Gospels have to say about Jesus and 'the kingdom of God'. But it hides the ambiguity between that concept and the politico-religious issues with which Jesus' adversaries entangled it and Pilate, with all his Roman instincts, was required to adjudicate the stakes. He opens his examination of his prisoner, Jesus, with the question: 'King of the Jews! is that what you are?' To this Jesus cannot respond with a straight 'Yes', or a straight 'No', without playing into the hands of Pilate's bias of mind. Saying yes to Pilate could mean only a political kingship, that of an insurrectionist against Rome. If, to exclude this as entirely false, Jesus replies 'No', he denies the sense in which indeed he is a king. All that Jesus can do – though, given Pilate's Roman pre-occupation at all times with politics and militarism, it is a forlorn proceeding – is to clarify the sense of the vital word. So Jesus asked: 'Pilate, are you using this word "king" as you would as a Roman, or do you quote from hearsay?' Impatiently, but sensing something alien and enigmatic, Pilate retorts: 'Am I Jewish? It's your own nation and priestly authorities who have handed you over to me. What's it all about?' Jesus, patiently, still pursues his concern for the sense of the word 'king': 'My kingdom doesn't tally with this world of yours. If it did, my followers would not have let me be arrested without battling it out. But, truly, that's not the sort of kingdom which mine is.' Pilate, in deepening confusion, asks: 'So you are a king then?' To this Jesus replies: 'King is your word. In my book it means bearing witness to truth, and that is the purpose in my very birth, my being here in this world. Those who heed truth hear me.' Pilate interjects here with soldierly scepticism: 'What is truth?'; and as the famous essayist has it: 'would not stay for an answer'.[9]

There are those who think that Pilate would not have 'stayed for an answer' from the very outset once this word 'king' was uttered.[10] By capital sentence, 'the case would have been closed forthwith.' But 'stay' he did, sufficiently to register in the bearing of Jesus, and in the context of the charge, something strangely awry and incongruous. When, later, his perhaps reluctant, perhaps expendable, scruples were overcome, he played ironically with the same haunting word in the *titulus*, or charge placard, over Jesus' cross.

It is a strange coincidence that this very passage is part of the earliest surviving manuscript of the New Testament. Dating from about 125 AD, the Rylands Papyrus 457 contains John 18:31–34 on the one side and 37–38 on the other.[11] The first fragment of parchment survival preserves the central 'crisis' of the New Testament and certainly of John's Gospel. What was at issue around this word 'king' between Jesus and his accusers, before the Roman procurator, had its sequel in the genesis of a living community of discipleship, of 'Christianity', whose allegiance was to a 'kingship' – divine and redemptive – evident, to their faith's sight, in the conduct of Jesus through the whole encounter. The Church was the answer Pilate would not stay for – the answer of corporate devotion to the meaning of his suffering as discerned from all that the encounter signified as to man and wrong and God and grace.

By virtue of its origin as such a faith, the Church inevitably became the focus of a resistance to that reading of the 'kingship', a resistance continuous with its rejection in the first context of Jesus' ministry. It is this continuity which explains the constant overlap in John's Gospel of the encounter, within Jesus' story, between himself and the religious leadership of his time, and that between their successors and the community whose faith held to his crucified 'kingship'. We see throughout the Gospel how events in Jesus' ministry are in juxtaposition with tensions and dangers of the church communities around the synagogue. The Gospel has, therefore, to be read, as it were, with bifocals, alert to both the immediate dimensions of the situation in which John's Christian readers found themselves, and to the narrative, dramatically and symbolically presented, of Jesus' own story.

It is in this sense that the crisis which had its climax in the trial and death of Jesus is continuous in the ongoing history. The immediate issue in that continuity – the issue between the new Church and the Jewish establishment – has to be seen within the all-embracing theme of a moral universe and the holiness of God. Nowhere has that final theme been more finely expressed than by Paul Winter in his study, *The Trial of Jesus.*[12]

> A hurried trial over, events moved swiftly on from the fatal moment when Jesus was taken away from Pilate, to a place called *The Skull*, to the moment when he inclined his head – and it was finished. It is not over ... Not Pilate's sentence, not the jostling of the soldiers who divided his garments, not even the cry from the cross was the last word. The accusers of old are dead. The witnesses have gone home. The judge has left the court. The trial of Jesus goes on. His is a trial

that is never finished, and one in which the roles of judge and accused are strangely reversed.

The sentencing of Jesus incriminates mankind. Surely it was this knowledge which caused John of Ephesus to present the vital scene in which Pilate proffers Jesus to the crowd assembled in the courtyard with the words: *Ecce Homo,* in Roman Latin: 'Behold the man'. The crown of thorns Jesus then wears takes care of the 'kingship'. 'Behold the man', in all its paradox, becomes a mirror in which we 'behold mankind', manifest, by this drama, in all the human potential for wrong – wrongs political, religious, personal and communal – as these so evidently conspire against Jesus. *Ecce Homines.*

iv

It is this which dominates and determines John's thinking and his Gospel. Does he not introduce the first disciples of Jesus, recruited from his namesake, John the Baptist, by linking their new master with 'the sin of the world'? That was always his stance. 'Not for our sins only,' he writes in his First Letter (2:2), 'but for the sins of the whole world.' He sees Jesus' response to his sentence at the hands of Pilate as a 'bearing' of those sins in the sense we have studied in Chapter 7. He finds them universal. The Christian Creeds never assume otherwise or associate the evil at work in the Cross with any particular reproach. The credal phrase: '... crucified *under* Pontius Pilate' serves to state fact as historical rather than spell condemnation.

For the New Testament the central meaning of the death of Jesus is a verdict against us all, a verdict which goes down in history as indictment of mankind, of human society *per se* as the place where such a one as Jesus is there in such a place.[13] It is this which forbids to Christianity any facile optimism about human perfectibility by law, or legislation, or religion, in themselves, which roots the Christian Gospel back in a radical realism about the world and humankind. The Christian faith only realises divine grace in realising human wrong. Jesus' Cross, as John sees it in his unison with his co-disciples, is where both realisations meet. The trial of Jesus continues wherever he is crucified afresh in the sin-proneness of that humanness by which he was crucified at Jerusalem.

It is this inner fact of things which characterises all else about Jesus and John. It is this fact which explains the constant sense of stakes at issue which, as we have seen, marks the 'divisions' over Jesus, the 'crisis' of his impact, the encounters and the confrontations that make the drama of his Gospel. The things *about* Jesus cannot be divorced from the themes *between* him and the people of his time and place. So it is that, within the universal terms we have just noted, there revolves continuing controversy, in his pages, with 'the Jews'. This is in no way the indictment of a whole people in and for themselves. John is no anti-Semite.[14] He is 'Semitic' to the core. But he writes and cares for, and in, a church community still at issue with others over their reading of the 'kingship' of Jesus and all its implications for the human whole and the Jewish future. It is in this sense that the 'trial' of Jesus persists in the local communal confrontation John's authorship faces between his circle of discipleship to Jesus and the Judaic loyalties which dispute it. As with Saul and Damascus, Christians are both the occasion and the focus of the same motives of rejection which were present in the scene before Pilate. However, 'extension' of the issue about Jesus' kingship in which John at Ephesus was involved as a church leader was very much a minor movement in the larger drama of the crisis about Jesus in its inclusive meaning arraigning all humanity. In John's understanding of the Cross as involving 'the sin of the world' there are no private indictments and no unilateral acquittals.

That central truth about the 'trial' of Jesus, however, did not preclude communal tensions between interpreters and followers committed to their contrasted loyalties over its actual, juridical verdict. 'The Jews', in John's writing, were a varied group within the synagogues – not Jewry as such or *in toto* – who resisted Christian (Jewish and Gentile) understanding of Jesus' significance, before, through and beyond his crucifixion. Some reached a private faith in Jesus but desired to retain their Jewish allegiance intact. The Gospel of John shows traces of the desire to bring them fully over.[15] There were others who did in fact leave the synagogue but were reticent, for example, about the Christian Eucharist and uncertain about how to define Jesus' Christhood. There were still others – the majority – who with deepening urgency wanted all compromising crypto-Jews out of the synagogue, just like the blind man healed in John 9:22. To take Jesus as Messiah, in any sense, was for this group an abnegation of Jewishness altogether. These irreconcilables saw God's stake in Jesus (as John received it) altogether devalidating the Jewish Temple (cf. John 2:19) and virtually abolishing all Jewish feasts (in which John took such clear but idiosyncratic interest). After the Fall of Jerusalem in 70 AD and the destruction of the Temple, Jewish fears intensified and attitudes hardened. Midrash-style debates between the parties grew more bitter and in the late eighties of the first century the synagogue authorities reworded the curse of deviators (*Birkat ha*

Minim), the twelfth of the eighteen *Shemoneh Esrreh* in the liturgical services, in order to identify and evict those who confessed Jesus as Messiah. Some of the so-called 'crypto-Jews' drew back into the synagogues. While Judaism was a *religio licita* (a tolerance not enjoyed by 'outright' Christians) such expulsion meant that all insurance against persecution ceased for those expelled. Further, Jewish authorities tried and executed some of the Johannine community's evangelists on the charge of misleading and corrupting Jews (cf. 5:18, 10:33, 16:2). 'Crypto-Christians' informed about 'full' ones and so heightened antagonisms further. All this is the background to the Gospel's concern for 'the true Israelite' (1:47), its pre-occupation with rejection (1:11, 17:14), its contrast between Moses' disciple and Jesus' disciple (19:28) and its caution about 'hatred from the world' (15:18).

Readers of the Qur'ān are very familiar with a strong emphasis on confrontation with the Jews in Muḥammad's own context both of expectation of their recognition of his mission and subsequent disappointment and embroilment with their non-recognition and its political, or tribal, sequel in the confiscations and conflicts. It is important to distinguish between the military hostilities of that Medinan context with its tragic blood-letting, and the theological tensions over Jewishness and Messiahship which belonged with the world of John. His was a struggle for spiritual meanings never entangled with political – still less with military – resistance or attack.[16]

V

From the primary drama of Jesus' 'kingship under trial' before the Roman Procurator and the emerging sub-drama about that same 'kingship' between John's community and his detractors, we must pass to the actual issue of the juridical story. There are several points of detail legitimately at issue among scholars and historians, particularly relating to the 'custom' of clemency under which Barabbas was released and to the speed of the sequences between Sanhedrin and Pilate.[17] These can be left with the researchers. The climax can well be set down in the words of a recent Jewish writer whose account tallies very closely with that of the Gospel according to John.[18]

> There is ample evidence in the Gospels and in what is known from other sources about Palestine under the Romans, to suggest that Jesus was executed as a Jewish trouble maker: as a man who had, or was reputed ... to have, messianic, and hence (from the Roman point of view) revolutionary pretensions. In carrying out this deed

> the Romans were at least helped, if not positively provoked, by Jewish sacerdotal officials, who held their positions by grace of the country's colonial masters and were anxious not to have the *status quo* disturbed by trouble in the streets both because they wanted to protect their own positions, and because they foresaw (rightly, as events were to show during the rebellion against Rome) the consequences of messianic enthusiasm among the populace.

Pilate, too, had his vested interest in keeping his area and his reputation clear of any suspicion of a compromise of Roman order such as leniency, or scruple, or sentiment might imply. Jesus was 'delivered into the will' of sovereignties – political and hierarchical – for which his own 'kingship' had been both a negligible episode and a strange judgement in reverse. That irony was in the very nature of their wrong and of the majesty they had failed to understand. From their verdict *against* Jesus, the Church, born in the very realisation of his glory and Lordship, lived by its verdict *about* him and grew in taking it to the world. That Christian acknowledgement of 'God in Christ', so central to the personality of John of Ephesus, perpetuated the crisis-situation about Jesus, no longer now a juridical climax to his ministry but an ongoing, present claim on the human spirit for love and for discipleship. In intimate experience, 'the disciple whom Jesus loved' wove together the climax and the claim and his Gospel is the fabric of his weaving.

His verdict about Jesus is both a work of creative literature and a travail of deep theology. To many it has seemed the major factor in what they see as the 'Hellenisation' of Jesus, the transformation – as it is alleged – of the Judaic prophet and preacher into an ontological 'mystery', a divine revelation, an incarnate lord. Such 'de-Judaising' of Jesus, if such it be, is of course a vital concern for Muslims with their firm convictions about the human Jesus as faithfully discharging a messenger's role among the Jewish people.[19] All their instincts would lead them to suspect any picture which found more than a speaking relevance in Jesus.[20]

If we take John of Ephesus intelligently, however, it becomes clear that his presentation firmly repudiates what such interpreters call, in the clumsily abstract terms, 'Hellenisation' and 'de-Judaisation', though it is understandable why they think so. John is Jewish to the end not only, as we have seen, in his conflict with the synagogue but in his cherishing of his heritage from Moses. He turns the flank of real 'Hellenism' by anchoring his Greek relationships of mind so firmly in the actualities of Galilee and Jerusalem. To present Jesus as 'the Word' *might* have meant Platonic notions of an immanent principle of reason, and/or gnostic insubstantiality and esoteric mystery known only to the élite of hidden knowledge. But to add '...was made flesh and dwelt among us' and to portray that 'dwelling' in act and symbol so that it continued 'among us' down the centuries was to be as unPlatonic as any mind could be. To communicate into the Greek world was one thing - to naturalise into it quite another. Was it not John's Judaic Christian genius to do the one and resolutely to exclude the other?

Comparably, to see the 'Logos' theme and all that goes with it in the Gospel as risking or disserving the Judaic is to isolate John from the long preoccupation, *within* Jewry, over the status, for example, of divine wisdom and the relation of divine sovereignty and providence to universal man. It can be claimed that John in his Gospel was in essentially Jewish travail over a consistent loyalty to his past once the significance of Jesus, however disconcertingly, as the Christ had been registered within the soul. We cannot credibly charge John as a 'de-Judaiser' unless we claim a warrant to silence the issues within Jewishness itself.

It is in fact arguable, though not proven, that John builds his whole authorship around the lectionary of the Palestinian synagogue. The Qur'ān divided into thirty or sixty equal parts for recital in the mosques, and privately, is familiar to every Muslim and the use of an annual calendar with the Feasts of *Al-Fitr* and *Al-Aḍḥā,* and the *Maulid* of Muḥammad. Jewish Festivals are more numerous and recitals sometimes extend beyond an annual recurrence. Detail here is not appropriate. What matters is the fact that the Gospel according to John can be fitted into the synagogue lections with the discourses of Jesus as his synagogue sermons in that context. If so, then the cluster of Jewish Festivals with which John associates his narrative could also 'situate' and illuminate those discourses, carefully dated as these are by the evangelist. 'I ever taught in the synagogues,' Jesus said (18:20), in repudiating the charge of secrecy and subterfuge. John refers to three Passovers (2:13, 2:23, 6:4, 13:1 with 19:14 and other references) and their incidence is linked with the cleansing of the Temple, the feeding of the multitude in possible association with the Eucharist in the long discourse of Chapter 6 about the bread of life, and the third with the crucifixion. The Feast of Tabernacles (7:2) is the setting for the discourse about water and light, while 10:22 notes the Feast of the Dedication *(Hanukkah)* whose readings in the lectionary show intriguing parallels with the shepherd theme in Chapter 10.[21] John's readers were no doubt primarily alert to what this pattern of exposition held for them as newly ousted from the synagogue. The writer's studied option for this pattern in the construction of his Gospel is eloquent of his devotion, for his own and for his people's sake, to the treasures of his Jewish nurture. Whatever the tensions, in no way does he shed them. He lives them.

vi

If, then, John is neither the 'Helleniser' nor the 'de-Judaiser' hasty or easy judgements have suggested, it is time to reckon, if only here in summary, with the portrayal of Jesus in his Gospel. To do so it is helpful to begin with the 'signs', to let them take us into the witness of the Prologue, and pass from there into the varied imagery of the evangelist and finally to the time-relationship which is so vital to his theme. The accent on 'remembrance' – another favourite dimension – will best follow in Chapter 10 in relation to the Paraclete. Throughout, the reader needs to be living in awareness of that crisis-situation which is everywhere implicit.

The 'seven signs' of John's Gospel are every commentator's care. They comprise a lively presentation of Jesus' ministry as both denoting and conveying joy and grace, sight and light, life and love, where acts of healing and words of interpretation combine, under the evangelist's hand, to express the 'kingdom' and the 'kingship'. This purpose of the 'signs' is all there in the word 'sign-ificance' and corresponds, in measure, to the central place of the *āyāt* in the Qur'ān. There the phenomena of the natural order not only alert and inform the observant 'scientist', the human *khalīfah* intelligently recruiting their potential for his ends: they also evoke his religious vocation to gratitude and wonder. In the second role they are joined by embodiments of significance within the historical order and prophetic mission. In that context, Jesus and Mary his Mother have honoured place, as Surah 21:91 declares: 'We made her and her son a sign to the worlds.' The *bayyināt*, or acts of expressive meaning, which the Qur'ān frequently attributes to Jesus, are close to the idiom of John for whom the deeds of Jesus, in healing and teaching, are disclosures, or manifestations, of glory and truth. In that sense, whatever the disparities, the Qur'ān-reader is on familiar ground when he comes upon the 'sign-structure' of John's writing.

The renowned Islamic theologian, Ḥamīd al-Ghazālī can afford us a clue into John in this regard, at least initially. In his famous *Iḥyā' 'Ulūm al-Dīn* (Book 8.3:1) he explains that the Qur'ān is given in letters and their sounds because, he says, these are 'attributes of human beings'. Only through his own human attributes, such as these are in language, is man able to reach an understanding of the attributes of God, 'the inmost majesty of whose speech is concealed in the garment of letters. Just as human bodies are the dwelling place of the soul, so likewise the sounds of the Arabic language become like the dwelling place of the divine wisdom which is the soul or spirit in the sounds.'[22]

John could have appreciated this analogy. In his Gospel we must read personality for language and acts in event for word-syllables. Truth, for him, is through personality. 'The Word was made flesh.' That wherein God addresses his world, his human creation, is not in the primary sense scripture or letters and sounds, but a life, a person and a history. The 'scripture', as we have seen in Chapter 4, derives, as record, from that primary revelation. Dependable access to it is made possible, Christians believe, by the enabling of the Holy Spirit in the writers. By virtue of his ripe retrospect and his critical leadership situation, John has a unique place in that vital 'scriptuarising', or documenting, of Jesus.

All his literary artistry and his feel for symbolism are dedicated to the task. Hence the sequence of signs, which one writer has described as 'a prism of words', filtering the light into sevenfold colour. The first two are in Cana of Galilee, the water and the wine at the wedding (2:1–11) and the healing of the nobleman's son (4:46–54); then: the cure of the paralytic at Bethesda (5:1–9); the feeding of the multitude (6:1–14); the cure of the blind man (9:1–41); the raising of Lazarus (11:1–46); and finally the ultimate sign of Jesus' Resurrection (20:1–29). There are other *bayyināt*, like the stilling of the storm (6:15–21), the encounter (8:3–11) with the accusers of the woman taken in adultery, and the feet-washing (13:1–17). There are, also, 'signs' which Jesus adduces in his sermons from earlier history, like that of Moses and the serpent (3:14–15).

Behind this presentation lies a double purpose, to link interpretation and meditation with event so that history is understood as much more than bare chronicle, and to bring 'reality' down from the 'ideal' realm where Greek thinking habitually set it into the living texture of earthly doing. Where Al-Ghazālī has 'letters and sounds' as the vehicle of divine communication, John has deeds and expositions. Even details of his narratives are sometimes invested with a significance, subordinate to the main purpose, but there for the taking if the reader will discern it. For example, the wedding feast in Cana of Galilee inaugurates Jesus' ministry as the joyous transforming word and presence of 'the kingdom'. Through the vine and its grapes the waters from cloud and soil yield the wine of celebration. But that central analogy of how life, too, is transformable and – transformed – is set in quite a cluster of other points, of which perhaps the sweetest is the note about how 'the servants which drew the water knew'. Those containing-jars, with the carefully noted dimensions, were there as part and parcel of the old order with its ritual washing before meals. The servants of a new situation proceed from the utensils of the old. The event sets an *imprimatur* (as long Christian marriage liturgy has repeated) on the hallowing of sexuality in wedding covenant, which Jesus witnesses 'with his disciples'.

There is one exchange in this narrative which has often puzzled Muslims and been the subject of frequent reproach, namely, Jesus' apparent curtness or discourtesy, with his mother, Mary, who is highly venerated in Islam.[23] The word translated 'woman', used also from the Cross in a moment of deepest tenderness in 19:26, is hard to turn into truly equivalent English. *Gunai* means 'mother' in this context and in John's usage is in no way a harsh or churlish word. The rest of Jesus' remark: *Ti emoi kai soi* means (lit.): 'What to me and you?' It is neither rude nor dismissive. The sequel immediately makes it clear that it was not a rebuff or a rejection. It does imply a divergence in their view of the situation. Mary is practical, may even be implying that it is Jesus' presence 'with his disciples' that has caused the embarrassing insufficiency of the wine. Perhaps he and they should leave? At least he should understand the situation. By contrast, John portrays Jesus as occupied with 'the hour', a theme which recurs throughout the Gospel (7:30, 8:20, 12:23, 13:1, 17:1). This does not have to do with fingers on a clock dial, but with the ripeness of God's will and his mission. So *Ti emoi kai soi* might be paraphrased: 'We are not seeing eye to eye here, Mother.' Mary does not read the comment as anything but a positive response and, whether or not she fully takes it in, she directs the servants accordingly: 'Whatever he bids you, do it.'

It is in these intricately rich ways that John intimates meanings to his readers and the latter need to be sensitively alert to his nuances. Examples are everywhere both through all the 'signs' passages and also in the other events of the story. Space here admits of only one other extended instance, namely the story of the call of Nathaniel in 1:45–51. Read without discernment it seems a strangely puzzling sequence of incident and verbal exchange, but with the clue of Jacob and Messianic imagery all falls into coherent place. Nathaniel as a name means 'honoured of God' – a sense close to the literal meaning of 'Muḥammad'. He is sceptical when Philip tells him of Jesus as Messiah, because of the origin in Nazareth, a place reputedly no nursery for a Messiah. Philip invites him to 'come and see'. Nathaniel has been 'sitting under a fig tree', traditionally the symbol of Messianic hope realised in Messianic security ('... every man under his vine and under his fig tree and none shall make them afraid': Mic. 4:4). When Jesus greets him, Nathaniel is taken aback by the salutation which reads so clearly into his thoughts about Messiah, recognises his integrity of mind and strikes a contrast with Jacob (a new strand in the encounter) who, far from being a genuine soul (in his old days) was guileful and devious. Jesus responds to Nathaniel's surprise, by taking further the Jacob allusions and assuring Nathaniel that something more surprising than character-reading is ahead, namely the transactions of grace of which Jacob's ladder could be held the symbol. Nathaniel's response to discipleship will involve him in the things of Christ where God's love reaches down to mankind and mankind has the open door to grace.

Read this way, as it is 'between the lines', the story is no longer opaque or clueless, but luminous and warm. It is this way throughout John's writing. For this quality of creative witness is what he does with history. It is so in the conversation with Nicodemus, the 'ruler who came by night', with the woman at the well of Sychar in Samaria, in the exchanges with the authorities after the feeding of the crowds, and after the healing of the blind man, in the reception of the inquiry of the Greeks and in all the features of the final week and of the crucifixion. It was this quality which enabled John to interpret in chapter 17 the intimate content of Jesus' communion with God in the final crisis and climax. When, in a telling but unobtrusive way, he notes the 'progress' of Nicodemus from 3:1 f. to 7:50 f. and 19:39, he obliquely charts the course of many timid souls mastering their fears in a later day. His whole authorship, he insists in 20:30–31, is for the delineation and evocation of faith that 'Jesus is the Christ, the Son of God,' the faith that means 'life through his name'. He intends his Gospel to be the place where the faith that writes it and the faith that reads it find and embrace each other. What this means in and through the 'signs' we must now explore in the Prologue which is both preface and summary of the Gospel.

vii

Given patience and perception 'the Word', as John has it, need not be unduly difficult of Muslim understanding. He brings together two distinct conceptions, Greek and Hebraic, marries them in his content of the term *Ho Logos*, 'the Word', and, in so doing, unites the meaning of two great Quranic terms – namely, *al-Amr*, 'the command', and *Al-Sakīnah*, 'the presence'. His Prologue (1:1–18), integrates in one deeply theological summary the import of the whole Gospel. He inserts the historical point of departure, 'a man sent from God named John (the Baptist)' (verse 6), which is Mark's beginning (1:1–8) into the divine initiative whence, for him, that history derives. The life-story he is presenting is set in the perspective of God's eternal purpose. *Ho Logos,* as a term, expresses this double reality – what is authentically divine operative and recognisable in that which is actually human.

It is, in its different way, the same relatedness which is understood in the Islamic concept of *Tanzīl,* or 'sending down' of the heavenly 'speech' of God as a 'Scripture' on earth. If we ask how this 'intercourse' of eternity and time, of the divine and the human, is feasible and actual, we say that that 'mystery' is hidden within the fact – if we are Muslims – of *Tanzīl* itself, or – if we are Christians – of 'the Word made flesh'. The difference is not, essentially, one of 'mystery' (for they are closely comparable) but one of form and manner. In the Islamic faith we have 'the words made Scripture', the Book: in the Christian faith we have 'the Word made flesh', the Christ who is Jesus. Many of the issues that made Muslim theologians adamant about the Qur'ān being 'uncreated' belong with John's concern here in his Gospel, in line with the whole Christian tradition, to insist that Jesus is divine. In either case the motive is not to ascribe to God what He does not eternally own, to be positively sure that we are divinely authenticated in recognising God's revelation. In that sense the pre-existent Qurān and the pre-existent Christ are respective areas of concern in a proper religious anxiety.

John in his Prologue associates intimately the word of command which inaugurated creation (verse 1) with the initiative fulfilled in the advent of Jesus (verse 14). Light and life, John's well-loved words, belong with both. God's intention – for, in and through creation – issues into the divine fidelity to man in creation which Incarnation and redemption embody. This clear parallelism between 'genesis' and 'grace' is comprised within the term Logos. It was 'by the word of the Lord the heavens were made', as Psalm 33:6 declares, by the *Amr* the Qur'ān understands as belonging altogether to God (11:123,13:31, 82:5 *et al.*) and descending through the seven heavens (e.g. 65:12) to bring the vital revelation by which man understands his creaturehood. This 'word' of command effectuates creation inasmuch as the utterance – the intention operating – translates the purpose into deed. John's Hebraic Logos has the same meaning. 'By the word of the Lord' all came to be.

The Greeks, whose language supplied that term, could recognise in this Semitic idiom the universal principle of reason which runs through the whole material world. Akin to the 'signs' (*āyāt*) of the Qur'ān Greek and Stoic thinking read an affinity between perceptive intelligence in man and perceivable intelligibility in things. The speech by which they formulated this rationality, and sharpened their awareness of it, meant that language in them teamed up with meaning in things. Logos denoted both and enabled their exchanges.

John in his Gospel is saying that this meaningfulness in creation, articulate in man, is taken up, like sound in music, into the total significance of Jesus. He states this very carefully and with, we can say, deeply Muslim susceptibilities. What speaks in Jesus is the divine 'Wisdom' (another of his germinal thoughts) spoken of, for example, in Proverbs 8:22 f. as being always in God's presence. The divine counsel which lies behind creation can be thought of distinctively from God Himself yet never divorced from Him, just as, grammatically, 'Him' and 'His' are distinguishable but never separable. This 'Wisdom' is akin to the Greek Logos, with the subtle differences belonging to the genius of either culture.

With all these associations of mind John says that 'there in the very initiative the Word was, the Word in the divine purpose and presence'. Then he adds, very carefully: '... and God was the Word.' His Greek is very important here. He is *not* saying '... and the Word was God' in the sense that there is no divine being other than, or outside Jesus. He does not say *Ho Theos*, 'the God'. There is no definite article and the omission is quite significant. He is not exhausting what we mean by God in what we have in Jesus. That would give no ground for what Jesus was, as if one could have some actual music without the arithmetic of sound, or a drama without a dramatist, or a building in the absence of architecture. 'And God was the Word' has a full and yet restrictive sense, as one might say: 'and music was the symphony.' These are differentiated, not in *what* they are, but in *how* they are – not in essence or quality, but in how these reach us in experience.

Further, John writes, 'without him [Christ] nothing came into being' in creation – a very Quranic exclusiveness. He denies all 'demiurges', intervening agencies, and plural or lesser deities. He is resolute for divine Unity within creation. Creation, in plan and in implementation, may be differentiated but certainly not divided into duality or plurality after the fashion of the pagan world.

This wondering interpretation of God and the world John complements with the meaning of what he believes to be God's purpose and action in Jesus. 'The Word was made flesh.' A divine initiative to reveal and to redeem was translated into history and event around a single personality in a living situation. He captures that sense of crisis which we have noted from the outset. 'He came to his own...' (*ta idia*) – his home, his world, his creation (as Greeks would understand), his kin, the Torah-keepers, those where 'wisdom had pitched tent' (as Jews would understand). He, too, 'pitched his tent' (verse 14) among them, but 'his own' (*hoi idioi*) (now plural) people 'received him not'. John is telling a story of rejection as the context of a story of grace. The light illuminates the darkness precisely in being at issue with it. The story of Jesus is for him God's penetrative love reckoning effectively with the human waywardness which mars the creative design. In so doing the Creator is known to be 'faith-keeping' and consistent.

The tent-imagery John employs here comes of course from his Hebraic roots, where the divine Presence, the *Shechinah* 'settled' upon the 'tent of meeting' (Exod. 40:34–35) just as it had hovered over Mount Sinai (Exodus 24:16). In Surah 2:248 there is a reference to the *Sakīnah* in a Judaic context and in 9:26 and 9:40 in incidents associated with Muḥammad. Without equating distinctive, and not easily ascertainable, meanings, it is possible to see at least a cognate theme in respect of divine presence for divine ends, within particular situations where those ends are involved. It is such a presence, in the sense of the *pleroma* we noted at the start of this chapter, that John identifies in the significance of Jesus and which his Gospel portrays. The care Muslims have always taken at all costs never to 'associate' the human and the divine in the way pagans do in no way denies or forbids that involvement of the divine with the human which is inseparable from creation, law, revelation and mercy. On the contrary, the Qur'ān itself assumes it as noted in Chapter 7. Were the divine and the human in dissociation, there could be neither prophethood nor Muḥammad. It is not the fact of that relatedness which is in dispute between us, but only its form, its intensity, its Islamic reservations, or its Christian decisiveness. John believes that the divine Presence, for deeply divine reasons, is equatable with Jesus in his story. No *Shirk* is here and no forfeiture of unity. All this is what he means by 'the Word made flesh' and this, following him, is what Christians have meant by the Sonship of Jesus. It is because it is so that he must embark on his narrative, dominating it all the time by the central 'crisis' of truth and love which it generates in the world, and deriving the whole from creation 'in the beginning'.

viii

It remains to examine briefly our final point about the time-relation in this Gospel according to John. All, of course, is retrospect – long retrospect, in the narrative sense – but all the time it is illumination of present experience within the Church. The present is there in the past or, if we read that past as present, i.e. as if we were actually living in the Galilee and Jerusalem of Jesus, then the future, i.e. the future where we now are, is there in that present. Sayings like 'I have overcome the world' (16:33) are true not simply as prospective assurance from Jesus talking with disciples: they express the present and past experience of the Church. As we must see in Chapter 10 in connection with the Paraclete, memory plays a crucial role in the Gospel. But it is not the memory that simply recalls what, otherwise, might suffer oblivion: it is the memory that relives and renews a sustained and sustaining significance. The story is told not, as all history is, merely with hindsight, but as a continuity in which the reader now stands.

This can be usefully illustrated in two passages, in default of many others, namely, 1:29–42, being the call of the first disciples, and 17:1–26 often called Jesus' 'High Priestly Prayer'. In the first the disciples follow and 'discover' Jesus in terms of 'the Lamb of God who bears away the sin of the world'. It would be hard to reconcile this with their obvious later incomprehension, in this and the other Gospels, of the real and ultimate significance of Jesus. *This* 'Lamb of God' significance was indeed 'ultimate' and only known after the Cross and Resurrection. How, then, could the disciples have heard it so and received it so, at the very outset of their non-acquaintance with Jesus? If we take the narrative as it stands we must disqualify much else elsewhere in the story.

It seems clear that John as writer is taking the final perspective. Indeed their discipleship *did* begin in initial unawareness, but that beginning had *this* future. They did, indeed, respond to 'the Lamb of God' but only in the event, here telescoped so that its climax is set into its origins. History is proleptic in this way. Was not the battle of Badr *Yaum al-Furqān?* (Surah 8:41). An immediate chronicler would have said that some three hundred Muslims, in a small skirmish, defeated a thousand Quraishī soldiers and that the dead were fourteen to fifty. It was far from a finish. The Quraish came back: Uḥud was dubious. Mecca resisted another decade. Nevertheless, a long-range historian would see that Badr was truly pivotal and that it had within its sequel, turning on its issue, the tide of Islam across Asia and Europe and even, given that tide, the factors inducing the discovery of America, and much else besides.

In such wise, all that the disciples came to be as leaders and to hold as theologians could be discerned in that first recruitment of their naiveté. They heard the Baptist speak and they followed Jesus and they belonged thereby to 'the Lamb of God'. In sowing a seed a farmer (given prospering weather, etc.) sows a harvest in one and the same activity. The harvest only comes in the sequel by being integrally there at the start. As Thomas Mann puts it in his monumental *Joseph and His Brothers:*[24]

> We see what is coming, what is already present because it happened when the story first told itself, and is only not yet come to pass because we give due heed to ... laws of time and sequence ... What we can do ... is to extend somewhat our notion of the present, to include in it somewhat larger entities of sequence, and make them a sort of loose coincidence in time.

John's coincidences, however, are far from 'loose'. They are purposive and controlled. He turns his past/present portrayal into direct speech when so many of his narrative occasions pass imperceptibly into discourses from Jesus, as we have seen. This does not mean that he is attributing things to Jesus unwarrantably. He is presenting events in meaning, meaning in events, not – manifestly not – like a secretary accepting dictated words, but as an interpreter realising the clues. His warrant, as with all historians, is the conviction that he is grasping and mediating the reality. This quality in John must be understood if we are not to accuse him, mistakenly, of transforming Jesus into an unrecognisable figure or falsifying his impact as retrospect, and only retrospect, could yield it. This is not to say that the reader now has no need to reserve any questions, taking everything blindly on trust. It is to say that he should understand the nature of the document he reads and appreciate that John is neither a ghost-writer, nor a verbatim reporter, but a disciple in maturity.

Nowhere is this situation of the Gospel clearer than in the long prayer of Jesus in chapter 17. Plainly, we are not reading an auditor's notebook jottings. We are reading an epitome of Jesus' mission, close to its climax, from within his inner consciousness, his sense of the future, as these are apprehended in John's own retrospect and reverie. His capacity for this role turns on that activity of the Holy Spirit, 'bringing all things to remembrance' awaiting us in the Chapter 10 to follow.

John chapter 17 is full of the characteristic words of John: glory, truth, life, the world, the work, the word, joy, love, unity – all words of Jesus. The prayer is full of 'completion', of a task fulfilled, a mission achieved. John, who had not stayed over the birth of Jesus (as Luke and Matthew did), sees the whole ministry within the framework of eternity. Even the Cross, so near at hand, is gathered without explicit mention into the theme of glory – glory tied back to the original divine purpose predating the world and finite history. There is a 'theology' of the knowledge of God and of eternal life, as indeed elsewhere in John, only articulate in the disciples after the birth at Easter of the Church. That Church is seen, in the prayer, anticipatorily, as it became, a given community – preserved, precarious, consecrated, commissioned, and yet to be tested, enlarged, hallowed and united. It would be artless not to read in all this the perspectives not of spiritual Gethsemane but of Ephesus and Rome and of Jerusalem after Titus.

Greek aorist tenses and phrases like 'they have kept my word', and 'the world has hated them', clearly imply a distance from Gethsemane, the point in time. Yet all has to do with those immediacies in their long significance. We have what one writer calls 'an eschatological continuum'.[25] Eschatology, or what has to do with 'the end' or 'the end-time', means climax, judgement and history's fulfilment. In John, eschatology, as the phrase goes, is 'realised'. What elsewhere is thought of as a future event to be awaited is here thought to be 'realised' in the ongoing 'judgement' – decision – being worked out in the world through the mission of Jesus, through the incorporation of the Church, and through the choices men make in that 'crisis' about themselves with which the Gospel confronts them by its invitation into truth and its challenge to 'the evil'. It is that issue which gives urgency to John's writing. What he sees as central to Jesus' whole 'trial' is essentially the 'trial' of the world. The themes in which God, in Christ, summons mankind to truth and love and glory are, by the same token, the point at which mankind is summoned to a verdict about itself. 'To as many as received him he gave the authority to become the sons of God, those, that is, who believe on his name' (1:12).

It is to that faith John ardently, gently, fiercely, patiently, wishes to guide his readers. That faith would be, for him, 'the baptism of God', the coming in to the fabric of the personality of each of us 'the grace and truth which came by Jesus Christ', because in him they had their divine abode. 'Thou in me,' he said, 'and I in them that the world may know' (17:23).

Notes

1 It is not meant to suggest that *Ṣibghah* and *Pleroma*, in Qur'ān and Gospel, can be aligned in any way except their common stake in comparable metaphor. Both are highly metaphorical terms in the sense of inter-fusion indicated here. In inter-faith meeting which respects doctrine and does not let sentiment discount it, there is need to experiment by exploring possibly kindred clues. The clue ventured here is the thought that there is a divine activity expressively proceeding within human personality, whether effectuating true religion (*ṣibghah*), or the declarative 'Word made flesh' in Jesus as the Christ (*pleroma*). See Chapter 2, note 10.

2 A habit of mind, like that normally brought to the Qur'ān in Islam (and by some Christians in relation to the Bible), which takes Scripture as meaning itself in explicit literalism, must find the kind of discerning readership proper to the New Testament a difficult hurdle to take. It is a very necessary one, though, if we are not to stumble and misread. John is the writer who surely stretches our intelligence and our will to comprehend.

3 It needs to be remembered that Surah 2:138 implies a restrictive sense to *Ṣibghat Allāh* ('Who is better than God in respect of *ṣibghah?*') which might be held to exclude the enlisting of its import made here. If the question in the passage is read, not as exclamatory but as exclusive, and if *ṣibghah* is taken to mean (God's) religion, then it will be read as stating, in that form, the familiar finality and ultimacy of Islam, leaving no case for Christian *pleroma*. The option here will depend on the readership, so option it remains.

4 It would be strange to list 'the sons of Zebedee' (21:2) and on the same occasion separately note 'the disciple whom Jesus loved', unless they were distinct identities. The latter, moreover, seems certainly to have been a late recruit among disciples. There is also evidence of the demise of John Zebedee prior to the time of the redactor here.

5 Perhaps the whole import of John is summed up in saying that 'what John has done is to make his Jesus the prime theologian and evangelist of the Christian *kerygma*'. George Johnston, *The Spirit-Paraclete in the Gospel of John* (Cambridge, 1970), p. 136. In so doing, if we comprehend his Gospel rightly, John becomes the prime theologian and evangelist of the *kerygma* as Scripture.

6 Nowhere in the New Testament is that opposition to Gnosticism clearer than in the First Epistle of John with its reproach of those who deny that Jesus is come in the flesh' (4:2–3). The Gospel clearly shares the same insistence on the actuality of Jesus and his history, on 'the Word ...made flesh' (1:14). Yet it also stresses that 'the flesh profits nothing' (6:23; cf. 1:13 and 3:6). Despite the tensions about the Gospel and its presence in the Canon, it is fair to say that there is no real contradiction here. The apparent one stems from the contrasted sense of the Greek word *sarx*, as physical actuality and the principle of self-centredness which the physical houses or embodies. There is a similar ambiguity in John and elsewhere, about *kosmos*, the 'world', which 'God so loved...' (3:16), but about which Jesus could also say: 'I am not of the world' (17:14, 17:16).

7 Among major recent works on the Fourth Gospel are: C.H. Dodd, *Historical Tradition in the Fourth Gospel* (Cambridge, 1963), and *The Interpretation of the Fourth Gospel* (Cambridge, 1955); C.K. Barrett, *The Gospel According to St. John* (London, 1978, 2nd edn), *The Gospel of John and Judaism* (London, 1975); *The Prologue of St. John's Gospel* (London, 1971); Raymond E. Brown, *The Gospel according to St. John* (New York, vol. 1, 1971; Vol. 2, 1970).

8 An Islamic theme in the sense that, as traced in Chapters 5 and 6, the sequence of confrontation and crisis is required by the Qur'ān. Hostility to prophets, Jesus included, is a deep theme in the Qur'ān, as is their ultimate 'vindication,' whether

by outward success, as with Moses, David and Muḥammad, or by 'rescue' as with Jesus, followed by exaltation.

9 See the careful paraphrase of John 18:33–37, by C.H. Dodd in *About the Gospels* (Cambridge, 1952), p. 33. The sense is very well brought out in the New English Bible version, doubtless by help of C.H. Dodd, its Vice Chairman and Director.

10 As urged, in the following sentence quoted from Paul Winter, *On the Trial of Jesus* (Berlin, 1961), p. 148.

11 Preserved in the John Rylands Library, Manchester, England, it measures 2.5 by 3.5 inches and is designated as P.52. It is a vital witness to the antiquity of the Gospel.

12 Paul Winter, *loc. cit.*, pp. 148–49.

13 Matt. 27:36, in the narrative of the crucifixion, graphically captures this in the words: 'And sitting down they watched him there...' or: 'They sat and watched him there.'

14 John's Jesus, for example, tells the Samaritan woman at the well that 'salvation is of the Jews' (4:22). However, that gentle emphasis in the drift of the exchanges is no bar to the conversation. It is only partisanship which makes it plausible to derive anti-semitism from the New Testament in general or this Gospel in particular.

15 Notably the long narrative exchange in Chapter 9, where the parents of the blind man (i.e. the Jewish stock of the new believing community) absolve themselves of any liability either to answer for him or to support him but refer their interrogators to the blind man himself (verses 18–23). The story of Nicodemus has implications in the same sense (3:1–13) where Hebraic learning is, nevertheless, imperceptive of the new life, but moves, hesitatingly towards it (7:50–52) and assists at the burial of Jesus (19:39–42). Whether, or when, Nicodemus finally became an avowed 'confessor' of Christ is left to silence. His story epitomises the open question, the limen, or threshold, where so much inter-communal relationship hovers in this Gospel.

16 The massacre of the Banū Qurayẓah under Muḥammad, within his Medinan story, was the extreme point of the element of ruthlessness within the *Sīrah* of the Prophet. According to the earliest chroniclers some eight hundred males of the Jewish tribe were killed in retaliation for their alleged complicity in hostilities against Islam. A recent writer believes that in fact the numbers were much less. See Barakat Ahmad, *Muhammad and the Jews: A Re-Examination* (New Delhi, 1982). Whatever the acerbities between John and 'the Jews' they were those only of unhappy mental tensions. If and where these became 'physical' it was John's community who were the victims.

17 See, for example, Paul Winter, *op.cit.*; A.N. Sherwin-White, *Roman Society and Roman Law in the New Testament* (1963), and A.E. Harvey: *Jesus on Trial: A Study in the Fourth Gospel* (London, 1976).

18 Dan Jacobson, *The Story of Stories: the Chosen People and Its God* (London, 1982), pp. 193–4.

19 See, for example, Ismā'il R. al-Fārūqī, *On Arabism: 'Urūbah and Religion* (Amsterdam, 1962), pp. 63–99; and *Christian Ethics: A Historical and Systematic Analysis of Its Dominant Ideas* (Montreal, 1967), pp. 74–135. That alleged 'Hellenising', however, is in direct line with the 'sign' quality of Jesus which is so central a clue to John's Christology, and 'sign-significance' (if the term may be permitted) is also a crucial theme in the Qur'ān. The Islamic desire to have Jesus only and wholly 'messenger' fails to reckon with his 'sign-significance' for the Qur'ān itself. Mere word transmission would reduce prophets to leaflet distributors. It is important to see that John's presentation of Jesus is his sense of the dimension of a relevance that does more than speak (cf. the serial 'I am').

20 Examples are legion. Cf. Fatḥi Raḍwān's comment on Jesus in Christology as 'a

god in spite of himself', in a play, so named, written in 1962. See *Journal of Arabic Literature*, vol. V, 1974, pp. 108–126.

21 See Aileen Guilding, *The Fourth Gospel and Jewish Worship: A Study of the Relation of St. John's Gospel to the Ancient Jewish Lectionary System* (Oxford, 1960): 'The Gospel might fairly be described as a Christian commentary on the lections of the triennial cycle' (p. 231). The author notes recurring parallels also in chaps. 15 and 16. It is clear that had John been the 'Helleniser' he is often surmised to have been, and had he gone for the Greek *ethos*, his Gospel would have been a very different book.

22 *Iḥyā' 'Ulūm al-Dīn*, Book 8.3:1. Al-Ghazālī continues: 'The inmost majesty of His speech is concealed in the garment of the letters.' It was in such terms that this pivotal thinker in Islam wrestled, *qua* the Qur'ān, with the issue that engages John *qua* the person and significance of Jews, namely how the temporal can enshrine the eternal, and the human 'carry' the divine.

23 See V. Courtois, *Mary in Islam* (Calcutta, 1954) and Chapter 3 earlier.

24 Thomas Mann, *Joseph and His Brothers*, Eng. trans. H.T. Lowe Porter (London, 1978), p. 557.

25 C.K. Barrett, *Commentary on St. John's Gospel*, 2nd edn (London, 1978), p. 90.

Chapter 10

The Abiding Spirit

i

> In Islam there is no such thing, in principle
> as conversion, but restoration, a returning, and
> a remembering...The greatest challenge upon this
> earth is not so much to explore God as to remember
> that there is one.

This summons to remember, Ḥasan Askarī[1] goes on, refers back not simply to mortal forgetfulness during life but has to do with recalling a primeval consciousness when all prospective humanity in the loins of the future acknowledged God's claim in response to the question: 'Am I not your Lord?' (Surah 7:172). Humanity has perpetually to remember that first original confession of tributary creaturehood.

Memory, then, is the clue to human awareness of God. Due obedience follows on renewed reminding. Prophethood was the means to counter forgetfulness. The Qur'ān itself is named *Al-Dhikr*, 'the Reminder'. Recital of it shares the same term. 'Remember Me,' says 2:152, 'and I will remember you.' Revelation, so understood, locates the wrong of the world not, essentially, in wilfulness but in heedlessness, not in waywardness but in thoughtlessness. Messengership in revelation, rather than saviourhood, is the right, sufficient corrective. To be sure, there are many times in Quranic situations when heedlessness is almost indistinguishable from wilfulness and the thoughtless are desperately perverse. The tribulations of the messengers say as much. There is an occupational hazard in prophethood which seems to indicate more than faded recollection in the hearers. Nonetheless, human mindlessness may be understood as a failure in awareness, a lapse of primeval memory.

The theme of the Holy Spirit in the Christian faith can well be introduced from this angle. Recollection is certainly to the fore in all the Gospels. 'He will bring all things to your remembrance,' says John 14:26. However, the bringing back to mind meant here is not some ancient cosmic destiny as such. Nor is it the content of some overlaid code. It is the gathering significance of the Christ-event as the *Sitz im Leben* of the world's salvation. The documenting of that conviction was studied in Chapter 4, and was a major concern in our attention to John in Chapter 9. The New Testament was itself the terms of the remembering.

That *Sitz im Leben* of salvation, as Christians hold it to be, certainly belongs with the cosmic destiny confessed in Surah 7:172. John's Prologue makes that clear in linking 'the Word' of creation with 'the Word' of grace in Jesus. Remembering also underlay the Gospels' presentation of the teaching of Jesus. But the drama of redemption embraces both cosmic destiny and the teaching that renews it and sets them in its own more radical context of redemptive love. It is more radical because it reads the human situation as calling for more than exhortation to a vocation that is more than overlooked. Thus New Testament *Dhikr* returns to a nucleus of historical events which it sees as having in epitome the whole issue of the human meaning as both cosmos and ethic define it. It is useful to note how the Qur'ān, too, in many situations has histories within its *Dhikr* where the prophets, especially Muḥammad, invoke the salutary warnings and examples of past generations in their heedless ways.[2] The New Testament is not unique in capturing as symbolic what is historical in form, nor in recalling events in order to learn of divine relationships. It is distinctive only in the inclusiveness and the character of the history that it holds in memory. The Gospels are the clear token of how this 'bringing to remembrance' availed in the genesis of a Scripture which housed it and made possible the renewal of the things remembered via a readership through the long centuries. Our purpose now is to study the activity of the Holy Spirit both in that Scripture genesis and in the other aspects of the *Dhikr* in community which the Church comprises. For 'things brought to remembrance' having to do with Jesus and, through remembrance brought into focus, are the works of the Holy Spirit, 'the Paraclete'.

ii

First it is useful to appreciate the different temper and concept within this corporate possession of what is decisive for faith. Islamic awareness of Islamic heritage is through the precise and constant memorising of the Qur'ān and its recital. That recitation of the text ensures, on Muslim premises, the standing in truth of its practitioners. Where Islam sets the recitation of a Book, the Christian faith sets the repossession of a personality. The difference belongs with the entire understanding of revelation itself in the two faiths.

It was not, of course, a distinction which could obtain in the centuries before Islam and the *Tanzīl* of its Scripture. But something comparable was consciously contrasted, between the Judaic tradition and Jesus himself, in the New Testament patterns the Church owed to him. For example, in John 5:39, Jesus is reported as inviting his hearers to give him a real hearing whereas instead they prefer to 'search the Scriptures' for proof-texts. Again in John 7:52, Nicodemus, who had been tentatively speaking up for Jesus, is silenced by the textual pundits who can find no reference to 'prophets out of Galilee'. Indeed, throughout the four Gospels – even in Matthew who is himself very fond of supportive citations – there runs this issue between textual *taqlīd*, or hidebound literalism, and the living, personal authority that liberates the mind. It would, therefore, be wrong to conceive of, or use, the New Testament Scriptures in a textual manner inconsistent with the usage of Jesus himself and with the way in which they came to exist. When Jesus taught, the Scriptures about him did not yet exist and he himself never wrote. That means a profound difference in the shape of Christian 'Scripturality' from the Quranic. The latter is itself the literal vehicle and not the means of access to that which is more ultimate than itself, as the New Testament is to Jesus. This cardinal fact, studied in Chapter 4, belongs with the role of the Holy Spirit in the documenting of the Christian ultimacy in Jesus.

iii

Study of 'the Holy Spirit who is to abide with the Church for ever' (John 14:16) brings us to several important issues which gather around the term 'the Paraclete' and the belief of some Muslims that it refers to the Prophet Muḥammad himself, in line with a prediction attributed to Jesus in Surah 61:6. We need much patience with each other to disentangle the strands in this theme.

The first is the meaning of the term Paraclete itself. The Greek is *Parakletos*, a derivative of the verb *parakaleo*, meaning: to call, or send, for; to desire of; to exhort; and to console. The word was transliterated into Hebrew and Aramaic and could well have been used by Jesus himself just as it stands in Greek. The nounal derivative *paraklesis* comes to mean 'consolation' or 'comfort' (in the old English sense) as that to which the appeal made invites, or in which it results. Since one situation in which aid has to come alongside is that of people in court, *parakletos* has then the meaning of 'advocate', either for defence or for prosecution. In non-juridical situations it may have simply the sense of 'companion', a word which means, quite literally, 'taking bread with'. There is nothing so close as a common table and the binding community of bread. The link between the Holy Spirit and the Eucharist will concern us later.

Times of persecution in the Church were frequent and intense at the hands of Roman authority. It has also been very evident from John, in Chapter 9, that sharp enmities against believers were abroad, embittered by the tensions between, or concerning, so called 'crypto-Jews' or 'crypto-Christians'. The borderlands of allegiance are always contentious. But it has to be said that these 'trials' of Christians were an extension of the essential 'crisis' developing in Jesus' ministry and culminating in his crucifixion. It was in this sort of context that we must understand the role of the Paraclete, as defender of believers, as their succour under false or confused accusations, their wisdom in the content and the temperance of their reply (e.g. Mark 13:11, etc.). There was certainly 'comfort' in such a reliance readily available according to the promise of Christ. This theme may be traced back to the Book of Job (Ayyūb) where (e.g. 16:8–11) the Targum, i.e. the Aramaic version, used the Greek loan-word *parakletos* for the Hebrew *melits*, meaning a witness on one's behalf in face of hostility. *Melits* is used, for example, in Gen. 42:23, with the sense of 'an interpreter' in the story of Joseph. The *parakletos* in that sense mediates between parties in a situation of estrangement.

The idea of a 'defensive counsel' in the word Paraclete can be turned into that of 'prosecution'. 'Defending' this often involves 'prosecuting' that. In John the Paraclete 'accuses' the world of 'sin, righteousness and judgement' (16:7–11), and John links that accusation closely with the reception the world gives to Jesus. This corresponds, but in its more radical way, with the thought of a divine *Dhikr* calling mankind away from what ought not to be (neglect, failure, compromise) and back to what ought to be (*islām, taqwā, falāḥ*, and the other concepts by which the Qur'ān defines man's true response to God). It is in this sense, among others, that the Holy Spirit is described as 'the Spirit of truth', under whose guidance and prompting true meanings are known and true living identified, against all calumny and distortion.

Such vital guidance involves the further idea of guardianship associated with the term *parakletos*. There are scholars who suggest that in the period between the two Biblical Testaments, and in the Qumran Community, such guardianship or spokesmanship was thought of as protecting true believers from 'the spirit of error'. The vindication which would result from such spiritual 'prosecution' of evil-doers is an experience the Qur'ān often emphasises as the right of the well-doers. In the Early Church it was the assurance that through the apostolic preaching truth was being heard in 'the courts of the world' and the Holy Spirit made it to be so by his divine presence there, through and on behalf of the believers and particularly their responsible leaders.[3]

All this is understood of the Paraclete in the New Testament because he is 'the Spirit of Christ' and 'another Comforter'. This word 'another' in John 14:16 clearly implies that Jesus was the first 'Comforter'. There is a close parallel in John between what he writes of Jesus and what he writes of the Spirit. 'I will come to you,' Jesus says (14:18) in the same context as his words about the coming of the Spirit. 'He will not speak of, or from, himself' (16:13), but will 'take and show' what is Christ's (16:14–15). The meaning is that the Paraclete is to be perennially to the Church what Jesus had been historically to the disciples. 'He will abide with you for ever' (14:16). The New Testament understands this as ensuring to the Church in sustained immediacy the finality of Jesus. There is no idea here of a successor, still less of a replacement. The Holy Spirit verifies, draws out and mediates the Christ-event. As the energy within the witnessing community the Paraclete perpetuates all that Jesus had been in a sort of living 'exegesis' (or 'drawing out'). That 'exegesis' would have had no theme without the great original ('the Word manifest in the flesh'); but the great original inaugurated that spiritual energy by which it would 'abide for ever'.

This explains why John, for example, declares that 'the Holy Spirit was not yet...' in 7:39, because Jesus was 'not yet glorified', i.e. the whole import of the Christ-event was not yet evident. The words do not mean that there was no prior activity of the Holy Spirit, in creation, in prophethood, in the baptism of John and of Jesus. They mean that the complete *régime*, or 'time' of the Spirit waited for, and waited upon, the fullness of Jesus' work. It is for the same reason that the Nicene Creed uses the technical term about the Holy Spirit 'proceeding'. It means 'issuing forth', 'ensuing' from an antecedent reality that both enabled and required it. The Eastern and the Western branches of the Christian Church have differed over what is called in Latin '*filioque*', i.e. whether the Holy Spirit 'proceeds from the Father and the Son' or '... from the Father through the Son'. The distinction need not detain us here.[4] Either way the Holy Spirit belongs with the Christ-event as interpretation belongs with music and both belong with God as music with musician. To mark that sequence the Creeds use a different term to say how 'God in Christ' and 'Christ through the Spirit' are understood.

iv

The ongoing relationship of the Spirit to Christ means that being Christian in the world is the vocation to be the extension, through the generations, of the significance of Christ. This is the point of the words '... that he may abide with you for ever'. It is for this reason that the metaphors under which the New Testament presents the work of the Spirit in the Church have to do with partnership and mutuality. Thus fire inheres in fuel, light in lamps and wind in sails. The person is always the prime unit of faith but only as truth indwells the mind. Fires reside only in fuels, but fuels are dead and cold unless fire possesses them. Thus Timothy is told in 2 Timothy 1:6 to 'stir into flame the gift of God which is in him'. Likewise, if we ask, with Surah 31:31, 'Have you not seen the ships riding the sea by God's grace?' we know it as a sign of God's mercy because we, for our part, hoist sails to harness the winds. It is they that propel the ships but only by dint of sails we spread – and both 'by leave of God'. What sails are to winds, souls are to the Spirit. It was just these metaphors of wind and fire which we find in Acts chapter 2 in the story of the first symbolic possession by the Spirit of the Church.

Later in the Book of Acts, the first recorded Council of the Christian Church took place in Jerusalem to decide a very crucial question, namely whether the new fellowship was genuinely open to non-Jews as well as Jews on equal terms – a decision definitive for the whole Christian future. When the Council set out its resolution of the matter in a positive inclusiveness of all alike its document used a striking phrase. They said of their ruling: 'It seemed good to the Holy Spirit and to us...' (Acts 15:28). Why 'and us...?' It could be argued that what is 'good to the Holy Spirit' is good and there is no occasion to add: '... and to us'. Can human authority improve on divine? Or even complement it? But no! The Holy Spirit is present, and works, through human minds and personal wills. How else, in time and place, are His purposes fulfilled? We have something of the same 'God and...' situation which we find in the Qur'ān: 'Obey God and obey the apostle.' The Book of Acts, from the beginning, has to do with partnership. The initiative is with the wind but the impulse is by means of the sails. 'The Holy Spirit and us' is the necessary pattern.

This explains why the Greek noun *parakletos* belongs with the abstract *paraklesis*, usually translated 'comfort' or 'consolation', or the sense of 'adequacy' that comes from the presence of the Paraclete. Barnabas, among the apostles, is described in Acts 4:36 as 'the son of comfort', this being the meaning of his Aramaic name, as Greek transliterated it – *bar*, 'son', and *nabas* feasibly from the root to 'exhort' or 'prophesy'. Barnabas was certainly a great encourager of people, drawing out the best in them. This, we may believe, is the surest and the wisest form of 'comfort'. If, boldly, we translate his name adjectivally, we would get 'Barnabas, the Holy-Spirited man' – a rendering which confirms all that has been said about the fire/fuel, wind/sails partnership in the Spirit's ways with man.

It is against the background of these brief studies in the New Testament meaning of the Paraclete that we must set the unhappy controversy between Muslims and Christians in respect of the word. According to Surah 61:6 a prophecy of the coming of Muḥammad is attributed to Jesus: '...a messenger coming after me whose name is Aḥmad' (or, if we so read, 'whose name is more praised').[5] It must be the task of Quranic exegesis to interpret this attribution to Jesus. What is certainly clear is that it cannot be related to the sayings of Jesus in the Gospels about the Paraclete. Those sayings in no way relate to a purely prophetic spokesman whose coming, six centuries after, would in no sense be relevant to Jesus' disciples in their immediate first-century situation. His promise was to them and to their posterity in unbroken sequence. It did not, in its Gospel context, relate to a generation fifteen generations on, and after a silent hiatus of non-fulfilment. Nor could its meaning of the steady recapitulation of the event of a personality (which is the point of the word 'another') be realised in a further, later, 'messenger', however noble.

One textual matter has in some quarters arisen in the problem of relating John 14:16 with Surah 61:6. It is the suggestion that the Greek word *parakletos* should be read *periklutos* – a term which would approximate to the meaning of *aḥmad*, 'more praised', or 'celebrated'. For those accustomed to Arabic consonantal words, with variable, unwritten vowels, this might seem plausible, with the 'e', 'i', and 'u' vowels replacing the 'a', 'a' and 'e' ones. There is, however, no textual evidence in any way sustaining such variant reading, and the manuscript texts of St John go back to the second century. Moreover, the two Greek words are themselves compounds and the prefixes and root verbs are both different. Suspicions of textual corruption here would be completely unfounded, on documentary, grammatical and exegetical grounds. Of course, any deliberate alteration to 'divert' *parakletos* into *periklutos* would be impossible before Muhammad's time – by which time the text of the Gospel had been known and fixed for four centuries.

The issue for Muslims and Christians today about John 14:16 and Surah 61:6, however, lies beyond the sort of interest in verbal foretellings which so attracted and pre-occupied early generations when controversies were pursued in, and provoked by, such trust in citation. It is not vital whether *aḥmad* (or *Aḥmad*) – Arabic lacking capital letters – should be read as an adjective or a name. 'Muḥammad' translates *periklutos* equally well.[6] It is *parakletos* with which debate has to deal. Controversy when not couched in the real terms tends to generate its own obscurities. The 'greater celebrity' status attributed to Muḥammad in 61:6 must be assessed in spiritual and religious, not in merely predictive, matters. That being so, whether predictive anticipation of such greater celebrity can be assigned to Jesus must be weighed, and rejected, on two grounds quite transcending textual argument. The one is that the birth of Christianity – and with it the New Testament Scriptures themselves – have to do with a sequel in the experience of the disciples which takes faith, and religion with it, beyond 'messengership' *per se*, into a realisation of 'God in Christ' where revelation itself has passed beyond 'law', and 'guidance' (and so beyond 'prophecy' as such) into redemptive grace. It is ultimacy in those terms which, for the New Testament, indicates the finality of prophecy and does not admit of Jesus being seen as one (even the penultimate one) in a series still capable of persisting. The Christian understanding of 'the Holy Spirit proceeding…' means, precisely, the ongoing significance and experience of a new order of grace, not the earlier order requiring something more final in its own kind. The difference, expressed in other terms, is that between 'inspiration' and Incarnation.

The other ground would be the issues, could we join them, between the actual shape of Muḥammad's mission as Prophet-ruler as it eventuated (as Muslims believe by divine guidance and will) and the different pattern of Jesus' ministry, as studied here in Chapters 5 and 6. The human 'Īsā (Jesus) of Surah 61:6 could only be understood as speaking proleptically of one whose actuality in history – indeed, whose date and place – were to him quite unknown. Apart from the question just considered as to *whether* a further, and final, instalment of prophethood could be meant, there is the question *what* that prophethood would be in pattern, strategy and ethos. This question would be all the more crucial because the one to come was the one to close the prophetic order (though 61:6 does not say so). The matter resolves itself into the painful question of whether Jesus could be understood as anticipating, in completion of his own mission, what in fact eventuated in the actuality of Muḥammad.[7] There is, here, not only the question of foresight divinely enabled to peer down six centuries: there is the question of congruity. It is plainly far more important to align John 14:16 and Surah 61:6 in this sense, taxing as it is, than to be occupied with verbal points about readings, vowels, and surmises, lively or inept, as the case may be.

Some readers may expect here a reference to the so-called Gospel of Barnabas, much quoted in Muslim circles and cited to support the *periklutos* reading instead of *parakletos*. Though much popular credence has unhappily been given to it, this 'Gospel' is a sixteenth-century Italian text, of which no Greek or Aramaic original has been found. Its credibility is deeply suspect on numerous grounds. It goes far beyond Surah 61:6 in having Jesus announce his ministry with the formula: 'In the name of Muḥammad, messenger of God . . .'[8] It has no sustainable relevance to our understanding of Jesus, his meaning in the Paraclete or, indeed, any of the points at issue between Islam and Christianity except, unhappily, that of ministering to confusion or abetting prejudice.

V

The New Testament, which sees the meaning of 'the Holy Spirit, the Comforter' in the way we have now reviewed is itself the evidence of that meaning made concrete in its own contents. 'Bringing all things to your remembrance', on this count, meant the authorship of the Gospels as the responsible, interpretative memory of the community through its Evangelists, setting down what they believed the reality of Jesus to be. This we have studied in Chapter 4. It was a process necessarily requiring a retrospect of time for, as the poet Robert Browning asks:[9] 'What truth was ever told the second day?' His 'John' goes on to say:

> To me, that story – aye, that Life and Death,
> Of which I wrote 'it was' – to me, it is:
> Is, here and now: I apprehend nought else.
> Is not God now i' the world His power first made?
> Is not His love at issue still with sin. . .?

Thus the Gospels came to be, as the *Dhikr* which the significance of Jesus crystallised in the mind of the first Church.

There was the Holy Spirit's *Dhikr* also in the Epistles. These, as we saw in Chapter 4, applied the claims and norms of discipleship to the situations confronting the first, ex-pagan, Christians in the Roman dispersion, and, indeed, the adjustments in outlook necessary for the Jewish Christians in their new perspective on 'the Gentiles' and their full inclusion with them in the new fellowship. One might fairly say that the initial fulfilment of the pledge about 'the abiding Spirit' in John 14:16, 15:26 and 16:7–15, occurs in the emergence of the New Testament writings themselves. Certainly the other meanings of the Paraclete as guardian, sponsor and enabler, were manifestly made good in the possession of those Scriptures.

It remains to consider the final sense of 'the comfort of the Spirit' which has to do with the Paraclete as 'companion'. It is well to link this with the two great Christian sacraments, baptism and the Eucharist. For it is in these that the Christian tradition sees both the symbol and norms of the Spirit's activity in the life of the personal believer.

What has been called 'the seal of the Spirit'[10] in baptism concerns that inter relation of grace and personality which was our preface to the Fourth Gospel, via the Quranic *Ṣibghat Allāh*, in the preceding chapter. Baptism might be described as the engagement of the human spirit with the Spirit of God. In Christian tradition it has three main features. It happens in the personal story by a personal decision. It is symbolised in a historic rite. It inaugurates and sustains a living partnership of the self and the Lord the Spirit. If we explore these three elements we will be close to the Christian significance of the Holy Spirit within the life of the faith.

Baptism is decision within the personality about personality. When John – called the Baptist in distinction from John the Evangelist – prepared for the coming of Jesus, as the first three Gospels describe, he posted himself in the wilderness of Judea on the banks of the River Jordan. The water he needed, as we shall see. But the point of the wilderness, in part, was to draw people away from the pre-occupations and deceptions of the city and the engrossing pursuits of a familiar world, in order to confront them with their real selves, to give them occasion to face the shams and deceits in which they hid from a true awareness of life. His preaching quickened that realism dramatically. 'The axe,' he cried, 'is laid at the root of the trees' (Luke 3:9). He demanded a real repentance coming from a real honesty about the self in all his hearers. For him repentance meant a radical acknowledgement of how far short they, and their societies, were from a true life. Only so could they be readied for 'the Kingdom of God' in the Gospel of Jesus.

This message had at its heart – and set at the core of Christianity – a deep conviction about human selfhood which perhaps we can illuminate from a source that may seem initially strange, namely

Buddhism. Buddhism is acutely concerned with the issues in our being individual selves. Given transience and flux in all our experience, and the futility he saw in these, the Buddha concluded that 'desire' was the sorry factor causing us to cling to this futility and so spelling our frustration. 'Desire' should be extinguished like an unfuelled fire, so that the self might escape from the illusion of significance which 'desire' mistakenly gave it. By a disciplined abnegation of 'desire' we could attain the truth of *anatta*, or self-noughting, which liberated us from the trap of being selves. In extreme form it said to humanity: 'Your very selfhood is a sin.'

For the Christian mind there is a deep truth here which needs rescue from a dark misreading. 'Transience', anyway is not all. There is mystery and quality within it. But it is only too true that certain forms of 'desire' will distort our humanity, deceive us into lust and satiety, blight our relationships and pervert our whole being. We do well to withhold fuel from such fires. 'To sow to the flesh is to reap corruption' (Gal. 6:8). But this is properly called 'selfishness'. It should not be assumed to be the only form of 'selfhood'. Our very existence is *not* a sin: it is the context of a decision, a crisis, by which it might become so. But there is a blessed other possibility: the option for a selfhood truly unselfish, a potential fulfilled in realisation of love, of the arts, of skills, of compassion, and so of genuine personality. Where Buddhism, by and large, sees selfhood and selfishness as metaphysically akin, Christianity sees them as morally distinguished. For the Christian the true *anatta* is *not* 'a not-self', in which our personhood, our individuation, are essentially negated, but a self-transcendence within the self in which a true and loving humanness may be attained.

If this is to happen those Buddhist warnings against the distorting, deceiving nature of *some* 'desiring' must be firmly made and heeded. This was the intention of John's preaching. We must be radical with what has been called: 'the deceitfulness of sin'. The self needs to take deep stock of itself, repent and set its face towards the good, and do so decisively with a sustained intention. This was the meaning and purpose of John's baptism as the soul's encounter with the Holy Spirit.[11]

That personal decision needed, and received, the focus of a symbolic rite. This – our second theme here – was vivid and sacramental. Baptism could well be described as a *rukn*, or essential part, of religion. It concentrates the *niyyah*, or 'intention', by giving it form in a public ceremony where, as in Islamic *wuḍū'*, or ritual cleansing, something done with and by the body transacts the intent of the soul. All faiths in some way know and use this sacramental dimension, housing what they mean in what they do and so thereby doing the meaning. The thing is not then only thought, intended, or willed: it is also realised and fulfilled. The doer becomes so in the doing.

The imagery in John's baptism was well drawn to this end. There was the river, like a spiritual Rubicon.[12] Like all water, passage through it cleanses. But that simple washing symbolism belonged with the history of transit in the Biblical narrative. Exodus out of Egypt under Moses, and then the crossing of Jordan, were memorialised among the Jews as the story of 'liberation'. They were out from the old and into the new, out from 'the house of bondage', into the land of freedom. The Christian faith saw that transit as a parable of new life in Christ. Jordan went down into Christian history as the symbol of entry into faith via 'the washing of regeneration'. That sense of decisiveness was closely linked with the still more crucial symbol of the death and resurrection of Jesus. These became not only historic events of our redemption but a paradigm of 'a death unto sin and a new life unto righteousness'. The Christian, in baptism, had to 'reckon himself dead with Christ', so that he might 'know the power of the resurrection'. The old symbolism of liberation acquired the new dimension of grace in its radical work in the soul.

That radical work contrasted with the Buddhist understanding yet heeded it in different terms. It told the Christian that he did not 'own' himself. If he acted as if he did he would forfeit true life. To take life as if it was essentially 'autonomous' – meant for the satisfaction of a self-sufficient, self-centred 'me' – was to ensure futility. 'He that loves his life shall lose it.' There *was* a death to self we had to die, if we were truly to belong to Christ. Such 'belonging', which baptism transacted, would give us back ourselves, but in a quite different idiom, as self-giving, self-transcending people whose selfhood would be spent and fulfilled in discipleship. 'Desire to belong', not 'desire not to be', would be the true and liberating thing, since the illusion in which futility lay was not the self but selfishness.

This explains why there is such a close parallelism in the New Testament between baptism and death. It is a simple fact about us all that we are mortal. 'We owe God a death.'[13] There comes a time when we have to concede that 'we are not our own', in that we must consent to surrender the shape of life as we know it in a physical 'house', by the demise of the body. With that demise goes everything we hold dear in its present 'feasibility.' Physical death is an inclusive focus of the self question.

> The grave's a fine and private place,
> But none, I think, do there embrace.[14]

Must we not anticipate, then, that final crux of our selfhood in a readiness to *live*, while life obtains, in spiritual terms of being 'dispossessed' of our selves – which is what death will mean anyway? This is not in any way to 'cheat' its finality. On the contrary, it is to defy its finality by experiencing, here and now, a life that is not in thrall to its threat or its veto. 'In the midst of life we are in death'; in the midst of death we are in life.

The symbolic rite, or *rukn*, of baptism from John through the Apostles and down the long centuries has transacted these meanings of 'newness of life' both by its graphic imagery and its actual incidence. It is the Christian's *wuḍū'*, the Christian circumcision in the inward self. As such it is our experience of the companion Spirit. So – our third aspect – it is the point of consecration for service. This is why Matthew, Mark and Luke begin their narrative of Jesus' ministry with baptism in Jordan at the hands of John. That meaning has concerned us in Chapter 5. The sign of the Cross, for the ordinary Christian, is the sign of recruitment to service. It is a hallowing and an enabling of personality in partnership with the Holy Spirit. That will to serve 'seals' the disciple in the calling 'never to be ashamed of Christ crucified ...' It makes us 'members of Christ', in a 'membership' which, by the imagery of the body, incorporates us in 'the fellowship of the Holy Spirit', which is a fellowship of ministry and action in the world.

vi

When the Apostles' Creed confesses faith in 'the communion of saints', these are often assumed to be people, the whole body of believers. The Latin *communio sanctorum* could equally well be 'the communion of holy things'. The Greek too has readings that are neuter as well as masculine, while the Latin does not distinguish. If we read 'things', the meaning could embrace the two great sacraments, which otherwise are not credally stated. Baptism is the first. The Holy Communion is the second. Here 'holy things' come very much into their own, within what is technically called the *epiclesis*, one of the main areas of the *paraklesis* we are studying. *Epiclesis* means 'invocation', the 'calling down of blessing upon' both communicants and the 'communicables' of bread and wine in what is called by Christians 'the Eucharist'. Holy Communion, 'the Lord's Supper' and 'the Mass' are other names.[15]

Celebration of this other *rukn*, or vital dimension, of Christian faith and worship could well be described as 'the sacrament of the Paraclete'. For the prayer 'Send Your Holy Spirit upon us and upon these Your gifts...' has a central place in the Communion Rite. The Spirit's *Paraklesis* belongs, we may say, in four dimensions which inter-depend in Holy Communion. They are: creation, redemption, participation and consecration.

The bread and the wine of the Eucharist are inclusive symbols of the Creator's world entrusted into the care, skill and techniques of man. The corn and the vine belong with all created things, being in Quranic terms *āyāt*, or signs, of God's gift and mercy. They yield bread and wine, however, only by the co-operating hand and care of man, partner with nature in husbanding its fertility, which – man apart – would languish in choking weeds. In bread and wine, then, we mean to hallow the whole economic order, the productivity of man recognised to be, as the Qur'ān has it, *min faḍli Rabbī*, 'of the goodness of my Lord'. The Qur'ān-minded Muslim, in that sense, should be readily at home in Holy Communion.

The bread and wine which represent the whole natural order were taken by Jesus, as recalled in Chapter 5, for a historical meaning. He made them symbolise the fact of his death, graphically enacted in 'the breaking of bread and the pouring of wine'. It is that redemptive meaning which Christians see at the heart of the sacramental situation at the holy table.

That table, in these meanings, becomes a place of fellowship. Hence the name 'Holy Communion', meaning communion with Christ and communion with one another. Where 'all partake of one bread and drink of one cup' they belong together thereby. Hospitality at a common board has always been a token of human community. Holy Communion believes the hospitality of God present in the mystery of the Cross and, therefore, gathers Christ's human guests around the memorialising of that Cross according to the ordinance of Jesus himself. This *anamnesis*, as it is called, incorporates participants into one, not merely of those who happen to be present but of all the centuries of their sequence.

This community awareness is very personal in that the bread is individually received and the cup personally shared but there is nothing solitary. The situation might be likened to the *taslīm* of Islamic *Ṣalāt*. Facing the *Qiblah* which belongs to all, each separate Muslim greets his fellow Muslims around the whole circle oriented to that *Qiblah*. He does so by turning his head fully round to left and right, with the words of peace and salutation. In so doing, he both discovers and affirms his community. The Christian does likewise at Holy Communion.

Finally, this Eucharist is a sacrament of consecration. In this it links with what has been said about a self-dispossession in baptism, for the sake of a true self-repossession, 'a death to sin and a new life in righteousness'. That double truth of a self to negate and a self to fulfil has to be steadily renewed. Holy Communion is where we are most able and alerted to do so. The reminder of our creaturely privilege within creation, our forgiven status in redemption, and our part in spiritual peoplehood, lays upon us the claim to service and fidelity. So Holy Communion is understood as 'our sacrifice of praise and thanksgiving' in which 'we offer and present ourselves a living sacrifice', this being 'our reasonable service'. There is strength to fulfil this dedication in the steadily renewed *dhikr* of the divine love which demands and deserves it.

Exposition of these two Christian sacraments in this way, brief as it is, is necessary to understand the role Christianity sees as belonging to the Holy Spirit, the Paraclete. For all these meanings are alive through His presence. Hence the invocation, the *epiclesis*, which asks the hallowing of the common elements of bread and wine that they may bear this large significance. We might, with proper caution, find something of a parallel to sacramental prayer for 'the coming down of the Spirit', in the Islamic practice of *Taṣliyah*. There, too, is invocation in which believers 'call down blessing' upon the name and memory of Muḥammad, because it is in him that the divine ways with mankind are believed to proceed. Those ways, Quranically, have to do with prophethood and guidance. But the prayer of *Taṣliyah* celebrates as well as confesses where it believes those ways to be. The Christian, for his part, invokes the divine benediction on the tokens of what he believes the divine way to be, in Christ and, with those tokens, on the community of faith which lives by their meaning.[16]

vii

This simple study of the Christian sacraments helps to illuminate what the Creed means by 'the Holy Spirit proceeding from the Father...' 'Proceeding' is a technical term, meaning that the hallowing, directing and enlightening activity of the Spirit issues from the reality of God as Creator and Lord. It will be clear how all this activity belongs integrally with the meanings of Christ. This is why the Creed adds: '... proceeding from the Father and [or through] the Son.' It is in those meanings that God the Creator is known as Redeemer in power and mercy. Their embodiment in Jesus we studied in Chapter 7.

It would be possible to express this understanding of divine action by means of three prepositions: God over us in sovereignty, God with us in compassion and grace, and God within us in truth and light. Some have found a clue in a literary analogy. A great creative work of art, music or drama belongs with the creating mind, the artist, musician or dramatist. But that source and ground of all gives being to that in which he is expressed and fulfilled – the work the artist begets. In it he is self-expressed. Without him it could not be, nor could he be what he is without it. In turn the work makes its impact, becomes realised for what it is, on the part of those for whom it was meant. Art lives to communicate. It is by nature self-expressive. Yet to be so it must incarnate itself in self-expression. Then there is realisation. In distinguishing these we do not pluralise or multiply. We comprehend a unity. It is a unity which is self-expressive, self-expressed and thereby self-expressing.

It is in something, dimly because transcendently, akin to this analogy that we can suggest what the Christian understanding of God means and how 'the abiding Spirit' fulfils in our experience what Christ fulfils in history and how both belong with the whole reality of God Whom, warranted by those fulfilments of Himself, we call Father.

Notes

1 Ḥasan Askarī, *Inter-Religion* (Aligarh, 1977), p. 18. Seyyed Ḥosain Naṣr is an eminent exponent of the idea that true Islam is the essential 'mindfulness' of right humanity, in contrast to the 'forgetfulness' which has overtaken empirical man, especially in the modern west. This 'forgetfulness', which only a true 'recollection' or *dhikr*, will overcome, explains the intrusion and specious authority of 'alien ideas' of which secularism is the expression. See e.g. *Islamic Studies* (Beirut, 1967), and *Islam and the Plight of Modern Man* (London, 1975).

2 Examples are many, such as the desolation which followed the collapse of the Ma'rib Dam, the condign fate of tribes like 'Ad and Thamūd and the evidence of decayed palaces and ruined shrines so vividly impressed upon Muḥammad by his travels. See this writer's *The Event of the Qur'ān* (London, 1970), chap.11, 'The Sense of History', pp. 166–79.

3 See George Johnston, *The Spirit-Paraclete in the Gospel of John* (Cambridge, 1970).

4 When the Western Church introduced and stressed *Filioque* the concern was to emphasise the essential relation of the Holy Spirit to Christ. The Eastern Church clung to what the verse in John 15:26 actually said, from which the clause derived, and its concern was to avoid any subordination of the Spirit which might be implied by *Filioque*, which was, for both west and east, a true statement about the activity of the Spirit, insofar as activity ought to be distinguished from status.

5 The distinction between a proper name and a comparative adjective can be made in English by capitalising the former. This is not possible in Arabic. *Aḥmad* in form is a comparative adjective from the root which yields *Muḥammad*, i.e. H.M.D.

6 For further discussion see W. Montgomery Watt, 'His Name is Aḥmad', *The Muslim World Quarterly*, vol.43, no.2, 1953, pp. 110–17.

7 See this writer's *Muhammad and the Christian* (London, 1984), chapter 3.

8 On The Gospel of Barnabas, see Laura and Lonsdale Ragg, *The Gospel of Barnabas* (Oxford, 1907), English trans. with critical Introduction; see also J. Slomp, *Gospel of Barnabas, and Essay and Enquiry* (being a revision of Salīm 'Abd al-Aḥad and W.H.G.T. Gairdner's earlier work) (Madras, 1908; Hyderabad, 1975).

9 Robert Browning, *Collected Poems* (Oxford, 1940), 'A Death in the Desert', pp. 488 and 486.

10 See G.W.H. Lampe, *The Seal of the Spirit* (London, 1951), for a classic study of this theme.

11 'The soul's encounter' may seem improper language in respect of Infant Baptism which many Churches practise. This has to be seen, however, in the context of the Christian family. The confession of faith, by sponsors and godparents, is prospective to its personal assumption by the child on reaching maturer years. For this personal acknowledgement of baptism the service of Confirmation exists with its opportunity to solemnise and make good the baptismal meanings. Meanwhile, the faith of the proxies has bound them over to ensure, as far as in them lies, a nurture of the child in the reality of that faith.

12 The Rubicon was the river in north Italy which Caesar crossed and burned his boats behind him to give his soldiers to understand that there could be no retreat.

13 William Shakespeare, *Henry IV*, Part 1, Act V, Scene 1, line 127, where Prince Henry says: 'Why, thou owest God a death', chiding Falstaff.

14 Andrew Marvell, 'To His Coy Mistress'.

15 The Mass as a name derives probably from the Latin conclusion to the Office: *Ite, missa est*, 'Go, it is the sending'. Hence the word Missal for the Office Liturgy.

16 On *Taṣliyah*, or the calling down of God's blessing upon Muḥammad, as enjoined in Surah 33:56, see Constance E. Padwick, *Muslim Devotions* (London, 1961), pp. 152–66; and this writer's *Muhammad and the Christian* (London, 1984), pp. 55–6.

Chapter 11

Islam and Jesus Now

i

'In certain states of the atmosphere ... the evening sun shortens the perspective' when Jerusalem looks towards 'the threshold of Arabia'. Chapter 1 began from this intriguing observation. Such vistas are, at most, only a parable. What of the view of the faiths, either into the other, in present states of 'the atmosphere', as current history finds it in the postures of politics and the prose of journalists? It is time to relate the issues of Scripture and faith, the mutual duties of scholarship and the interplay of theology, to the tensions of the time. Our concern for the New Testament to be understood around the mosque can only be realist if alert to the mosque's situation. We cannot reckon well with how Islam sees Jesus apart from its debate within itself about contemporary affairs. Our purposes throughout have not been only academic but vital and open to the world. It remains to ask whether there is any shortening of the perspective to be discerned across the territory between Muslim and Christian which all the foregoing – from either view-point – has served to map? If, in so many ways as we have seen, what has to do with Jesus is clue to all else between us about God and man, are there any signs of hope of closer understanding?

The answer is Yes and No. Jerusalem is as good a symbol of the ambivalence as any. Having opted to begin there for imagination's sake, let us stay briefly with its image in Islam. Aside from constituting the first *Qiblah* of Islam, *Bait al-Maqdis*, as Muslims name the Holy City, quickly established its fame in the Islamic soul. Mu'āwiya, the first Ummayyad Caliph, took his caliphal oath of office there, rather than in Medina from which – or Damascus to which – he transferred the Caliphate. Traditions circulated widely about its merit and its celebration. Ka'b al-Aḥbar said that God Himself looked towards it twice a day. Other cities gained esteem by claiming to be built of its clay. All the world wept when Nebuchadnezzar destroyed it. Books of *faḍā'il*, or praises of its excellence, came into currency, the most famous being that of Abū Bakr Muḥammad al-Wāsiṭī, preacher of the Al-Aqṣā Mosque, a decade after the Fāṭimid Caliph, Al-Ḥākim, had destroyed the Church of the Resurrection. Eschatologists averred that the *Ka'bah* itself would journey to Jerusalem for Judgement Day, to be preceded by the bones of Muḥammad for re-interment there. Its streets and minarets were beloved of Sufi saints and scholars, like Al-Ghazālī, Al-Saqaṭī, Al-Thaurī and Al-Ḥārith, who found inspiration in its association with Elijah, with Al-Khiḍr, and with Jesus, and in the mystery of the Prophet's Night Journey and ascension into heaven.

However, there were counter-voices and, as in several other fields, the most strident of them was the redoubtable Ibn Taimiyyah (1263–1328). He decried the *faḍā'il* literature. He insisted that there was no *ḥaram* in Jerusalem and no sacred enclave to be revered. He was adamant that a visit to Jerusalem should never be combined with a pilgrimage to Mecca. To violate this rule was equal to a renunciation of Islam. On no account must visitors perform a circumambulation of the Dome of the Rock. In all things the unparalleled distinction of Mecca must remain supreme.[1] Ibn Taimiyyah's rigorous jealousy for Mecca at least demonstrates that the attitudes he castigates were common. Otherwise his vetoes would have had no cause. We meet his temper on other fronts and in the current scene.

It is likely that the wealth of Islamic tradition extolling Jerusalem owed much to Jewish and Christian influences bearing on Muslims, either from converts who acceded to Islam or *dhimmis* who did not. This could not have happened if the fascination had not been congenial to Muslim loyalties. Yet, at the same time, there was the instinct to be vigilant for the self-sufficiency of Islam and wary of what might seem, or serve, to impugn it. The parallel, on both counts, with the Muslim attitude to Jesus is obvious, and the reasons comparable.

ii

Through all we have reviewed there runs a great tenderness for Jesus, yet a sharp dissociation from his Christian dimensions. Islam registers a profound attraction but condemns its Christian interpretation. Jesus is the theme at once of acknowledgement and disavowal. Islam finds his nativity miraculous but his Incarnation impossible. His teaching entails suffering but the one is not perfected in the other. He is highly exalted, but by rescue rather than by victory. He is vindicated but not by resurrection. His servanthood is understood to disclaim the sonship which is its secret. His word is scriptuarised into the incidence of the Qur'ān fragmentarily. He does not pass as personality into a literature possessing him communally. Islam has for him a recognition moving within a non-recognition, a rejectionism on behalf of a deep and reverent esteem.

We are, of course, setting down these items of ambivalence from within Christian criteria, but then these are the only ones we can bring. Without them we have no mutuality. With them our mutuality becomes tense, not quiescent – an active responsibility, not a casual relation. That active responsibility is as testing as ever. Recent developments within Islam have done nothing to ease it, while the mutuality is now conditioned by political, commercial and technological factors at once more tangled and more entangling than they have ever been. If we are looking for a drawing together of the two faiths, their theologies and their communities, the immediate signs are encouraging only in respect of sophisticated and studious contacts between the few, while the evidence from the many, and in the large, remains daunting and disappointing.

It was a significant development which brought a Muslim representation to the inter-faith participation in the 1983 World Assembly of the World Council of Churches.[2] But the temper and perception present there find little echo in the reverberations from Teheran or Islamabad. The qualities of Ibn Taimiyyah are more widely admired and his rigorism preferred. It is noteworthy that several of the practitioners of articulate relationships, wrestling with intellectual mediation between us, are exiled or isolated in the western world, be it Philadelphia or Lyon, and need for their occasions the context they call into question. Their deep and sincere commendation of the Islamic, as they believe it to be, is articulate outside Muslim régimes.[3] Since it is from thinkers such as these that we must draw, in part, in this chapter, it is well to appreciate how far current patterns in the Muslim world, geographically defined, all too often run counter to their mind. Only in such realism can hope properly obtain.

iii

Once obvious factor in the assertion, today, of the self-sufficiency of Islam is its expression in the nationalism of state-creation. The emergence this century of numerous nation states, in the wake of the collapse of the caliphal system and the recession of western empire, has been the salient external feature of the Islamic history. Though it breaks up the ideal structure of Islamic unity, assigning this to pan-Islamic sentiment, it certainly obeys the characteristically political instincts of Islam.[4] Pakistan is, of course, the most conspicuous example of both the insistent sense and the human cost of Muslim separateness politically sanctioned and embodied. One cannot create states in the name of Islam and escape the urgent necessity of defining and exceptionalising, *vis-à-vis* all problems, the Islam one has affirmed. Current nationalism, therefore, serves strongly to accentuate Islamic identity and to bind it over to assertive moods and minds. There is a sense, perhaps, in which it *need* not be so. Muḥammad 'Alī Jinnah,[5] for example, speaking in 1947 to the new Constituent Assembly of Pakistan, declared:

> We may belong to any religion, caste or creed. That has nothing to do with the business of the State. ... We should keep that before us as an ideal and you will find that in the course of time Hindus would cease to be Hindus, and Muslims would cease to be Muslims, not in the religious sense, because that is the personal faith of each individual, but in the political sense as citizens of the State.

The stresses of Pakistani self-definition soon overtook such irenic ideas. Indeed, their logic would have suggested non-partition in the first place, a united India being a far more appropriate - not to say more merciful - fulfilment of them. Though the boundaries drawn necessarily included non-Muslim subjects and excluded vast numbers of fellow-believers left outside its 'protection', they symbolised and required a political will to be Islamic, however and through whatever tensions that will might be defined. Such political will, in such deliberate form, inevitably involved an acute assertion of identity and a sharp internal experience of identity-making. In the event - through many vicissitudes of constitutional discussion, formulation, and abrogation, and a sequence of régimes, elected and imposed - that identity has tended, perhaps inevitably, towards the more rigorous forms. The incompatibility requiring the statehood, because Islam is not a religious community but a religious nation, makes for a comparable sharpening of distinctiveness in its interior definition - so at least it has proved in the story of Pakistan.

That creating via partition is not, of course, the experience of states such as Iran and Malaysia. In their different context the nation–state–faith structure is the same. In the case of Iran the strong emphases of the Āyatollāh Khomeinī, in the given circumstances of his long resistance to the Shah, have welded into a powerful revolution the intense conservatism of Shī'ah Islam and the passion of Iranian national exclusivism, responding to the inroads of the secular and alien world. Indeed, one of the main thrusts of his philosophy was that *taqiyyah* –

the traditional Shīʻah posture of outward acquiescence in what it inwardly deplored – must be decisively repudiated and reversed. This in itself enabled him not only to disqualify those *ʻulamā'* minded to maintain *taqiyyah* but also to centralise rejectionism at the very core of Islamic Shīʻah consciousness. As elsewhere, this meant a depreciating of the real issues of modernity and a passionate exclusion of human and religious openness to everything outside its own lights and its own criteria. By the same token, it also meant a powerful sense of assurance-in-identity, and an emotional truculence feeding on rejection, given and received. In no way, therefore, has this brand of Islamic nationalism conceded genuine co-existence, spiritually or intellectually pursued.

To diagnose the religious blight of statehood in these terms is not to deny the inevitability of the political order nor to ignore the fact that all socio-religious identities instinctively seek, or enjoy, the sanctions of power. Judaism in the shape of Zionism has resolutely recovered them. What matters, plainly, is the temper of such amalgams of the politico-religious order. Given a tolerant temper, the state 'establishment' of a faith can usefully serve to affirm the non-ultimacy of the political, the liability for power, and the precious controlling truth of the sovereignty of God. However, unless that equal citizenship and common humanity are enshrined within the faith, the sovereignty of God is itself usurped and assumed by the state.

By the nature of its origins Islam has been distinctly prone to this pattern of things. It *can* be interpreted in solely moral terms.[6] But its instincts are more with the realism of that aggressively political thinker, Machiavelli,[7] who scorned unarmed prophets and saw the state as an organism intending at all costs to survive, an entity absolutely given to its own necessities, the exclusive judge of what is at enmity with it and of how the enmity is to be overcome. Religion, exclusively allied with such ultimacy, becomes thereby the criterion of enmity and the theme of assertion which demands survival. *Verita effettuale*, Machiavelli called it: truth which knows how to look after itself and the state as its means and end.[8]

If this power-reliance of religion suggests that the great hope of inter-religious meeting must be an effective 'secularising' of the state (in the strict sense of the word) as the primary factor in its feasibility then it has also to be confessed that, within Islam, it is still far to seek. Nor, as Lebanon proves, are the Christian minorities, in their exposure or their docility, really ready for it. Indeed, the Maronite/Christian separatism in the Lebanon is a minor leaf out of the same book of religious enmity politically defined and pursued.

There are, happily, Islamic countries, like Egypt, where non-Muslim citizens, living within the assumptions of *dhimmī* status, have reasonable religious occasion to be themselves. But there are pressures everywhere, hard to resist and to be undergone, for increasing rigorism in the equation between the state and Islamicity, with the latter more sharply defined. Régimes, as of late in the Sudan, are liable to concede some tightening of *Sharī'ah* law as the price of avoiding yet more rigorous demands. Almost everywhere the strains of contemporary history tend towards a sharpened defensiveness, cultural self-sufficiency and religious conservatism.

To analyse this situation realistically is not to deny to those caught in it a genuine sympathy and a perceptive reckoning. It is always humanly easier to consolidate familiar securities when the unknown threatens, to cling to traditional instincts when the uncongenial insinuates itself. Political defensiveness, even aggressiveness defensively assumed, are understandable in the long retrospect of imperialism from the west. The enviable, yet also disruptive, advantages of technology in all its forms could hardly fail to prove disturbing of the equanimity of cultures, absorbing them at stressful speed, and with all the psychic complications of their external origin. It is not congenial to the human spirit to be at once in political rejection and technological dependence. The very need to relate Islamic economics, Islamic education, Islamic sociology, and Islamic ethics – separately and all together – to conditions of unsparing and unrelenting change naturally generates in many minds an instinctive protectionism which is either facile about the solutions, or negligent of their range, in primarily asserting its own confidence, however paradoxical. Though the issues are deeply inter-religious the instinct to 'solve' them unilaterally within Islam is strong. Where there is most need to be objective and open, there is the steady impulse to be subject only to one's own.

iv

It follows that the climate for any lively reckoning with the significance of Jesus, which has been our pre-occupying concern in all the preceding chapters, is hardly propitious. There are countries where no Christian presence or worship is tolerated, or is rigorously restricted to foreign nationals. It is impossible to have a place of public Christian worship in Saudi Arabia and a facility for certain alien personnel is strictly confined and private. The exclusion of all non-Muslims from the environs of Mecca and from any experience either of the pilgrimage locale or the pilgrimage liturgy remains utter and absolute. In Kabul, Afghanistan, an expatriate Christian Church was bulldozed into the ground in 1974, shortly after its inauguration, despite the fact that verbal permission had been given for its erection and supplies for its construction had been passed, as such, through the official customs. In Malaysia, draft legislation purports to forbid, under severe penalties the use of certain vocabulary by Christian theology and liturgy. It includes basic terms, like *Allāh, īmān, rasūl*, and *injīl*, all of which are authentic Christian usage in the Arabic and some other eastern languages. The demand to enforce a monopoly of them, by Islam, measures the degree to which some in Islam wish to isolate faith from faith and preclude altogether the sort of mediation which a common currency of words both enables and suggests.[9] The idea is a melancholy commentary on the mentality which conceives it.

These examples, at random, of the hardness in the scene are, happily, not the whole story. There are instances, for example, within the United Arab Emirates, where generous help and hospitality have been extended to the Christian presence. The fact that large Muslim communities in Europe, on the receiving end of minority status, expect generous allowance of their ritual and cultural claims helps to the idea of reciprocity. Cathedrals in Cairo and Lahore may 'balance' cathedral mosques in Washington and London. But the inner attitudes which might surmount the ghetto concept, preferred or sought, are hard to come by. It is, no doubt, easier to concede a physical facility than to open mind and society to genuine mutuality. For many in the Islamic world, for reasons implicit in the nature and history of Islam, the sense of exclusiveness and superiority is instinctive. Nothing can well stand on equal terms with the final religion and the perfected faith, and whatever *de facto* serves others as religion must do so on terms of political subordination and spiritual inferiority or of reluctant concession to foreign practitioners. Colonel Qaddāfī opened a Muslim-Christian conference in Tripoli, Libya, by asking his Vatican guests why, Islam being the final revelation, they did not accept it.

Such inferiorising of what is not ourselves is, doubtless, an attitude to which more than Muslims are prone. There are adherents who demonstrate it in all faiths. What we have also to ask is how far faiths are capable inwardly of calling it in question. Hinduism, in a way, has the ability by dint of its otherwise disconcerting relish for the plural and the relative. India has had Presidents who are not Hindus, a phenomenon scarcely to be anticipated of non-Muslims in Pakistan. There are accents about patience, gentleness and vulnerability, in Christianity, which have checked in some quarters the ready superiority of Christian tradition. The self-doubt of which Christians are capable has, indeed, been noted and reproved by Muslims on many occasions.[10] One urgent question in the present is how far Islam will prove capable of the interior self-criticism which will interrogate and restrain its characteristic assurance that it has no need to relate beyond itself, or that at most it may confine relationship to matters purely pragmatic or practical.

Meanwhile its reactions are those, all too often, which register provocation rather than identify mutual vocation to honesty and vision. For example, Masih Muhajeri[11] writes in *Islamic Revolution: Future Path of the Nations:*

> What has taken place in Iran is a revolution... unparalleled in the world and unprecedented among the revolutions in contemporary history. It can be proudly stated that nothing matches it except the movement of the divine prophets. ... This revolution came to destroy the existing anti-human values in today's world and to restore the divine human values to humanity.

A comparable temper of complete self-sufficiency may be cited from Kalim Siddiqi[12] of the Muslim Institute in London.

> The position that has to be taken now, and only the Islamic Movement can take it, is that the western civilization is in fact a plague and a pestilence. It is no civilization at all. It is a disease. It feeds upon itself to its own detriment. The west today is qualitatively no different from the *jāhiliyyah*, the primitive savagery and ignorance that prevailed in Arabia and the rest of the world at the time of the Prophet Muhammad.

Insisting that 'Islam is incomplete without the Islamic State', this writer continues with perhaps the most chilling of all observations.

> Allāh is an active partner and participant in the Islamic movement ... by being ever present in the consciousness of the individual Muslim as well as the *Ummah*. Allāh (*ta'āla*) makes an active contribution to the strength and commitment of Muslims. The awareness of His constant presence removes the fear of death or of material loss. Martyrdom becomes the highest prize life has to offer. In cases of extreme danger to the Islamic movement, He actively and directly intervenes. ... The knowledge that Allāh is an active

> participant in the Islamic movement gives [it] a metaphysical dimension and quality which is unique.

Such entire cultural annexation of God (we will return to the phrase) is not unknown in other spheres, whether Joshua, the Maccabees, the Crusaders or the Inquisition. The dimension, significantly, in every case is militarist and coercive. To be sure, *Issues in the Islamic Movement* is by no means representative of all Islam. Indeed, it includes within its new *jāhiliyyah* many exponents and rulers in the current Muslim scene. The 'issues' it handles are often internal. Yet its forthrightness and its rejectionism *vis-à-vis* others give little ground for hope, at least in this milieu, of the kind of attention to Jesus in New Testament terms which we await. That it should be so is both their privation and our pain.

V

One recent example of the melancholy tangle in which popular Muslim premises and eclectic handling of sources are involved over the person of Jesus is Muḥammad 'Aṭā al-Raḥīm's *Jesus: A Prophet of Islam.*[13] The author makes the familiar case that Islam effectively rescued Jesus from Trinitarian travesty and restored him to his pure, Semitic, prophetic, teaching status. Everything other than this is the knavery or stupidity of Constantian bias and confusion surrendering to divinising instincts of paganism. The faith in the Incarnation, the Holy Trinity, the sacraments of Baptism and the Eucharist, and the whole structure of the Church, are a ghastly error. When 'Aṭā al-Raḥīm uses the Gospels, which he mostly scouts, he cites them only for his own prior conclusions, ignoring the evidence they bear against his cavalier rejection of their reception of the impact of Jesus. He fails to penetrate the significance of Christian wrestling with the integrity of faith, reading *into* Christian unitarian liberalism, not a tension within a mystery, but an evaporation of it. He lifts George Orwell's double-think incrimination of mind-perversion out of Orwell's context and applies it wantonly as follows:[14]

> Doublethink lies at the root of a Christian's basic assumption that Christ is God. It is around this assumption that the controversy of the two natures of Jesus has raged. One moment he is human. The next moment he is divine. First, he is Jesus, then he is Christ. It is only by the exercise of doublethink that a man can hold these two contradictory beliefs simultaneously. It is only by the exercise of

doublethink that belief in the doctrine of the Trinity can be maintained.

For Orwell, the very possibility of doublethink stood in the laziness which refused to think at all and to start from the beginning with an honest will. 'Aṭā al-Raḥīm claims T.S. Eliot, without reference, for the 'statement' that 'Christianity is always adapting itself into something that can be believed', but he has quite failed to penetrate either the irony, or the misery, of *The Wasteland*. He relies on the *Gospel of Barnabas*, discussed in Chapter 10, but nowhere explores its credentials. He does not grapple with the continuing formulation of Christian theology within the New Testament and after it, as one discernible sequence, nor with its roots in the experienced significance of Jesus as the 'prophet' he sees him to be. His rescue-act on behalf of Jesus does not pause to consider how far it might be a mutilation. As T.S. Eliot has it elsewhere (*The Cocktail Party*): 'Most of the time we take ourselves for granted ... nothing but a set of obsolete responses.'[15]

Is the whole controversy too painful, too parlous, to pursue? Had we not better let it rest in hopelessness or indifference? Can it usefully obtain outside the partisans? Will Islam ever be intelligently open to the Christian significance of Jesus? Or, since controversy cannot be dismissed from what is at issue, can it ever be worthy of his quality? Controversy will never be what it must be, unless such misgivings register all the time in its pursuit.

Yet will such diffidence ever elicit the penetration that must be forthcoming? Consider this bland dictum of 'Aṭā al-Raḥīm:[16]

> The effective abandonment of the teaching of Jesus was largely due to complete obscuring of his historical reality. The Church made religion not only independent of the Scriptures but also independent of Jesus, so that the man Jesus became confused with the mythological Christ.

Again, how should response be made to the cast of mind behind the following?

> There is no record of how Jesus walked, how he sat, how he stood, how he kept himself clean, how he went to sleep, how he woke up, how he was with old people, how he was with young people, how he was with old women, how he was with young women, how he was with strangers, how he was with guests, how he was with his enemies, how he conducted his transactions in the market place...

Similarly, how should we respond to the reason for such knowledge:[17]

> Extracting a moral principle from the Gospels and trying to live by it is not the same as acting in a certain manner because it is known that Jesus acted that way in that situation. One course of action is the fruit of deductive knowledge, the other course of action is by revealed knowledge.

As long as we are in common humanity with Muslims whose minds are so, it seems important to sustain a travail for the New Testament to be read, to let it be seen how Jesus was with the leper and the Samaritan, how he was with estranged publicans like Matthew and Zaccheus, how awake he was in Gethsemane, how he conducted himself in the market-place of the Temple and how he responded to a stranger on the Cross. If only they were deepened, liberated from sheer traditionalism, and lifted into true drama, 'Aṭā al-Raḥīm, with his items of curiosity, is really probing for what Christians have always received as the meaning of the Incarnation. Jesus is to them the inclusive 'sign' – a life lived as the clue to God.

vi

It is the insistent requirement of the concept of prophethood in Islam that it must exclude and negate the concept of Incarnation, whereas, as Christians see it, prophethood deepens and climaxes into 'the Incarnate Word'.[18] Theology and Christology then require each other. By contrast, in Islam, spokesmanship comprehends all that may be done for God in this world. This is held to underwrite what Muslims see as a 'pure monotheism'. It is pure because (to return to an expression used in reference above to *Issues in the Islamic Movement*) it does not 'annex' God, as Judaism 'annexes' him to things Judaic and Mosaic ('God and His people'), nor as Christianity 'annexes' Him to things Messianic ('God in Christ'). As we saw, there *is* an 'annexation' of God in things Islamic, in the cause of the Prophet and his *Jihād* ('God and Muḥammad'). Clearly, any theological faith must involve recognising the how and where of His relation to the world. God, in utter isolation, would be not only meaningless but irrelevant. Theology has, in some way, to be 'transitive', whether via Moses and peoplehood, or Muḥammad and prophetic finality, or Jesus as the Christ. What is between us all about God, and in the kindred faiths in people, Prophet or 'Son', is not this essential relationality to humankind but the degree of the relationship, its measure, its reservation or its generosity within transcendence. Islam is categorical that only the prophetic is consistent with a right monotheism.

That it is held to be so is a matter of dogma. Perhaps that is where we should leave the matter as being irresolvable for lack of agreed categories of thought. But it must be seen that what *is* agreed categorically is God as One. About Him the question is in no way 'whether'; it is only 'how?' It is this which, for the unity's sake, makes it necessary to retain the controversy, however reluctantly, or, better, to relate to each other without ignoring the issue. Both Judaism and Islam have been minded to claim that they and they alone are exclusively monotheist.[19] Divided as we are in our respective 'God and...' positions, we must all agree to share the faith in unity. For only so can we hope to dispel the distortions to which we are prone and thus serve the right worship to which all theology is bounden.

Otherwise we are liable to deep travesty in our notions of the other. For example, Frithjöf Schuon remarks:

> Christianity is not directly based on the idea of Unity and need not insist upon it, since its essential basis is the Mystery of Christ. ... The essential basis of Christianity is a fact, whereas that of Islam is an idea.

This opinion leads him into an unhappy depreciation of the Christian situation in other respects. 'Jesus Christ is God institutionalised,' he avers and so it follows, for him, that the Church excludes the world from its inner life and 'has left the entire laity outside itself'. Hence its Gospel has no social application. Warming to this thesis, he concludes that 'a lay Christian is by definition a peripheral being', and is moved to add, in that insidious self-approbation which at times besets us all: 'No Muslim can be a layman.'[20]

The last comment ignores the long tussle within Islam about the door of *Ijtihād*, whether it was open and to whom, and what were the items of expertise required for its exercise. Plainly, all faiths have their pundits and their experts, and – by the same token – their lay folk, their non-experts. To opine that 'the idea of redemption' (from which Schuon argues all the rest about Christian world-renunciation and social unconcern) 'is not necessarily linked to the conception of divine unity and might be associated with a polytheistic doctrine', is to make a valid comment about pagan saviour-cults and about esoteric redeemers. It is, however, contrary to the emphatic, and integral, place of Christian redemption within the Christian theology of unity. There, redemptiveness as a quality in God is inseparable from the reality of His unity, not to say inseparable also from the credibility of His sovereignty. The undefeated sovereignty to which redemption witnesses is the very gist of the meaning of the unity.

vii

As long as writers so widely and justly respected in contemporary Islam as Frithjöf Schuon are capable of such misconstruings of Jesus, the New Testament and the Christian meanings, it must remain important to sustain the will, and care for the means, to correct what is awry and restore what is lost – and all for the sake of those profoundly Islamic ends, the unity of God and the true being of man.

What hope is there of the enterprise being realised within the passions of politics, the stresses of society and the prejudices of faith? Clearly it brings us back to the four areas at issue which were broached in the initial concern of Chapter 1, namely the nature and authority of revelation, the human situation, Jesus and Christology, and our understanding of God. As we have seen throughout, the issue about Jesus comprehends them all. It is fair to say that what divides Muslim and Christian – how to recognise revelation, what constitutes 'Scripture', the measure of what humanity entails for God and God requires of man – can all be seen as implicit in the question of Jesus.

Let us see what bridge of interpretation we can build by focusing the question of Jesus in the term 'Sonship'. To do so has at least the merit of grasping the controversial nettle firmly, of incurring the risks – which other language might lessen – where they are most emotive. We can agree to explore the metaphor from within two aspects to which Islam and the Qur'ān are thoroughly committed, namely the Virgin Birth and the theme of 'obedience'.

Christian theology has consistently understood the Virgin Birth of Jesus as *within*, and never apart from, the larger mystery of the Incarnation. It is seen as the 'way' of something greater. If this were not so, faith would be on a merely biological level. Plainly, birth is on behalf of life: nativity serves biography. The Nativity has never been a faith-inducing thing in itself. Nor was it in the forefront of the message of Jesus or of the early Church. He was never announced in Galilee or across the world as one whose credentials belonged in his infancy. A right exegesis of a vital passage in Isaiah 7:14 readily acknowledges that the term there which played so large a part in the faith in virgin birth does not itself carry such significance.[21] The understanding of Jesus' birth which Luke and Matthew in their Gospels share with the Qur'ān has vitally to do with life and personality, with who and how Jesus was, whether as teacher or as Saviour. Our common faith as to the manner of his birth has meaning as the conviction of something purposive in the divine economy, of a gift to the human scene which merited this pattern of being given. Our differing faiths as to what the gift was are at least one in recognising that it is not a mere biological wonder with which we have to do. Perhaps this sense of a divine intention in making Jesus present to our history may help to mediate to Muslim reverence the Christian perception of what that intention may have been. In the confession of the Virgin Birth of Jesus, Muslims share, as it were, the prelude to Christian Christology.[22]

To follow it into its Christian completion involves us all in the vexed questions about 'Sonship', what they can and cannot mean and how they might be translated into intelligible - if not acceptable - Islamic norms of thought. For these, submission to divine will is, of course, the ruling theme, the defining dimension, of theology. Can 'submission' be understood as a ready identity of will with will, so that 'obedience', as it were, achieves and does not merely conform? If so, we may be able to mediate into the Islamic sense of divine sovereignty *over* human will the Christian sense of divine sovereignty *through* human will. The distinction, properly understood, will be the clue to Christology. Plainly, any divine purposiveness within human history, in time and place, will need a human agency - whether prophetic or redemptive, whether speech or personality - recruited to its ends. Such 'needing' is a corollary of time, of history and the created order, and so, too, a corollary - not a compromise - of divine omnipotence. The only issue within such recruitment will be, not its necessity, but its quality, how intimately related to God and how apprehended within the human spirit. What obtains for Islam in the Qur'ān via Muḥammad obtains for Christianity in Christhood via Jesus. There is a clear kinship in the fact of divine purposive action in history. The difference has to do with how the partnership, the eternal and the instrumental, is conceived and fulfilled.

It would be foolish, therefore, to stumble over the term 'Sonship', and fail to penetrate this situation inter-will, as it obtains in our theologies of God and the world. For the Christian faith the inter-will situation means the God-in-man seen in Jesus as the Christ. We might take a way into the meaning by pondering, for example, the familiar Muslim concept of *khalīl Allāh*, 'friend of God' (4:125: 'God took Abraham as friend'). We can find encouragement in so doing from mediaeval Muslim writers. Al-Jāḥiz, theologian-grammarian of Basrah in the ninth century, wrote:[23]

Inasmuch as God took one of His servants as a friend, is it possible that He should take one of His servants as a son, so intending to signify God's pity and love for this servant and the excellent upbringing and education He gives him and the grace of the rank which the servant holds in relation to God?

Al-Jāḥiz himself rejects the possibility but cites, nevertheless, a Muslim writer approving the argument from 'friend' to 'son', if it has to do with vocation and upbringing with a view to a divine purpose.

'Abd al-Jabbār, in the eleventh century, picks up the same idea and links it to the usage whereby 'son' or 'sons' could be applied to individuals or peoples in the sense of righteous obedience, and the term 'Father' to God as of an owning and a ruling Master. The Torah, he argues, can be cited in this sense, and the Lord's Prayer, and, indeed, Romans 8:16 where 'the Spirit bears witness with our spirits that we are children of God'. Reporting on Christians, 'Abd al-Jabbār says they use the term 'son' in the meaning of a faithful devotee (*wālī mukhliṣ*), and the term 'Father' in the sense of a sublime Master.[24] Al-Ghazālī, in the same century appreciates the metaphors in the same reverent sense and adds. 'If you obey Him [God] He will act towards you as the begetter acts with a child begotten of him.'[25]

Such welcome appreciation, within Islam, of positive possibilities in this field of metaphor, as distinct from its outright, unthinking rejection, may not go very far. Christian doctrinal guardians will be wary. It might be claimed that the appreciation only wards off more adequate meanings, and that, as they stand, these thoughts leave ample room for adoptionism or other vagaries. Yet, in our dour situation, they afford some hope of mediation of meaning, through the core-concept of 'obedience' and divine purpose presiding within a human biography to achieve a servanthood. Is it not the integration of 'servant' and 'Son' which is the heart of Incarnation as the New Testament comprehends it and the Creeds define?

Through all the foregoing chapters we have noted this dimension of 'obedience' in the self-consciousness of Jesus acting within the actualities of his context by the light of Messianic vocation. The concern of Christian theology to lift the formulation of that 'obedience' into ontology, and thus to speak of 'God from God, light from light' credally is simply to acknowledge that what happened in Jesus takes God to explain – indeed takes God to achieve. Its happenedness, in other words, is not only human and historical, but divine and eternal. It could not well be characterised as an 'obedience' unless there were a divine referent. Incarnation is simply the divine reference within the active love of Jesus' obedience in the measure of the Cross. It would be a grossly unworthy, un-Islamic thing to comprehend Christhood as a merely human dimension. That is why Christology belongs within theology, why theology must take in the Christ. For the Christ makes good in history the very sovereignty of God, but only because that sovereignty, from infinite resources of love, makes good the Christ. This inter-situation is what Incarnation means.

It is an inter-situation we can understand by reflection on 'the obedience of Christ', which is central, for example, in the Epistle to the Hebrews (5:8) and always evident in Jesus' language referring to God as his Father and to his inner decisions as those of 'His son'. 'The cup my Father has given me' was how he understood and accepted his suffering. An inter-acting 'good pleasure' is the theme of the baptism in Jordan and controls the crisis points of all his ministry. 'In whom I am well pleased' (Matt. 3:17; Mark 1:11; Luke 3:22) does not refer to some external admiration or arbitrary favour. It means in an inseparable way 'By whom I am well served', in the inward, reciprocal sense that what God wills Jesus wills, and what God desires he desires. There is thus the entire satisfactoriness of a confluence of purpose whereby what is eternally willed is historically fulfilled because in Jesus, where and how he is in the living context, what is eternally fulfilled has been historically willed. Throughout his ministry the 'sonship' of Jesus is this confluence of wills freely responsive to what he understands as the intentions of his 'Father'. This is real and concrete in the events before it is enshrined in the ontology of doctrine. It is Palestinian actuality before it is Greek formulation. As we saw in Chapter 5, Jesus' correction of Peter's mistaken instinct about 'rescue' from Messianic travail turned on what Jesus called 'the mind of God', with which, he said, his sense of vocation tallied, not Peter's (Matt. 16:21–23). Peter did not have 'the mind of God'.

It is this free, faithful concurrence of mind that holds the clue to Fatherhood/Sonship in the Gospels and in the Christian faith. The distinction between Father and Son is there because the sphere of the original is eternal, while the sphere of the translation is historical. Jesus, in the flesh, accomplishes the eternal mind, just as the poem translates into accessibility the mind of the poet. Both elements in the inter-situation are vital. We cannot divorce all that Jesus was from the great original, the divine original of love; but we do not know and recognise the eternal original, this manifestation apart. It is in this sense, within our knowing and loving, that 'the Father sent the Son', that 'the Word was made flesh', that 'God was in Christ'. The inter-situation is of the very nature of eternity and time. What the Incarnation means is that they are significant for and of each other. The significance is fulfilled and measured in Jesus as the Christ.

These meanings are implicit in the term 'obedience' we are considering, as applied to Jesus in the New Testament. It is a term with something reciprocal at its core. What is translated *in* the doing – be it command or law, duty or love – is translated *from* the will, the obligation and the intent. Right obedience is transitive: it effectuates the very nature of what is obeyed. The desire which wills to be obeyed, when obeyed, translates itself by and into the conformity which fulfilled it. Even bare laws have their way, so to speak, only in the way of the law. The submission is their only empire. How much more in the things of love and personhood? In that sphere the desire which instigates and the desire which implements are distinguishable by being one.[26] We Christians are saying that the love of God is transitive in 'the obedience of Christ', and that Jesus, in his doing, is index to God's translation of His nature and His meanings into our ken.

What Christian doctrine about Jesus' Sonship means, therefore, is that in the definitive quality of his Messianic history we identify obedience of the Father in the obedience of the Son. There is the human on behalf of the divine: there is the divine on account of the human. If, for whatever reason, one would prefer to have the divine *not* thus reciprocal to the human, one 'must needs go out of this world'.

It is illuminating to realise that when the New Testament speaks of 'the obedience of faith' (e.g. Rom. 16:26) and of 'the obedience of Christ' (2 Cor. 10:5), something of the same transitive situation recurs as studied between the Father and the Son. Our 'obedience' in these passages is 'Christ's' as the one who has right to it and is fulfilled in it, not his as brought by him. Just as the mind of God finds translation in and through the mind of Jesus, so the mind of Jesus finds translation in and through the mind of the Christian. Or, as John has it in the great prayer of Jesus to the Father: 'Thou in me and I in them' (John 17:23).

Whether these thoughts of the inter-will situation in the Incarnation bridge effectively into Islam only Muslims can say. They certainly hope to exclude those unhappy and extraneous notions of paternity which have too long persisted in some quarters, distorting the whole meaning and being no more relevant than they would be in discerning the Qur'ān's own language about *ibn al-sabīl*, 'son of the road' (Surah 2:177, 2:215, 4:36). Nobody there inquires about tramps as born of the road's wedlock. More importantly, the Qur'ān lays great store by obedience to God. 'O you who have believed, obey God ...'

(4:59 *et al.* repeatedly). Numerous passages join such obedience to God with obedience to Muḥammad, linked as they are inseparably in the *Shahādah.* It may be that this prominence of 'obedience *to*' may conduce to thought about an implicit unity of will and desire, between obedience willed by God sovereignly and obedience willed by man co-agently, as we have studied them in the case of Jesus and in the understanding of Christianity. The wonder of their being one obedience is what Incarnation has always meant.

viii

The credal phrase 'begotten of His Father' no doubt presents a stumbling-block on account of Surah 112:3, which seems to contradict it. *Lam yalid wa lam yūlad*, however, in that verse ('He neither gives birth, nor is given birth') must be taken in comment on the previous *Huwa Allāhu aḥad, Allāhu-l-ṣamad* ('He is God the One, God the ever self-subsistent'). *Al-Ṣamad*, used only here in the Qur'ān, means one who has all resources in himself, who is not in a chain of contingency, deriving being like humans and like humans giving it, in the sequence of procreating and being procreated. God is eternally ever-living, a truth in no way impugned by the Father/Son relationship we have studied. The 'begetting' to which the Creed refers is not the passing on of being, thus superseded, within contingency. It is the time-expression, because of all that God is, of His self-giving within the order of human history. All self-expression is 'begotten' of the self, whether art or drama or symphony, where desire conceived becomes desire fulfilled. The duality in no way offends the unity. The faith is simply saying that God, by His very nature, actualises in history the enterprise of love we identify in Christ as His. In so doing, like an artist in his art, He is known for who He is.

Indeed, the term 'only begotten' in the Creed is directly concerned with unity. It should be read as 'one-ly'. If the One God is revealed, then His revelation is one. He does not contravene His own consistency, or reveal in fickle inconsistency. 'Only begotten' means 'unreservedly given', without stint or ambiguity. 'Before all worlds' in the Christian Creed means that the nature of God was ever and always what it has become known to be. There is nothing innovative about the Incarnation. It belongs with the sense of the Arabic term *azalī*, 'eternally from before'. That we necessarily think of it as an occurrence – an initiative – is because it is relating to history and in history things always supervene. The issue here is precisely that of *Tanzīl*, occurring in the seventh century, of the eternal Qur'ān. The paradox is not explained, but contained, within the doctrine, whether of Incarnation, or of *Tanzīl*. To believe in the pre-existent Christ is simply to affirm that the divine nature, historically revealed in him, has ever been eternally so.

In these ways the Christian faith is witnessing that the servant obedience of Jesus as the Christ is counterpart to the Lordship that wills to be so served, in what is thus reciprocally accomplished. This is how, for Christians, Jesus belongs in God and God with Jesus.

ix

'For Christians': why not leave it there, living and letting live? Why be concerned that the impact – better, the imprint – of Jesus, as the New Testament knew it, should be felt and received by the world of Islam? Are not the obstacles too massive, the deterrents too formidable? Is zeal in the matter ill-judged, or misplaced? Is evangelism somehow a partisan pursuit – an enthusiasm which has not taken the real measure of the world? Is there not something plainly God-meant in the pluralism of religions and all the psychic, cultural, language, diversity of the world, and the seeming irreconcilability of faiths within societies? To the committed the quality of Jesus may be altogether ultimate, 'the joy of man's desiring'; but should not their commitment concede, about irreversible postures of religions: 'It is not so with them'? Are there not, in fact, far more immediate concerns in the current situation of poverty, injustice, illiteracy , oppression, tragedy, where action together should certainly precede, and may well exclude, doctrinal witness?

Such misgivings are familiar enough and there are indications that they are widely held, though some in the Christian allegiance react by a stronger re-avowal of a countering assurance. To all their reading of 'the mind of the Spirit'. But those who register the misgivings cannot leave them there. Sincerely understood, they are not misgivings that terminate vocation: they only search and test it. The question about witness is never 'whether'; it is only 'how?' The very factors, which are rightly read as daunting it, also call for it more truly. A world in which Jesus and the New Testament were effectively muted would scarcely be well served. The issues which many like to call practical are always spiritual, and therefore also doctrinal, in their diagnosis and their satisfaction.

Through and within them all, it may be said, run four related facts of our time which are clearly central to the core and care of Islam, and in which Jesus and the New Testament, as we have now inquired of them, belong squarely and urgently. To explcre them in conclusion will be the surest way in which to relate Islam and Jesus now.

They are the drift to secularity, the new pluralism, the tendency to extremism and the menace of idolatry. The first is obviously more intensively the experience of the west and so of Christian minds. It is easy for Muslims to assume that they can, or do, stay immune; but the signs, and the precedents, are not with them in so thinking. Wherever its incidence may most strongly fall, the burden of the secular condition is with us all.

While it gravitates to irreligion it is kindled in part by religious pluralism itself. There is bewilderment from the sheer variety, and the sharp disparity, of faith-options. It is highly disconcerting for the religious temper, in many cases, to find alternative systems of belief and ritual commanding allegiance and to come to terms with the discovery. Religions have, of course, long been present to each other and there is nothing new in the fact of their encounter. What is new is, rather, the degree of their physical inter-penetration and the wider awareness of their coexistence.[27]

The pull of extremism is one evident result of both accelerating secularity and cultural pluralism read as a threat. The hardening of Islamic attitudes, as earlier noted, is a sombre feature of the contemporary scene. Jewry and Judaism, not least in Israel, exhibit comparable trends towards strident rejectionism, a fear of assimilation, and a preoccupation with threat and survival. Within the Christian churches also strong conservatism responds to unease or fear of the times by postures of defensive aggression or heightened sectarianism, taking refuge in rigorous tests of faith and citadels of authority. For more than half a century, the Muslim Brotherhood has exerted a sturdy influence - dogmatic, social and often political - in the cause of a tightly disciplined, doctrinally assertive and intensely self-conscious expression of Islam in the Arab world and beyond. It has its counterparts elsewhere.

This intensified conservatism, in whatever faith, inevitably raises the crucial issue at the heart of religion itself, namely its own understanding of its liability as religion, its capacity for radical humility and honesty about itself. It is here that we come to the menace of idolatry - the temptation of a faith-system, precisely because it believes itself custodian of truth, to make an absolute of its own custody. When this happens it is near to idolatry, the worship of itself. The paradox is that it is constrained in this temptation by perceiving the other idolatry of contemporary humanity which is the temptation of secular technology. Whether in panic or in pride, religious faith may behave as if the interests of God were somehow so vested in itself as to warrant an absolute authority to pursue them. Secularity will then be the evident contemporary target of such a militancy in a guardianship for God which will brook no question, and will seek no partners in its exclusive sponsorship of the divine. The real tasks of spirituality will be disserved by such unilateralism on behalf of God, and the true measure of secularity will be misjudged.

It is here that Jesus and the New Testament relate so deeply to the current scene in the care, whatever the faith-system may be, for a right response to the secular and a right temper in the religious. They relate deeply because of their realism about the potential perversity of religion and the radical necessity of the redemptive meekness so central to the word and work of Jesus and so often reversed in the temptations to which Christianity has succumbed. That the custodial faith from Jesus, and about him, should demonstrate so deeply the nature and guilt of such disloyalty only underscores how real is the perversity and how crucial the work of grace. Christians have no warrant to be complacent about religion for they have at their faith's heart the event, in Cross and Resurrection, that most surely measures the reach of the shame and the hope of the truth.

What matters is what faiths find and enshrine as definitive in their origin, and the resultant capacity for self-accusation. It seems fair to surmise that the setting of Islamic origins in power-assumptions and the assumption of power has predisposed it – Sufis apart in respect of the inner self – to self-confidence and unhesitant religious assertion. The secular impact, perceived as threatening, tends in most cases to be read as requiring – indeed vindicating – this stance of custodial pride of truth, and of countering self-assurance, in which the real measure of the secular situation is not taken. It need be no surprise that modern secularity arouses in authoritarian religion the mood and substance of reaction least adequate to meet it. The more anathemas a zeal for truth inspires in us the less likely are we to sense the deeply religious reasons, and dimensions, which attend the secular development, both critical and wistful. There is a sense in which irreligion is a religious protest, a negation pleading for an affirmation, the religious theme of life being inescapable. To believe ourselves possessed of the key to it, dogmatically fitted and institutionally turned, may tempt us into usurping what can only be God's, by pretending to own what faith – and faithfulness – can only serve. *Allāhu akbar* can never rightly come to mean *Islāmu akbar*. The latter is what some contemporary Muslims are heard saying in the intensity of their anger or the urgency of their reaction, whether to the fact of pluralism or the fear of secularity. It is precisely this temptation which makes the person of Jesus, and the New Testament patterns that express him, in their primacy to gentleness, humility and grace, so crucial a witness where Islam obtains.

It is a witness whose distinctive themes of Incarnation and the Cross can joyfully salute and share the splendid resources of Islam in answering that other idolatry of the age into which technology tempts us all. Islam is a vibrant demand to 'let God be God'. This demand, originally heralded in the *Shahādah's* 'There is no god but God', is equally authentic where the context is saying 'There are no gods but...', and these are: market forces, human rights, national interest, technological efficiency, scientific dominion, party dogmatism, the pursuit of happiness, or the secular autonomy of man. Whether crude or subtle, these are all repudiated by the Islamic affirmation: 'God alone is God.' His worship must effectively relativise all other loyalties which will find their due and their propriety only under His sovereignty. It takes God, we may say, to dethrone gods; but it happens only through His witnesses and their submission. This is *islām* and Islam.[28]

That central meaning of divine Lordship is blessedly corroborated in the Qur'ān by the kindred theme of man's *khilāfah*, or dominion, of human competence over nature as a divine design – a divine generosity – to be received and implemented as an entrustment, or a privilege.[29] That authority to be scientific, to attain techniques and so to achieve civilisation, is further confirmed in the Qur'ān by the interpretation of nature as a realm of 'signs' (*āyāt*). These are, at one and the same time, the means to science and the spur to reverence. The laboratory is also the sanctuary. The natural order houses both the technological dominion and the sacramental mystery, with humanity the sphere of the cognisance of both. In a sacramental earth we only rightly possess ourselves in loving the Lord. Our autonomy is real, but only by gift received. The only right receiving is wonder, thankfulness and prayer.

It is within this mutual understanding of the divine/human mystery, as disclosed in nature and discerned within ourselves, that Muslims and Christians together are equipped to face the current menace of idolatry and beyond it the vocation to be rightly under God and with the changing scene as technology reshapes it. The equipment which is conceptual and definitive is still, therefore, only hortatory, commendable, descriptive and authentic. When it passes, as it must, to translation into fact, into substance, into the effective discipline of man's perennial impulse to arrogance and perversity – both religious and secular – it is then that the significance of Jesus and the New

Testament becomes crucial. Jesus and the Gospel – uncompulsive, non-coercive, patient, forgiveness-seeking, forgiveness-making, long-suffering and redeeming – measure our situation and undertake its salvation in the love which bears and hopes all things. Because that love can allow itself no illusions about the fallibility of law and the limitations of power, it must be steadily renewed in the pattern of the Cross as 'the power and the wisdom of God'. Such constant renewal is the meaning of the Resurrection. It is the heart of Jesus' relevance, via the New Testament, to things present, religious, secular and plural.

In a mood of yearning and tragedy, the poet, explorer and philosopher, Sir Walter Raleigh, wrote:[30]

> O had truth power, then gentleness could not fall,
> Malice win glory, or revenge triumph:
> But truth cannot encounter all.

His perception has a strangely Quranic ring: 'O had truth power!' Yet, empower it, as yearning pleads, and its tasks persist and deepen. As love shows how, truth must 'encounter all', 'truth as it is in Jesus'.

Notes

1 See L.I. Levine, ed., *The Jerusalem Cathedra*, No.1 (Jerusalem, 1981); Isaac Hasson, 'Muslim Literature in Praise of Jerusalem', pp.168–84. Also S.D. Goitein, *Studies in Islamic History and Institutions* (Leiden, 1966), pp. 135–48. On one aspect of the influence of Ibn Taimiyyah this century, see this author's *The Pen and the Faith* (London, 1985), chap. 4: 'Sayyid Quṭb'.

2 The Muslims present were: Muhammad Talbi (Tunis), Shaikh Yusuf Khan Shakirov (USSR), Muzammil Siddiqi (USA) and Aziz Khaki (Canada). They were among a total of fifteen representatives of faiths other than Christian. Whereas at the Third Assembly in New Delhi in 1961 the idea of such representation had been dismissed as impracticable and undesirable, the Vancouver Assembly of 1983 sought 'to hear the voices of people of other faiths on the theme, the sub theme and the issues'. In preparation for the Vancouver Assembly a multi-faith consultation was held. See Report in *The Ecumenical Review*, vol. 35:3, July 1983, pp. 246–64. Dr Talbi contributed a Paper on the *Ummah*, in which he wrote: 'It marks the transition to a complete openness to universalism ... The *Ummah* is defined by its mission. ... This mission consists in realizing the universal plan of God. It welcomes in its embrace all those who respond to the original founding call and thus become part of this plan.'

3 One example is Seyyid Hossein Nasr, of Temple University, Philadelphia, a recent Gifford Lecturer, former Chancellor of the Arya-Mehr University of Technology, Teheran, and author of *Islam and the Plight of Modern Man* (London, 1975) and numerous other works; also Muhammad Arkoun, of the University of Lyon.

4 See e.g., *Muhammad and the Christian* (London, 1984), chap. 3.

5 Translated from the Cairo edit. of *Ihyā' 'Ulūm al-Dīn,* AH 1346, p.285.

6 As, for example, by Justice S.M. Murshid, writing in *Hamdard Islamicus*, Karachi, vol. 2, p. 231: 'The Basis of Pakistani Nationhood': 'An Islamic state is

a "secular" state in the broadest connotation of that expression.... What it signifies is a state which creates conditions for fruitful realisation of the Islamic faith. Islam is a frame of mind, an outlook on life and a way of thinking upon which our lives are to be patterned.... A Muslim undertakes to live in accordance with God's plan and to participate in the enterprise of realising God's will. In this orientation, human destiny is fulfilled insofar as individual and corporate activity approximates to goodness.' Hasan Askari, comparably, denies that Muḥammad ever founded a state or that the state is crucial to the realisation of Islamic norms. See his contribution in Y. Moubarac: *Verse et Controverse: Les Musulmans* (Paris, 1971), p. 132.

7 His name is cited in no sinister sense, but as that of a powerful, forthright exponent of a political philosophy. He reproached Christianity for what he called 'lazy ambition' and want of realism. Its compassion was a defect and a delusion. History is necessarily a conflict of forces. Security may well turn on 'the one man' who is confident enough not to be deterred by scruple and who, on behalf of the general good, takes responsibility for flouting ethics and does 'necessary evil' with a decisive, political will. This, if any, is Machiavelli's notion of 'redemption' and a 'redeemer'. Its affinity with the *Sīrah* is evident.

8 See *Discourses*, 1:34, 1:102, and *The Golden Ass*, 106–114. For Machiavelli there is 'evil' which is 'good' politically speaking. Since power is indispensable the pursuit of it, if successful, atones for whatever evil it entails.

9 A draft Law (1984) in some Malaysian States; an enacted law in the States of Kelentan and Trengganu.

10 Not least the self-doubt which must be read into what holds back from the attitude above (notes 8 and 9). Ibn Khaldūn, for example, in his *Muqaddimah* sees Christianity as not fully 'missionary' because it does not admit the duty of *Jihād*. See Franz Rosenthal, ed., *The Muqaddimah* (New York,1958), vol. 1, pp. 415, 473. Ibn Taimiyyah, likewise, quoting Surah 57:25 about God sending down 'iron, a redoutable thing, to mankind's great profit', observes: 'The right religion must have in it the guiding Book with the helping sword.' See Qamaruddin Khan, in *Islamic Studies,* vol. 3, no. 4, 1964, pp. 521-30. Despite the many indictments of alleged 'mission *cum* imperialism' in modern times, Muslim writing on Christianity still echoes, from time to time, the view that disowning a polity and the political arm, Christianity lacks the courage of its own faith and is not truly a religion fully willing what its being one demands, and, therefore, contrasting with Islam.

11 Masih Muhajeri: *Islamic Revolution: Future Path of the Nations* Teheran, 1982), p. 151.

12 Kalim Siddiqi: *Issues in the Islamic Movement 1980–81, (1400–01)* (London, 1982), pp.4–8.

13 Muḥammad 'Aṭā al-Raḥīm, *Jesus, a Prophet of Islam* (London, 1977).

14 Ibid, p. 198.

15 T.S. Eliot: *The Cocktail Party*, London, 1950, p. 31.

16 'Aṭā al-Raḥīm, *Jesus*, p. 12.

17 Ibid, p. 200.

18 One of the finest expositions of this conviction is Donald M. Baillie, *God was in Christ* (London, 1948). Using the term 'annexing', in this paragraph may be harsh as well as graphic, but it is intended to capture sharply the inescapable 'God and...' situation diversely obtaining in the three Semitic faiths. The 'association' of God with covenanted people, with Messianic action, or with prophetic, political agency, shapes the respective theologies and is shaped by them.

19 This follows since chosen peoplehood unilateralises a full, authentic experience, and worship of God, and excludes other peoples from its essential intimacy. 'In Jewry is God known' (Psalm 76:1). Islam exclusifies monotheism on the principle of finality and on the ground of the alleged implicit or explicit distortions of Christian theology.

20 F. Schuon, *The Transcendent Unity of Religions,* trans. P. Townsend (New York, 1953), pp. 128–31.

21 In the passage in Is. 7:14, from which the doctrine may have taken its form and sanction, the Hebrew word *almah* ('maiden') means simply a young girl or a recently married woman. It does not denote what the Greek *parthenos* does, used to translate it. Also the context of Isaiah chapter 7 does not make the 'sign' to King Ahaz turn on a miracle birth but on the fact that, in the brief interval before the weaning of the child, the hostile foreign alliance which made the king panic will have disintegrated and the dangers will be passed. Meanwhile, the perennial wonder of a birth, any birth, and the simplicities of womb and family, assure us of the abiding trustworthiness of God, of 'God with us', *Emmanuel*, the name bestowed on the child.

22 'Prelude' is used here historically not essentially. Faith about the birth is shared: faith about what it inaugurates is not.

23 See *Al-Radd 'alā-l-Naṣārā*, ed. J. Finkel: *Thalath Rasā'il* (Cairo, 1965), pp. 10–38. See also, on Jāhiz, via 'Abd al-Jabbār, in S. Pines, *Studies in Mysticism and Religion*, in honour of G.G. Scholem (Jerusalem, 1967), pp. 177–90.

24 See note 23, Pines, p. 183 f.

25 Al-Ghazālī's *Al-Radd al-Jamīl li-Ilāhiyyat 'Īsā bi Ṣarīḥ al-Injīl* ('The Comely Refutation of the Divinity of Jesus by Exegesis of the Gospel') was edited by R. Chidiac (Paris, 1939). See p. 40.

26 That 'the obedience of the Son' *is* 'the obedience of the Father' will be clear (and the point is important) only if one appreciates the difference in the sense of 'of' *and* the mutuality. 'Of' is 'to or for' in the one use, 'by' in the other. What Jesus does is the Father's doing. Christologies of 'substance' and 'being' develop from that of 'doing'. 'One in deed with the Father' helps us to understand whence the Creed came and why.

27 See *Towards a Theology for Inter-Faith Dialogue* British Council of Churches (London, 1984).

28 Distinguishing the common noun (small 'i') from the institutional, definitive proper noun, the faith, rite, law, polity, in which due submission is duly made.

29 A Semitic theme developed in my *The Privilege of Man* (London, 1968), and *The Mind of the Qur'ān* (London, 1973).

30 The poem 'Petition'.

Index

Incidental references have been excluded. For broad, major themes, difficult of detailed listing since they are perennially in the presentation, the full table of Contents may be found useful.

Passages cited from the Qur'ān

Passages cited from the New Testament

The Gospel according to Matthew

Citations

Citations

The Epistle to the Romans

Chapter	verse(s)	page(s)
7	1–24	10, 225, 228
8	16	291
	28	120
11	33	10
12	1	93
	16	50
15	19	2, 113
16	26	293

First Epistle to the Corinthians

3	32	5
	23	196
8	5, 6	195, 227
11	23	215
12	4	195
15	3–4	177, 215
	28	11

Second Epistle to the Corinthians

4	6	33, 229
5	14–16	11, 193, 215
6	6	80
	12	35
9	15	231
10	5	293
12	1–5	230

Epistle to the Galatians

2	20	230
3	13	212
	28	123
4	8	227
5	23	80
6	2–5	223

Epistle to the Ephesians

3	19	229
4	8–10	204
4	22 to 6.9	98

Epistle to the Philippians

1	21	230
2	5–11	29, 30, 93, 177, 204

Epistle to the Colossians

1	24	183
	27	229
3	5	227

Other Biblical Passages cited

Power, Participation and Ideology

Readings in the Sociology of American Political Life

Edited by CALVIN J. LARSON and PHILO C. WASBURN

PURDUE UNIVERSITY

Bringing together outstanding statements concerning three central topics in political sociology—power, participation and ideology—the editors present the major divergent views on basic topics in political sociology and reveal the complexity and interrelatedness of political structures and processes through a comprehensive look at American society and its political system.

Part I presents a common sociological approach to the study of decision-making at the national and local levels. Part II reveals the interplay of psychological, social-structural and cultural influences in the determination of patterns of political participation. The interplay of personality, social structure and culture with respect to their influence on ideology is presented in Part III.

behavior and comparative political sociology.